TRAILBLAZERS
Caroline Chisholm to Quentin Bryce

SUSANNA DE VRIES

© Susanna de Vries, this fourth updated edition published 2015

This book is copyright. Apart from any fair dealing for the purposes of study, research, criticism, review, or as permitted under the Copyright Act, no part may be reproduced by any process printed or digital without written permission. Inquiries for reproduction by any means whatsoever should be made to the publisher.

First published in 2011, second edition 2012, third edition, 2013.
Published by Pirgos Press, Cutty Sark Studio, 10 Matingara Street, Chapel Hill Brisbane, 4069.

National Library of Australia
Cataloguing in Publication entry: De Vries, Susanna.
TRAILBLAZERS — Caroline Chisholm to Quentin Bryce

FOR OTHER BOOKS BY SUSANNA DE VRIES, SEE AMAZON KINDLE
ISBN 9781925280180 (4th Edn)

1. Women pioneers, Australia.
2. Early settlers – Australia – Biography
3. Women and travel
4. Women in politics

Under the Australian Copyright Act all photos taken before 1934 are deemed to be out of copyright.

Front cover: H.E. Quentin Bryce, photograph by Marcus Bell and Adam Finch, Studio Impressions, Brisbane;
Rear cover images: Vida Goldstein courtesy National Library of Australia, Hilda Rix Nicholas courtesy the Rix Nicholas Archive, Canberra and Bronwyn Wright, photos of Nell Tritton, courtesy Mrs Lavinia Tritton.t
Cover and book design by Jake de Vries.
Index by Jake de Vries

Contents

Introduction   1

CHAPTER 1
Caroline Chisholm   3

CHAPTER 2
Elizabeth Hawkins   37

CHAPTER 3
Mary Gaunt   68

CHAPTER 4
Hilda Rix Nicholas   124

CHAPTER 5
Sister Anne Donnell   160

CHAPTER 6
Nell Kerensky (née Tritton)   197

CHAPTER 7
Marie Louise Mack   240

CHAPTER 8
Margaret Ogg & Emma Miller
Vida Goldstein & Edith Cowan
Irene Longman
Dame Enid Burnell Lyons
The Right Hon. Julia Gillard   297

CHAPTER 9
H.E. Governor Quentin Bryce   324

Dedication and Acknowledgements   348

Endnotes   349

Author Details   371

Nell Tritton

INTRODUCTION

The Macquarie Dictionary defines the term trailblazer as 'a leader in various fields'. This book profiles 15 Australian women who blazed a trail for the younger generation. It shows how far women have come over the past 100 years and highlights their difficulties to be taken seriously in politics, law, writing, exploration and art.

Caroline Chisholm has become famous for establishing hostels and ran an employment agency for young migrant women at a time when the government did nothing for workhouse girls who arrived penniless in Australia. Caroline's employment agency offered destitute women jobs on country properties where many of them found husbands and wrote letters thanking her.

Caroline's contemporary, Eliza Hawkins, deserves to be known as the first white woman to cross the Blue Mountains, travelling in a covered wagon over treacherous roads with a baby on her lap.

In the 1880s, Mary Gaunt was one of the first women admitted to Melbourne University. Miss Gaunt's desire to study law was denied since male academics believed women incapable of studying 'difficult' subjects. In 1909, Mary, now widowed, led her own expedition into the West African jungle, staying in remote villages to gather information for her book *Alone in West Africa*. In 1913, in the absence of sealed roads, Mary travelled in a bone-shaking mule cart from Peking to the edge of the Gobi desert and returned to Europe on a Russian troop train. Her amazing experiences in China and Russia produced two more travel books. Mary donated her royalties to the Red Cross to help Belgian refugees. For many years she lived in Italy and, during World War Two, died in France.

Melbourne artist Hilda Rix Nicholas battled against the notion that painting in oils was reserved for men so women artists should limit themselves to painting small watercolours. Hilda blazed a trail for Australian female artists in the 1920s by holding a series of successful exhibitions of her large oil paintings in Paris and London before returning to Australia and paint Australian subjects.

In 1914, Sister Anne Donnell went to Lemnos Island to nurse wounded Anzacs from Gallipoli. Due to the inefficiency of the

British War Office her unit was desperately short of beds, sheets, and drinking water. Working long hours under harsh conditions Anne Donnell's courage and compassion inspired younger nurses.

Brisbane journalist Nell Tritton married Alexander Kerensky, Russia's Prime Minister in exile. Living in Paris, she helped the exiled Kerensky run a newspaper that exposed the fact that Stalin's *gulags* were killing thousands of Russians. Stalin retaliated by sending henchmen who tried to assassinate Kerensky. On several occasions, Nell, a skilled rally driver, saved her husband from being killed. In 1940, the Germans invaded Paris. Kerensky, aware he was on the Nazis' death list for denouncing Hitler's concentration camps, fled south in a car driven by Nell. During their nightmare journey their car was bombed by German planes. During the escape, the stress and lack of drinking water shortened Nell's life.

Sydney journalist Louise Mack, was honoured as one of the world's first female war correspondents. Disguised as a peasant girl, Louise was smuggled out of German-occupied Antwerp by Belgian patriots who took her to neutral Holland. She donated the royalties from her war memoir to help Belgian war victims and became a celebrity in Britain. Finally, she returned to Sydney. ple

Margaret Ogg and Vida Goldstein remained undaunted when men mocked them as they demanded women be given the vote. Men jeered again when these dauntless ladies claimed that women were clever enough to hold parliamentary office.

It took many years before Edith Cowan and Irene Longman managed to enter Parliament. Enid Lyons, mother of 12 children, became Australia's first Cabinet Minister. It would take a further 67 years for Julia Gillard to become Australia's first female Prime Minister. As Margaret Whitlam memorably observed, 'No matter what our politics, we all admire a dauntless woman'.

The final chapter relates the story of Quentin Bryce, lawyer and human rights activist, who has blazed a trail as Australia's first female Governor-General and works extremely hard for causes in which she believes.

SUSANNA DE VRIES, AM.

CHAPTER 1

Caroline Chisholm
1808–1877

THE WOMAN WHO CHANGED AUSTRALIA'S POLICY ON MIGRATION

The distinguishing characteristic of Mrs Chisholm is philanthropy — directed by a degree of common sense that amounts to genius... Thousands have reason to bless Mrs Chisholm. From Sidney Solomon's *Emigrant's Journal and Traveller's Magazine*, August 1849.

Caroline Chisholm, once as famous as Florence Nightingale, died in poverty, almost forgotten, but today is reckoned among the world's greatest social reformers.

In 1838, Captain Archibald Chisholm and his wife Caroline arrived in the penal colony of Sydney on long leave from India, where Caroline had run a school for destitute girls. On their arrival they were confronted by a shabby town where men outnumbered women by almost four to one. The ratio of men to women was even more extreme in rural New South Wales, where, in some places, there were more than 10 times as many men as women of marriageable age. The result was many abductions of Aboriginal women or incidents of rape by shepherds, stockmen and settlers.[1]

In an attempt to create a more stable and thriving colony, the British government set up what was known as the 'bounty scheme' to send single working-class girls as migrants to Sydney, where domestic labour was needed and bachelors wanted wives who did not have a convict background. This bounty scheme gave workhouse girls and orphans a free passage to New South Wales as well as providing a set of new clothes and two pairs of work boots. The scheme was funded with money raised by selling land to wealthier immigrants to pay the fares of the girls from workhouses and orphanages. Some had been evicted from their homes in an era of recession in the British economy. There were no welfare benefits for the homeless or unemployed.

As Charles Dickens recorded in *Oliver Twist*, the parish council was responsible for supporting those who could not look after themselves and councils regarded these women as a burden. When homes were repossessed or families could not pay the rent, families were sundered, and family members incarcerated in Victorian workhouses. Men and women were segregated in these harsh places, where the poor were regarded as little better than criminals.[2] The idea of emigrating to a sunny place where food was plentiful and with a chance of a better life was attractive to many orphanage and workhouse girls.

Poster, displayed in orphanages and workhouses, advertising single women could emigrate to Australia for five pounds

Unknown to them the British government had another agenda. They wanted to reduce the numbers of destitute and unemployed in Britain by sending them to New South Wales, which, at the time, included what would after separation become known as

Queensland.

Bounty agents received a commission for each girl they persuaded to emigrate. Ships to transport the girls were chartered by the British government. Bounty agents were instructed to tell the girls that they would have a good chance of finding a husband in a colony where there was such a shortage of young marriageable women. Many destitute and half-starved young Irish women signed up by the boatload.

The unfortunate Irish girls, most of whom had received only a minimal education and could scarcely write their names, encountered intense discrimination once they arrived in Sydney, tousled, friendless and with no money. Ireland was then a British colony where Catholics suffered intense discrimination and were barred from education. Many Irish Catholics lived under primitive conditions, in huts with very little furniture, surviving on a diet of potatoes and black tea. The 'bounty girls' were dismayed to find no hostels to accommodate them and that prospective employers had not been advised of their arrival. They were placed in tents erected in the Domain by the colonial authorities. Lacking washing facilities and wearing soiled clothes, as the migrant ships also lacked washing facilities, these girls found it very hard to obtain domestic work. Brothel madams and pimps tried to seduce them with offers of money and gifts to become prostitutes.

One of Caroline Chisholm's many achievements was to save over a thousand of these destitute girls from being lured into working as prostitutes in brothels or on the streets and find work for them as domestic staff in respectable homes.

※

William Jones, the father of Caroline, died when she was six. She and her sisters and brothers were raised by their philanthropic widowed mother, who did her best to imbue her children with her own sense of responsibility for the poor and disadvantaged.

Miss Caroline Jones and Lieutenant Archibald Chisholm first met at a regimental ball held near Caroline's family farm in Northamptonshire. Like many other Scottish people who migrated to Australia, Archibald Chisholm's grandparents were Highlanders, who had lost their money and lands supporting the Jacobite cause. Archy Chisholm had grown up in a large family who found themselves *nouveau* poor. He joined the Indian Army instead of a Highland regiment, because he lacked the money to buy a commission. Unlike the prestigious English or Scottish regiments, the Indian Army did not demand up-front payment called 'commissions' from young officers.

Archibald's playmates had been the children of crofters (tenant farmers living on small holdings and growing subsistence crops). For centuries these Highland crofters had fought loyally for their feudal lairds and in return had been given small plots of land to farm. But once the lairds became absentee landlords in Edinburgh they lost connection with their clansmen or sold out to English landlords. Meanwhile, demand for wool by the mills in the new industrial towns made sheep rearing more profitable than having tenants for the new English landlords who took over in the Highlands.

In what became known as 'the Highland clearances' bailiffs were sent to evict the crofters from their tiny cottages and when they met resistance they burned the roofs over the crofters' heads. Archy Chisholm's Gaelic-speaking clansmen found themselves homeless through no fault of their own and were forced to leave the Highlands and emigrate to North America or Australia.[3] This explains why he would loyally support his wife's work on behalf of penniless migrants.

Archibald and Caroline not only loved each other, but had a great deal in common. Both had lost a parent when young and both came from backgrounds where rural poverty was prevalent.[4] Caroline had always been encouraged to think for herself and to care for others. Her family were evangelical Christians and family meals were often shared with those in need.

Lieutenant Chisholm had to return to his regiment in India after a brief courtship. Before his departure, he formally asked Mrs Jones for Caroline's hand in marriage. Initially, Caroline had reservations about the marriage. As well as making stipulations about being allowed to continue her philanthropic work, she made it clear she had no intention of entering the social merry-go-round of dinner parties, race meetings and regimental balls which was part and parcel of the life of the wife of an officer stationed in India. Caroline, realising her request was unusual, gave Archibald a month to make up his mind. In stipulating what was in effect a 'pre-nuptial agreement', it would allow her more freedom than the average wife, which was a very modern attitude for her era.

Archibald Chisholm accepted Caroline's demands. However, Caroline made one important concession to her future husband. Like most of Clan Chisholm, Archibald Chisholm was a Catholic, the 'auld' religion of Scotland. Caroline Jones was an Anglican Protestant, but decided to convert to Catholicism so the couple would have no religious dissent when raising their children. But she believed in a non-denominational God and all her life she would help those in need regardless of their beliefs, despite the fact that most Catholics and Protestants distrusted one another.

Their wedding took place in Northampton's Church of the Holy Sepulchre on 27 December 1830. A wedding portrait shows Archibald Chisholm in uniform, a tall, dark, slim young officer. Caroline Jones was thirteen years younger but nearly as tall as Archibald, with a curvaceous figure, clear grey eyes, auburn hair and a creamy complexion.

Caroline had a strong and warm-hearted personality and a great deal of charm, which she used to raise funds for charitable causes. Her portrait by Michelangelo Hayes shows her in midlife, wearing a lace hair net and a dark, unflattering dress emphasising a large bosom. Comparing this portrait with contemporary descriptions of the 'very attractive Mrs Caroline Chisholm' suggests the portrait fails to do her justice. We know that once her husband had left Sydney to return to India, she was pursued by an ardent admirer, but she repulsed him by insisting how happily married she was.

Following their marriage, the couple spent some time in England, where Caroline fell pregnant. Archibald was able to extend his leave by six months, so was present at the birth of their first child, who died after six weeks, leaving Caroline grief stricken. Archibald applied for an extension of his leave and was granted another six months in England before sailing to India in 1832, where he was promoted to the rank of captain.

It had been arranged that Caroline would board the ss *Elphinstone* and join Archibald in Madras. Wives of officers from her husband's regiment welcomed her and introduced her to the social round of tea parties, polo and regimental balls. Life in the garrison town of Madras was a different world to quiet, rural Northampton. Social life among officers stationed in India during the 1830s (when well-trained native servants, costing only a few rupees each month, were plentiful) was lavish.

Civil wars in India's long history, which led to desperate poverty and hunger in some areas, contrasted with enormous displays of wealth by the maharajahs. On outings to the bazaars, Caroline was surrounded by ragged, begging children covered in sores, some deliberately maimed by their parents to attract sympathy. Indian and Anglo-Indian child prostitutes lurked in the shadows in this garrison town and children sleeping in the streets on pieces of cardboard was a familiar sight.

The enormous contrast between the idle, gossipy lives of officers' wives, devoted to dinner parties and regimental balls, and the grinding poverty around her shocked Caroline, although the other officers' wives accepted it as the natural order of things. Caroline prayed for guidance that she might be shown what she could do for the hordes of discarded, unwanted mixed-race girls who were the illegitimate offspring of British soldiers forbidden to marry Indian girls. Some of the illegitimate sons of soldiers were employed by the army in humble capacities, but the army authorities did not care that the daughters of British soldiers were begging in the streets, many of them ending up as prostitutes.

Caroline decided to start a school for these street girls. At that time, the British Army did not provide education for children of common soldiers, who were meant to remain single. The sons of British officers were sent back to English boarding schools. Officers' daughters were educated by their mothers, who had a governess imported from Britain, or were sent 'home' to school. Children of Indian women and men serving in the British Army ran wild — the girls, with their gipsy looks, huge dark eyes and delicate limbs, were very attractive and often used as sex slaves.

Mrs Chisholm became convinced that saving these children from prostitution was part of God's plan for her life. When she proposed to open a residential school for the daughters of soldiers and live in the school while she ran it, her fellow officers' wives were horrified. Archibald Chisholm was warned that this plan was unsuitable for any officer's wife. The Chisholms would become outcasts should they move out of married quarters into smelly, overcrowded Madras and carrying out their plan could jeopardise his prospects of being promoted.

Captain Chisholm honoured the promise he had made when he married Caroline. He agreed to finance part of the expenses of setting up a school from his pay, while Caroline raised the rest from donations including a large one from the Governor of Madras. She realised that young part-Indian girls lacking a dowry needed education in budgeting, bookkeeping, cookery, cleaning and ironing, enabling them to secure paid employment and, hopefully, suitable marriages.

Mrs Chisholm's Female School of Industry for the Daughters of English Soldiers was quite progressive, as the girls governed themselves through committees. The elder girls acted as 'assistant housekeepers', ordering and cooking food for the younger ones. Caroline taught the girls to read and write and the basic principles of home nursing and child care.

In May 1836, Caroline gave birth to a son, who was christened Archibald after his father.

The following year, she bore a second son, named William after her dead father. The rigours of army life and the hot and humid climate of Madras adversely affected the health of Caroline and her husband. Archibald applied for long leave and was allowed to spend the next two years in the colony of New South Wales, where the climate was milder.

The couple arrived in Sydney in September 1838 and settled into a comfortable house in rural Windsor, where they employed a housekeeper. Ten months later, Caroline gave birth to their third son, named Henry. After years in the humid heat of Madras, she enjoyed living in New South Wales.

In 1840, Archibald was recalled to active service and sent to fight against China in the Opium Wars. As he could be away for a long time, they decided it was best for Caroline and their children to stay on in their rented home in Windsor. She was certain she would find philanthropic work in the penal colony and thought of setting up another school. Before Archibald left, he alerted Caroline to the fact that unemployed Scottish immigrant girls who slept in streets and doorways around The Rocks area were in urgent need of help. He convinced his wife to channel her energies into caring for them. English and Irish girls who slept in tents in the Domain were also in need of assistance.

The wool boom was ending, but bounty immigrants still flooded into a greatly reduced labour market. The colonial authorities had closed the Sydney Immigration Barracks and the new arrivals were required to leave their ships within 10 days as the chartered vessels had to return to England. So penniless girls camped in two large government-owned tents in the Domain or slept in doorways while they tried to find work. After a three-month voyage without washing or laundry facilities in the dark and overcrowded sleeping quarters, the girls had lank, greasy hair and looked bedraggled in their soiled clothes. Some had been sexually abused by the ships' crews, because discipline was lax and the captains chose to ignore what was happening. Their main concern was delivering the bounty immigrants alive so that they could collect the price of their passage from the British government.

Caroline soon realised that girls who were clean and tidy and spoke well could find jobs as housemaids, while the rest were forced to beg or enter a life of prostitution.

None of the government officials' wives or the squatters' wives who sat on charity committees seemed concerned about the welfare of these girls. Caroline managed to find some of the girls work as domestic servants and took several others to her Windsor home, where she gave them exactly the same practical education in cookery and thrifty housekeeping as she had given her pupils in India.

***

The catalyst that turned Caroline from a teacher into a fiery activist urging reform of the entire system of emigration was her meeting with a penniless Highland lass who was seduced with gifts by a wealthy married man. Flora (who never revealed her full name to Caroline) and her widowed mother had been evicted from their Highland croft and arrived penniless in Sydney under the 'bounty' scheme. They camped in a large tent in the Domain, where Flora's beauty and obvious innocence attracted the attention of a wealthy man who, Caroline noted, had bought her expensive clothes and 'trinkets'. Flora was flattered and fancied herself in love with her admirer. She did not heed Caroline's warnings that he was married and gave in to her admirer's wishes for intimacy, believing he would propose marriage.

Caroline continued visiting the immigrants' tent and kept an eye on Flora. 'Each time I visited, I observed a little more finery on her,' she commented. But Flora turned a deaf ear to Caroline's warnings and continued the romance.

Months later, Caroline spotted a pregnant Flora standing on the edge of a cliff overlooking the harbour. Caroline persuaded her not to commit suicide and realised she must set up a properly supervised women's refuge so that vulnerable girls had somewhere to live while looking for work.

Caroline knew that many men in the bush were very keen to marry. Some went to the Female Factory and asked the matron to recommend them a suitable wife. If the girl accepted, she was free to leave with him provided they married immediately. Caroline decided to initiate a plan whereby girls could be taken to the bush to work as domestics and milkmaids and could meet bachelors in need of a wife.

Always a believer in starting at the top, she asked the Governor's wife to intercede with her husband, Sir George Gipps, for the use of a large abandoned timber barracks formerly utilised to house convicts as a temporary home for the migrant girls.

Caroline sought help from the Governor's wife rather than from the Anglican Church. Although she intended her hostel to take in women from all denominations, she realised that, being a Catholic, she would automatically make Protestant clergy hostile to her scheme. She told Lady Gipps that the government tents in the Domain were overflowing with migrants. One group of 64 orphaned girls had only fourteen shillings and one penny between them — not nearly enough to pay for the cheapest of lodging-house accommodation.

When Mrs Chisholm was finally granted an audience with a very reluctant Governor Gipps, she knew that she must speak out clearly about the dangers to young girls from sexually transmitted diseases and produce facts and figures to support her plan for re-opening the former convict barracks as a hostel for immigrant women.

Sir George Gipps wrote how he expected to see 'an old lady in white cap and spectacles, who would have talked to me about my soul. I was amazed when my aide introduced a handsome, stately young woman, who proceeded to reason the question as if she thought her experience worth as much as mine'.[5]

So 'handsome, stately young' Mrs Chisholm won the first round of her battle. Although Governor Gipps did not believe her scheme would succeed, he agreed to let Mrs Chisholm use the deserted convict barracks in Bent Street. The barracks was nothing more than a 45-foot-long, very draughty shed filled with rats.[6] The wooden slab building had a dirt floor and was partitioned into several small rooms. The old storeroom served as Caroline's combined bedroom, pantry and office. She worked very hard and soon more than 100 women were living in the new hostel.

Caroline described her terrible first night in the old barracks:

> I retired weary to rest. Scarce was the light out than I fancied dogs were in the room and in some terror I got a light. My first

act was to throw on my cloak and get out the door. My second thoughts were, if I did so, my desertion would cause much amusement and ruin all my plans. I lighted a second candle and seating myself on my bed, kept there until three rats descending from the roof alighted on my shoulder. I feared that I would catch a fever. But to be 'out generalled' by rats was too bad. I got up, cut bread into slices, placed the whole in the middle of the room, put a dish of water convenient and sat on my bed reading and watching the rats till four in the morning. At one time I counted thirteen. The following night I gave them a similar treat, with the addition of arsenic.[7]

Worse than the rats were the male prowlers who visited the hostel by night and by day hoping to lure away one of the girls or rape them. Caroline wrote:

When I first opened the Home, the greater part of my duty was of a very unpleasant nature — sailors, soldiers, draymen and gentlemen would visit the Home; and, as there were several doors, I had no sooner turned one party out, than it was reported that another [had arrived]. I was almost weary of telling them, 'these are the single women's quarters, you cannot stay here'.[8]

Her experiences in India had taught Mrs Chisholm that the best way to protect girls from an unfortunate marriage or falling pregnant to men who offered money for sex was to provide them with paid work. To find work for 'her' girls, Caroline decided to activate a network of contacts in the bush and see if jobs as maids, cooks or nursemaids could he obtained. Once working there, most of them would find husbands.

Caroline continued to protest against the system whereby young, innocent girls on arrival in Sydney Harbour were visited aboard the ships by brothel madams in all their jewellery and fine clothes and who impressed the poverty-stricken girls with talk of an easy life. She knew they remained silent about the dangers of infection from sexually transmitted disease which was the fate of many of these girls. At a time when 'ladies' did not mention such matters, Caroline outraged delicate sensibilities by relating the full facts in her report to the Land Immigration Commissioners.[9]

To forestall the brothel madams, Caroline met every ship that arrived, taking new arrivals back to her hostel. She received an offer of the loan of a bullock dray for use by girls looking for work in the bush. But the girls were frightened of going to the bush. A bushranger named Jackey-Jackey had robbed and murdered an elderly woman returning to Sydney from Bathurst. It was not an isolated incident and the Sydney newspapers had been full of stories of rape and robbery in the bush.

Faced with the prospects of a long journey on an open dray, the girls' fears of rape and murder by armed bushrangers, of venomous snakes that dropped from trees and dingoes that hunted like wolves made them refuse to travel to the bush. Caroline had to send the empty dray back to the bush again, since there were no takers for her employment plan.[10]

She was anxious that no word of this should reach Governor Gipps or he might withdraw his reluctant support for her plans. So she sat the girls down and explained that dingoes did not hunt humans and that most bushrangers had been captured. There were good men out in the bush who needed wives and perhaps they would be lucky enough to find a husband very soon. With a flash of her old humour, Caroline noted that the thought of finding husbands seemed to conquer the fears of the girls and finally they volunteered to go out to the bush by dray.

The next day, she ordered two drays instead of one, which gave her the services of a second burly 'bullocky' whose job was to protect the girls from marauding bushrangers and outlaws. The girls were driven on the lumbering bullock drays to various homesteads and placed in homes where the wife needed domestic help. Caroline was nobody's fool and insisted there was a wife in each house where she left a girl to supervise and protect them and refused to leave teenage girls in homes or bush huts of single men.

Although the number of immigrant ships coming to the colony decreased during the wool depression of the 1840s, Caroline's journeys to the interior became longer and her parties larger. She had one with 147 women in search of work on one journey. Caroline's rural background in Northumberland ensured she was an accomplished and fearless horsewoman. She bought a large white horse she named Captain and rode into the bush at the head of the drays, wrapped in a cloak like a crusader leading her troops.

Back in Sydney, to put her case to the people of New South Wales and government officials, Caroline wrote pamphlets and letters in clear, concise language. She developed good relationships with newspaper editors and owners, not to publicise herself but to advance the humanitarian causes in which she was involved.

The Sydney Morning Herald published her emotive appeal for better conditions and paid work for immigrant women and asked for more drays to help transport them to the interior. The following day, she received offers of help and gifts of food and money from farmers and settlers, stunned to realise just how bad the situation was for female immigrants. Gifts of money, tins of biscuits, tea and coffee were delivered to the hostel. The gifts of tea were vital, as Sydney's water supply was contaminated and boiling the water for tea sterilised it.

Over the years, Caroline received and answered mountains of letters from intending immigrants, 5,000 of them from famine-ridden Ireland. Letters from parents distraught with worry and grief at separation from their children went straight to Caroline's heart and received her immediate attention. She was an excellent organiser and enlisted others to her cause through her gift for public speaking. Caroline had a wonderful sense of humour, she was warm-hearted, loyal and supportive. She persuaded women in the country towns to form Ladies' Committees to find jobs for 'her' migrant girls and, because the trips on the drays could last several days, established a system of what became known as 'Mrs Chisholm's shelter sheds'.

Caroline's aim of finding her girls employment won wider support. Soon voluntary committees were set up to act as employment agencies and place girls in country towns ranging from Port

Macquarie, the Moreton Bay Settlement (Brisbane), Wollongong, Maitland, Scone, Liverpool, Campbelltown, Goulburn, Yass and Mittagong (see inset map on the next page). Even though roads were bad, Caroline visited these towns herself by road or, where there were no roads, by boat.

Several branch hostels were set up under the supervision of clergymen. Initially, the Protestant churches had reservations because Mrs Chisholm was a Catholic, but when they realised that she was helping migrants of all denominations, they joined her in what they recognised as valuable work. There was continued resistance from Anglo-Saxon Protestant 'ladies' against employing Irish Catholics. They believed that Irish girls were slovenly and unused to laying tables and making beds properly as most came from homes too poor to afford a dining table, cutlery and proper beds.

As her workload increased, Caroline was torn between her love for her own children and her duty to the hundreds of daughters of Irish peasants and dispossessed Highland crofters. She soon realised it was hard to fulfil the duties of manager and matron of the large Immigrants Home (as the old barracks was renamed) and to supervise her own lively boys. After she had found the two eldest playing in the street by the hostel, strictly against her orders, she sent two of the boys back to her housekeeper at Windsor.

Caroline could not bear to part with her youngest son, Henry, a sturdy toddler, so he remained with his mother at the Female Hostel. Fears for the safety of her own children during a cholera epidemic climaxed when Caroline found a distraught woman in her office asking for a white gown in which to bury her dead child. Aware that Sydney was rife with cholera, dysentery and various infant fevers, Caroline described how 'A lady whose esteem I value told me I should not risk my child's life, I must either give up the Home (her hostel) or my selfish feelings for my child.'

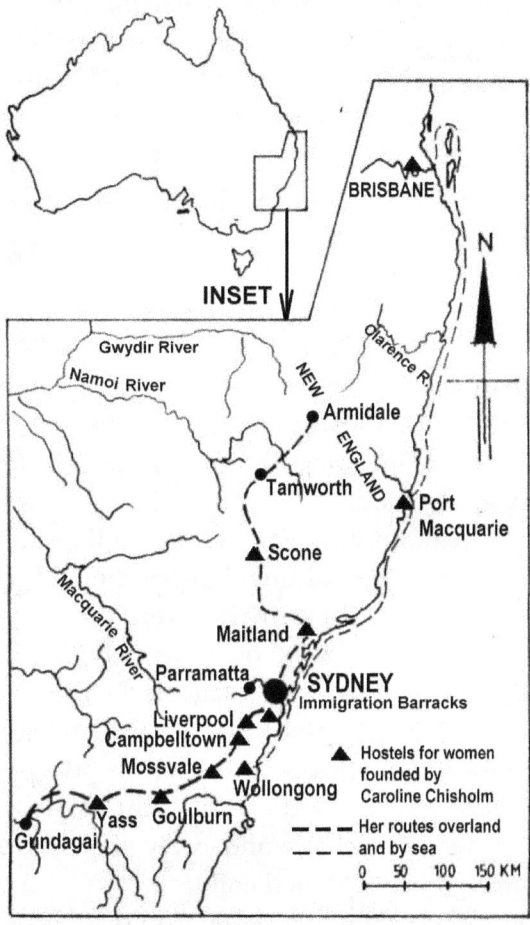

Believing the woman's child had died from typhus acquired from the lice that infested the old building — or even bubonic plague — Caroline packed up her son's clothes and sent Henry to live with his brothers at Windsor in the care of her housekeeper.[11] She was deeply distressed at having to send her youngest child away, but she had to continue her philanthropic work in the belief it was what God intended her to do.

The fact that Caroline and Archibald were separated by his military duties meant that she could focus on her work as a voluntary social worker. In the mid- nineteenth century, when contraception consisted of *coitus interruptus* or douching with a solution of vinegar, alum and water, most married women bore a child every eighteen months or two years.[12] Free from the pains and dangers of childbirth and released from the time-consuming breastfeeding and care of babies and infants, Caroline could devote her time, energies and organisational skills to improving conditions for other women.

Mrs Chisholm, riding her white horse at the head of a convoy of bullock drays laden with girls, became a familiar sight in the bush. She made frequent journeys to place her girls in homes which she had usually investigated beforehand. If she found a wealthy bachelor or widower with a farm she would try to place a girl on a neighbouring farm. From this clever stratagem, many happy marriages ensued.

Caroline Chisholm was good at persuading tough ex-convicts to help with the yoking and unyoking of the bullocks. Setting out from Sydney at dawn, her journeys were long and tiring; in the wet season, the drays struggled over boggy bush tracks knee- deep in mud. When the going was particularly rough, the girls and widows with children would climb down and walk beside the drays. When fording a stream, to lighten the load on the bullocks, Caroline would put a toddler in each of her white horse's enormous leather saddlebags and carry them across the stream while comforting the frightened children.

Her determination and endurance on these gruelling trips into the bush was remarkable. In the days before refrigeration, they could not take fresh meat with them. Salads were thought to be harmful to the digestion so the travellers lived on the traditional stockman's diet of roast mutton, salt beef and damper, washed down by black tea made in a billycan and, on occasions, biscuits donated by the public.

Eventually, the stress and responsibility of organising these journeys and the work involved in running the Female Hostel and a diet often lacking in fresh vegetables or milk would take their toll. Unknown to her or to her doctors, Caroline Chisholm drove herself so hard that slowly she developed kidney disease.

By December 1841, she added the setting up of a school to her workload. Between 1839 and 1842, 23,705 Irish immigrants arrived in Australia, outnumbering the influx of 5,986 Scots and 12,227 English and Welsh.[13] In 1843, the potato blight had started to ravage Ireland, whose peasant population lived off potatoes. Starvation soon followed in Irish rural areas and emigration seemed the only escape from misery and starvation.

The numbers of Irish unemployed and destitute arriving at Australian ports soared. Members of one migrant Irish family were so short of money on arrival in Sydney, they were reduced to eating potato peel that their children scavenged from dustbins.[14]

Caroline became convinced that the greatest force for good was family love and male convicts could be redeemed by wives and families. Her philanthropic work had given her a good understanding of human nature. She realised that it was necessary for children to have love and security so that they, in their turn, could *give* love and security, thus breaking the vicious cycle of child abuse and exploitation.

The penal system separated men from their families as a punishment, but Caroline knew that mere punishment would not rehabilitate them. She began to work to achieve family reunions for convicts and became involved with a scheme to send entire families of emancipists or free settlers to settle on small farms in the bush near Wollongong.

By 1844, the unemployment situation in the colony was so serious that a government Committee on Distressed Labourers asked Mrs Chisholm to give evidence. This was remarkable, as previously women had never been taken seriously enough to be asked to provide figures to government committees. Caroline had already collected statistics on the numbers of unemployed through placing notices in the *Herald*, inviting them to register with her. In her report, she told the Committee on Distressed Labourers she had recorded 2,034 unemployed men and women and dependent children, all needing government support. She urged that many of the unemployed be resettled by the colonial government on small blocks of vacant Crown land.

It was a brave and ambitious plan that would later be incorporated into the Selection Acts of 1860-61, but her proposal aroused hostility among the wealthy squatters who wanted to lock up all the land for themselves. When this proposal was rejected by the government, Caroline opened an employment agency in Bent Street, Sydney, close to her Female Hostel, staffed by volunteer workers from various churches.

To protect 'her girls' from unscrupulous employers, she drew up employment contracts which were revolutionary for the era in providing better conditions for workers. Over the years the agency she started found jobs in the bush for some 14,000 young women, some of whom showed their appreciation of Caroline's help in gaining a chance of better lives by sending her pieces from their wedding cakes!

Archibald Chisholm returned to Sydney in March 1845. He had retired from the army with the rank of Major and a small pension. Together they drew up a plan to open their own loan society (which they named the Family Colonisation Loan Society) as Caroline was convinced that the corrupt government bounty system, if restarted, would take advantage of the migrants.

In 1846, the Chisholms returned to Britain to run the Family Colonisation Loan Society and planned to send their own migrant ships to Australia. Caroline looked forward eagerly to seeing her mother again and introducing her sons to their grandmother for the first time.

A few months before leaving Australia, Caroline had become pregnant and, on 6 August 1846, their fourth son was born aboard the ship that took them 'home'. They christened the little boy Sydney, after the harbour city Caroline had grown to love.

In Britain, they found a small house in the north London suburb of Islington. Caroline's mother, Mrs Sarah Jones, came to live with them to look after the boys, leaving Caroline free to lobby the government through the press, publishing pamphlets and having interviews with influential reformers like Lord Shaftesbury.[15]

Caroline aimed for the Chisholms' Family Colonisation Loan Society to raise funds to be able to help poverty-stricken families who were young enough to start new lives to migrate to Australia relatively cheaply. She hoped that, if her society chartered ships, paid the wages of their captains and crew, she and Archy could supervise better conditions than those of the government 'bounty' scheme. Someone from the Family Colonisation Loan Society would meet migrants on arrival, have suitable accommodation waiting and help them find work.

Caroline spoke about the new society at meetings, answered mountains of letters, wrote pamphlets giving advice to migrants on everything from footwear and clothing to surviving on a diet of salt beef, damper and black 'billy tea' out in the bush. She also interviewed intending migrants who swarmed to her home seeking information. During this busy period, she once again fell pregnant and bore a daughter, whom she named Caroline.

Between 1850 and 1854, she convened and spoke at numerous emigration meetings in cities all over Britain. In 1852, she supervised the departures of the migrant ships *Slains Castle, Blundell, Ballangeich, Peru, Lindsay* and the ss *Ballarat*. In 1852, she visited Ireland, held a pro-migration meeting in Cork and visited several convents which cared for orphans to tell them of the possibilities for emigration to Australia. She hired several matrons to travel on the emigrant ship ss *Peru* from Queenstown, near Cork, for Australia. In 1853, she and her husband were in Glasgow supervising the building of a ship on the Clyde designed for emigrants to their own specifications.

When Mrs Chisholm had turned 43, Monica, her last child, was born. During the pregnancy Caroline had kept herself busy writing books and pamphlets.[16] So much work meant that she had little free time for her housework and relied on servants.

When Charles Dickens visited the Chisholms' north London home, he commented on the fact that the brass plate by her front door needed cleaning. Very impressed by Caroline Chisholm's desire for reform, Dickens, in search of picturesque characters for his novels, used aspects of Caroline's story to create a memorable character known as Mrs Jellaby for *Bleak House*. Mrs Jellaby was, like most of Dickens' characters, a composite of several people the author met and was a courageous female reformer who spoke on platforms but hated housework.

While he used some aspects of Caroline Chisholm in Mrs Jellaby, he did praise Mrs Chisholm's work for immigrants. Dickens was fascinated by tales of transportation and emigration. He knew for himself the grim realities of grinding poverty. As a child, he had worked long hours in a blacking factory when his father was in the debtor's prison and he had been withdrawn from school. He described this poverty in *David Copperfield* in which two families, the Micawbers and the Peggottys, emigrate to Australia.

In *Great Expectations* Dickens created the most famous convict in fiction — Magwich, who terrified little Pip on the marshes, was brought food by Pip, was recaptured by the police and transported back to Australia. Dickens gained much of his knowledge of convict transportation and emigration from the writings of Caroline Chisholm. Dickens' magazine *Household Words,* for March 1850, contains an anonymous article entitled *A Bundle of Emigrants' Letters* with an enthusiastic description of 'Mrs Chisholm's work' and her founding of the Family Colonisation Loan Society.

A week later, Dickens published an article influenced by a letter Caroline Chisholm had sent him, which he called *An Australian Ploughman's Story*.[17] The hero of the story, a convict who finds work once he becomes a ticket of leave man in Australia, pleads for a wife to share his simple home in the bush so he can start a better life and raise a family. Jem, the ploughman, claims '...virtuous wives in a lonely land make all the difference between happiness and misery'.

Caroline's publicity for the cause of well-regulated emigration was assisted by Charles Dickens and other generous benefactors.

Her pamphlets and public speeches and Major Chisholm's organisational skills ensured widespread support for better conditions for government-assisted migrants and changed what had been a terrible migration system for the better. Many of the points Caroline Chisholm suggested in her pamphlets and reports.[19] These would be incorporated into the British Passenger Acts of 1852 and 1855.[20]

Fearlessly, Caroline dared to tackle another subject that 'nice' ladies were not meant to know about — the sexual abuse of vulnerable females on board immigrant ships. Archibald stuck to his promise and helped his wife mount a campaign for better conditions for the bounty girls who had no means of redress against the captains and crews who saw them as fair game. The Chisholms decided they would lobby the British government for a better deal for migrants.

While running her hostel in Sydney, Caroline had been angered by the number of women seduced or raped on board ship. She was so incensed by the harsh treatment suffered by a teenage rape victim, an orphan named Margaret Bolton, that she helped the penniless girl bring a lawsuit against Captain Robert Richardson. He had raped Margaret and his friend, Dr Richard Nelson, the ship's doctor, covered up the incident. Mrs Chisholm's involvement and the ensuing publicity ensured that Dr Nelson and Captain Richardson were tried, convicted and fined.[21] Sexual abuse had been so widespread on convict ships that they were known as floating brothels. Migrant ships lacked a female matron to supervise and protect the girls. Mrs Chisholm would change all that by daring to publicise the abuse of these girls and young women.

In the landmark case of raped teenager Margaret Bolton, Mrs Chisholm used the guilty verdict to lobby the British government for protection of female migrants against sexual harassment and, as a result, the employment of female matrons on board migrant ships became compulsory.[22]

Caroline was determined that the abuse of what the government referred to as 'immigrant paupers' must end. She demanded and won the right for inspectors to check each government migrant ship, and for improvements to the bleak living conditions bounty migrants had endured for more than a decade, which included a lack of washing or cooking facilities and a shortage of bunks. In a pamphlet Caroline Chisholm published at her own expense, *The ABC of Colonisation,* she explained how emigration should operate when bringing out migrants on assisted passages. Practical as ever, Caroline told intending migrants what sort of clothes and footwear to bring with them.

The poor and needy flocked to Caroline's north London home for information about emigrating to Australia through the Chisholms' emigration society. She interviewed prospective migrants, gave them practical advice on the price of food and tools in the colony and discussed what work was available. If she thought they were employable and sufficiently resourceful and stable to withstand the stresses of migration, she helped them emigrate with assistance by the Chisholm's Family Colonisation Loan Society.

Caroline held public meetings all over Britain demanding better food and a proper dining room for the immigrants on government ships. Previously, ship owners, greedy for profit under the 'bounty' system, had filled their ships to overflowing with migrants, making women and children share bunks on the long sea journey in the dark and reeking holds of the vessels. While one shift was sleeping, the other shift would cook food in a makeshift galley or huddle together on the swaying deck to keep warm. Sanitation on board was rudimentary, to say the least — usually one slop bucket between 20 migrants and infection from dysentery was rife.

Working together, Caroline and Archibald Chisholm were responsible for changing a brutal government-run emigration system for the destitute into one that was more humane. Caroline's pamphlets insisted the government allocate each woman or child older than 12 a separate bunk, which should not be shared. Sufficient bedding, cutlery and 'privies' were to be provided, with separate privies for women and children and no more slop buckets filled with excrement in the sleeping areas. The Chisholms' Family Colonisation Loan Society raised money through loans and public donations. Soon they were able to charter their own ships, funded by the generosity of benefactors including Charles Dickens' friend and supporter, the philanthropic Miss Angela Burdett-Coutts.

Before there was such a thing as telegraphic transfer of money, Caroline talked with bankers and arranged transfers whereby emigrants working in New South Wales could send relatively small sums (which banks had previously refused to handle) back to parents or relatives in England.

From 1850 onwards, Caroline and her husband worked hard for their Family Colonisation Loan Society entirely without a salary or benefits of any kind. Archibald Chisholm supported his wife and children from his meagre army pension and every penny they raised went towards providing better conditions for migrants. As applications from working-class migrants continued to pour into the Islington house, Caroline drew up plans to charter two twin-screw steamships. They were to be named the *Caroline Chisholm* and the *Robert Lowe* to take migrants to the new colony of Port Phillip (soon to be known as Melbourne) under far better conditions than the old government 'hell-ships'. But there was a need for a reliable person to run the Melbourne end of the society.

After lengthy discussions, it was decided that Archibald should go back to Australia and run this important side of their joint operation and Caroline would join him later. Between 1851 and 1854, Caroline and Archibald were separated. She remained in Islington and interviewed women who wished to emigrate, using the Islington house as an office.

During its first four years under Caroline's direction, the Chisholms' Family Colonisation Loan Society sent seven ships to Australia, containing 1,288 adults, 475 children and 68 infants.[23] Caroline ensured at the society's chartered ships had one matron on board for every 50 females to 'instruct them in housewifery'. The ships were provided with bathrooms, wash-houses, irons and stoves.

Funds raised were used to help migrants rather than employing new staff. Archibald ran the Australian side of the organisation single-handed, which put a great strain on his health. He welcomed migrants on arrival and collected repayments on their loans once they found work. This commitment to their society meant that, although husband and wife were extremely fond of each other and were best friends as well as partners, this devoted couple had to spend four years apart.

Once again, Caroline, having spent her money on her philanthropic work, was embarrassingly short of money for her own living expenses. An old friend of Florence Nightingale wrote to Miss Nightingale, then in France, telling her in confidence that Mrs Chisholm needed financial assistance. On 2 June 1853, Florence Nightingale wrote to her mother, Mrs Fanny Nightingale, asking her to send money to Mrs Chisholm for her own use. She implored her mother to be very tactful as Mrs Chisholm would not appreciate being regarded as a charity case. Caroline had hoped to return to Australia on the maiden voyage of the steamship named in her honour, the ss *Caroline Chisholm*, which was built to Caroline's specification. However, in a time of crisis, it was requisitioned by the British government to carry British soldiers to the Crimea.[24]

Caroline's travel plans had already been delayed once when she had to visit Rome to collect young William, who was boarding in a seminary and studying for the priesthood. The head of the seminary feared William was not robust enough to enter the priesthood and decided he should terminate his studies and accompany his mother back to Australia in the hope a long sea voyage would improve his health. Caroline's parish priest had written to the Vatican telling them about Mrs Chisholm's dedicated work with the poor and dispossessed and requesting the honour of a papal audience.

This request was granted and Caroline travelled overland through France to Rome. On arrival at the Vatican, she was thrilled to have a private audience in which Pope Pius IX who gave her a gold medallion and a white marble bust he had commissioned from an Italian sculptor. It showed Caroline in profile. She was elated when His Holiness took her by the arm and praised her. Caroline had learned a little Italian, and understood the words *excellentissima, perseveranza* and *brava*.[25]

The fact Britain was at war meant more delays for Caroline and her sons. Eventually, they were given passages on the ss *Ballarat*, sailing for the newly created colony of Victoria in the late spring. One of the conditions of sailing at a reduced fare was that Caroline was to act as matron to the young women on board.

Parting from her mother was terrible — both women realised it was unlikely they would ever meet again in this life. The evening before the ship sailed, Caroline was asked to make a speech to the assembled migrants. She intended to refer to the difficulties all of them faced when leaving elderly parents behind in Britain. She started by saying 'I have an aged mother', but tears filled her eyes and she could not continue.[26] Only too well she understood the anguish of women torn between loyalties to parents, husbands and children. But at least she knew that their Family Colonisation Loan Society was in the capable hands of a trusted friend named Samuel Cogden and a committee composed of influential people such as the explorer Count Strzelecki and Sir Stuart Donaldson, a future Premier of New South Wales.

In July 1854, Caroline, her husband and children were reunited in Melbourne, where she found that the discovery of gold had made a great difference to New South Wales and the new colony of Victoria. Migration soared with men who hoped to get rich and workers in Sydney and Melbourne flocked to the goldfields.

> Cottages were deserted, houses to let, business is at a standstill, and even schools are closed. In some suburbs there is not a man left. The ships in the harbour are, in a great measure, deserted. Both here and at Geelong all building and contract works, public and private, almost without exception, are at a standstill. The price of provisions in the towns is naturally on the increase, for

although there may be an abundant supply within reach, there are not sufficient hands to turn it to account.[27]

The population of Victoria tripled as daily bulletins appeared on billboards and in newspapers about the latest gold strikes. Unskilled men and tradesmen in Sydney and Melbourne left work and wives to cope with chopping wood and drawing water and headed off to the diggings to live in tents. Some women followed their men onto the gold fields. Caroline recorded that

> ... for every respectable woman on the goldfields there were two of the other kind, temporary brides and. housekeepers who went when the money went. Diggers' weddings were an uproarious feature of life in Melbourne as men back from the goldfields, flourishing champagne bottles, lolled in carriages with brightly dressed brides as they raced along Collins Street. Some lodging houses in the town would supply a young lady who, for a 'consideration' would act the role of a bride. Carriage and footmen would also be provided for the bridegrooms, who lit cigars with banknotes, waved flags, dressed ostentatiously and behaved outrageously.[28]

By that time, Major Archibald Chisholm's health had been badly affected by the years in India, making him unfit for heavy work. His army pension had to support a large family of teenage boys, six-year-old Caroline and three-year-old Monica. The Chisholms still refused to take any payment from the society they had founded but they soon discovered war in the Crimea and the gold rush had changed the patterns of emigration. Now single men in search of gold were pouring into Victorian ports, but there were very few single women.

Caroline employed a widowed migrant named Ann Clinton to act as governess to her daughters. This left Caroline free to continue working, as she felt personally responsible for the large number of girls and married couples she had encouraged to migrate when she had interviewed them in London. Some of them had not found work and others were having difficulty repaying their loans. Caroline could understand their problems. She and Archibald had their own money worries. For years, they had been renting houses and now they lacked sufficient capital to buy a house in which to spend their old age. But, as always, Caroline trusted that God would provide a solution.

Some women told Caroline that they wanted to rejoin their husbands at the goldfields, but feared the journey was too expensive and too dangerous. She did not want to let these women down and decided to see life on the diggings for herself. She and one of her sons set off to the goldfields in a horse-drawn cart with horsehair seats and worn-out springs. They travelled over rough roads and bush tracks to Bendigo, Kyneton and Castlemaine.

Each time Mrs Chisholm spoke in public, some man would tell her she had encouraged him to send for his wife and children, but complained that there were no cheap inns on the way and that the price of family reunion was too high.

At the diggings, Caroline saw drunken women selling their bodies to the miners while others sold sly grog at the back of refreshment tents. All this made her keener to reunite gold diggers with their families as she jolted over bumpy roads, facing danger from bushrangers or from drinking infected water.

Caroline became convinced that she must do something to help reunite miners with their families and decided to raise funds to build shelter sheds to provide cheap overnight accommodation for women and children en route to the goldfields.[29]

She wrote to the newly appointed Governor of Victoria, Sir Charles Hotham, urging him to establish inexpensive shelter sheds to act as staging posts at Essendon, Keilor, Sunbury, Gisborne, Wood End, Carlsruhe, Malmsbury and Elphinstone. Other rural areas where Caroline stayed volunteered to raise funds for what became known as 'Mrs Chisholm's Shelter Sheds'.

On her return to Melbourne she was asked to talk at public meetings about the goldfields. She started one speech by saying,
'I am not one of those who like to ask "What will the government do for us?" For us the question is, "What shall we do for ourselves?"'

Mary explained how grasping landlords were taking advantage of the influx of new diggers to raise prices of food, rooms and water to extortionate levels. At the diggings, men lived in tents, ate cold food and had no washing or toilet facilities.

By that time, Archibald was ill and keen to retire from public life, so they rented a house in Melbourne's Elizabeth Street North where he could live. It became apparent that the Chisholm family was now short of money. They had worked for many years for others without thought of any payment for themselves.

Friends, well-wishers and the Legislative Council of Victoria donated money to Archibald Chisholm to establish himself in a small business. With the money, he bought a general store in East Kyneton, hoping to benefit from the gold rush by selling food and tools like picks and shovels. Archibald and his three eldest sons, Archibald junior, William and Henry, worked in the store and lived nearby.

Meanwhile, Mrs Chisholm's Shelter Shed Committee was still busy raising funds. Caroline and the girls stayed on in their rented house in Melbourne to oversee the equipment of the shelter sheds. Caroline intended to rejoin Archibald at Kyneton once the work for the shelter sheds was completed.

Each shelter shed had a paid keeper who charged overnight guests a very small fee for very basic accommodation with dirt floors. These shelter sheds became very popular with travellers short of money and families content to sleep on bunks and straw mattresses.

During this busy time, Caroline made frequent visits to her husband and sons at Kyneton. The delicate William married an Irish girl and moved back to Melbourne.

Caroline wanted to change the law to help the many innocent girls who had been drawn into a life of prostitution in Melbourne's brothels. She was frustrated that women had no voice in Parliament (colonial Melbourne was not exceptional in the amount of prostitutes working there; London was estimated to have had 80,000 prostitutes and Paris, a smaller city, had even more).[30]

The gold rush meant that the number of brothels increased due to so many diggers — men with money and no women. The 'lucky diggers', flaunting their wealth, hired or 'married' prostitutes for a day or a week. Caroline wrote an angry letter to the press when a girl of 13 was found dead in a house of ill repute in Little Bourke Street. The teenage girl had died of a heart attack, a one-pound note on the bed beside her. Once again, Caroline demanded homes or subsidised lodging houses for 'females and distressed families' on their arrival.

By now, Caroline's health was failing and she realised she could no longer run a women's hostel in Melbourne as she had done years ago in Sydney.[31]

In December 1857, she gave up their rented home in Melbourne and joined Archibald at Kyneton in accommodation close to the family's general store. Unfortunately, the store was doing badly due to competition from rival businesses.

The following March, Caroline and Archibald were delighted to find themselves grandparents when William's wife had a son.

Caroline was often in pain and the doctor believed that the harsh winters at Kyneton adversely affected her health. Leaving the boys in charge of the store, she and Archibald returned to Sydney, where they rented a shabby weatherboard house in Redfern. Archibald, gaunt and pale but still distinguished with an upright carriage and silver hair, managed to find work in a draper's shop. It was not the kind of work he wanted, but they needed money badly. Their small capital was still tied up in the Kyneton store, which, due to low turnover, proved hard to sell.

The family settled into a routine but were soon jolted out of it by the shock of the death of their delicate son William. He had never been strong since living in Rome and, to make matters worse, William's baby died the following day. The bereaved Chisholms were too short of money to return to Melbourne for the joint funeral of their son and grandson.

However, living in Sydney's milder climate improved Caroline's health. As soon as she was well enough, she accepted invitations to speak at public meetings about the free selection of blocks of Crown land for immigrants, who would receive extended credit terms to pay for their land. Caroline spoke on a platform with John Robertson, Premier of New South Wales, who was attempting to pass the Land Selection Act. This allowed settlers without capital to take up relatively small blocks of land on favourable mortgage terms.

Caroline also crusaded for the right of unmarried mothers (meaning those who had been raped or seduced and became pregnant as a result) to receive government assistance and spoke out in favour of early closing of shops and stores. Some employers made their staff work 10- and 11-hour shifts on the shop floor for low wages.

Eventually, the younger Chisholm boys sold the Kyneton store for less than they had paid for it and joined their parents in Sydney. The rented Redfern house was too cramped for all of them so Mr and Mrs Chisholm rented a larger home in Stanley Street. By now the gold rush had changed Sydney. The former barracks on the corner of Bent Street, where Caroline had operated her Female Hostel, had been demolished. In its place was the handsome new Subscription Library. Migrant ships were now powered by steam and Caroline had ensured better sleeping conditions including separate cabins for female migrants and matrons to look after them on board ship.

In July 1862, Caroline started a girls' school in Stanmore, attended by her daughters Caroline and Monica and paying pupils. Later, the school moved to larger premises at Tempe but Caroline's failing health meant she rarely taught pupils.

She still received appreciative letters from women whose lives she had changed for the better. By now her fame had spread as far as France. In 1862, the French historian Jules Michelet devoted a chapter to *'la glorieuse Madame Chisholm'* in a book titled *La Femme* describing Caroline Chisholm as a 'living legend' and as a suitable candidate for canonisation.

By now, Caroline was in pain from what would eventually be diagnosed as kidney disease.[32] Alarmed by the swift deterioration in her condition, her husband and her doctor advised she must return to London to consult a specialist.

In 1866, the Chisholm family arrived in London without their son Harry, who had married and remained in Sydney. But, instead of improving, Caroline's health worsened. 'Dropsy' or severe swelling in her legs caused by kidney failure made walking very difficult.

Major Archibald Chisholm was now over 70, still erect but unable to work. Caroline was forced to rest in bed for long periods but, as always, detested being idle. When she felt well enough, she took up her pen and earned a little money from journalism. But it was obvious to visitors that their funds were low and Caroline lacked many comforts. Friends lobbied for government support, stressing that Caroline had dedicated her entire life to the needs of others.

Eventually, the British government awarded Caroline a small pension in recognition of her outstanding service to humanity and improving the Australian emigration system. As yet, she was not totally bedridden and spent the next few years in a small back bedroom in a dingy little house at Highgate Hill, north London, where she was delighted to receive visits from her children and adored grandchildren.

In spite of pain and discomfort from her illness, Caroline was consoled by her religious faith and the fact that she had fulfilled God's plan for her life. She prayed something would happen to improve their living conditions.

Caroline was right. Eventually, she did receive some financial assistance. In the last year of her life, their married daughter Caroline (Mrs Charles Gray) paid for her parents to move to a larger and more comfortable home at 43a Barclay Road, Fulham. Caroline's bed was placed beside a large bay window so that she could look out over the street lined with beautiful trees, which gave her pleasure.

Caroline died of bronchitis aged 68 on the Feast of the Annunciation and the last sound she heard was the ringing of church bells.

Her body was taken to the Roman Catholic Cathedral of St Felix in the town of Northampton, near the farm where she was born and raised. Her husband, distraught over Caroline's death, was deemed too frail to attend the funeral and died a few months later. Their joint tombstone, a white marble cross in Northampton's Billing Road Cemetery, was engraved with the words

> Of your charity pray for the souls of Caroline Chisholm, the Emigrants' Friend, who died 25 March 1877 aged 67 years and of Archibald Chisholm, Major, Madras Native Infantry, who died 17 August, 1877, aged 81 years. Rest in Peace.

Caroline Chisholm was a woman of the 19th century, but, in the skilful way she organised support and publicity for her cause, she seems very modern and was a trailblazer for her era.

She was in advance of her times in insisting her future husband sign a prenuptial contract which gave her the right to pursue her interests in philanthropy. She carried on her life's work with her husband's support and promoted the cause of families in need in the press in an era when wives were meant to remain silent.

Caroline Chisholm's achievements were praised by the French historian Jules Michelet, who called her a saintly person, and described how

> ... lacking wealth and without any financial assistance [Mrs Chisholm] has done more for the people of the New World [meaning Australia] than all other emigration societies and the British government put together. This great lady succeeded in her aims by strength of character and vigour of soul.[33]

Oil painting showing the tragic plight of widows and children evicted from their homes and sent to workhouses. Those who emigrated to Sydney had nowhere to live, which prompted Caroline Chisholm to set up hostels for them. Painting in the Queensland Art Gallery, photographed by Jake de Vries.

Engraving showing the cramped sleeping arrangements below decks on an emigrant ship, which lacked privacy or space to wash or dry clothes.

Engraved portrait of Caroline Chisholm by Michelangelo Hayes, with a map of Australia behind her. Private collection.

A Sydney employment agency and the kind of men from whom Mrs Chisholm protected 'her' young women. Engraving owned by Pirgos Press.

CHAPTER 2

Elizabeth Hawkins (née Lilly) (1783–1875)

THE FIRST WHITE FEMALE TO CROSS THE BLUE MOUNTAINS [1]

On Easter Saturday, 5 April 1822, Sydney's Lower George Street was bustling with activity. Bullock carts, drays, wagons and horses were lined up near the horse-troughs in readiness for an early departure. Thomas Hawkins was loading the last few crates of stores onto the drays with the help of half a dozen convicts assigned to him.

Mrs Elizabeth Hawkins helped her 70-year-old mother mount the steps of a covered wagon, then she and seven of her children climbed in as well. Elizabeth's eldest son, 12-year-old Tom, would travel on horseback.

Elizabeth, her husband Thomas, her mother and their eight children were ready to set off on their hazardous journey to a remote military settlement of Bathurst.[2] It was a leap into the unknown, fraught with danger. 38-year-old Elizabeth and her elderly mother, Mrs Lilly, were destined to become the first white women to cross the Blue Mountains.

With a creaking of harness and cracking of rawhide whips, the procession started off. Elizabeth's husband headed the procession on a bay horse, accompanied by his eldest son and two convict supervisors, all on horseback. After them came a bullock-drawn cart with a tarpaulin over its load and two open drays carrying crates of stores and household goods — another cart loaded with farm implements followed. In the rear came the covered wagon in which Elizabeth, her mother and the seven younger children were travelling. A canvas canopy, known as a tilt, sheltered them from the elements. In addition to their luggage, they carried an emergency supply of drinking water in earthenware storage jars. The tilted wagon, the carts and the drays were all driven by convicts, assigned to Thomas. Their journey was supposed to take a week, but it would be 17 harrowing days before they reached their destination.

Elizabeth had promised her sister in England to make notes about the journey, so she could write a long letter 'home' about it.

Thomas Fitzherbert Hawkins had been employed as a paymaster in the British Navy. Throughout the Napoleonic wars, Thomas had been attached to H.M.S. *Berwick*, a 74-gun ship. During the Battle of Waterloo the *Berwick* was engaged in transporting troops across the Channel when Hawkins was wounded. He also had his leg broken and now walked with a slight limp.

Six years after Britain had won the Battle of Waterloo, the British Admiralty retrenched or placed on half pay hundreds of officers, including Paymaster Hawkins. Having excellent character references and experience in bookkeeping, Thomas Hawkins had expected to find a suitable job in Britain. But after six months of fruitless job hunting his savings were dwindling and he and his family had to live on a meagre pension from the British Navy.

In desperation, Thomas considered emigrating to Australia. He had been told that in the penal colony of New South Wales former army and naval officers were eligible for land grants. He was also aware that the sheep and wool industry was booming in the colony and that free convict labour was available.

However, by the 1820s, the best grazing land in the vicinity of Sydney Town had already been taken up by free settlers and serving officers. Therefore, newly arrived settlers had to look for suitable pastures further inland, including the plains beyond the Blue Mountains.

In the early years of the 19th century, attempts had been made to cross the Blue Mountains by following the valleys which meandered between its steep slopes, but all of them had failed. In 1813, the courageous explorers Gregory Blaxland, William Wentworth and William Lawson decided to follow the ridges rather than the valleys and succeeded in crossing the barrier as far as Mount Blaxland. Soon after, surveyor George W. Evans extended the exploration to what was later called the Bathurst Plains. Evans reported that beyond the Blue Mountains excellent pasture land was for the taking.

Soon after that discovery, William Cox had built a road that provided access to the western slopes of the Blue Mountains and the Bathurst Plains. The road, which was built by convicts, was in part extremely steep and dangerous to travel on.

While still living in Britain, Thomas had made inquiries about a land grant in the newly developed Bathurst Plains, where he was told the soil was fertile and water plentiful. He was assured that he would have no difficulty in obtaining a land grant there.

As this information sounded most promising, Thomas decided to take the big step and start a new life in the Antipodes with his large family. Elizabeth realised that she would have to face many hardships, but, with eight children to feed, she accepted her husband's emigration plans and was prepared to become a trail-blazing farmer's wife.

Goodbyes were said and Thomas Hawkins and his family boarded the sailing ship *Minstral* in July 1821 and sailed to the penal colony of New South Wales.[3] On board the ship they met fellow migrants going to join relatives on the land and Australian residents returning from a visit to their home country. They heard stories of beautiful birds and flowering trees, but also of severe droughts and devastating floods. However, everyone reassured them that the colony offered wonderful opportunities.

Despite the occasional bout of seasickness, the Hawkins children, who had always loved hearing their father's stories of life at sea, greatly enjoyed themselves aboard the *Minstral*.

It was only when they arrived at Sydney Town, early in January 1822, that Elizabeth and Thomas heard disquieting stories about settlers and shepherds being attacked by Aborigines.[4] They were also told that settlers' children had died after being bitten by poisonous snakes or spiders. Elizabeth had always fussed over the health of her children — she was aware that out on the lonely Bathurst Plains the nearest doctor would be a week's ride away on horseback. She wondered whether they could manage until the new settlement was large enough to warrant a resident doctor and a proper school for the children.

In Sydney Cove, the Hawkins family lodged in a boarding house in the most salubrious part of The Rocks, high on the hill overlooking Sydney Cove. A friend from navy days came to see them and expressed grave concern about Thomas's rash decision to take his young family on such an arduous journey.

To keep them solvent until they could make their farm self-supporting Thomas had applied for the job of Government Storekeeper at the new settlement of Bathurst . The job was way below his capabilities but it would give him the right to live in a timber dwelling owned by the government and to employ convicts to work for him in the government store and on his land. Thomas's application was granted, which meant that on arrival in Bathurst he and his family would have a roof over their heads until he had obtained his land grant and built a house on it.

Thomas was told that the street plans for the proposed new town had been prepared. With an eye on his own career prospects, Governor Macquarie had cannily named the projected new town 'Bathurst' in honour of Henry, Earl of Bathurst, who, as Colonial Secretary, was a powerful political figure.

To build a courthouse, a jail and other public buildings, the British government was storing building equipment, bricks and other building materials in the government store and its yard. A few ticket of leave men had settled there already and were chopping down trees and starting to build houses.

During their stay in Sydney, Thomas and Elizabeth were warned that William Cox's road over the Blue Mountains was extremely dangerous, especially the part that led to the top of Mount York and down the other side. 'Good luck' everyone wished them, adding they certainly would need a lot of luck. But it was too late to withdraw — the die was cast.[5]

Before setting out on their journey, Thomas and Elizabeth spent three months selecting and buying horses, bullocks and cows. To ensure that sufficient milk would be available for the children they decided to take two milking cows with them as well. They had to hire drays and fit out a tilted wagon.[6] They also had to purchase provisions, tools and other equipment to set up home in the outback and start a farm of their own.

While staying in Sydney, Elizabeth had enough spare time to go for walks with her children. They went sightseeing around the harbour and in town, where they saw gangs of convicts breaking stones and toiling on roads. Sydney Town was an open jail and convict cottages, occupied by slatternly convict women, straggled along Lower George Street. There were public houses, frequented by convicts and seamen. It was a most unsavoury place, so Elizabeth avoided that area on future walks with her children.

Thomas Hawkins was allotted nine 'trusty' convict men to accompany them on their journey across the Blue Mountains — two were sufficiently skilled to act as supervisors.[7] These convicts had been released from hard labour and assigned to him to work in the government store in Bathurst and later as farm labourers. These men did not inspire trust in Elizabeth, but Thomas assured her that the men assigned to him had been hand-picked from the Hyde Park Barracks and regarded by their jailers as 'trusty' prisoners.

On Good Friday, 4 April 1822, the Hawkins family attended morning service at St James Church in the centre of Sydney before making final preparations for their departure. Free settlers came to their lodgings to farewell them and to wish them good luck in their pioneering venture.

By the following morning, everything the Hawkinses had brought out from England or bought in Sydney was packed and loaded on the wagons. Their supplies included sacks of flour, raisins and sugar which Elizabeth hoped would not turn sticky in the heat and the rain. They took beef, tins of treacle and jam, shovels, picks, hay rakes, hoes, scythes, clothing for summer and winter, a compass, a map and a precious tinderbox which was essential to start a fire.

Shortage of space meant that the only furniture Elizabeth could take was a table and eight chairs — some of which would be used to sit on inside the tilted wagon. She worried about the effect this journey would have on her children, the oldest being only 12. But she had to take heart, the arduous journey was about to start.

The first day took them to Rooty Hill, a 40 kilometres journey. They travelled along 'a turnpike road as good as those in England'. When they were near Parramatta, Thomas rode on to the 'Female Factory' to select a convict girl who would help Elizabeth to cook, wash, clean and look after the children. He chose a pleasant country girl convicted for stealing some small items. The girl seemed most suitable to Elizabeth, but she was worried that her new servant might swear and be a bad influence on her children.[8]

Thomas had arranged to stay for two nights at Parramatta in a government-run hostel for travellers, which Elizabeth called in her letter 'the Government House'. There they spent Sunday resting and recovering in the parklike grounds surrounding the hostel.

The Hawkins family made an early start on Monday to cover the 21 kilometres distance to the Nepean River and Emu Plains. For another 15 kilometres, the road was still in a good condition.

The Nepean River had to be crossed to reach Emu Plains. There was a cross-river ferry, but it was too small to take the large bullock-drawn carts and drays across. Only the tilted wagon could be ferried to the other side of the river, but not until the horses had been unharnessed.

The women and children had to wait for hours in a small hut while their possessions were unloaded from the carts and drays which had been hired to take their luggage this far. Everything had to be ferried across and reloaded on a second lot of carts and drays which were awaiting them on the other side of the river. Before nightfall, they managed to get part of their luggage across the river, while the rest had to wait until the next day.

That night they stayed at a government-owned rest-house and depot at Emu Plains. During that stay, Elizabeth wrote down the previous days' events in what would become a very long letter to her sister in England. The following page shows Elizabeth's record of those events in her own handwriting.

The following morning, rain came pouring down, wetting most of their luggage and delaying the loading of it. Finally, by five o'clock in the afternoon, the rest of their luggage had been ferried across and loaded on the drays. They now had one cart fewer than when they started, so some of their possessions had to be left behind at Emu Plains in the government depot. Because there was insufficient grass for their cattle in the mountains, they had to take extra fodder, reducing room for their luggage even further.

Before starting the most difficult part of their journey the Hawkinses decided to stay at Emu Plains for another four days, probably spending more nights at the government hostel.

At Emu Plains was a splendid mansion, called *Regentville*, where Sir John Jamieson lived. *Regentville* was surrounded by ornamental flower gardens, terraces and miles of orchards. Portly Sir John was known as 'the Knight of *Regentville*' and was the largest landowner for hundreds of miles.[9]

When within a few miles of Parramatta, Hawkins rode on to the Factory for a female servant who had been selected for us. He rejoined us whilst we were partaking our dinner at the foot of a tree. We arrived rather late in the evening at Rooty Hill a distance of 25 miles, the Government House was ready to receive us. The next day being Sunday we rested partly to recover from the fatigue we had previous to leaving Sydney, and because the general orders were there should be no travelling on Sunday. I could have been contented to have remained there for ever, the house was good & the land all around like a fine wooded Park in England. On Monday we resumed our journey and for 9 miles found the road the same as before, we had now reached the Nepean River, which you cross to Emu Plains where there is a Gov. House & Depot

On their final night, Elizabeth and Thomas were invited to dine with Sir John Jamieson at his residence, which was greatly appreciated. Sir John was a generous host and his guests were offered mock turtle soup, boiled chicken, beef, fish and curried duck, all served by female convict servants. The guests washed their meal down with several bottles of excellent burgundy. After the dessert, Madeira wine as well as liqueurs were served by Sir John's convict housekeeper. Elizabeth did not know that the housekeeper was Sir John's resident mistress — all he talked about was his intended engagement to one of the Macleay girls, daughter of the Colonial Treasurer.

Sir John congratulated Elizabeth for her fortitude in going out to such a remote spot and opening up 'civilisation in the wilderness'. In the letter to her sister Elizabeth related how

> I was told I would be immortalised for the attempt to get [to the settlement of Bathurst] and that the government should be grateful for taking such a family to a place where no family of free settlers had gone before.[10]

After a four-day stay at Emu Plains, Elizabeth went to say goodbye to Sir John. He wished her and her family good luck for the future. He assured her that the land around Bathurst was beautiful and fertile, which raised Elizabeth's confidence that their new life as pioneers might turn out well. At least, at Bathurst, they would be independent and the government would give them a dwelling, however basic. Until they were ready to start farming, there would be 'a secure government job for Mr Hawkins, a secure future for all of us'.

When the Hawkins family were about to leave, Sir John instructed his housekeeper to give them a cooked haunch of mutton, two dressed chickens and some freshly churned butter to take with them on the journey.

The government hostel at Emu Plains was the last decent place that would shelter them until they reached the settlement of Bathurst and for the rest of the journey they would have to sleep in a tent or in primitive lodgings.

On Saturday 12 April, the Hawkins family left Emu Plains early in the morning.[11] After travelling less than a kilometre they encountered a shallow stream, where one of the bullock drays got stuck in the soft sandy bottom. It took them more than an hour to pull the dray out of the stream by using two additional horses.

The road to the fledgling settlement on the Bathurst Plains had been completed only a few years earlier and most of the bridges were still unfinished, which meant that crossing some of the rivers was extremely hazardous.

The new road had been cut through the bush by unwilling convicts who were flogged if the overseer thought they were slacking. Not surprisingly, the convicts did not care about the long-term quality of the road — their main concern was to get enough tobacco and sleep and to avoid the lash. In some places the new road was already potholed. Convicts were lugging heavy baskets of stones to fill in the worst holes to keep the road trafficable.

The first major hurdle was encountered on the ascent at Lapstone Hill, the slopes of which gradually grew steeper and steeper. It soon became clear that the bullocks would be unable to pull the heavily loaded carts up the steep incline, so some of the luggage had to be unloaded and taken back to the government depot at Emu Plains. Thomas rode back and organised a cart and horses to collect the abandoned luggage.

Fortunately, the horses were strong enough to pull one of the drays right up to the top of the mountain. But even with a reduced load, the bullocks were still in trouble, so the horses were brought back from the top of the mountain to assist them. They made little progress that day, advancing only some five kilometres.

On Lapstone Hill, they pitched their tent for the first time. The weather had cleared and the moon shone brightly. It must have been an unforgettable evening for Elizabeth and the children. In her letter, she writes enthusiastically about the experience.

> It was a lovely moonlight night, and all was novelty and delight to the elder children. Immense fires were made in all directions. We gave them their supper, and after putting the younger ones

to bed, I came from the tent, in front of which was a large fire. The men – nine in number – were busily employed in cooking in one place, our own men roasting a couple of fowls for our next day's journey.

I turned from the view, took the arm of Hawkins, who was seated at the table with the storekeeper [who had joined them from Emu Plains], and went to the back of the tent. Here we saw Tom and the three eldest girls trying who could make the best fire, as happy as it was possible for young hearts to be. Then I seemed to pause. It was a moment I shall never forget. For the first time for many a long month I seemed capable of enjoying and feeling the present moment without a dread for the future. Hawkins was again an officer under Government, a home to receive us, and the certainty under any circumstances of never wanting the common necessaries of life.

After a little while we returned to the table. These were moments of such inward rest that Hawkins took up a flute belonging to one of the party, and, calling Eliza [their eldest daughter] to us, she danced in a place where perhaps no one of her age had ever trod before.

The next morning, when preparing to depart, Thomas discovered that during the night a team of bullocks and his horse had disappeared and, doubtless, had returned to Emu Plains. While Thomas and some of the convicts went to collect the animals, the rest of the party continued their journey to the small settlement of Springwood.[12]

It was an exhausting journey of nearly 16 kilometres over a steep, stony road. At Springwood was a wooden hostel, which provided basic accommodation for travellers. It consisted of a large room, a spacious kitchen with a fireplace and two small bedrooms. The 'furniture' was made of tree stumps fashioned into rough seats and one of the bedrooms had a primitive type of sofa-bed cushioned with strips of bark. A corporal, his wife and two soldiers lived in that barn-like structure. The corporal's wife, an ex-convict woman, ran the place.

Thomas, having had to return to Emu Plains to retrieve his horse and the stray bullocks, did not arrive until later that night. In the absence of his father, 12-year-old Tom took charge. The boy may not have realised that their landlady was working as a prostitute, but Elizabeth certainly did. In addition to serving beer and spirits, the landlady was providing sexual favours to the soldiers for a fee and neglected to do any housework.

Elizabeth described their landlady as 'slatternly and dissolute and the place with its tattered furniture and blackened sheets as some sort of disorderly house', being too prudish to call it a brothel. She was disgusted by the whole place — the beds were damp and dirty and crawling with bed bugs, so she got her own mattress and unrolled it on the floor.

> The earth was dirty, damp and cold. We could not think of undressing the children and when in bed all looked most miserable. I lay down with my baby... The bugs were crawling by hundreds. The children were restless with them and the confinement of their clothes. The old woman had contrived to steal some spirits from our provision basket, which made her and the soldiers tipsy. All was noise and confusion indoors... Never did I pass a night to equal it.

Arriving very late, Thomas Hawkins spent the rest of the night in the wagon, keeping watch on the soldiers, fearful for the safety of his wife and young daughters. Modesty would have prevented Elizabeth revealing the real reason for her husband's fears, but, reading between the lines, it is obvious he was concerned that she and the girls might be raped.

Most nights Thomas Hawkins, as head of the party, did not get to sleep before three in the morning. Then one of the convicts took over the night watch, keeping guard against attacks by bushrangers or marauding Aborigines.

Elizabeth wrote admiringly that 'my husband only twice took off his clothes; as we and the children occupied the tent his only resting place was the wagon'.

The whole family were delighted to depart the next morning.

On the ninth day of their trek, the road became steeper and steeper and they all had to dismount from the covered wagon. Elizabeth carried baby Edward in her arms while the two eldest girls supported their grandmother, and in this fashion they walked behind the wagon to lighten the load on the bullocks.

In her letter Elizabeth described that

> ... the road from beginning to the end of the mountains is cut entirely through forest, nor can you go in a direct line to Bathurst from one mountain to another, but you are obliged to wind round the edges of them and at times to look down on precipices which make you shudder. Our cart [the tilted wagon] had now three bullocks as we had so much trouble to get on with two, but we were worse off than ever. As the ascent became worse they refused to drag, and every few minutes first one and then another would lie down. The dogs were summoned to bark at them and bite their noses to make them get up. The barking of dogs, bellowing of bullocks and the swearing of the men made our heads ache, and kept us in continual terror. That was exactly the case every day of the journey.

Although desperately weary, they had to push on with their gruelling journey to find a suitable camping site before nightfall.

That day, the journey took them through soaring mountain passes and down steep slopes. Elizabeth was overawed by the sight of the towering peaks of Mount York and Mount Tomah, which loomed in the distance.

To reach their next destination, the Hawkins family had to travel along sheer gorges in which the wagons could have plunged hundreds of feet down, had the bullocks slipped on the narrow track. Apparently, this had happened to some unfortunate settlers who had preceded them. At a sharp curve in the road, they saw a cart that had slipped over the edge of a sheer precipice — a warning of what could happen to them if they were not extremely careful. It was highly dangerous, but awesome and breathtaking.

There was another delay when an axle of one of the drays broke. Elizabeth recorded,

We were on the side of it [the mountain]; in front it was almost perpendicular; behind was a valley so deep the eye could hardly distinguish the trees at the bottom. To gain the top of this mountain the road wound along the side. The first dray with the horses got up. They were then brought back to assist the rest with the bullocks, but they could not succeed in raising them from one rock to another. With great noise a sudden effort was made, and one shaft was broken. This had to be repaired as well as we could, some of the luggage was taken off, and with the assistance of the other horses it was got up.

Finally, they were able to continue and covered another three kilometres to a place where water could be obtained. In pitch darkness and pouring rain, they pitched their tent in the middle of the road, the only open and level spot they could find. Elizabeth and the children were obliged to remain in the wagon until the bedding was put in the tent. Although that day's journey had been extremely tiring, they had managed to cover 16 kilometres.

Fortunately, they had still plenty of provisions: half a pig, some beef, flour to make bread, tea, sugar and butter. Breakfast and supper were their only daily meals. Elizabeth used to take a small basket in the wagon to keep her and the children from getting hungry during the day.

The next morning, it was still raining, making life most uncomfortable for the travellers. Once again the men had to search for stray bullocks. After waiting some time, they decided to proceed, leaving a dray behind, guarded by one of the overseers. Meanwhile, the men kept searching for the bullocks and trekked through virgin bush where now the towns of Lawson and Katoomba are located. That day, the road was slightly better. After travelling for 16 kilometres they arrived at two bark huts, which had large slabs of bark tied to wooden frames with strips of stringy bark. These huts, erected for the convicts who had worked on the road, were now vacant.

As it was still raining, the women and children were happy to have a roof over their heads, rather than sleeping in a leaking tent.

Elizabeth and her mother were kept awake by bugs and fleas — to make things worse, two of the girls fell through a gap in the wall.

> Helen and Louisa were laid head and foot. Finding them restless, we looked, and found, poor things, that from some of the pieces of bark not being close to the outside, they had tumbled through, and, being suspended by their arms, we had some difficulty to drag them up.

Early in the morning, an overseer arrived from Emu Plains, telling them that the lost bullocks had again returned 'home'. Hawkins directed the overseer to collect the animals and take them to the dray they had left behind. Due to that delay they were obliged to wait that day for the arrival of the bullocks and the last dray, so another restless night had to be spent in the flea-infested hut.

In the morning of 17 April, Elizabeth, her mother and the children climbed into the tilted wagon once again and departed from their abominable shelter. The hills were not excessively steep and no major problems were encountered, so good progress was made. After covering almost 19 kilometres, they pitched their tent near the present-day town of Blackheath.

When the Hawkins family continued their journey, they were only 11 kilometres from the summit of Mount York. The road skirted the steeper slopes of Mount Victoria and was tolerably good. The weather was fine and in anticipation of something wonderful, their spirits were high — they expected that after that day their main difficulties would be over.

Thomas shot some birds and the boys hunted and killed a kangaroo-rat. They were all cheerful until they were a few kilometres from Mount York, commonly called 'The Big Hill'.

Elizabeth asked Tom to ride and see what lay ahead of them. He soon came galloping back and yelled out,: 'Oh! Ma, you will never get up, I am sure you won't. I can't see much of the road, but I can see the valley you are to reach — it is dreadful.'

To return at this late stage was out of the question — they *had* to continue. It was too dangerous to stay in the tilted wagon, so once again Elizabeth, her mother and children dismounted and started to climb the steep hill. Elizabeth worried that their boots and walking shoes, which she had planned to hand down from child to child, were becoming worn and badly damaged by sharp stones. To repair the damaged boots and shoes, they would need a cobbler, but it seemed unlikely that one could be found among the soldiers and rough ex-convicts who made up the population of the fledgling settlement of Bathurst.

The ascent of Mount York was so steep that the carts and drays had to be hauled up with ropes using a system of pulleys, which had been specially installed on posts and trees beside the road.

Totally exhausted, but without any mishaps, they all managed to get to the crest of the mountain. Once on top, they had a good rest while Elizabeth gave everybody food and wine.

Thomas realised that the way down would be even more difficult than the ascent. Precautions had to be made to stop the carts and drays from running out of control when descending. The men began cutting down trees to be chained behind the carts and drays. On the way down, these trees acted as brakes — men were standing on them to increase the braking effect.

The women and children continued to walk, as sitting in the wagon during the descent was even more dangerous than when going up the mountain. As Elizabeth looked down into the ravine-like valley below, she feared the younger children would never manage to get there on foot.

They left the narrow road, finding it too slippery, and walked down a steep tree-clad slope. With the danger of spraining their ankles, they slipped and slid while clinging to the trees to support themselves. Little Ann burst into tears and had to be carried by the maid, while Elizabeth and her mother carried the baby in turn.

> How we got down I cannot tell, but I believe the fear lest any accident should happen to him [baby Edward] gave us strength and resolution to keep our own footing. We were often obliged to sit down on a fallen tree, but when we did the pains in our legs and the violent trembling all over us made it difficult to get up again. We at last reached the bottom in safety. The descent is

about a mile. It is four thousand feet above the level of the sea, all rocks and cavities, awfully grand to behold.

Somehow or other, they managed to get down the steep descent in one piece, their cumbersome long skirts and tightly laced bodices impeding the movements of the women. In those days, conventions did not permit a respectable woman to wear trousers, which would have made the lives of Elizabeth and her mother easier.

It was about three o'clock when they sat down on some fallen trees. The autumn weather was still hot. By now, Elizabeth was so exhausted and stressed, she was on the verge of tears, but she had to keep up a brave face in front of the children and held her tears back. Tom and Eliza found a spring and the party quenched their thirst with crystal-clear water. Then they waited and waited for the cavalcade to arrive.

> We waited a considerable time, could hear nothing of the rest, and then desired Tom to go and meet them, and when he found them safe, to call out. An hour passed and still we heard nothing. Mother and I then thought to walk a little way and listen. Sometimes we could just hear the sound of voices, and all again was still. We returned to our children. It was nearly sunset, and in this country it is dark almost immediately. I asked Eliza if she would venture up with the female servant to inquire what we were to do, as I was convinced some accident had happened. It was nearly dark when they returned with two cloaks, lantern, and tinder-box, on account of the first dray having upset at what is called the 'Forty-nine mile pinch'.

The dray had been manoeuvred too close to the edge of the road and was in danger of slipping over the sheer precipice below them. Fortunately, a tree stump by the roadside saved their goods and the lives of the horses. The dray came to a standstill, half-suspended over an immense precipice. So all the stores had to be unloaded before the horses could pull the dray back — then everything had to be packed again.

The convicts had performed very well during the ascent and descent of 'The Big Hill'. One man, who was the head driver of the cavalcade, had behaved particularly well when the dray slipped off the road. This man, who came from Folkstone (the same town Thomas Hawkins used to live in), climbed on top of the dray and, hanging by ropes, laboured hard to unload the luggage. Later that night, he was also the one who brought some of their provisions down. Thomas promised he would try to get the best-behaved convicts their most wanted passport to freedom: 'a ticket of leave'.

It was obvious that they still had to wait a long time before the cavalcade would arrive, so they collected wood and made a fire. It was completely dark when finally the tilted wagon arrived with warm clothing and food.

By nine o'clock, two of the drays arrived as well, but the last one was still at the top of the hill, guarded by Thomas. Due to the darkness and fatigue of the horses, the last dray would not come down that night. An hour later, two of the convict men walked up the hill again and relieved Thomas, who, totally exhausted, came down to join his family.

Finally, at eleven o'clock, they had supper, then pitched the tent and went to sleep. Next morning, they woke up after about six hours' sleep, still exhausted from the previous day's exertions.

> The next morning we all felt the effects of being exposed so long to the night air, and the great fatigue we had. After breakfast we walked up to a small rock, and, sitting down, viewed the scene around, and felt thankful that the little property we possessed was safe, for the injury caused by the dray's upsetting was trifling.

While enjoying the scenery, they saw three persons on horseback coming down the valley. When meeting the Hawkins family, they stopped and a chubby-faced gentleman in his late 50s dismounted from his thoroughbred horse. He introduced himself as the Reverend Samuel Marsden of Parramatta, clergyman and magistrate.

The clergyman appeared to know a great deal about farming and the wool industry. He told Thomas that he had collected samples of wood and had shown them to King George during a visit to England. Reverend Marsden explained that he had been visiting convict labourers and ticket of leave men who made up most of the population of the settlement of Bathurst. The clergyman had been favourably surprised by the fertility of the area and how suitable the land was for grazing cattle and sheep. He was amazed to find that Thomas had brought his wife and children with him to this isolated settlement of convicts and soldiers.

Wishing to praise the brave 'wagon-woman', Reverend Marsden said to Elizabeth, 'Mrs Hawkins, I congratulate you'. Reassuringly, he continued, 'You are going to the Land of Goshen' (a Biblical term which referred to the fertile land near the Nile given to Joseph by the Pharaoh: 'a Land of Plenty'). Elizabeth was relieved to hear such encouraging words.

Around the fire that night, Elizabeth's servant from the Female Factory told her that the Reverend Samuel Marsden was known as 'the flogging parson of Parramatta'. While handing out Bibles as a parson, he took great delight in passing sentences for severe floggings as a magistrate.

Once the three horsemen had departed, Elizabeth went back into the tent and lay down, still feeling ill from the previous day's exertions. Once inside the tent and out of sight of the children, her tears started to flow. She wrote, 'I sat in the tent and cried and sobbed like a child.' Eventually, she fell asleep and did not wake until the last dray had rumbled past.

By about one o'clock, they were finally ready to proceed. After that good cry and restful sleep, Elizabeth's cheerfulness returned. Once again, she was spellbound by the fascinating Australian flora and fauna which surrounded them in the lush Cox River Valley — the colourful birds enthralled her most of all.

> There are but few birds on the mountains, but their plumage is more beautiful than I ever beheld before. They are called 'Blue Mountaineers'. Then, with a green variety of parrots, which may be heard chattering in the trees, there are also birds called

'Laughing jackasses', which startled us the preceding evening just at sunset. They appeared to be all round us, making their horrid noise.

After a trouble-free journey of some 13 kilometres, they reached the Cox River. Fortunately, a new bridge had recently been completed, so to Elizabeth's relief they were able to cross the river relatively easily, although descending the steep bank created trouble. Precautions had to be taken to stop the drays from tumbling down the bank into the river.

They had now reached what they thought to be a suitable resting place with good grass for the cattle. They decided to stay there for two days to recover and pitched their tent in a field in front of a house occupied by a corporal and his wife. These people, who had been informed that the Thomas Hawkins and his family would be coming, kindly offered them a bucket of milk, which Elizabeth appreciated very much.

In the evening, a gentleman named Mr Lowe arrived and joined the Hawkins family, who were sitting around a blazing campfire. Mr Lowe, a Chief Magistrate, was on his way to Sydney, returning from his property at Sidmouth Valley, where an overseer lived and looked after his stock. Mr Lowe invited the family to stay at his property the following night, as it would be too far to travel to Bathurst in one day. His offer was gratefully accepted.

The following morning, Elizabeth took the opportunity to give the children a good washing and changed their clothes. As the day was extremely sultry, she felt hot and tired. By now, all were exhausted from the long journey and longed to reach their destination.

Early in the morning of 21 April, they set off again over another series of hills.[13] Up one steep hill, down the other side, then up the next. Wagon wheels creaked and jolted over rutted ground and rocks, jarring the travellers' spines. The bullocks were tired and required even more urging than before. It took a long time for the drays to get up the steep hills and some of the horses had to be returned from the top to assist the bullocks with the ascent.

Elizabeth thought in despair that the journey seemed neverending. It was now the 16th day of a journey which was supposed to have taken them 10 days.

At the top of the highest hill, they paused to let the animals get their breath back. In the distance, beyond the Fish River, they saw the lush plains of the Macquarie River area. Elizabeth was thrilled and thought that at last all their worries might be over. However, more hardships lay ahead.

Eventually, they arrived at the Fish River and found there was no bridge. At the ford, they had to urge the horses and bullocks into the water with the younger children still inside the tilted wagon — the adults and the older children waded across through waist-deep water.

Having crossed the Fish River, they reached Sidmouth Valley, a beautiful and lush region. They had to cross a swamp, where one of the drays became bogged. Once again, the horses had to come to the assistance of the overtired bullocks. At last, by late afternoon, they arrived at the resting place to which Mr Lowe had directed them. Mr Lowe's overseer kindly offered them his tent for the night. As it had begun to rain again, they were very glad to accept his offer, thereby avoiding having to pitch their own tent on the soggy ground. After a restful night, they set off on the last leg of their journey. The road was good and they were determined to reach their new home that night. To cover the remaining 29 kilometres in one day.

> ... we almost trotted, which jolted us so dreadfully that I thought every bone would be disjointed. It was as much as we could do to keep ourselves on the seats and hold the children. As if to the very last our journey was to be made uncomfortable, a fine rain began, which beat in our faces, and made us very cold.

At last, they could see some structures in the distance. Surely, it had to be the settlement of Bathurst — without doubt, one of the houses they saw had to be their future home. What a welcome sight! However, yet another river had to be crossed before they reached their destination.

> Before we could reach home we had to cross the Macquarie River, the most dangerous of all. You descend a steep bank, and suddenly plunge into the water, which was as high as the bottom of the cart. The first dray got over, but the rest, being lower, we were obliged to seek another ford for them. We remained alone. The driver of the first brought one of his horses over, put it to ours, and in we plunged. We felt more alarmed for our personal safety at that moment than we had done during the whole journey. We reached the opposite side, and all at one moment exclaimed, 'We are over'. A few minutes brought us to our house, where there was a blazing wood fire to warm and cheer us up.

Rather than the projected 10 days to cover 220 kilometres (137 miles), the journey had taken 17 days.[14] Today, a car can do this journey in a matter of hours, but it was a major endeavour for pioneer settlers, who had to negotiate an unsealed road in horse- or bullock-drawn carts.

On their arrival at Bathurst, William Lawson, one of the explorers who had first found a way across the Blue Mountains, was waiting to meet them. Lawson, the new commandant of the area, welcomed everybody and shook hands with Elizabeth, her mother and Thomas. As commandant and government representative Lawson gave a particularly warm welcome to Elizabeth and her elderly mother, as they were the first female free settlers in the area. Thomas Hawkins was delighted to meet Lawson with whom, as Government Storekeeper, he knew it was important to form a good relationship.

In 1813, Lawson had been one of three explorers who crossed the Blue Mountains for the first time — his contribution as a surveyor had been invaluable. Three years before the Hawkinses' arrival, he had been appointed commandant of Bathurst by Governor Macquarie and now lived in the settlement's Government House.

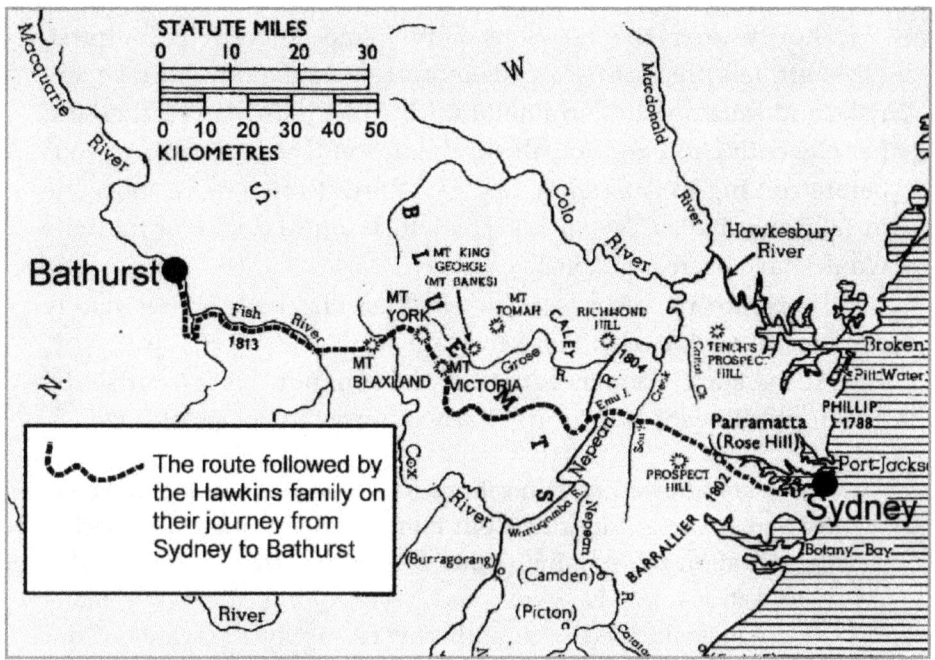

The route followed by the Hawkins family on their journey from Sydney to Bathurst

Next, Elizabeth and Thomas went to inspect their house, which was the former storekeeper's residence, a timber structure with brick floors and a roof covered with timber shingles. It contained three rooms and a pantry, with access to a loft for additional sleeping accommodation. Commandant Lawson promised that two additional rooms would be added, but in the meantime some of the children had to sleep in the covered wagon.

Thomas and the convicts unloaded and unpacked all the luggage. Because they had left much of their belongings behind at the Emu Plains depot, their new home could be only sparsely furnished. Nevertheless, Elizabeth managed to create a comfortable and cosy home with the few things they had brought. It took months before the rest of their luggage arrived.

Now Elizabeth's only worry, knowing there was no doctor in Bathurst, was the possibility that one of the children or her mother might fall sick or break an arm or a leg. She knew very little about medicine and had only a few simple remedies in her medicine chest.

Shortly after the Hawkins family had arrived in Bathurst, Elizabeth fell pregnant. Records indicate that she did not take any risks and returned to Parramatta for the birth of Allan Fitzherbert, her eleventh child and fourth surviving son (she had lost two sons before coming to Australia). She gave birth to two more sons, one in 1825 and the last one in 1827, by which time a doctor or midwife would have been available.

There are no records as to whether Elizabeth or her family ever needed a doctor in those early days.

At the start, Thomas earned a pittance, but this was offset by generous allowances in kind. Elizabeth wrote to her sister how

> ... we are allowed certain rations for six months, of meat, wheat, tea and sugar, sufficient for our family and servants. In respect of the situation the nominal value of it is but five shillings a day with rations for Hawkins and servant, but there are many advantages attached to it, sufficient to supply the wants of our family and prevent our wanting any ready money for housekeeping. We live very well, get excellent fish, and the wild ducks are delicious. We are supplied with vegetables from the Government garden, and we are allowed the use of two cows, which, with two we have of our own, give us butter and milk.

Thomas inspected the vast pastoral regions on the northern side of the Macquarie River, selected an area of land facing the river and submitted an application for a grant. In the meantime, the Hawkins family had free access to government land on the southern side of the river, where their cattle could graze.

> The land on this side [south of the Macquarie River] is so good for rearing cattle that nearly the whole consumption of the colony depends upon it. In addition to our cavalcade, we had thirty-four head, which belonged to our landlord, on the following terms: One third of the produce to be ours, to be divided at the end of seven years. Although we have not got our own land marked out for us yet, Hawkins has selected his spot, and applied for it, still until then we can have the use of as much as we want for any cattle we may possess. I think there is no

doubt we shall do well and prosper, but I would never persuade anyone with such a large family as mine, and the slender means we possessed, to leave England… Without the assistance of the Government to bring us here we never could have come.[15]

On 30 June 1823, just over a year after their arrival, Thomas received a Crown grant of 800 hectares (2,000 acres) in the area called Kelso, near Bathurst. But initially he did not have the financial means to build a house on it.

It was the Hawkinses' good fortune that, a year later, Thomas inherited £3,000 from a cousin of his father, also called Thomas, who owned a property in Sussex called *Blackdown*. On receiving the bequest, Thomas was finally able to start building a house on his own land. In memory of his Sussex namesake and benefactor, he decided to call his house *Blackdown*.

Whenever Thomas had free time from running the government stores, he and his son Tom crossed the river and went to work on their own land with the help of several convicts. Out there, they worked like navvies, cutting down trees and grubbing out stumps. They also erected fences and built stockyards.

Thomas Hawkins built a two-storey brick dwelling on their land at Kelso. Convicts helped with the construction and made the bricks to pave the veranda — these bricks have lasted to the present day. On completion, the family finally moved to their new property and started farming in earnest. They were delighted that the soil was as rich and fertile as they had been told it would be. As it was close to the river, water supply was never a problem.

The only worry was the fact that the Wiaradhuri tribe of Aborigines lived in that region and resented white people settling there. The Wiaradhuri were the traditional owners of the land and feared that sheep and cattle would pollute their drinking water from the Macquarie River. It was not uncommon for the settlers' livestock to be speared and eaten by the Wiaradhuri.[16]

Dairying was seen as women's work. Elizabeth ran the dairy section of the farm most efficiently.[17] She had to learn new skills as a farmer's wife, such as separating cream from milk, churning butter from the cream and cheese from the milk. The elder girls and Elizabeth's convict maid had to help her milk the cows twice a day.

They also had to light a fire every morning so scones and damper could be baked in a camp oven. Elizabeth made money selling their cheese and butter to other settlers. She also taught her younger children to read and write in between cooking, washing, ironing and carrying out her farming duties.

Thomas and Elizabeth Hawkins became important figures in the new settlement of Bathurst.

***

Sadly, Thomas Hawkins had been farming for only 13 years before he died at the age of 56 on 27 May 1837, during a stay in Sydney. His remains were brought back to Kelso for burial.[18] There is no record of the cause of his death.

When Thomas died, his affairs were reported to be in confusion.[19] Nevertheless, Elizabeth, most likely with the help of some of her older children, continued to run the farm for another five years. But it seems that she was dogged by misfortune. The district experienced a prolonged and severe drought. In spite of all Elizabeth's efforts to 'nurse' the animals through bad times, *Blackdown* eventually had to be sold to a magistrate by the name of John Savory Rodd.

Subsequently, the property changed hands many times and through the years improvements and extensions to the house were carried out. Today, *Blackdown* has been converted into a hotel and is included in the National Trust Register as it is one of the earliest land grants to the west of the Blue Mountains.[20]

After the sale of the property, the Hawkins family broke up. Elizabeth, her mother and the younger children were spread amongst the homes of four married daughters. Later, Elizabeth and her mother spent time with the eldest son, Tom, at his home *Walmer* in Bathurst, before moving to Sydney, where Elizabeth stayed for the rest of her life.

At the age of 89, Elizabeth wrote:

> I will only add that my troubles then began [after arrival at Bathurst]. I lost my husband, my home and three sons, but I have never felt the want of kindness from all connected with me, and whatever I might have thought at the time, it has pleased God to spare my life until I can now say from my heart, all things have been wisely ordered.[21]

Despite her loss of five sons (two died before she arrived in Australia) and the loss of a daughter, Elizabeth's large family must have given her great joy. In old age she wrote how:

> I am now in my eighty-ninth year. I have 7 children, 44 grandchildren, and 59 great-grandchildren living in many parts of the world: England, Denmark, India, New Zealand, New South Wales, Victoria and the Fiji Islands. The God who has protected me through all these long years, may He be the God of them all, protect and bless them for ever.

Ironically, Elizabeth lost another son shortly after she wrote those words.

Elizabeth Hawkins died on 6 April 1875 at Surry Hills, Sydney, at the ripe old age of 92. It was more than 53 years since she had blazed a trail as the first white woman on that hazardous road across the Blue Mountains.

TRAVEL RECORD OF THE HAWKINS FAMILY WHEN CROSSING THE BLUE MOUNTAINS IN 1822

	Date of departure	Approx distance travelled	
		Miles	KM
Sydney Town	Saturday 5 April		
↓		25	40
Rooty Hill hostel)	Monday 7 April		
↓		13	21
Emu Plains hostel)	Saturday 12 April		
↓		3	5
Lapstone Hill (camping)	Sunday 13 April		
↓		10	16
Springwood (lodging house)	Monday 14 April		
↓		10	16
Near Lawson* (camping)	Tuesday 15 April		
↓		10	16
Near Katoomba* (bark huts)	Wednesday 17 April		
↓		12	19
Near Blackheath* (camping)	Friday 18 April		
↓		10	16
West of Mt York (camping)	Saturday 19 April		
↓		8	13
Near Cox River (camping)	Monday 21 April		
↓		18	29
Sidmouth Valley (camping)	Tuesday 22 April		
↓		<u>18</u>	<u>29</u>
Bathurst (arrival on 22 April 1822)	total dist. travelled	137	220

* These are names of present day towns and mountains

THE CHILDREN OF THOMAS FITZHERBERT HAWKINS AND ELIZABETH HAWKINS (NEE LILLY) WERE:

1) George John Hawkins, born 1803, probably in Deal, and died in 1811.

2) Henry Fitzherbert Hawkins, born 1805, probably in Deal, and died in 1812.

3) Thomas Jarman Hawkins, born 1809 in Deal, married Ann Bowling (his cousin) in 1838 and had 5 children; he died in 1885.

4) Elizabeth Hawkins, born 1811 in Deal, married John Piper Mackenzie in 1827 and had 9 children; she died in 1899.

5) Mary Jane Hawkins, born 1812 at Deal, married (1) Thomas Evernden in 1830 and (2) Johan Bertlesen. She had 1 child by Thomas and 3 children by Johan; she died in 1866.

6) Helen Hawkins, born 1815 at Drayton, married William Henry Mackenzie in 1832 and had 10 children; she died in 1894.

7) Louisa Hawkins, born 1817 at Chelsea, married James Garnett Ewer in 1855 and had no issue; she died in 1902.

8) George Daysh Hawkins, born 1818 at Chelsea, not married; he died in 1842.

9) Ann Hawkins, born 1819 at Newark, married John Francis McArthur in 1838 and had 12 children; she died in 1911.

10) Edward Brace Hawkins, born 1821 at Newark, drowned 1849 in California.

11) Allan Fitzherbert Hawkins, born 1823 at Parramatta, not married; he died in 1847.

12) William Lilly Hawkins, born 1825 at *Blackdown*, married Elizabeth Ann Simpson in 1853 and had 8 children; he died in 1872.

13) Sarah Hawkins, born 1827 at *Blackdown*, married James Henderson in 1849 and had 12 children; she died in 1907.[22]

Sydney's Lower George Street with bullocks and horses, around the time when Elizabeth Hawkins and her family departed from there. Engraving by J. Carmichael.

Elizabeth Hawkins and her children travelled in a similar covered wagon, pulled by bullocks instead of horses. Watercolour by colonial artist Harold Brees. Courtesy of Christopher Deutscher Fine Art, Melbourne, from the Deutscher Gallery 1986 exhibition.

Engraving, showing travellers bound for Bathurst ascend Mount Victoria with a dangerous precipice beside the road to which a barrier has been added.

Mount York seen from Mount Tomah. Painting by Conrad Martens. Courtesy National Trust of New South Wales.

CHAPTER 3

Mary Eliza Bakewell Gaunt
[1861–1942]

TRAVEL WRITER, EXPLORER AND NOVELIST

'Gaunts *never* give up', the motto of Mary's ancestor, Prince John of Gaunt, (1340–1399) was quoted by Mary's father, William Gaunt, to his children.

Over a century ago, Mary Gaunt, educated at Ballarat's Granville College for Young Ladies, became a trailblazer for female education and one of the first women permitted to study at the all-male bastion of Melbourne University in the 1880s.

Mary was a member of a very distinguished and clever family who claimed descent from the Plantaganet Kings of England, through Prince John of Gaunt's third wife, Lady Katherine Swynford.

William Gaunt, Mary's father, having been a Goldfields Commissioner in the Victorian gold rush, eventually became a judge in Melbourne. Two of Mary's brothers would become admirals of the fleet, knighted for their services to the crown while two younger brothers became lawyers. Mary also hoped to study law so she could earn enough money to visit Africa and China, both countries which had fascinated her since her Ballarat childhood.

In 1882, advised by university officials that women lacked the brains to study 'hard subjects' like law or medicine, Mary enrolled in the Faculty of Arts to study literature, her other interest. Soon she and the other eleven women who had enrolled with her realised that their written work was marked down by biased male academics, keen to prove that women were not clever enough to be awarded degrees and should never have been admitted to university.

By the end of her first year, Mary realised that none of her intake would be awarded degrees, no matter how hard they worked. Unwilling to be rejected as unworthy of a degree, Mary left the university in protest, but her professor of literature assured her that she had a talent for writing and should become an author.

Mary defied her mother's attempts to marry her off and decided to embark on the hazardous career of a writer, hoping it would give her the opportunity to travel overseas.

Strong-minded and ambitious, Mary Gaunt was brave enough to write under her own name. Initially she made her name with short stories and novels. Her Australian novels were based on tales of the early days of the goldfields of Victoria, related to her in her childhood by her father William Gaunt.

In his early 20s William Gaunt emigrated from Shropshire to Victoria and dug for gold at Indigo before being appointed Goldfields Commissioner in charge of a band of mounted troopers. Mary's short stories in the *Melbourne Age* and *The Argus* about diggers, bush rangers and women on the goldfields proved popular with readers, as did three subsequent novels set on the goldfields of Victoria. The female protagonists of her novels were feisty young women in search of financial independence, just like their author.

Unlike many sentimental romances by female writers of the Victorian era, very few of Mary Gaunt's novels had happy endings. Instead the novels described the harsh life of women living in tents on the goldfields.

William Gaunt told his daughter that Katherine de Roet Swynford, one of her ancestors, was the third wife of Prince John of Gaunt, son of King Edward III, a Plantagenet monarch. Katherine de Roet was orphaned, brought to court at the request of Queen Phillipa and appointed governess to the children of Prince John of Gaunt and his wife, Blanche, Duchess of Lancaster, who died of the plague. She and Prince John fell in love but as a commoner Katherine could not marry into the royal family. Katherine bore Prince John four children out of wedlock and shocked the English court by becoming John of Gaunt's third wife.[1]

William Gaunt's children inherited their father's sense of adventure. As a law clerk in training William migrated to the colony of Victoria, just before his 21st birthday. William dug for gold without success, so he joined the Goldfields Department and was sent to Beechworth. Later, he was created Magistrate and Goldfields Commissioner on the Indigo goldfields near Chilton.

Mary and her brothers Cecil and Ernest were born at Chilton. When William returned to Beechworth as magistrate, the family went to live there. Later William Gaunt moved his young family to the gold rush town of Ballarat where he bought a weatherboard home and opened a legal practice. After a fire caused extensive damage to their wooden home at Ballarat, William Gaunt rented *Strathalbyn House*, a stone, 15-room lakeside mansion. The property was surrounded by extensive grounds and an orchard. The Ballarat mansion had a central tower where the children played on wet days, a library, a schoolroom, a ballroom and stables for their horses. The owner had gone bankrupt and during a temporary recession the bank rented it to William Gaunt and his family. By now, they had seven surviving children and Mary was the eldest daughter.[2]

The *Strathalbyn House* property (now *Bishopsbourne*, the official residence of the Bishop of Ballarat) was cheap to rent but needed a large staff to run it and maintain the extensive grounds, vegetable garden and orchard. The need for kitchen staff, housemaids, gardeners and grooms and school fees for seven children meant that William Gaunt was often short of money to pay his domestic staff. Meanwhile, William Gaunt was doing further legal studies to be admitted to the Bar in Victoria (which eventuated in 1873).

Near the end of a pregnancy or recovering from a recent birth, Eliza was frequently confined to bed. She often complained that the family lacked the money to educate their sons properly, but did not believe her daughters should have tertiary education.

In an era when most girls were married by the age of 20, Mary and her younger sister refused all her mother's attempts to marry them off to the sons of Ballarat worthies. Mary insisted she would either marry for love or remain single, a statement that angered her mother who told Mary she was stupid — a 'good marriage' was the only way she would survive when her parents were dead. She prophesied that Mary would never succeed as a writer, a career reserved for men. Like her sister Lucy, Mary should concentrate on getting married as soon as possible.

In the 1880s, women's writing was seen as second rate and vastly inferior to anything produced by men. Women were pigeonholed into writing romantic novels or articles about the latest fashions or recipes. To avoid the disdain of male critics, talented women like 'Henry' Handel Richardson, 'Miles' Franklin and 'George' Eliot wrote under male pen names.[3] In the final years of Queen Victoria's reign, Mary was expected to make a marriage of convenience, but she refused to do so.

In spite of her mother's attempts to discourage her, Mary continued to write short stories and worked on a novel. The short stories she wrote for the *Melbourne Age* and *The Argus*, published under her own name, became very popular.

In 1887, Mary was thrilled to receive a commission to write seven chapters on aspects of the colony of Victoria for *Australia Illustrated*, a lavish two-volume publication to celebrate Australia's first centenary, for which she received a handsome fee from its London publishers.

Living at home, Mary saved up her earnings until she had enough to sail to Britain, taking with her the manuscript of a novel set in Ballarat. She found that London publishers were not interested in her Ballarat novel, but there was interest in a novel on the Australian goldfields. Mary received a commission from London publisher Edward Arnold to write a goldfields novel with a female protagonist. Mary had a great deal of material to draw on from events in her father's years as a Goldfields Commissioner. He had been in charge of a band of mounted troopers and sat in judgement on rogues, robbers and murderers. William Gaunt had helped quell the Buckland River riots where Chinese gold miners were in danger of being drowned by their Australian counterparts and his intervention saved the lives of many Chinese miners.

In London, Mary joined the British Society of Authors and made contacts with editors. Eventually she acquired a literary agent who would prove of invaluable assistance in what would become a remarkable literary career. The result was that Mary Gaunt would become Britain's most popular 'quality' novelist and travel writer in the Edwardian era and beyond. At one period, she and her contemporary, the English novelist and travel writer William Somerset Maugham were respectively the most popular female and male writers in Britain and both writers had good sales in Britain, America and Australia. But while Somerset Maugham achieved great success with his first novel, *Liza of Lambeth*, success was slow in coming for Mary Gaunt. The advance on her goldfields novel was tiny and her funds were low while living in London. She could not obtain a loan to tide her over as, in the era of Queen Victoria, banks refused to lend money to women.

Mary had just enough money to return to Australia. Her parents and their youngest sons, Clive and Lance, were living at 15 Moorhouse Street, Malvern, a Melbourne suburb, so the boys could attend Melbourne Grammar School. By now, William Gaunt had been made a County Court judge by Premier Graham Berry.

Mary's sister Lucy had married an engineer who worked in Malaya. Her favourite brothers, Lieutenants Ernest and Guy Gaunt, were serving in the Royal Navy and sent her long letters about their exploits.

In 1875, Judge Gaunt and 79 senior public servants, were suspended from duty for lack of government money to pay them, due to the refusal of the upper house to grant supply to Premier

Berry's government. In spite of protest marches and a petition to Queen Victoria, Judge Gaunt received no income for ten months but still had to pay school fees and maintain his family. Mrs Gaunt turned sour and complained that Mary as a single girl cost the family money, but Mary still refused to marry unless her husband would treat her as an equal.

Short of money, in 1879 William Gaunt and family returned to Ballarat, where, instead of working as a solicitor, he set up in practice as a barrister specialising in mining laws.

Not until she turned 29, did Mary fall in love. She took a short holiday to see an old school friend who lived in the pleasant seaside town of Warrnambool. Here, Mary met Edinburgh-trained Doctor Lindsay Miller, a tall, good looking physician whose wife had died two years previously. Dr Miller had established a solo general practice in this small seaside town, hoping its mild climate would help his ailing wife. He had given up a senior teaching post at the Royal Melbourne Hospital. But despite their move to Warrnambool, Lindsay's wife had died soon afterwards. When Mary met the doctor for the first time, he was still grieving over his wife's death.

Dr Lindsay Miller was seven years older than Mary. He was good looking, intelligent and a man of wide interests. The couple had a mutual passion for books. After her return to Melbourne, Mary continued their friendship by letter and gradually a romance evolved. To avoid her mother meddling in her affair, she kept quiet about Lindsay until he proposed. Mary was happier than she thought possible, treasuring the ruby and diamond ring he gave her to mark their engagement.

On 8 August 1894, at a quiet wedding at St George's Anglican Church in Malvern followed by a reception at the family home, Mary Gaunt became the second wife of Dr Hubert Lindsay Miller. Their honeymoon was spent in Brighton before they returned to Dr Miller's combined home and surgery at Warrnambool.

Mary enjoyed the happiest period of her life. She helped her husband in his home-surgery and became very popular with the patients. When not working in the surgery or in their home and garden, Mary continued to work on her goldfields novels and had success with them. During this happy and tranquil period, Mary completed a number of novels, including, *Dave's Sweetheart* (1894), *Kirkham's Find* (1897) and *Deadman's* (1898), which was named after a goldfield called Deadman's Creek. The last two books became best sellers in Britain, Australia and America.

Unlike many husbands of that era, Lindsay had no objection to his wife using her own name on her books and provided support and encouragement to her while writing them.

Lindsay also suggested Mary use her writing skills to help the newly established Melbourne Women's Hospital, staffed entirely by women doctors, to receive donations. So Mary, always interested in causes to benefit women, wrote articles for the Melbourne press about the fledgling Women's Hospital and other charities staffed by women.

Encouraged by excellent reviews, Mary started planning her fourth novel, *As the Whirlwind Passeth,* set in Sydney at the time of Governor Bligh. However, due to the onset of her husband's decline and mental instability, caused by symptoms of tertiary syphilis acquired many decades earlier as an Edinburgh medical student, she had to stop work on her Sydney novel for decades and deal with the worst crisis in her life.

What had been a very happy marriage turned into a nightmare as Dr Miller exhibited signs of erratic behaviour. Mary, worried by events she did not understand, consulted his former colleagues at the Royal Melbourne Hospital. To her horror, she learned that her dignified and widely respected husband was suffering from premature senile dementia. Without doubt, this was the tertiary stage of syphilis, a fatal disease which could take many decades to emerge and cause what was known at the time as 'paralysis of the insane'. The public mental hospitals were a nightmare, as, before the invention of tranquillisers, mental patients were kept in padded cells or chained to 'restraining chairs' in lunatic asylums.

Dr Miller was admitted as a private patient to Kew Lunatic Asylum. Syphilis was considered scandalous, so Mary told as few people as possible what was the *real* cause of her husband's gradual decline into insanity and paralysis. As medical fees for a private patient at Kew Lunatic Asylum were high, Mary had to sell their Warrnambool home and rent a small house in an adjacent street to the Kew Lunatic Asylum to be close to her husband.

Each day, Mary visited the grim asylum to bathe her husband's wasted and paralysed limbs to give him some relief. She endured the nightmare of watching the man she loved descend into insanity while trying to hide what doctors believed was caused by syphilis. At that time this sexually transmitted disease was not only scandalous but also fatal. As yet the Wassermann test for syphilis had not been discovered, so there was no mention of the word syphilis on his death certificate. Instead Dr Lindsay Miller's death certificate, dated 13 October 1900, gave the cause of death as 'disease of the brain and spinal cord'.[4] Since syphilis was a scandal for a respected physician, Mary was careful not to record anything about this bleak period in her life.

As she had no say in his estate, her husband's financial affairs were placed under the control of the Master in Lunacy and took a long time to be sorted out. Widowed Mrs Mary Miller was now homeless and, having spent all their savings on her husband's treatment, retreated to her parents' home while the Master in Lunacy settled what little money was left.

After running her own home at Warrnambool, Mary found it impossible to endure her mother's constant criticisms. She wanted to make a new life and was determined to support herself in the hazardous world of writing, the only world she knew.

Aged 40, and still grieving over the death of her husband, Mary returned to London, the centre of the publishing and literary world. She found life in crowded, foggy London expensive and lonely and missed the tranquillity of Warrnambool. She rented a cheap bed-sitter in Kensington and managed to survive by writing short stories for Melbourne papers.

As the result of a chance meeting with retired colonial official John Ridgewell Essex, who had written scholarly articles on African tribal lore, Mary's interest in Africa revived. As a young girl, she had read the story of a cabin boy named Carlos who worked on a Spanish galleon wrecked off Africa's Slave Coast. Carlos and several Spanish sailors had been rescued by members of the Ashanti tribe, but their king's sorcerer ordered them to be tied to the 'fetish tree' and be sacrificed. However, little Carlos was spared because the king wanted to learn Spanish from him. After reading that story, Mary vowed that, one day, she would travel through Africa and visit Ashanti Land.

Together, Mary and Ridgewell Essex wrote three novels set in colonial Africa which received excellent reviews. With this success, Mary wanted to explore West Africa herself and write a book about her experiences. However, several ex-colonials to whom she confided her plan were horrified that a white woman would even consider exploring the wilds of Africa unchaperoned with naked African porters carrying her camping equipment and other baggage. Nevertheless, Mary was determined to go there.

Her publisher, Mr Laurie, of Werner Laurie, found her desire to visit West Africa, the 'white man's grave' strange, but was happy to commission a novel and a book about her planned travels, which was to be illustrated by Mary's own photographs. But Mr Laurie was worried that one of their most popular authors might die from some tropical fever before completing the manuscript, so he paid her only a very small advance.

In November 1907, Mary Gaunt boarded the Elder Dempster liner ss *Gando*. A free passage in return for writing about what was known as 'the Dark Continent' had been offered to her. She took with her a tent, a folding canvas bath and a trunk full of linen safari suits, a long elegant evening dress, taffeta petticoats and her jewellery. Friends in London had ensured she would be invited to stay as a guest at governors' residences in various African colonies and told her that even in the tropical heat the dress codes demanded full evening dress, jewels and decorations for the gentlemen. Having been taught to shoot by her brothers, she also took a small pistol.

Mary Gaunt (often called by her married name of Mrs Miller) had her first port of call at Bathurst, the capital of Gambia. After a week's excursion up the Gambia River, Mary took a coastal steamer to Freetown, capital of Sierra Leone, where she was a guest at Freetown's Government House.

Mary learned that several of the married British officials at Freetown lived with African women who were never acknowledged by the white community. This adulterous lifestyle gave her an idea for a novel featuring a British colonial officer who takes an African mistress as a convenience. He scandalises the British community by falling in love with her and wanting to divorce his wife and marry his mistress.

Mary's next port of call was the colony of Liberia, which had been founded by America's President Monroe as a place where freed slaves could rebuild their lives. Mary expected to find Liberia a tropical paradise, but was disappointed to see that Monrovia, the capital, was seriously neglected. She described the town as

> ... an outrageously ill-kept town with no proper roads, only dirt tracks knee deep in weeds, the houses built of wood or corrugated iron with broken windows and crumbling wooden balconies... The inhabitants of Monrovia are eternally at war with the tribesmen in the land behind them [many of whom they had captured and enslaved].[5]

Delighted to be leaving Liberia, Mary boarded the ss *Chama* for the voyage to the former Portuguese settlement of Axim. From there she took a coastal steamer to Sekondi, a port founded by Dutch slavers in the sixteenth century. As the only hotel in town was full of drunken gold miners, who leered at her suggestively having not seen a white woman for months, she went to stay with the Australian-born Matron Oram at the Sekondi hospital.

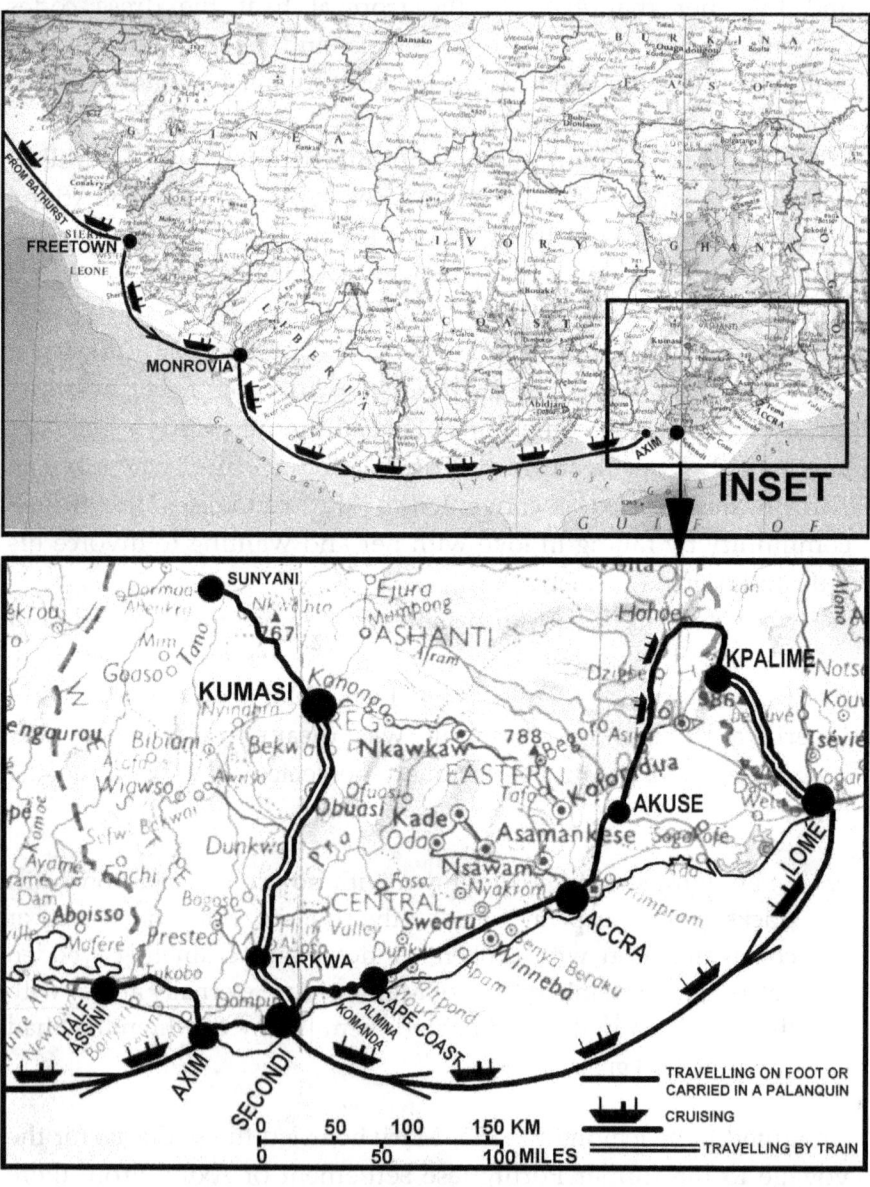

Map showing Mary Gaunt's routes in West Africa

Mary intended to visit the coastal settlement of Chama, 15 kilometres to the east of Sekondi. To get there she had to hire 17 naked Mendi warriors to carry her baggage along an overgrown jungle track. The Mendi tribesmen wore necklaces of boars' teeth round their necks, but nothing else. As the Mendi had a fearsome reputation, Mary engaged an African policeman from a rival tribe to protect her. As another precaution she employed an African servant-cum-interpreter who had been educated by missionaries and was warmly recommended by them.

On the long walk to Chama, Mary, overwhelmed by the tropical heat and humidity, feared she would have an asthma attack. Exhausted and feeling faint, she ordered the four strongest African warriors to carry her in a hammock.

As they approached the next village, the chanting and beating of drums signalled a funeral in progress. The Mendi warriors put down Mary's hammock and vanished in the direction of the drums. Alone in the jungle, Mary waited and waited. Her unease mounted as the hours went by and the sounds of drunken revelry grew louder and louder.

At last, the Mendi warriors staggered back with bloodshot eyes and hands waving — clearly they were intoxicated by palm wine. Staggering and stumbling, the porters continued their journey over the potholed jungle tracks. By nightfall, Mary and her party arrived at a deserted government rest house on the edge of the jungle. Mary decided to spend the night on the veranda, sitting in her folding chair and listening to the soothing sound of the nearby surf. Exhausted by the stresses of the day, she eventually fell asleep.

The next day, they followed the 'King's Highway', which in spite of the grandeur of its name, grew worse and worse. The porters with their heavy burdens had to struggle through deep sand and rocky outcrops so steep that Mary was in danger of being tipped out of her hammock.

Chama, a jungle village, was nothing but a straggle of thatched huts and one street filled with scrawny goats, chickens and smiling children. Mary had to spend the night in a dirt-floored hut with a thatched roof, where she was bitten by fleas and driven mad by the whine of mosquitoes.

The next day Mary felt ill, but insisted on continuing her journey over hilly country to Kommenda, where they halted for lunch at a decaying stone fort. Mary hoped to reach the slave fort at the port of Elmina by nightfall, but her porters wanted to spend the night at Kommenda, claiming they were 'no fit' to continue. Mary went to see the village headman who agreed to supply her with fresh porters. But with the prospect of being dismissed the Mendi warriors announced they had made a miraculous recovery and were now fit enough to take her to Elmina.

They left Kommenda in the afternoon for the 10 kilometres trek to Elmina and arrived there by nightfall. Mary was carried down the main street, which was bordered by large stone houses built during the Portuguese occupation. Crossing the drawbridge, they entered the central courtyard of St George's Castle, the largest and most imposing former slave fort on what was formerly known as 'The Slave Coast of Africa'.

Mary decided to spent the night in a government rest house, built into one of outer walls of the fortress. She was greeted by Dr Duff, an Edinburgh-trained historian who was acting as curator of the fort and conducted research on the slave trade. Dr Duff was amazed to find a lady so far off the beaten track and said admiringly, 'Madame, not one woman in ten thousand would have endured the journey you have just made. You have the heart of a lion and the brain of a man.'[6]

Mary was fascinated by Dr Duff's knowledge as he told her about his researches into the African slave trade. They talked until late at night while Mary made notes which she would use in several future books.[7]

The following morning, Dr Duff showed Mary around St George's Castle, reputed to be haunted by the ghosts of slaves who had died in the cellars, chained to rings in the wall. The Scottish historian explained to Mary how on arrival the captives entered by 'The Door of No Return', which had a human skull embedded in the wall above the door as a warning to the captives not to try to escape. They were taken to a special cell and branded with an identification number on the arm. The condemned cell had another skull and crossbones inserted into the stone lintel. Any slaves who caused trouble were starved to death and their corpses thrown into the sea as a warning to the other inmates.

Only one African in three survived imprisonment in the slave forts of Elmina. The more attractive female slaves were given a bath and then taken to the apartment of the Portuguese governor for his sexual gratification. If they fell pregnant, they were given a house in Elmina Town, taught to speak Portuguese by Jesuit priests and became housemaids to Portuguese traders.

After expressing her gratitude to Dr Duff for his hospitality and sharing his knowledge, Mary and her porters set off for Accra, the capital of Cape Colony (now part of Ghana). They followed a track that led through sand dunes covered in coarse grass. They passed scattered fishing villages where thatched mud huts nestled among groves of coconut palms.

Eventually, Mary and her porters arrived at the town of Cape Coast, an untidy straggle of woven huts and shanties. Mary received a warm welcome from the local medical officer and his wife, who invited her to stay with them in their bungalow.

To obtain new porters at Cape Coast turned out to be difficult, so Mary asked the Mendi warriors to continue working for her. They agreed on the condition that Mary increase their fees. Having no choice, she accepted their demands.

The 115 kilometre journey from Cape Coast to Accra over rough tracks took several days. Through an interpreter Mary learned that Accra had been quarantined in an epidemic of yellow fever. Fortunately, by the time she and her porters reached the coastal town the epidemic was almost over.

The acting governor of Accra regarded Mary's arrival with mixed feelings, believing that an unchaperoned white woman, travelling with naked African porters, was scandalous. But having learned that she was the daughter of a judge, the widow of a doctor and a well-known writer, he decided to invite her to stay at

Government House (a former Danish trading fort), situated about five kilometres outside Accra.

> I really think it was noble of the Acting Governor to invite me, for he had no sympathy with my mission, and though far too polite to say so, regarded a woman travelling on her own a pernicious nuisance... Government House at Accra, known as *Christiansborg*, had been bought from the Danes sometime in the 1870s, [converted to] a Government House, and then, because some governor did not like it, became a lunatic asylum before reverting [it] to being a Government House [again].[8]

Mary was exhausted from travelling in blistering heat and humidity. She was glad to have brought her long evening dress and jewellery, because dinner was very formal. She spent a month resting and recovering at Government House preparing for another arduous journey to the upper reaches of the Volta River.

Once again, obtaining porters was a problem as the natives flatly refused to work for a woman. In desperation, Mary had to deplete her funds and hire one of the few lorries available in West Africa. With Mary sitting beside the driver, the truck lurched and bumped over the rough track to Dodowah. On her arrival, Mary requested the local chief to contract a number of porters to accompany her on her 44 kilometre trip to Akuse. Soon she was confronted by 16 tall Kroo warriors, who, apart from wearing penis sheaths, were stark naked.

Although Mary was exhausted from her bruising journey, she wanted to leave for Akuse immediately, so they could travel during the coolness of the night. On their way they had to pass Krobo Hill in the tribal lands of the Krobo, who, for centuries, had been enemies of the Kroo. Through her interpreter Mary was told that Krobo Hill was called 'Murder Hill', because every Krobo youth underwent a rite of passage to manhood, which required him to kill a man on Krobo Hill and donate the corpse to sorcerers for use in 'fetish magic'.

> On Krobo Hill the fetish priests [sorcerers] held great orgies, and for their ghastly ceremonies and initiations caught any stranger reckless enough to pass the hill... at the end of the last century the British government intervened. Their soldiers took Krobo Hill and scattered the fetish priests... [but] only three years ago a negro clerk on his bicycle was traced to that hill and no further trace of him found.[9]

Mary's Kroo porters were frightened of the murderous Krobo warriors and insisted they wait for daylight before entering the haunted area of 'Murder Hill', where many from their tribe had vanished. Mary reluctantly agreed to leave the following morning and, without any incident, they reached Akuse before nightfall. From there they continued along the banks of the Volta River, which Mary described as

> ... entrancingly lovely. Its quiet reaches are like deep lakes in whose clear surface is mirrored the calm blue sky, the fleecy clouds and hills clothed in the densest green. Beneath the vivid blue sky are tangled, luxuriant feathery palms, tall cotton trees bound together with twining creepers and trailing vines. Men fish from canoes, boats return with cotton cloth for the factories run by negro agents of the great trading houses.[10]

The porters carried Mary's hammock across wild and sparsely inhabited country. Along the remote upper reaches of the Volta River, she visited a hospital and research station run by the Basel Mission. Here, dedicated medical missionaries were trying to discover how to prevent the sleeping sickness that had killed many Europeans and Africans. Mary was told by mission doctors that this dangerous disease was caused by the flukes of the 'guinea worm', an organism prevalent in most African rivers. They warned her about the importance of boiling all drinking water.

Mary and her African porters boarded a river steamer that took them even further up the Volta River. After spending an uncomfortable night in a disused cocoa store, the journey continued to the border of German-owned Togoland. The porters had to hack their way through unmapped jungle.

> I had been warned I should have to walk across the Eveto Ranges as no hammock-boys could possibly carry me. I decided the walking had better be done very early in the morning and arranged to start at half past five as soon as it was light. I cannot think the Eveto Range is perpendicular but it seemed to be so… The track twisted and turned among holes and roots and rocks. After ten minutes it was brought home to me I was a fool to have even attempted to travel in Africa.[11]

After crossing into German territory Mary noticed a great difference between the German-run colony and colonies run by the British. Unlike most of the African villages on the British side, the first village on the German side of the border was neat and well maintained. The streets were bordered by flame trees with orange flowers. Underneath the trees were rustic seats made from split logs. Even the goats and sheep looked neater and cleaner in Togoland than in the British colonies.[12]

Mary's next destination was the neat little town of Kpalime, where she dismissed her porters and travelled by train along the newly built railway line to Lomé, capital of Togo.

Lomé, situated on the Bight of Benin, was built on a swamp, drained under the supervision of German engineers. It had attractive gardens and modern bungalows for resident German officials. The neat streets were maintained by African prisoners from the local gaol. Mary was full of admiration for the cleanliness and orderliness that prevailed and how well the Germans had preserved the natural beauty of the countryside. She wrote,

> A beauty spot to the Germans *is* a beauty spot, whether it be in the Fatherland or in remote West Africa, while in contrast the English in Africa seem indifferent to aesthetics or beauty.[13]

From Lomé, Mary returned by steamer to Sekondi, intending to travel from there to Kumasi, capital of the Ashanti Protectorate. She boarded the train at Sekondi for the 200 kilometre trip to Kumasi, thrilled she was about to achieve her childhood dream to visit the mud brick palace of the king of the Ashanti and see the 'fetish tree' under which men had been sacrificed to pagan gods.

At Kumasi, Mary was escorted to the Chief Commissioner's residence, where she was welcomed by the commissioner and his young wife. She explored the town and visited small shops full of imported goods such as kerosene lamps, brooms, brushes and sewing machines. Under British rule, Kumasi had become a thriving trade centre for rubber and gold.[14] British officials lived in pleasant bungalows surrounded by trees and shrubs and the streets bore British signs with names like 'Kingsway' and 'Stewart Street'.

It was clear that the export of gold had brought great wealth to the Ashanti and some of them could even afford to employ men from the Hausa and Krepi tribes to act as salesmen or porters.

Many Ashanti women had won the right to considerable independence and conducted business on their own account. Mary greatly admired the spirit of these women and described them as 'rich and self-supporting, happy, and sure of themselves', in contrast to downtrodden wives from many other tribes.[15]

Mary tried in vain to find records of little Carlos or the Spanish sailors sacrificed under the 'fetish tree'. She was disappointed to learn that the palace of King Prempeh (the saviour of young Carlos) had been burned down by the British and that the king's collection of rare books had disappeared. On the site of King Prempeh's palace, a smaller one had been built by a subsequent king.

With a retinue of naked warriors from the Krepi tribe, Mary went to the remote forested area known as 'the Northern Territories of the Ashanti'. With the help of a porter, who spoke broken English, she wanted to communicate with local chiefs and their sorcerers, who had the power over life and death of the villagers.

After several days travelling, they reached the remote village of Potsikrom, where goats, pigs and scrawny chickens wandered down the only street. The natives of the village were excited to see their first white woman. To honour Mary's arrival, Ashanti warriors fired their muskets into the air and the chief presented her with a sheep and some ripe bananas. She gave the sheep to her native porters, who killed and roasted it for dinner.

As they departed the next morning, a procession of villagers followed Mary and waved her goodbye. After crossing the Tano River by canoe she reached Sunyani and stayed there in the thatched bungalow of the Provincial Commissioner.

The last stop on Mary's journey was Odumanse, which was no more than a straggle of thatched round mud huts with holes for windows and doors. The women, tall and statuesque, wore nothing but strings of beads cut from bamboo.

Eventually the time had come for Mary to return to Kumasi from where she caught the train back to Sekondi. Once again, she stayed in the hospital compound as the guest of Matron Oram.[16] After a brief stay there, she readied herself for her return voyage to England. The luxurious Elder Dempster liner ss *Dakar* lay at anchor off shore, so Mary and what remained of her luggage had to be paddled out to the ship in a small canoe through the heavy surf — it was the final exhilarating experience of her African expedition.

After Mary returned to London she spent the next six months at her desk writing her travel book *A Woman in Africa* and a novel, *Every Man's Desire*, as well as short stories set in Africa. The literary critic of *The Telegraph* called *A Woman in Africa* 'a remarkable book of energy and vision' and it became a best seller in Britain and America.

With royalties from her African books, Mary was able to escape from London during the winter months to a small hotel in Nice, while keeping up the payments for the construction of her new house in Eltham in Kent.

She had great success with another West African novel, *The Uncounted Cost*. At a time of great sexual prudery Mary Gaunt dared to write about the 'double standard.' This referred to the different sexual standards demanded of unmarried men who could 'sow their wild oats' with impunity, while single girls of good family had to guard their virginity or men would regard them as 'spoiled goods'.

The Uncounted Cost featured a girl whose family, having lost their money, wanted her to marry a wealthy man before he set off for tropical West Africa, where few men took their wives. Urged on by her family, the girl gave in to the young man's request to have sex with her on the night before he departed, promising to marry her on his return. In West Africa the man took a black mistress and on his return refused to marry the girl, with dreadful consequences.

The Uncounted Cost was banned by prudish British circulating libraries due to its sexual frankness and became a *success de scandale* and a best seller.

Having satisfied her curiosity about West Africa, Mary hoped to visit Peking and the Silk Route and obtain material for another travel book and a novel set in China. She wanted to follow the route she and her brother Ernest had planned to do together many years before.

Ernest Gaunt's friend, the famous explorer and writer, Dr George Morrison, had been appointed to the post of advisor to General Yuan Shi-kai, President of the new Chinese Republic. As Morrison was regarded as the western world's greatest expert on China, Mary was keen to become acquainted with him and obtain useful information for her forthcoming expedition.

In 1912, George Morrison returned from Peking to London for his wedding, giving Mary the opportunity to meet him. Morrison was intrigued by Mary's plan and invited her to stay with him and his new wife in Peking, an invitation Mary eagerly accepted.

Mary's British publisher had heard a great deal about 'Chinese Morrison' and was impressed he had invited Mary to stay with him in Peking. The publisher agreed to commission a travel book on China, illustrated by Mary's own photographs.

On 31 January 1913, Mary Gaunt began her 20-day train journey across Russia to Peking. After crossing the English Channel by ferry, she caught the express train that took her across the vast plains of Tsarist Russia and the Central Siberian plateau. 10 days later the train reached Irkutsk, known as 'the pearl of Siberia'. After another 10 days, the train finally reached the ancient imperial city of Peking.

As arranged, Mary went to stay with Mr and Mrs Morrison. As the policy advisor to the fledgling Republican government of President Yuan Shi-kai, George Morrison was under a great deal of stress. But despite his worries about the possibility of civil war, 'Chinese' Morrison still found time to be a kind and generous host.

Mary learned that on the day of her arrival, Empress Long Yu had died. Her sudden death bore an unnerving resemblance to the death of Long Yu's husband, the young Emperor Zaitan. He was rumoured to have been poisoned on the orders of the Dowager-Empress Cixi.[17] George Morrison explained that Empress Cixi, who had died four years ago, was a former concubine and had risen by guile and ruthlessness to become the most powerful woman in China.

After staying with the Morrisons for two weeks, Mary moved into the 'Hotel Wagon-Lits' inside the high-walled Legation Compound, which was patrolled by British and American soldiers acting as sentries.[18]

Escorted by one of her new friends, Mary explored Peking's crowded streets, where vendors sold sweets, toys and rice cakes and acrobats and jugglers performed. The overwhelming stench of unwashed bodies, garlic and tobacco made her feel nauseated.

Small wooden carts drawn by mules or sweating coolies tangled with each other in the unpaved roads, donkeys staggered past her under huge loads and doe-eyed camels from Mongolia were tied to posts in dusty streets. Not only was Peking dusty, but

Mary discovered it had even more flies than the Australian outback.

Shortly after Mary's arrival in Peking, President Yuan Shi-kai announced that the deceased Empress Long Yu would be given a lying-in-state ceremony inside the Forbidden City, followed by a large funeral procession through the streets of Peking.

Mary, desperately keen to enter the Forbidden City, obtained an invitation to attend the funeral ceremony of the empress. She recorded that the Forbidden City

> ... was thrown open for three days to all who could produce a black paper chrysanthemum with five leaves — red, yellow, blue, black and white — fastened to a tab of white paper with a mourning edge and an inscription in Chinese characters. The foreigners had theirs from their Legations, and the Chinese from their guilds.
>
> All must walk — old and young, great and lowly, representatives of the mighty nations of the world and tottering Chinese ladies swaying like 'lilies in the wind' upon their maimed feet — only one man, a Mongol Prince, an Incarnation of a Buddha, a living Buddha, was borne in a sedan chair. But every other mortal had to walk.[19]

Soldiers of the New Republic in full marching order guarded the entrance to the Imperial City. Mary and thousands of other wearers of a paper chrysanthemum entered the first courtyard through a huge archway. On both sides of the vast courtyard were low, dilapidated buildings with fronts of lattice-work. Some of the buildings were guard-houses, others had been the sleeping quarters of the 6,000 eunuchs who had attended upon their rulers.

After passing through several more archways, Mary and the other mourners came to the courtyard where lay the body of the late empress.

> The third courtyard was spacious as Trafalgar Square, and round three sides was a wide raised platform of stone reached by broad and easy ramps, and all across it ran a canal held in by marble

> banks, crossed by graceful bridges. Two colossal bronze monsters with grinning countenances and curly manes, conventional lions, mounted on dragon-carved pedestals, stand before the entrance to the fourth temple or hall of audience, and here was what the crowd had come to see...
>
> To the sound of Eastern music a yellow-clad Buddhist high-priest went to make his reverence. He was taken op the steps in his yellow sedan chair, carried by four bearers in dark blue gowns with Tartar caps on their heads.[20]

The funeral procession of the Empress Long Yu was originally planned to take place shortly after the lying-in-state ceremony. However, on 20 March 1913, the popular left wing politician Sung Chaio Sen was assassinated, which had such profound political ramifications that the arrangements for the funeral procession were delayed.

George Morrison was shocked when he learned that President Yuan was involved with Sung Chaio Sen's assassination, which spelt ruin to hopes of a well-run reformist republic. Morrison feared that it would lead to civil war between the two factions.

Finally, on 3 April 1913, the funeral procession of Empress Long Yu took place. Mary obtained a good view from the top of the Legation Compound's wall. The procession started from the Eastern Gate of the Forbidden City and advanced down Morrison Street on its way to the railway station.

> I looked down into the walled-in space between the four gateway arches, as into an arena, and the whole pageant passed below me... Slowly, slowly, the procession moved on, broken now and again by bands of soldiers in full marching order. There was a troop of cavalry of the Imperial Guard, they told me, but how could it be imperial when their five-coloured lance pennons fluttering gaily in the air clearly denoted the New Republic. There was a detachment of mounted police in black and yellow, the most modern of uniforms... Near the Chien Men Gate and the railway station, people were crowded together like Chinese flies in summer, and that is saying a great deal. They were cleared away by the soldiers, the bier was lifted onto a car, bands struck

up a weird funeral march, soldiers presented arms and the priest-

Map by Jake de Vries of the routes Mary Gaunt followed and the main cities and towns she visited in China

like lamas fell on their knees.

And finally very slowly the train steamed out of the station, and the last of the Manchu Empresses was borne to her final resting place.[21]

A few weeks later, Mary went to visit the Great Wall. Accompanied by two young officials from the British Legation, she went by train to the small town of Nankou, from where she was carried over rough stony ground in a mule litter. On her own feet again, Mary struggled up the steep steps that led to the top of the Great Wall.

Mary learned from an English-speaking guide that the Great Wall had been designed so that entire companies of Chinese archers could stand on top, protected by chest-high parapets with slits through which they could fire arrows at their enemies. The wall sprawled across hills and valleys, bridging vast gullies, climbing up and dipping down as far as the eye could see. Over two million labourers had died during the building of the wall, described in a Chinese poem as 'built on skeletons'.

Mary saw gaping holes where peasants had removed stones to use for building their homes. Mules, donkeys and horses carried sacks of grain and hides along a track beside the wall. Blue-coated coolies trudged along with bamboo poles across their shoulders. Camel trains from outer Mongolia padded past, just as they had done for centuries.

Exhausted from so much climbing, Mary and her companions returned to Nankou where they stayed at the only hotel in the town. It consisted of one large room, divided into many smaller ones by large sheets of paper, so the smallest whisper could be heard in every room.

The following morning, Mary went to visit the tomb of Yongle, the most famous emperor of the Ming dynasty. Ever since her grandmother had shown her a blue and white porcelain plate from one of Yongle's dinner services, Mary had wanted to visit the emperor's tomb, high in the foothills of the Jundu and Tianshou Mountains.

Mary had read how the warrior Prince Yongle had seized power from his feeble-minded nephew, Jianwen.[22] To eliminate potential rivals, the new emperor had ordered the murder of two thousand of the late emperor's eunuchs and concubines and watched the beheading of nine young princes of the blood royal. Early in the 15th century Emperor Yongle had ordered the building of the Forbidden City — no expense had been spared in creating one of the world's most magnificent palace complexes and making Peking the capital of Yongle's China.

Mary was carried to the Ming tombs in a palanquin, a type of sedan chair on poles borne on the shoulders of four burly coolies. After covering several kilometres over stony ground, she and her party came to the 'Holy Way', an avenue guarded by stone lions, camels, elephants and warriors, all larger than life. Eventually they arrived at a red painted arch which gave access to a huge natural amphitheatre.

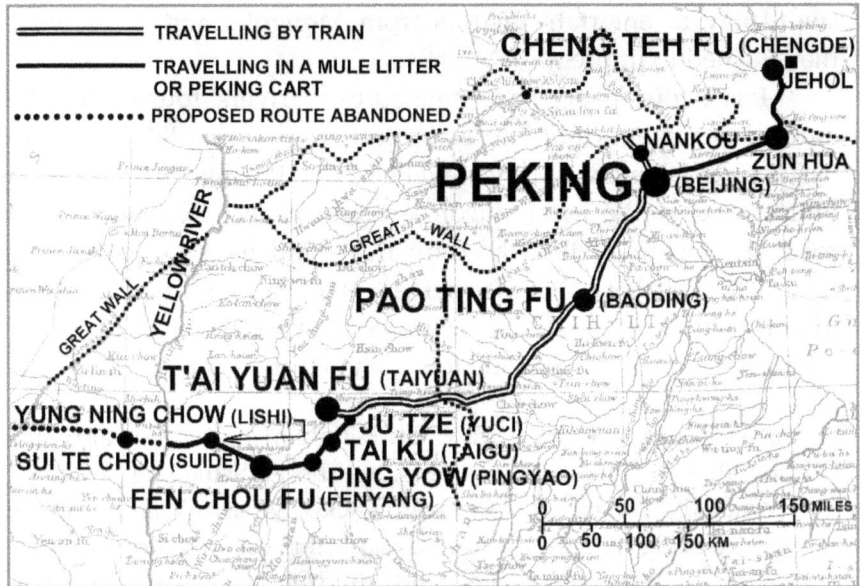

After dismounting from her palanquin in front of the imposing Emperor Yongle's Memorial Hall, Mary entered through a huge wooden door studded with bronze knobs. She walked into the Hall of Eminent Favours, where stood a gigantic gilded dragon with five claws — the symbol of imperial power. Beside it was an enormous prancing horse, carved in stone, the Chinese symbol for good fortune.[23]

Later, at Mary's request, the guide unlocked a small wooden door in the burial mound and ushered her inside. They walked along a paved passage that led down to a stone chamber in the heart of the burial mound. Inside was a plain granite tablet with an inscription, but to Mary's disappointment there were no golden artefacts as described in ancient manuscripts in George Morrison's library. The guide told her that Yongle's treasures had been stolen by tomb robbers.[24]

After her return to Peking, Mary undertook an uncomfortable and hazardous expedition to 'Jehol', the Mountain Palace complex of the Manchu emperors (now known as Chengde Imperial Park). The park contains hunting lodges, temples and ornamental gardens, where emperors used to organise displays of archery and swordplay to entertain visitors from Mongolia and Tibet whom they wished to impress.

Mary's tour leader had engaged two drivers, four porters and an interpreter and took secret commissions from all of them. On her way to Chengde, Mary travelled in a 'Peking cart', drawn by mules, one of the most uncomfortable means of transport. The road was no more than a stony track and each jolt of the cart reverberated along Mary's spine. After a few days of great discomfort, Mary and her team arrived at the walled city of Zunhua. Unimpressed by the town, she wrote,

> ... once inside Tsung Hua Chou [Zunhua] I saw no beauty in it, for all the romantic walls outside. The evil-smelling streets we rumbled through to the inn were wickedly narrow, and down the centre hung notices in Chinese characters on long strips of paper white and red, and pigs, and children, and creaking wheelbarrows, and men with loads, blocked the way. But we jolted over the step into the courtyard of the inn at last, quite a big courtyard, and quite a busy inn. The courtyard was crowded. There were blue-tilted Peking carts, there were mules, there were donkeys, there were men of all sorts; but there was only one wretched little room for me. It was very dirty too, and I was very tired.[25]

The following day Mary's small expedition arrived at the River Lahn, where they were hit by a dust storm that covered Mary's clothes and hair with a layer of yellow grime from the Gobi Desert. After crossing the river, they entered Inner Mongolia, where the track became so bad that one of the mules stumbled and Mary's flimsy Peking cart overturned.

> I was [thrown] out onto the hillside before I had time to think, and presently was watching those mules make hay of my possessions. They didn't leave a single thing either in or on that cart — camera, typewriter, cushions, dressing-bag, bedding — all shot out onto the road... It took us over an hour to get things

right again, and my faith in the stability of a Peking cart was gone for ever.[26]

Despite all the hardships, Mary's team eventually reached Chengde, where they went to stay at the Anglican Hsi An Fu Mission in the town's centre. Mary had a letter of introduction to the Military Governor of Chengde, whose permission she needed to visit the adjacent Imperial Park. The governor treated Mary with great courtesy and issued passes for her, her team and some of the missionaries who hosted her. He ordered his private secretary to accompany Mary and her group to the Imperial Park.[27]

Mary had read that the Imperial Park had an evil reputation as a place cursed by the gods. In 1820, the Manchu Emperor Jiaqing had died there, as had Emperor Xianfeng, the elderly husband of the Dragon Empress Cixi. It was rumoured that the spirits of the dead emperors haunted the area and brought bad luck to all those who visited the Mountain Palace of the Manchu.

But Mary was not discouraged by these rumours and wrote

> ... we went along a sordid, dusty street to the principal gate, a shabby and forlorn-looking gate, and the watch-tower over it was crumbling to decay, and we entered the courtyard, a forlorn and desolate courtyard, where the paving-stones were broken, and the grass and weeds were coming up between the cracks... No one save the servants who keep the place, live in the grounds now. No one has lived there for over fifty years, not since 1860, when the reigning Emperor fled there from the Allies who sacked Peking, and died there. Perhaps it was for that reason that his secondary wife, the great Dowager-Empress [Cixi] disliked the place, and went there no more.[28]

Although many buildings were decaying, Mary was impressed by the beauty of the Imperial Park and the restrained elegance of the many pavilions and pagodas. Acres of gardens, ornamental pools and eight small lakes were dotted with single-storey wooden pavilions, linked by 26 causeways or highly decorative bridges.

The gardens and ornamental pools were tended by a few resident gardeners, but several of the beautiful pavilions and temples had been allowed to go to rack and ruin. The largest pavilion was built entirely of sweet scented cedar and inside was a carved throne draped in tattered yellow silk. There was also an Imperial Bedroom, into which eunuchs used to carry the selected concubine for the night. Mary was told that the eunuchs would throw the concubine naked on the imperial bed, so she could not attack the emperor with a concealed weapon.

On an island in the middle of a lake, Mary visited the pavilion where Cixi had lived with the senile emperor and her infant son. The building contained exquisite carved wooden furniture, copied by Chinese craftsmen from original designs by Thomas Chippendale, sent out from England.

After her visit to the mountain palace complex, Mary and her party returned to the Anglican mission. She had a few days rest before exploring another temple complex in a nearby valley, known as the 'Valley of the Dead Gods'.

> ... we went up a valley for perhaps eight miles [and] embosomed among the folds of the hills — hills for the most part steep, rounded, and treeless — are the temples, red, and gold, and white, against the green or brown of the hills.
>
> To the glory of God! Surely. An ideal place for temples whoever placed them there, artist or Emperor, holy man, or a grateful son.[29]

By mid-June, Mary returned to Peking. To avoid another uncomfortable journey in a Peking cart, she decided to hire a boat called a *wupan*, which would take her down the River Lanho. Two missionaries, who went on leave, would accompany her and hired their own *wupans*. After an 11 kilometre trip in a mule litter, Mary reached the river and boarded one of the flat-bottomed *wupans*, fitted with a large cotton sail. At night the sail became a makeshift tent.

After several enjoyable but cramped days in her *wupan*, Mary arrived at the port of Lanchou at the mouth of the Lanho. From there she took the train to Peking and returned to the comfort of the Hotel Wagon-Lits in the Legation Compound.

By now it was mid-summer and extremely hot in Peking. Fortunately, Mary received an invitation from a friend to stay with her at Tong Xian on the eastern outskirts of the city. Her hostess had several servants and entertained many friends, which made it difficult for Mary to concentrate on her writing. So she decided to rent a disused temple in Peking's Western Hills, which would be a much quieter place. The temple was called *San Shan An*, or *Temple of the Three Mountains*.[30] It was set among oaks and maple trees, some 30 kilometres from the centre of Peking.

> ... the valley was lovely [in] that autumn weather. Day after day, day after day, was the golden sunshine, the clear, deep blue sky, the still, dry, invigorating air — no wonder everyone with a literary turn yearns to write a book in a valley of the Western Hills. And this valley of the San Shan An was the loveliest valley of them all... I have seen nothing to match autumn in the Chinese hills and I had not thought to see beauty like this in China![31]

Mary employed two Chinese 'boys' as a house servant and a cook. She was surprised to find that their combined wages plus the rent of the temple and all her food cost far less than staying at the Hotel Wagon-Lits. Several of Mary's friends from the British Legation spent weekends as her guest. She described her stay at the *Temple of the Three Mountains* as one of the happiest times in her life.

> ... those sunny days in the mountain temple when we read poetry, and told stories, and dreamed of the better things life held for us in the future! They were good days, days in my life to be remembered. Was it the exhilarating air, or the company, or the temple precincts? All thanks give I to those dead gods who gave me, for a brief space, something that was left out of my life.[32]

While Mary was staying at the old temple, an English friend gave her a small fluffy black and white dog, found wandering the streets of Peking. She called him Buchanan and he soon became her devoted friend. Since the death of her husband, Mary had gone through times of loneliness and misery, so the dog's company and affection meant a lot to her.

Once Mary's manuscript was typed up, she had time to concentrate on plans for her journey home across the Gobi Desert and along the ancient Silk Road, which would be the subject of her next travel book.

※

After three months living at the *Temple of the Three Mountains*, Mary travelled by train to the American Mission in Baoding, run by Doctor Lewis and his wife. During her stay there, she heard a great deal about the miseries of foot binding, a subject that touched her heart. In Peking she had seen many Chinese women hobbling around on feet that had been bound in childhood and felt deeply sorry for them.

Doctor Lewis acted as interpreter when Mary interviewed women with bound feet. She was told that the pain and the tears began when little girls were between five and six years old. To soften the child's feet, the mother soaked them in a mixture of herbs and water before the toes were bound tightly under the foot with bandages. These long bandages were rewrapped and tightened every day so the pressure caused the delicate bones to break. Then the feet were bound even more tightly and eventually the bones of the centre of the foot would also break. The toes were then bound back, with the result that they curled below the sole of the foot. Eventually, the arch of the foot was forced into the desired 'golden lotus' shape, which meant that these unfortunate girls would have to walk in pain throughout their lives. The only way they could gain any relief was to sit on the edge of the stone *k'ang* or heating platform and press their calves against the edge to stop the flow of blood to the feet and, as a brief respite, numb the pain.

Chinese girls were taught they must never complain in order to prepare themselves for childbirth. They were raised with the idea they must obey their parents and then their husbands without question. Mary wrote,

> ... the pity and the horror of it never failed to strike me. If the missionaries do but one good work, they do it in prevailing on the women to unbind their feet, in preventing unlucky little girls from going through years of agony. There is no mistaking the gait of a woman with bound feet, she walks as if her legs were made of wood. Her feet are tiny, shaped like small hoofs, about four inches long encased in embroidered slippers... Four [mission] doctors who came into contact with these women told me their sufferings were great and after the process was finished the feet were often sore and ulcerated and the least exertion makes them ache.[33]

Doctor Lewis told Mary that foot binding in childhood often led to sores and gangrene in the women's feet — when that happened one or even both feet had to be amputated in order to save the woman's life. Women whose feet had been bound often developed hip and spinal problems due to the fact that tiny feet, only 10 cm long, had to bear the full weight of an adult body. As a result, many of these women had difficulty giving birth.[34]

Chinese mothers knew that, unless their daughters' feet were broken and bound, their chance of marriage was poor. In a country where poverty was endemic and children could be sold into slavery during a drought — an early marriage was the best chance of survival for most girls from large families with little money.

On one occasion, Mary was present when a mission doctor examined the leg of a woman with bound feet.

> ... the whole limb from the big toe to the knee was hard and immovable as stone. If you press ordinary flesh anywhere it pits, yields a little, but a woman with a bound foot has a leg that is thin, perished, hard as marble. Once having seen a foot unbound, it is a wonder to me that any woman should walk at all. And yet they do. They hold out their arms and walk, balancing

themselves and to do this use a stick. Sometimes they walk on their heels, sometimes they try the toe, but once I realised what those bandages concealed it was a dreadful thing to see a Chinese woman walking. In spite of the hardness of the flesh, or probably because of it, they get corns on the spot upon which they balance.[35]

During her stay at the mission, Mary made plans for her journey home across the Loess Plateau to Xi'an and along the most southerly of the three Silk Routes to Lanzhou, the capital of Kansu. When she outlined her plan to the missionaries they were pessimistic and warned that the murderous thugs and bandits in the area were as cruel as the Boxers. Pai Lang, or 'White Wolf', employed henchmen notorious for raping female prisoners before torturing and murdering them. One woman missionary said, 'If I wanted to die I'd choose an easier way of doing it!' The only person at the mission to be fascinated by Mary's proposed trip was Doctor Lewis. He said he would have loved to join her, if only his patients did not need him so badly.

While in Baoding, Mary was introduced to the British botanist and botanical artist Reginald Farrer and his younger associate, William Purdom. They were aiming to collect samples of plants and seeds in north-eastern China and intended to send them to Kew Gardens. As Mary told the famous botanists about her plans, they encouraged her and provided useful information about travelling through the western regions of China.

Reassured by the British botanists, Mary wrote to various mission stations along her route, telling them of her plans and offering to pay something towards the work of the missions in return for their hospitality. One of the missionaries at Xi'an warned Mary by telegram, 'Do *not* come here. Xi'an threatened by White Wolf'.

Mary took this warning seriously and considered taking an alternative route to Lanzhou, via Fenyuan, Lishi and across the Yellow River to Suide. It was a shorter but far more difficult route. From Suide it would be another 800 kilometres to Lanzhou.

✸
✸✸

Once Mary had made her decision, she prepared for the long and arduous journey west. In early spring 1914, she went by train to Taiyuan, an ancient walled city at the end of the railway line in a south-westerly direction from Peking. She wrote,

> I was met at the station [of Taiyuan] by some of the ladies of the English Baptist Mission who had come to welcome me and to offer me, a total stranger to them, kindly hospitality, and we walked through the gate to the mission inside the walls. It was only a short walk, short and dusty... All the roadway was crowded with rickshaws and carts waiting in a long line their turn to go underneath the gateway over which frowned a typical many-roofed Chinese watch tower... The ladies lived in a Chinese house close under the walls. There is a great charm about these houses built round courtyards in the Chinese style.[36]

Taiyuan, capital of Shanxi province, did not welcome foreigners, especially women travelling solo. Mary was warned by the missionaries that, if she ventured outside the walls of the Baptist mission station, she could be at risk.

> 'This town,' said the missionaries, 'is anti-progressive and anti-foreign.' You feel somehow the difference in the attitude of the people the moment you set foot inside the walls. It seems to me that if trouble really came it would be an easy matter to seize the railway and cut off the foreign missionaries from all help, for it is at least a fortnight away [from Peking] in the mountains.[37]

After her stay at the Taiyuan mission, Mary continued her journey west. She intended to travel in a mule litter, but, as none was available, she had to sit on a chair on the back of a mule. Dressed in her long skirt and high button boots, she was hoisted by her porters onto the pack on top of the mule, who disliked this arrangement just as much as Mary and succeeded in throwing her off, so she had to remount. She wrote,

> I know of no more uncomfortable method [of travelling]. There are neither reins nor stirrups, and the mule goes at his own sweet will, and in a short time your back begins to ache, after a few hours that aching is intolerable... I wanted to cross Asia and was faced with disaster at the outset! Finally I was put upon the pack minus the chair, Buchanan was handed up to me and the procession started.[38]

Despite Mary's discomfort, she reached the mission at Taiku before nightfall. The following day, she and her party set off in a south-westerly direction to Pingyoa. Fortunately, the missionaries at Taiku had been able to find some improvised mule litter for her.

> ... it cannot be repeated too often that as a conveyance a mule litter leaves much to be desired. Sitting up there on my bedding among my cushions, with Buchanan beside me, I was much more comfortable than I should have been in a Peking cart, but also I was much more helpless... The missionaries had told me whenever I came to a bad place to be sure and get out, because the Chinese mules are not surefooted enough to be trusted... [39]

After a few days stay at a Pingyoa mission, Mary continued her journey to the 4,000-year-old hill town of Fenyang, where she had arranged to stay at the American mission run by Protestant missionaries from Oberlin College, Ohio.

Mary was told by the missionaries that the Boxers had arrived there in 1900 and declared that all foreigners had to die, because they regarded them as evil. The local people liked the American missionaries, who had been very kind to them and did not want the Boxers to behead them within the walls of their city. So Boxer troops took the missionaries seven miles outside the city and butchered them there. To Mary, this showed how the citizens of Fenyang managed to square their conscience and avoid 'blood guilt'. Despite the massacre that had taken place in Fenyang, Mary felt safe there, as the people were much friendlier than in other Chinese towns she had visited.

On the next leg of the journey, Mary and her porters had to cross a steep mountain range before reaching the town of Lishi and the eastern part of the Loess Plateau. They passed strings of ragged camels, pack-mules, donkeys and men with bamboo poles across their shoulders, carrying heavy loads. Most inns on the way had been built underground and were little more than caves, often with high-sounding names such as *The Inn of Increasing Righteousness* and *The Inn of Ten Thousand Conveniences*.

After staying for one night at the Scandinavian mission in Lishi, Mary and her team set off to the village of Liu Lin Chen, where they learned more about the dangers ahead of them. They were told that the gates of Suide (Mary's next destination) had been closed for the last four days as its townsfolk were terrified of an attack by White Wolf and his cruel henchmen. Suide was on the other side of the Yellow River and the main caravan route in the westerly direction crossed that town. Mary realised that straying from that route was impossible, so she had to abandon her plan to travel further west into Shaanxi. Nevertheless, Mary was determined to see the great Yellow River before turning back.

> Almost immediately we left the village [Liu Lin Chen] we began to ascend the mountain pass. Steeper and steeper it grew, and at last the opening in my mule litter was pointing straight up to the sky, and I, seeing there was nothing else for it, demanded to be lifted out and signified my intention of walking. There was one thing against this and that was an attack of breathlessness...
>
> And at last through a cleft in the hills I saw the Yellow River, one of the world's great rivers. The setting was ideal. The hills rose up steep and rugged on either side, pheasants called, rock-doves mourned, magpies chattered, overhead was a clear blue sky just flecked here and there with fleecy clouds, beyond were the mountains of Shensi [Shaanxi], the golden sunlight on their rounded tops, purple shadow in their swelling folds, far away in the distance they melted into the blue sky... Close at hand they were green with the green of springtime, save where the plough had just turned up patches of yellowish-brown soil. At their feet

rolled a muddy flood, the mighty Hoang-Ho, the Yellow River, China's sorrow.[40]

The phrase 'China's sorrow' referred to the fact that the Yellow River transported the soft yellowish fertile silt of the Loess Plateau away from the areas where peasants needed it to grow rice to feed their families.

The hills of Shaanxi beckoned Mary and she was tempted to carry on with her journey across the Yellow River and beyond. But reason prevailed. To continue would be madness — the *tufeis* or armed bandits of White Wolf were swarming all over Shaanxi. They had captured several cities, shot or beheaded prominent citizens, raped their wives and stolen money from the banks. If they found a European woman, the end of her would be very unpleasant.

Mary had to come to terms with the fact that she had failed to reach her goal. However, she did not want to give up altogether and considered to make her way back through eastern Siberia, where mighty rivers were flowing.

⁂

On Mary's return to the American Mission at Baoding, the missionaries were delighted to see her alive. She spent several weeks with them and during that time her plans to travel northeast to the Russian border and into Siberia crystallised. She was interested in taking a boat along the River Amur, part of which forms the border between China and Russia.

After her stay at the mission, Mary accepted Dr Lewis's invitation to join him, his wife and several friends to travel to Tianjin on houseboats.

> Dr and Mrs Lewis and their children had the largest [houseboat], with their servants, and we made arrangements to eat together on board their boat. Miss Newton and a friend had another, with more of the servants, and I, like a millionaire, had one all to myself.

> They were pleasant days we spent meandering down the river. We passed by little farms, we passed by villages, by fishing traps, by walled cities. Hsi An Fu, with the water of the river flowing at the foot of its castellated walls, was like a city of romance, and when we came upon little marketplaces by the water's edge the romance deepened. Sometimes we paused and bought provisions; sometimes we got out and strolled along the banks in the pleasant summer weather. Never have I gone [on] a more delightful or more unique voyage. And at last we arrived at Tientsin [Tianjin] and I parted from my friends.[41]

Tianjin was the second largest city in northern China and, like Peking, had a special compound where foreigners were allowed to live. Mary stayed at the Astor Hotel, the best in the city, where they kindly allowed Buchanan to sleep in her room. She enjoyed her stay in the cosmopolitan trading centre and felt safe there.

After a short stay at Tianjin, Mary travelled by train to Harbin, a Chinese City with a large Russian population. Many of these Russians were Jews who had fled from persecution in Russia. The day after her arrival at Harbin, she went to see Mr Sly, the British consul, who happened to know Mary's brother Ernest. The consul asked Mary to dinner and introduced her to the local elite. The following day he showed her some of the most spectacular sights and they ended the day with a party of friends in the exquisite public gardens. Mary felt that cosmopolitan Harbin bore some resemblance to Monte Carlo.

Mary's next destination was Vladivostok, a two-day train journey from Chinese owned Harbin and described it as

> ... a beautifully situated town set in the hills alongside a narrow arm of the grey sea. The hills around were covered with the luxuriant green of midsummer, a land where it is winter almost until June. The principal buildings in Vladivostok are all along the shore lined with all manner of craft. The British fleet had come on a visit, and grey and grim the ships lay there on the grey sea, like a Turner watercolour and for a dash of colour, they flew brightly coloured Union Jacks.

Map showing the routes Mary Gaunt followed and the main cities and towns she visited in south-east Siberia.

steamer *John Cockerill* and boarded her the following evening for a three-day voyage along the Amur River to Nikolayevsk.

> ... it was delightful moving along [the Amur River] — the great crowded steamer but a puny thing on the wide river, the waters still and clear, reflecting the blue sky and the soft white clouds and the low banks far, far away. The hills were densely wooded, mostly with dark firs, with an occasional deciduous tree showing up brightly among the dark foliage... What struck me was the vastness and the loneliness of the mighty Amur River.

From Nikolayevsk Mary made a brief visit to island of Sakhalin, which was used by Russia as a penal settlement. Convicts, ex-convicts and their descendants still formed a large part of the island's population. At the time of Mary's visit, the northern part of Sakhalin belonged to Russia while Japan occupied the south.

On 25 July 1914, Mary left Sakhalin and, after 18 months of travelling in the East, she was finally on her way home. From Nikolayevsk, she sailed upstream along the Amur River to

Blagoveschensk, a town with large weatherboard houses and wide streets. The town boasted an enormous emporium where Mary purchased a few small gifts and a dog-collar with a bell, so she could not easily lose Buchanan.

While shopping, Mary met some English-speaking people who told her that Russia and Germany were at war, which was the first time she heard of it. Russia, as the protector of the Serbs, had come to the defence of Serbia after the country had been invaded by Austrian soldiers seeking revenge for the assassination of the heir to the Austrian empire at Sarajevo. As a result, the generals of Tsar Nicholas were mobilising their forces to fight the Kaiser's Army and were busy recruiting young men for the Russian Army.

As a foreigner Mary stood out in the crowd and drew her fellow shoppers' attention. Some suspected her of being a German spy and were openly hostile to her. A store manager, who spoke a little English, advised Mary to see the provincial governor and get a protection order, written in Russian, which would indicate she was travelling on a British passport. Mary took the advice, hired a horse-drawn *droshky* and drove to the governor's official residence, where anxious people were crowding his office.

After spending several hours in the reception area, a tall, good-looking officer in the dark blue and gold uniform of a Russian Hussar entered. He clicked his heels, bowed low and informed Mary in excellent English that he was the Boundary Commissioner for this part of Siberia. Mary explained that she was Australian travelling on a British passport and needed a protection order written in Russian. The Boundary Commissioner complied with Mary's request and provided her with the Protection Order, so she was free to go wherever she pleased.

The Boundary Commissioner told Mary that German soldiers had invaded Belgium en route to attack Paris. Having violated Belgian neutrality they were killing Belgian citizens, so Britain had declared war on Germany. Mary's homeland of Australia had entered the war in support of Britain, 'the mother country'. The Russian officer kissed Mary's hand to celebrate the fact that they were allies.

Mary became acquainted with Paul Barentzen, the regional head of the Chinese Customs Service who lived at the Chinese side of the Amur River. After staying for a week with Mr Barentzen and his wife, she continued her voyage along the Amur River in a north-westerly direction. Seven days later the river steamer arrived at Sretensk, which was one of the centres of recruitment for Tsar Nicholas's troops. For the first time, Mary saw how the excitement of war affected young men who had not the slightest idea of the dangers involved and regarded enlisting as a big adventure. All these young Russian recruits could think about were cavalry charges and glory and, like the Anzacs, they had no idea of the havoc caused by German machine guns that awaited them. Mary wrote

> ... down the road came endless streams of square khaki-coloured carts, driven by men in flat caps and belted khaki blouses, big fair men, often giants with red, sun-tanned faces and lint-white hair, men who shouted and laughed and sang and threw up their caps... these men were delighted with their lot. I wondered was it a case of the prisoner freed or was it that life under the old regime in a Russian village was dull to monotony and to these recruits was coming the chance of their lifetime. Some will never come east again, never whether in love or hate will they see the steppes and the flowers and the golden sunshine and the snow of Siberia, they [would] have left their bones on those battle-fields...[43]

Years later Mary would learn from Australian friends that young Australian soldiers, departing for Gallipoli or the trenches of northern France, behaved in exactly the same way.[44] The young Anzacs left their home towns by train, laughing and singing with no idea that many of them would be dead within a year.

Mary had to cross the river by ferry to reach the railway station from where the train to Irkutsk would depart, but as the train was not bound to leave until the following evening she was in for a long wait. There was no hotel in the area, so Mary had no choice, she had to stay at the railway station.

> I set myself to make the best of the situation. The station was crowded with all sorts and conditions of people, and a forlorn crowd they looked... To wait a night and day for a train in a railway station was surely a little sacrifice to what some people were making. How cheerfully and patiently that Russian crowd waited! There were no complaints, no moans, but here and there a Russian woman buried her head in her shawl and wept for those loved ones who had gone to the war...
>
> I went into the refreshment-room to get some food, and had soup with sour cream in it, and ate chicken and bread and butter and cucumber and drank *kvass* as a change from the eternal tea. I watched the people on the platform and as the shades of night fell began to wonder where I should sleep. I went into the ladies' waiting room, dragged a seat across the open window, and spread out my rugs and cushions and established myself there... The sanitary arrangements were abominable, and what the atmosphere would have been like with the window shut![45]

It was evening before the train finally arrived. Mary, who travelled second class, spread out her rugs and cushions. As her compartment reeked of body odour she opened a window, which was against the wish of the other passengers. At a small station, she was promoted to first-class, so she and her dog had the compartment to themselves all the way to Irkutsk, where she arrived two days later. The station was a surging mass of noisy, chattering people. Mary and a Swedish naval officer had breakfast together — fresh bread rolls with butter and honey and the luxury of coffee with cream.

During breakfast Mary learned that the train to St Petersburg was reserved for the Russian army and that the military authorities would not allow civilians on board. Fortunately, through mediation of the naval officer, she could board the train and was permitted to use one of the compartments allocated to the officer. Mary realised that he was indeed 'a very great officer', and how lucky she was to have met him.

The journey seemed interminable. The train, loaded with Russian conscripts, crept slowly across the steppes, past lakes and rivers, herds of cattle and mobs of horses and companies of Russian soldiers learning to use arms for the first time. Buttercups, daisies and purple vetches were trampled underfoot at areas where armed men were drilling before going off to the trenches.

After changing trains at Chelyabinsk and once again at Moscow, Mary arrived at St Petersburg at long last. She bundled her luggage together and descended from the train with Buchanan under her arm. She was dressed in the only respectable clothes left to her after more than a year travelling along dusty roads and sleeping in filthy inns.

For years, Mary had wanted to see the magnificent city designed by Tsar Peter the Great in 1793. The city had been built amid drained marshes, alongside the Neva River, which provided valuable access to the Baltic Sea. The original wooden structures had been replaced by Empress Catherine the Great with stone palaces. St Petersburg had become known as 'the Venice of the North'. The city lived up to Mary's dreams and she described it as 'the most beautiful of cities in the world'.

After a four-day stay at the Astoria Hotel and a quick look at the wonders of the Hermitage, Mary took a train to Raumo in Finland. Its second- and third-class carriages were packed with men, women and children, desperate to get out of Russia.

The railway officials refused to allow Buchanan to stay in Mary's compartment and banished him to the luggage-van. Because Mary felt her dog would be lonely, she went to the van and kept him company.

The passengers in the train spoke many different languages, but not one amongst them spoke or understood Finnish, while the Finns spoke no language but their own and seemed to have a grudge against all foreigners. In the middle of the night, all passengers had to disembark at a railway station in the heart of Finland. As every hotel in that little Finnish town was full, Mary was again faced with spending the night at the railway station.

> The refreshment rooms were shut, the whole place was in darkness, but it was a mild night, with a gorgeous September moon sailing out into the clear sky, and I should not have minded

spreading my rugs and sleeping outside…, but the tales of the insecurity of Siberia still lingered in my consciousness. …[When] one of the porters [offered to] put us up in his house I went with all the others and took along my bundles of rugs and cushions. How many strange places I have slept in!

That porter had a quaint little wooden house set in a garden which might have been lifted from a story by Hans Christian Andersen. We had the freedom of a very clean kitchen. We made tea there and ate what we had brought in our baskets. …the best sitting-room was turned over to the women and children and myself. Two very small beds were put up close together and into them got the two women and three children, and I was accommodated with a remarkably Lilliputian sofa.[46]

The next morning, the train continued its journey across Finland and reached the coast of the Baltic Sea two days later. The following afternoon, Mary boarded the *Goathied*, a Swedish steamer that would take her to the far side of the Baltic Sea. There were Customs inspections and all luggage was examined before it was allowed to leave Finland.

Mary heard a broad Scottish accent and watched as 50 Scottish sailors arrived on board. They were part of the crews of four British ships that had been laid up at St Petersburg. Now they were returning to Britain, leaving their ships behind in dry dock in St Petersburg until the war ended.

The captain announced that he had received orders to change course — instead of going to Stockholm they had to sail further north to the Swedish harbour of Gefle.

As the *Goathied* was halfway across the Baltic Sea, a German torpedo boat approached. Mary recounted that

… from the torpedo boat came a voice through a megaphone. 'What are you doing with all those young men on board?' it asked in English with a German accent, English being the language of the sea. The sinister black torpedo boat was lying up against us. Sea-sickness was forgotten…

Leaning over the rail of the *Goathied*, we could look down upon the black decks of the torpedo boat, blacker than ever now in the dusk of evening, A rope ladder was flung over the side and up it climbed a couple of German naval officers armed with pistols. They spoke very correct precise English, and went below, demanded the passenger list and studied it carefully.

'We must take those young Englishmen,' said the leader, and he went through every cabin to see that no more were concealed.

The captain made as much remonstrance as an unarmed man can make.

'We are at war,' said the German officer curtly.

In the dusk he ranged the sailors along the decks, all fifty-five of them, and picked out those who were between nineteen and forty… It was tragic. There must have been treachery at work or how should a German torpedo boat have known that British sailors were on board?

But a few moments before they had been counting on getting home and now they were bound for a German prison! One by one they went [down the rope ladder], landing on the hostile deck, and were greeted with jeers at their misfortune by the German crew.

As the German torpedo boat drew away, the captain of the *Goathied* said he was relieved that the boat had not blown a hole in the side of his ship and thankful that none of *his* crew had been taken.[47]

Several hours later the *Goathied* entered the neutral Swedish harbour of Gefle where all passengers were instructed to bring their belongings onto the lower deck for a Customs examination. Mary piled her luggage, including Buchanan, onto a handcart. She had been told that dogs were not allowed to enter Sweden, so she hid Buchanan under her luggage and managed to smuggle him into the country.

Later in the day, Mary boarded the night train to Oslo and continued her journey through Buskerud, an area of snow-capped mountains. Arriving at Bergen, a city of wooden houses set at the head of a fiord, she and the other passengers boarded the *Haakan*

VII. On board ship Mary learned to her amazement that British and Anzac troops had landed in France and were fighting against the Germans.

The Norwegian ship took them to Newcastle-on-Tyne and from there Mary caught a train to London. At that time there was no quarantine for dogs in Britain, so she was able to bring Buchanan into England without any problems.

※

After years of travelling, Mary enjoyed the rural atmosphere of Eltham, centuries earlier the site of the Palace of Eltham owned by Prince John of Gaunt. From Eltham Station she could take the train to central London to visit her literary agent, old friends and favourite bookshops and attend meetings of the Royal Geographical Society.

Mary was concerned about the plight of Belgian refugee families. The Germans had sent thousands of Belgian men in cattle trucks to Germany to work in ammunition factories. Belgian women and children fled on ferries or fishing boats to Dover and Folkestone from where they were directed to Dartford to work in factories, because most male factory workers had enlisted to fight the Germans.

Mary and other kind-hearted residents formed a committee to raise money and rent homes for the refugees, provided them with food and warm clothing and gave English lessons to French- or Flemish-speaking children.

In 1915, a hospital for crippled and shell shocked Anzacs was established at the industrial town of Dartford, near Eltham, using Australian nurses. Mary volunteered to become a regular visitor at the convalescent home for amputees and went there to write letters for disabled Anzacs to their families in Australia. The Australian nurses, many of whom had been nursing under terrible conditions in France, were overworked, so civilian volunteers like Mary Gaunt helped out by taking the wounded for walks in wheelchairs, read to them and wrote their letters. Young wounded officers well enough to leave the hospital were entertained by Mary and other volunteers in their homes.

Mary read to the wounded in the convalescent home and organised a library for them. She supplied most of the books and her sister Lucy sent parcels of Australian books from Melbourne where she was working.

On the night of 8 August 1916, the Germans Luftwaffe launched 13 Zeppelins on southern London, aiming for Deptford Dry Dock and the factories of Dartford. Some of the Zeppelins went off target with the result that Mary's house was hit by a bomb and had its roof blown off, so she had to rent other accommodation.

The spring of 1917 was one of the coldest ever recorded in Britain and coal was scarce. Mary was working on another novel, but wartime paper rationing meant that few books were published, so her income from royalties plummeted. Despite her meagre income, she could not ignore the plight of the homeless refugees and continued to donate her time and what remained of her savings to help Belgian war victims.

*
**

Finally at 11 am on 11 November 1918, the Germans requested an armistice and the fighting ended. Subsequently, the wounded Anzacs at Dartford's Australian military hospital were invalided home on transport ships.

Meanwhile, Mary's asthma became worse and she suffered a severe attack of bronchitis. In the cold winter of 1920 she decided to sell her home at Eltham and move to the south of France. She rented accommodation at St Agnesse en Provence and lived on income from her investments and her now declining royalties.

Two years later Mary moved again, this time to Bordighera on Italy's Ligurian coast, where she rented the *Villa Camilla*, with its view over the magnificent yacht harbour. Around the harbour were wide boulevards, known as *lungarnos*, lined with palm trees. Bordighera had a mild climate and an excellent international library, which attracted Mary. The nearby harbour tempted Mary's brother Ernest and his wife, who loved sailing, to come and stay with her.

Bordighera was an affluent holiday resort. It had a large British community and many interesting people of other nationalities. Mary's next-door neighbours were a couple of charming Russian-Jewish artists who had worked in Paris. They gained a precarious living by selling paintings and doing some work in local antique shops. Mary enjoyed sharing meals with the two of them, hearing their memories of Russia and Monparnasse where they had known the Russian-Jewish artist Moise Shagall.

At the *Villa Camilla,* Mary was cared for by Anselma, who was an excellent cook and housekeeper. Anselma enjoyed telling Mary's neighbours that she worked for a famous author.

Following a lean period during the post-war years, Mary had two more successes in April 1925 when *The New York Literary Review* and *The Saturday Review of Literature* acclaimed her powers of narration when reviewing her latest book, *Where the Twain Meet.*

In 1926, Mary had an unexpected success with a crime novel, *The Mummy Moves,* which had been inspired by her many visits to the Egyptian galleries of the British Museum. To Mary's surprise, the book became a best seller in America and Britain.[48]

In the winter of 1930, after a severe bout of bronchitis, Mary Gaunt sailed to Jamaica for a holiday in the warmth of the West Indies. On Jamaica, Mary wrote more travel books, but they are not nearly as fascinating as her earlier works set in Africa and China. Her novel *A Tale of the Slave Days* roused a furore in Jamaica and in England. Scores of England's titled families had made their fortunes out of the slave trade, from which they had extended or built stately homes and become inordinately wealthy. Mary depicted British colonists using their female slaves as sex objects at a time when such things were covered up in 'polite society'.

Fears of yet another world war preoccupied Mary's brothers Guy and Ernest, both of whom had close contacts with British Naval Intelligence. They realised that Hitler was building up his armed forces in contravention of the Treaty of Versailles. Sir Guy

Gaunt wrote letters to *The Times* warning of the dangers of National Socialism and Fascism.[49]

From time to time, Guy visited his sister at the *Villa Camilla*. As he had been involved with the British Naval Intelligence, his presence at his sister's home alerted the Italian Organisation for Vigilance against Anti-Fascism (OVRA), who suspected that Mary was a British spy.

When Mussolini declared war on Britain, Guy strongly advised his sister to return to England, but well cared for by Anselma, she was reluctant to do so. However, when she learned that Mussolini's secret police were about to intern all foreign residents of Bordighera, she changed her mind.

Mary's neighbours, who were Jewish artists from Russia, had been beaten up by Mussolini's Blackshirts. On the night of their assault they decided to escape to France and invited Mary to come with them. Realising she could spend the rest of the war in an Italian jail, Mary saw the wisdom of leaving while escape was still possible, so she accepted her neighbours' offer gratefully. In a hurry she packed a few valuable possession into a suitcase and waited for her neighbours to pick her up. It was well after midnight before the two Russians arrived in their heavily loaded car. Anselma, who agreed to look after Mary's remaining possessions at the *Villa Camilla*, wished them good luck and waved goodbye.

To avoid being stopped by border guards, they followed the old inland road and managed to cross the French frontier without a problem. Once in France, the Russians headed for St Paul de Vence, in the hills north of Nice, believing they could stay there with a Jewish friend who was an art dealer.

As they arrived at St Paul de Vence, Mary made inquiries about renting a house. She was advised that it would be cheaper to find accommodation in the adjacent village of Vence. So they drove to the hilltop village of Vence where Mary rented a tall stone house in a narrow winding street.

By now France was divided into two zones — the north occupied by the German army while southern France with its capital at Vichy was supposed to be neutral. However, the French secret police in southern France worked hand in glove with the Gestapo. As a result, Mary's Jewish friends, who had saved her, were in danger as Jews were being rounded up and sent to internment camps. Finally, the Russian artists (whose names were never revealed) were able to board a boat for New York, having obtained forged papers with the help of Varian Fry, an American who ran an escape network from Marseilles.[50]

Several months after her arrival in Provence, Mary and her brother Guy decided to return to the *Villa Camilla* in an attempt to retrieve Mary's manuscript of her memoirs and other papers. Guy hired a yacht in Nice and he and Mary sailed to Bordighera. Unfortunately, their dangerous mission was unsuccessful — the documents and manuscripts Mary valued so much had vanished.

Only a brief record of Mary Gaunt's final years can be gleaned from letters written to her brother Guy and her niece Sheila. These letters reveal that, although she became frail and was confined to a wheelchair, her mind remained alert.

In 1941, Mary suffered a heart attack and was taken by ambulance down the steep road from Vence to an English-funded hospital in Cannes. On 19 January 1942, Mary died there at the age of 80. She had given most of what she had earned to those in need, so there was very little left in her bank account.

Although raised an Anglican, Mary had lost her faith in God and became an agnostic. On her deathbed, she expressed the wish to be cremated and her ashes scattered in the St Paul de Vence cemetery. Her obituary in *The Times* of 5 February 1942 called Mary Gaunt a 'cosmopolitan Australian writer whose hard work and talent had given her considerable success in Britain, America and Australia'. *The Times* praised her for her courage in travelling alone through some of the world's wildest areas. But in Australia, where Mary had lived until she was in midlife, little mention was made of her remarkable career or her Australian novels.

Top: The Ballarat lakeside house rented by William Gaunt for his family. This historic image shows the small tower in the centre where Mary and her brothers played as children on rainy days. *Strathalbyn House* was demolished and a smaller residence built on its site for the Bishop of Ballarat.

Left: A signed photograph of Mary Gaunt used as a frontispiece in one of her Australian novels. It is the only available portrait of Mary Gaunt. The photograph may have been taken shortly before her African expedition when she was in her 40s.
Courtesy the State Library of Victoria, who owns copies of many of Mary's first editions.

In the jungles of West Africa Mary was often carried by porters in a hammock.

The town of Elmina, with its former slave fort seen against the skyline.

Peking in the early 20th century, at the time of Mary Gaunt's arrival.

Mary Gaunt overseeing the loading of a flimsy 'Peking cart', which would take her to Jehol (Chengde). Peking carts were drawn by mules.

Mary Gaunt returned from Jehol in a 'wupan' on the River Lanho.

Top left: As there were no proper roads, Mary was carried in a mule litter on parts of her journey.

Bottom left: When visiting the remote Ming Tombs, Mary was carried by porters in a chair mounted on bamboo poles.

Mary and two friends take tea outside her home at the *Temple of the Three Mountains*.

Left: Chinese women with bound feet. The picture below shows the terrible effect of foot binding.

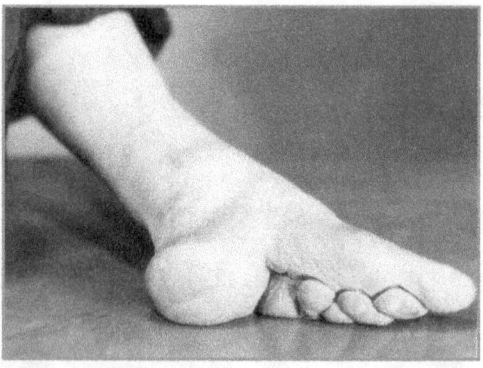

The ancient hilltop village of St Paul de Vence behind the French Riviera. Mary Gaunt rented a stone house in the neighbouring village of Vence rather than face chilly English winters. Photograph Jake de Vries.

The cemetery of St Paul de Vence where Mary's ashes were scattered. It is also the burial place of Chagall and D.H. Lawrence. Photograph Jake de Vries

CHAPTER 4

Hilda Rix Nicholas (1884–1961)

BLAZING A TRAIL IN FRANCE AND AUSTRALIA

'I'm going to paint things typical of my country... I'm the man for the job.' Hilda Rix Nicholas, on returning home to Australia from her successful exhibitions in Paris.

In the 1970s, the Queensland Art Gallery asked visitors to name their favourite Australian paintings. Those the public selected were *Monday Morning* by Queensland-born artist Vida Lahey, *Under the Jacarandas* by local art teacher Godfrey Rivers and *The Fair Musterer* by Melbourne-trained artist Hilda Rix Nicholas. Hilda blazed a trail for Australian artists with her successful solo exhibitions in Paris. Her third exhibition consisted of 'scenes of Australian life' which were shown at the most prestigious private gallery in Paris before being exhibited in the centre of London and touring British regional galleries.[1]

At the start of the twentieth century, Vida Lahey and Hilda Rix studied together under Frederick McCubbin at Melbourne's

National Gallery School. At that time, for reasons of modesty, female students, when drawing from the nude, had to work in a separate room from their male counterparts. Talented young men were encouraged to take up art as a career and paint large works in oils. Young women like Hilda and Vida were advised to limit themselves to small watercolours, usually of flowers or landscapes. Painting was regarded as a hobby for women, rather than a profession.

Vida Lahey never married. Since Queensland had few really wealthy art patrons, she taught painting to children and adults, limiting herself to small but exquisite watercolours of flowers, views of the buildings of Brisbane and the occasional beach scene. Vida's masterpiece, a life-size portrait in oils of two women washing clothes, titled *Monday Morning* was commissioned by a French lady named Madame Congerau and eventually ended up on the walls of the Queensland Art Gallery.

The life of the extroverted adventurous Hilda Rix was very different from that of the far more reserved Miss Vida Lahey. Hilda dared to defy the rigid conventions of her era. She enjoyed a very successful career in Paris exhibiting large dramatic portrait studies in oils, the kind of paintings usually reserved for male artists. Miss Rix wanted to shatter the convention whereby young ladies painted as a hobby rather than a profession, holding solo exhibitions and earning money like male artists.

'Mlle Rix paints like a man!' wrote a French art critic, amazed by the power of Hilda's art.

Hilda's achievements were impressive. In the 1920s, she blazed a trail for women with successful one-woman exhibitions in Paris and London. Returning to Australia, she espoused the cause of rural women and her paintings like *The Fair Musterer* re-enforced this concept that women played an important role in life on the land. This was one reason that this large oil was so popular with visitors to the Queensland Art Gallery at a time when Queensland was largely rural. In this painting, Hilda depicted a capable-looking girl in jodhpurs and riding boots beside a magnificent horse (see page 159). The central figure of an attractive young woman shows that she has just finished mustering a flock of ewes.² In 2010, *The Fair Musterer* was loaned by the Queensland Art Gallery to an important Rix Nicholas retrospective exhibition at the Ballarat Fine Art Gallery, where it was exhibited and illustrated in the catalogue.

The powerful portrait studies of Rix Nicholas were acclaimed for her mastery of drawing and her sense of colour and drama. A scholarly monograph of the life and work of Hilda Rix Nicholas, by the acclaimed art historian Dr John Pigot, has increased interest in Hilda's work and her major successes in Paris and London. ³

Hilda Rix was born in Ballarat and raised in Beechworth and South Yarra. Her mother came from the affluent Sutton family, who, in the colonial era, made their fortunes from selling pianos at a time when most middle class homes aspired to own one.

Hilda's mother, Elizabeth Sutton, married Henry Rix and studied art at the National School of Victoria in 1882, in order to enrich her life. She fostered the artistic talents of her daughters, Hilda and her older sister Elsie. Both children were encouraged to engage with art and music, to dress up and play charades or act in little plays performed at home. All her life, Hilda loved dressing up and collecting exotic clothes, which she used as props for her paintings. Elsie Rix, a very pretty girl and a good singer with some talent for writing, enjoyed acting as Hilda's unpaid model.

Hilda was educated privately at Merton Hall, in South Yarra, which became part of Melbourne Grammar School. Like her elder sister, Hilda was attractive in looks and personality and showed a great talent for drawing, even as a child. On leaving school, Hilda studied painting and drawing at the National School of Victoria under Frederick McCubbin, who praised her talent for drawing. Hilda's parents encouraged her to become an illustrator and felt that her elder sister should take up singing.

Hilda earned a little money by making line illustrations for school textbooks, which was seen as an acceptable career for young ladies. However, the life of a professional artist, exhibiting paintings and charging the public for them, was considered too raffish for a young lady of Hilda's background.

Mrs Rix hoped Hilda might be able to earn an income from her illustrations and paint in oils as a hobby. Arthur Streeton realised Hilda had exceptional talent and advised Mrs Rix that her daughter should study with several different artists to avoid being influenced by any one teacher. She must develop her *own* style.

Hilda's father, Henry Finch Rix, worked very hard as an inspector of schools. As Henry Rix's health was poor, he and his wife planned to take a long restful holiday overseas with their daughters and let Hilda express her creativity by taking classes in drawing and painting in London and Paris.[4]

This eagerly anticipated educational trip was put on hold as in 1906 Hilda's father suffered a massive heart attack and died. His premature death meant that Hilda's mother, who did not receive a widow's pension, had to delay plans to go overseas with her daughters. Fortunately, Mrs Rix had inherited money from her mother and planned to use it for their projected visit to Britain, France and Italy.

In spite of the fact they were in mourning, an exhibition of 100 watercolours and drawings by Mrs Rix and Hilda went ahead in Flinders Street, Melbourne. At their exhibition mother and daughter sold some artworks, which helped to finance their overseas tour. Trading in their first class boat tickets for a cheaper tickets in second class provided extra money and Mrs Rix, Elsie and Hilda boarded a passenger liner for England.

In May 1907, they arrived there and stayed in the London suburb of Forest Hill. It was springtime and the three of them enjoyed train trips into the neighbouring countryside, which Hilda found very different from the Australian bush. In her travel journal she wrote,

> Ye Gods! How neat it is! Even the lanes [are] kept clean by a man with a broom and I suspect a feather duster for the hedges. I sigh for our big wild bush, the smell of gum leaves and wattle after a storm.[5]

The journals kept by Hilda and Elsie record visits to the main tourist sights — Westminster Abbey, St Paul's Cathedral, Tower Bridge, the British Museum and the Royal Academy. They made an excursion to Kew Gardens, which Hilda loved for its colourful displays of rhododendrons.

Britain was enjoying the opulence of the Edwardian era when elegance in art and fine draughtsmanship was admired. The doyen of portrait painters was the expatriate American artist John Singer Sargent, who made dramatic portraits of British aristocrats in gorgeous costumes. Hilda's taste for this kind of art was nurtured by portraits she studied on the walls of London's Royal Academy. She also loved the fluidity and precision of drawing, which was her strong point.

Hilda's plan to take additional tuition in drawing led her to enrol at the Kensington Art School. On her first day, the director, John Hassall, examined Miss Rix's portfolio and asked her mother, 'Why bring this talented girl to me? She already draws *far* better than I do!'[6]

Nevertheless, John Hassall was able to teach Hilda a great deal more about the technique of drawing and its use in posters and illustrations. Hilda enjoyed searching the second-hand shops in Kensington High Street where she bought colourful costumes which she draped over her elder sister when Elsie acted as her unpaid model.

Hilda's daily journey from Forest Hill to Kensington and back required her to change buses several times and proved tiring. The family's modest budget prevented them from hiring hansom cabs for Hilda. They decided to move to slightly more expensive rented rooms in a Kensington lodging house to make Hilda's journeys to her art school shorter and less tiring.

The following year in October, at the start of the new academic year, Mrs Rix and her daughters exchanged their Kensington lodgings for a relatively inexpensive *pension* in Paris. They chose to live in Montparnasse, on the Left Bank of the Seine, near the studio of their family friend, Rupert Bunny. Rupert's father, Judge Bunny, and his wife had lived near the Rix family in Melbourne.

Rupert Bunny had shocked his conventional family by marrying Jeanne Morel, a young French artist who gave up her career to act as his model. He and Emanuel Phillips Fox were managing to make a living in Paris. Bunny was the most financially successful of all of them. He was lucky to have a clientele of wealthy South Americans who commissioned portraits from him. Like Hilda's mother he had studied at Melbourne's National Art School.[7] Rupert Bunny told Hilda, 'Nobody can have any idea of the intense vitality of art here — in Paris art is a living breathing thing.'

In that exciting first year in Paris, Hilda spent a great deal of time in the Louvre studying the classical masterpieces of French art. She loved the delicate but precise drawings of Ingres and studied the oils of the great French classical artists David and Gericault. The trustees of the Louvre were dedicated academics keen to preserve the conventions and, as such, refused to admit the work of 'modern' or contemporary artists. They excluded all the Impressionists, except Renoir.

Monet was no longer starving in a garret, but as yet not fully accepted by the conservative art establishment. The Gustave Caillebotte Bequest of early Impressionist masterpieces, donated to the French nation by the wealthy artist-collector, had been rejected by the trustees of the Louvre who regarded the paintings in Caillebotte's impressionist collection as unfinished works — an opinion echoed by the academic teachers of Hilda Rix and by Rupert Bunny. Early works of the Impressionists were on view in the Luxembourg Gallery, situated in the Luxembourg Palace on the Left Bank, near the inexpensive pension where the Rix family were staying.[8]

In her journal, Elsie Rix described Hilda and herself visiting the Caillebotte Bequest, but the Rix sisters echoed the opinions of Hilda's academic teachers that these were purely 'unfinished' studies. It would take another decade for fashions in art to change and major private and public French collections to regard the work of the Impressionists as exciting and desirable. London's Royal

Academy, where Hilda hoped to exhibit, was even slower to acknowledge the power of impressionist techniques.[9]

In 1907, most collectors and museums bought paintings for public and private collections at the Paris Salon. The jury of the Salon were elderly and conventional in their approach and their word was law in deciding which of the many artists who submitted paintings would have their work displayed. Exhibiting at the Paris Salon or the Beaux-Arts Salon was the only way to have paintings bought by France's lavishly government-funded art galleries. The jurors of the Salon, favouring paintings in the academic style, rejected modern impressionistic works. They considered that impressionism broke the strict rules that governed academic painting, a theory followed by Hilda.

Mrs Rix, having studied with Emanuel Phillips Fox at the National Art School, decided to pay him a visit in the studio he rented at 65 Boulevard Arago, near the Jardins de Luxembourg. The Rix family knew that Emanuel had married an English lady artist and wanted to meet her. The block of residential studios on the Boulevard Arago had a large courtyard garden which was shared between the artists and sculptors who lived and worked there and is now preserved as a national monument. Hilda wrote

> ... entering through an archway from the Boulevard Arago with a surprise of quaint courtyards and creepers, twisting cobbled paths, wicket gates and quite the loveliest little garden. [10]

Seeing small, highly coloured oil paintings by Emanuel's wife, Ethel Carrick Fox, Hilda realised that the older artist worked in the impressionistic style.[11] Ethel Carrick had not enough money to pay for models — their limited funds were reserved for paying professional models for the large oil paintings Emanuel hoped to exhibit in the Paris Salon. So, Ethel Carrick painted small rapid oil sketches of children and their nursemaids in the Luxembourg Gardens.

Hilda decided she would also go to the Luxembourg Gardens, but instead of using oils would make pencil drawings. She fell in love with the Jardins de Luxembourg which had wide avenues bordered by marble statues. Turn-of-the-century Paris enchanted Hilda with its boulevards bordered by elegant shops and terraced cafés and the narrow cobbled streets and ornate street lamps of Montparnasse. She was surprised to find Paris much smaller than London and far more rural. Fresh milk was delivered from the farms surrounding Paris in the morning by goatherds who milked their goats in the street and sold it.

An unexpected pleasure was the arrival of Hilda's former teacher, Frederick McCubbin, who arrived in Paris to stay with his friend Emanuel Phillips Fox.[12] McCubbin had taught Hilda to paint in oils, using muted colours, but, after seeing Impressionist works in the Luxembourg Museum, elderly 'Prof' McCubbin, loosened his brushwork and brightened his palette.

Hilda brightened her palette slightly but continued to paint in the academic style of her London and Parisian teachers. Not until 1912 would she paint in strong Moroccan sunlight and lighten her palette. But all that lay ahead.

In November 1907, Hilda enrolled at the Atelier Delecluse in Montparnasse, where classes with Auguste Delecluse started early in the morning. Hilda was in her element. She had originally enrolled for day classes only but enjoyed working at the *atelier* so much she paid a supplementary fee to continue working there during evening sessions with her teachers. Often she was so involved in drawing or painting she would forget to eat lunch.

In mid-July, art classes ended and the *atelier* closed as most Parisians took long summer holidays until September. The Rix sisters and their mother, having no car, toured Switzerland and northern Italy by train. Thrilled by what they had seen of the great art treasures of Italy in the Uffizi and other galleries, they vowed to return there the following year.

Back in Paris, Hilda managed to sell drawings made in the Luxembourg Gardens, which helped to pay her for her studies in the autumn term at the Atelier Delecluse.

The Rix family spent Christmas 1907 with friends who owned a chateau near Rouen.

In 1908, still living in the *pension* near the Jardins de Luxembourg, Hilda enrolled at the Académie de la Grande Chaumière for classes with Claudio Castelucho. One attraction of this Montparnasse art academy was the fact that pupils with limited funds, like Hilda, could pay the fees weekly rather than a year in advance, which was what most art schools demanded.[13]

At the Académie de la Grande Chaumière, Hilda was lucky enough to study with Richard Emil Miller, an American of Germanic background. Miller had made his name with colourful oils of superbly dressed women seated in Paris cafés. Like Manet, who he admired, Richard Miller saw himself as a realist artist, recording the real street life of Paris where large numbers of prostitutes solicited openly for trade. Miller's *Night Café* became a *success de scandale*, featuring expensively dressed 'ladies of the night', seated outside the Café de Flore. Miller's favourite models were courtesans, some of whom were part-time actresses and singers.[14]

Shocked by the large number of street walkers who solicited for custom in the cafés and streets, Hilda wrote in her journal that 'rottenness lurked under the glittering surface of French society'. She and Elsie had led sheltered lives and were shocked by the fact that Paris was now the sex capital of Europe, after the French economy had been shattered by France's defeat in Franco-Prussian war.

Hilda and her mother were worried that her choice of Richard Miller as a teacher would reflect badly on her morals and affect Hilda's marriage prospects. Although she regarded Miller's choice of subject matter in poor taste and *louche*, Hilda realised his value to her as a teacher. He taught Hilda to present her sitters in the most dramatic way possible, using colourful costumes as a revealing expression of her sitter's personality, which would become an important characteristic of Hilda's portrait studies in oils.

The other thing Miller taught his pupil was that, rather than grinding up pigments and mixing them with linseed oil, she should use oil colours in small metal tubes with removable tops. Miller taught her to employ the latest development in oil colours

— a brilliant lemon yellow, the intense green of jade, pale lavender and a deeper yellow that could be effectively shaded with raw umber to create the effect of gold. Hilda used this in her major work, *The Golden Cloak*.

Hilda followed the wise advice of Arthur Streeton and took lessons from a variety of teachers, including the celebrated illustrator Théophile Steinlen whose brilliantly coloured drawings, reproduced on posters all over Paris, had made him famous. Steinlen's bold handling of line was a source of inspiration for Hilda, as were some of the Japanese prints Steinlen encouraged her to study in the Musée Guimet.

One of Hilda's best portrait studies, made at this time, was titled *Sleepy*. She painted her sister wearing an antique kimono purchased in a street market. Hilda painted the softly faded silk kimono in delicate tones of blue, green, lavender and umber. It was one of the best of her early works.[15]

In April 1908, Mrs Rix and her daughters spent the Easter holidays in Nice. They enjoyed visiting the colourful flower market held each morning in the Cours Saleya.[16] The three of them went by train to San Remo where Hilda made pencil sketches of market women and donkeys. In Rome they saw the Vatican's magnificent art collections and marvelled at the Sistine Chapel. They caught a train to Naples, visited picturesque Amalfi and the isle of Capri. In Venice, they were awed by the magnificence of the gold-ground mosaics in St Mark's Cathedral.[17] Aided by Elsie who had a way with words, Hilda wrote up her impressions of the art treasures they had seen in an article titled 'In Search of Beauty'.[18]

Back in Paris, Hilda fell in love with Wim Brat, a handsome Dutch architectural student. The conventions of the era were strict and Mrs Rix insisted the couple must be engaged before they were allowed to spend a great deal of time alone. So Wim (pronounced Vim in Dutch) asked Mrs Rix's approval to marry Hilda. The young man's mother was wealthy and Mrs Rix considered his background suitable, so she agreed to the match. Wim gave Hilda an engagement ring and they enjoyed happy weeks together, visiting art galleries and planning their future.

All went well until Hilda's went to Holland to meet her future mother-in-law. Mrs Brat was a wealthy domineering widow who made no secret of the fact she did not approve of her only son's choice of bride. She had already selected a suitable Dutch girl for her son and heir and was angry that he had not obeyed her. She made it quite clear to Hilda that she was not welcome in the Brat family.

After much heart-searching and several more visits to Holland, in which it became apparent that her handsome fiancé was completely under the thumb of his possessive mother, Hilda broke off their engagement. She was now convinced that, although Wim claimed to love her, their marriage would never have worked.[19]

Back in Paris, Hilda consoled herself by throwing herself into her work and made more sketches in the Luxembourg Gardens and started another large portrait study modelled by Elsie.

The art academies and *ateliers* of Paris were closed from 14 July until the end of September, so the Rix family visited Picardy in northern France during the summer of 1910. They travelled by steam train to the small fishing port of Etaples, a few kilometres south of Boulogne, hoping to find somewhere quiet where Hilda could hire an inexpensive studio with sleeping accommodation. They wanted to spend the summer away from Paris as it was full of tourists.

The whitewashed cottages and narrow cobbled streets of Etaples where local costumes were worn by market women, attracted many artists. Peasant women wore picturesque white cotton bonnets, long skirts and wooden clogs. These were necessary when it rained as the unsealed streets were ankle-deep in mud. At Etaples, the cost of living was far cheaper than in Paris —the market sold plenty of inexpensive freshly caught fish and fresh vegetables. The market women were happy to act as models for a few *sous* per hour. Paris models charged much higher fees, because there was a greater demand for their services from the many artists working there.

Mrs Rix rented a large studio with sleeping accommodation from widowed Madame Monthuy-Pannier, who had four purpose-built studios in her garden which she hired to French and foreign artists during the summer months. The studio rented by Mrs Rix for Hilda was fitted with three truckle beds and heated by a pot-bellied stove. It had good lighting and room to store Hilda's finished paintings.

The market place of Etaples and the peasant women who worked had gnarled hands and weather-beaten faces. Hilda drew and painted the peasant women in their work clothes and in the colourful clothes they wore for the local *kermesse* or annual fair.

The Rix family returned to Montparnasse at the end of September 1910, so Hilda could take more classes before setting up in business as a professional artist.

In 1911 she sent a portrait study of her elder sister in a green riding habit to Society of French Artists.[20] Hilda's large oil *Retour de la Chasse (Return from the hunt)*, with its classical allusions to Diana, goddess of hunting, appealed to the academics on the jury. *Retour de la Chasse* was hung at eye level 'on the line' in their autumn exhibition. To have a painting 'hung on the line' in a prestigious exhibition was considered a great honour for a female artist, all the more so since she was a foreigner.

London's *Studio* magazine and Paris's *Notre Gazette* were intrigued by the attractive young Australian girl, starting to make a name for herself in Paris, and they published articles about Hilda's work.

That summer Hilda Rix made friends with the owner of a large house just outside Etaples where she was invited to paint a large oil, showing servants washing dishes. She depicted one maidservant pouring water into a bowl from a large copper kettle while the second girl washed the plates.[21] The subject matter of Hilda's painting was intended to highlight the laborious work of peasant women in rural areas.[22]

In this and subsequent summers, Hilda took her sketchbook with her in the streets of Etaples. She drew women wearing clogs, their long blue skirts covered by white aprons as they bargained with street vendors. By now, her command of the French language was excellent and this, coupled with the charm of her personality, made her a favourite with the locals so Hilda had no trouble finding local women who were happy to model for her for very little money.

Hilda was well regarded by her fellow expatriate artists who also rented summer studios at Etaples. They invited her to design a poster for their annual exhibition, which was to be held at a beach on the outskirts of fashionable Le Touquet.[23] The lithographed poster Hilda designed for the group reveals how well she had absorbed the tuition of Steinlen regarding the importance of strong line and boldness of composition (see page 157).

Elsie Rix wrote an article titled 'An Artists' Colony in Picardy', illustrated with Hilda's drawings of peasants and submitted this to Sydney's art magazine *Triad* so that friends in Australia would learn about their life at Etaples.[24]

⁂

In 1912, Hilda planned to visit Morocco with a group of male artists. In those days, travelling as a single girl with a group of men could ruin Hilda's reputation and wreck her chances of marrying a respectable man. Hilda's mother, mindful of her daughter's reputation, insisted she be chaperoned at all times. So it was arranged that Hilda would travel to Morocco in accompany of Mrs Tanner, wife of the American artist Henry Osawa Tanner, who rented a summer studio at Etaples.

The group landed at Tangier on 5 February 1912 and stayed in the pleasant surroundings of the Hotel Villa de France for the next two months. Like Ethel Carrick Fox, Hilda was inspired by the dazzling white light of Morocco.[25] Up to now she had little experience of painting in the open air, but lacking a studio she began painting out of doors. She wrote in her journal that Tangier was

> … like a beautiful dream [so] that I'm afraid to wake up in the morning and find it gone. Oh! It's impossible to give you the faintest impression as it's *much* more splendid than I thought… Every way one turns the head there is a new picture.

Hilda's creativity was stimulated by the cobalt blue of the sky and the intriguing shapes of archways, mosques and minarets. In her *plein air* works she painted veiled women lurking in shadowed archways and scenes in crowded markets. In spite of the flies, mosquitoes and the dust, she produced many superb and very original paintings in Morocco.

Returning to Paris, Mademoiselle Rix was given a one-woman exhibition of her Moroccan paintings in a commercial gallery, named Chaine et Simonsen. The exhibition proved to be a great success. The director of the Luxembourg Gallery attended the opening of Mlle Rix's show. He purchased one of her larger canvases *Grand Marché de Tangier*, to hang in this important public space seen by a great many Parisians and visitors to Paris.[26]

Art critics enthused over the work of the young Australian woman. They claimed Mlle Rix was a young artist with a brilliant future. More of Hilda's Moroccan canvases were exhibited with the Society of Orientalist Painters. The celebrated Paris dress designer, Worth, purchased several of Hilda's colourful Moroccan paintings which helped to make them fashionable. [27]

In February 1913, Hilda managed to persuade her mother to let her return to Tangier, accompanied by Elsie as chaperone and assistant. The sisters stayed at the hotel where Hilda had stayed on her previous visit. Its owner, impressed by the success of Mlle Rix — which had brought visitors to his hotel — provided free of charge a second room for Hilda to store her paintings and painting materials.

Working in the streets and markets of Tangier was not easy. Pickpockets and thieves were everywhere and artists' materials or water bottles left unattended were stolen. Elsie stood guarded over their belongings and did her best to fend off the flies with a horsehair switch. In Morocco, even though it was a very poor country, Hilda found it hard to hire female reliable models. In this male-dominated Muslim society where women rarely ventured outside the home, their male relatives refused to allow their wives and daughters to pose for her. Hilda employed young men to model for her but after receiving payment for the first sitting, the models, many of them young homosexuals, failed to return for a second sitting.

Annoyed by the waste of her time and money, Hilda ventured into the crowded market place and returned with a handsome Negro boy, who agreed to pose for her in one sitting, no matter how long.[28] Hilda was worried he too would vanish into the crowds. As she had to work fast, she used pastels and managed to complete a superb sketch of the Negro boy (see page 158).

For two young women without a man to protect them, crowded *souks* could be dangerous. Aware of the dangers, Hilda chose to paint in the open sheep market or the Soko, which was near their hotel. She claimed that

> ... in the heat of work I am not conscious of the ring of people until with a snap a pencil breaks and I hear a chorus of gentle groans of sympathy. When I dropped a pencil the other day an Arab picked it up and seeing the point was broken whipped out his large knife and sharpened the pencil and presented it to me with a beaming smile.[29]

After a few weeks painting from dawn to dusk with only a short break for lunch, Hilda felt she had enough paintings for a second exhibition. They were even brighter in colour than her previous Moroccan works. She had the canvases crated, shipped to Marseilles and sent by road to Paris, so they would be there in time for her next exhibition.

Despite the warning that foreigners were robbed and murdered if they ventured outside Tangier, the Rix sisters caught a ramshackle bus to Tetuan, a city once owned by Spain. Tetuan proved to be a wonderful area to paint with Spanish-style buildings tiled in shades of cobalt blue and turquoise. Braving danger, Hilda and Elsie hired donkeys and a donkey-driver and rode into the Rif mountains, hoping to see the famous Blue Men of Goulimine, whose skins were stained deep blue by the indigo used to dye their robes. Their dangerous journey produced more fine paintings.

Back in Paris, Hilda had an second success exhibiting her Moroccan paintings at the Society of Orientalist Painters and selling nearly all of them.

※

The Rix family spent a bitterly cold winter in Paris where Hilda rented a poorly heated studio with very primitive bathroom facilities. She painted a winter landscape titled *Snow in Montmartre,* which was impressive in its handling of the coloured blue and pink shadows she saw in the snow.[30] Artists invariably painted Paris in spring or summer so Hilda's snow scene attracted a great deal of attention. Her colours suggested the crispness and coldness of winter and, unlike most of Hilda's paintings, showed the influence of the Impressionists. The unusual scene of Montmartre under snow was bought by a major French collector. (It would eventually be purchased from his estate by the National Gallery of Australia).

Hilda had another success early in 1914 at a private gallery in Paris. Her large oil called *La Robe Chinoise* depicted Elsie wearing a magnificent scarlet and blue silk robe of the Manchu era and a long necklace which Hilda painted in her favourite jade green. In the painting Elsie wore the traditional black headdress of an aristocratic Manchu lady. This was regarded as one of the highlights of the exhibition. A private collector loved the work and paid a high price for it.[31]

In the summer of 1914 Hilda and her mother and sister returned to their rented studio at Etaples. They had no idea that their pleasant world would collapse when the Kaiser's army invaded neutral Belgium *en route* to capture Paris and avenge the humiliating defeat the Germans had suffered in the Franco-Prussian war.

As the French Army mobilised to fight against the Kaiser's army, British expatriates in France were warned by radio to return home. German soldiers had executed unarmed civilians in Belgian towns and they risked being shot as enemies of Germany.

As a result, the roads were jammed with farm carts, motor cars, cattle and frightened people desperate to escape. The Rix family decided to leave for England taking only the minimum of luggage. It was impossible to take Hilda's large paintings with them. She packed only a few of her sketch books and left her oil paintings in the care of her friendly landlady, telling her the war was not expected to last long and they would soon be back.[32]

The Rix women, like all Australians of that era, were travelling on British passports. When they finally managed to reach Boulogne they had great difficulty securing places aboard the last ferry to Folkestone. There were rumours that the Kaiser's soldiers would arrive and imprison all English-speaking people on French soil.

Amid widespread panic and confusion, standards of hygiene on the crowded ferry from Boulogne to Folkestone left much to be desired. The drinking water, always a problem in France, was contaminated with dangerous bacteria. Unaware of this, Mrs Rix and Elsie drank the infected water. Mrs Rix soon developed symptoms of 'enteric fever', as typhoid and paratyphoid were known. Some sufferers developed a raging fever and intestinal cramps and died in a few days, while others resisted far longer. Elsie was in the second group and her 'enteric fever' was slower to develop.

On their arrival at Folkestone elderly Mrs Rix was rushed to hospital in a critical condition. Elsie and Hilda were worried about their mother, fearing she might die. Slowly her fever abated, but soon Elsie was suffering stomach pains and her temperature was high. Unselfish as ever, Elsie had said nothing about this, until finally she collapsed.

> I got a nurse for her [Elsie] and her doctor said that awful word 'Enteric'. She too was carried away in an ambulance followed by two ghastly weeks of terror. I flew from one to the other, trying to cheer up both [of them] in the terrible consciousness that at any moment one or both of my loved ones might leave this world.[33]

Although Elsie had contracted a slower acting form of paratyphoid, her attack became so severe doctors feared for her life. Hilda's beloved sister and best friend died in hospital on 2 September 1914. Her mother was still on the danger list. So Hilda had to face the ordeal of organising and attending her sister's funeral alone with no relatives or friends to help her.

Fearing the shock of Elsie's death might kill her elderly mother, Hilda withheld the news for three months until the doctors considered Mrs Rix well enough to bear the news of her daughter's death. Hilda had to break the news to her mother in the nursing home. In the midst of so much personal tragedy, the daily casualty lists of war victims in *The Times*, grew longer and longer. Imported food became scarce. Hilda had rented a small apartment in London and saw searchlights that illuminated the sky searching for zeppelins as London and its suburbs became targets for German bombing raids.

Eventually, Mrs Elizabeth Rix was released from the nursing home and Hilda became her nurse. Aware that her life had been shortened by the attack of paratyphoid, Elizabeth Rix urged her daughter to draw her portrait so she would have a memorial of her. Realising that her mother did not have long to live, the final drawings of Hilda's mother are imbued with love and sadness.

In 1916, Elizabeth Rix died, leaving Hilda to organise her funeral. Hilda's strength and energy had been sapped by the stress and strain of acting as sole carer for her mother until she died. Hilda's grief was intense. She became so depressed, she could not eat and grew very thin and had sleeping problems. Once so lively and active, Hilda now lacked the energy to draw or paint and claimed she was unable 'to put one foot in front of the other', so great was the pain of losing the two people she loved most in the world.

A fellow artist named Mary Raphael took pity on Hilda and invited her to stay at Mary's country house in Kent to help her recuperate. Mary Raphael provided the support and encouragement Hilda needed at this very difficult period of her life. Eventually, Hilda recovered and felt well enough to return to

London where she rented a studio with living accommodation in Warwick Avenue in Maida Vale, determined to resume her career as a professional artist.

***

The fact that a handsome young Anzac officer, named George Matson Nicholas, saw and admired the paintings Hilda had left behind in her Etaples studio would change her life. Before the war, George Nicholas had been employed by the Education Department of Victoria. He volunteered to join the Anzacs, was wounded at Gallipoli and evacuated to a military hospital in Egypt before serving in northern France. At the battle of Pozieres, his courage under fire when leading an attack on a German machine gun post saw him promoted to the rank of major and recommended for a Distinguished Service Order.

Posted to Etaples, the art-loving Anzac officer heard about the attractive young Australian artist who had left her paintings in Etaples when forced to flee to England.[34] Major Nicholas was intrigued. He sought out and found Hilda's former landlady. Madame Monthuy-Pannier. She showed him Hilda's canvases, told him what a lovely girl Miss Rix was. Major Nicholas was impressed by Hilda's talent and wanted to meet her.

In September 1917, given leave from the trenches to attend his investiture at Buckingham Palace, Major Nicholas took the time to seek out Miss Hilda Rix. He found Madame Monthuy-Pannier had been correct — Miss Rix was a most attractive and charming young woman. It was love almost at first sight for both of them. At their third meeting Major Nicholas confessed he was in love with Hilda and she felt the same. He was due to return to the front a week after his investiture. The average life span of an officer on the Somme was less than a month. Hilda had no relatives in England and needed no one's permission to marry. They could marry in church once the banns were called.[35] George Nicholas gave Hilda an engagement ring and she made a pencil sketch of him, a leather 'Sam Browne' belt across his chest emphasising his broad shoulders (page 157).

On 4 October 1916, Major George Nicholas went to Buckingham Palace to receive the DSO, accompanied by his fiancée. Hilda sat on a spindly gilt chair in a vast reception room of Buckingham Palace and watched the man she loved walk down the long expanse of red carpet to have a medal pinned to his chest by King George V. A photographer caught George Nicholas and Hilda Rix walking happily hand in hand through the elaborate gates of Buckingham Palace and out into the Mall.

Three days later, they were married at St Saviour's Anglican church in the borough of Paddington. Their church wedding was followed by a reception at London's Hotel Cecil. Hilda's mother and sister were dead and she had no father to give her away or cousins or close friends to act as her bridesmaids. Once married, George Nicholas would be her sole relative in England.

George asked one of his brothers to act as his best man and chief witness. His two younger brothers acted as ushers and a few fellow officers and some of Hilda's friends were the only guests.

After a short and blissfully happy honeymoon at Hindhead, a rural beauty spot in Surrey, Major Nicholas had to return to the front at Poperinghe and take command of his battalion.

In a letter to her new husband, dated 15 November, Hilda enclosed photos of her late mother and sister and told George Nicholas how much she loved him.

> Your letter with news that you have gone back to Battalion has come and frightens me. Oh my dear, dear love, it's terrible. You are in danger and I am far away... Dear husband be brave and splendid and [do] your best but don't be reckless. I need you and love you utterly. Your wife, Hilda. [36]

Tragically, Major Nicholas was killed before he received Hilda's loving letter, struck down by a German bullet while bravely leading his battalion 'over the top' at Flers.

Hilda's poignant love letter was returned unopened, accompanied by her husband's personal belongings including his watch and military greatcoat. Hilda's journal recorded how without him she no longer wanted to live. Initially, she was supported by Major

Nicholas' brothers, Bryon, Frank and Athol, but once they returned to the front line she was alone with her grief.

Hilda vented her despair by creating a bleak painting of a woman in black on a battlefield, titled *Desolation*. She also painted a portrait of a young woman cradling a ghostly child and added a line from a poem by the late Rupert Brooke, *And those who would have been their sons*.[37] Her future, once so bright was destroyed. She would never have a child. Hilda could not bear to part with the possessions of the man she loved. She wore his watch and for years she slept with her late husband's Army greatcoat beside her on the bed.

By the end of 1917, Hilda had recovered sufficiently to draw a self-portrait, showing her as a grieving widow in a black dress (page 157). The drawing board beside her represented her main source of income. But the insecurity of war meant that there was little demand for paintings by collectors and public galleries.

Hilda was determined to continue painting under the name of 'Hilda Rix Nicholas', so that her dead father and her husband would not be forgotten. As German zeppelins made bombing raids on London and southern England fewer people bought art.

Hilda narrowly avoided being killed in a zeppelin raid. She had no reason to stay in London now that her husband was dead, so put her name on a waiting list to return to Melbourne, keen to return to her family home and visit relatives.[38] However, waiting lists for cabins were long in war time.

Eventually, Hilda was able to return home in May 1918. As a war widow she was entitled to a passage and she returned on a troop ship full of wounded soldiers, escorted by her brother-in-law, Athol Nicholas.[39]

In receipt of a small war widows' pension Hilda lived in the family home at South Yarra. In November 1918, she held a solo exhibition of European and Moroccan paintings at Melbourne's Guild Hall. These Moroccan works with their bright colours and broad brushwork were regarded as too *avant garde* for Australia. But

Hilda was determined to succeed in her homeland. She held a successful solo exhibition at the Society of Women Painters in Sydney's Queen Victoria Building and made new friends.[40] Some critics admired her colourful palette, but there were still many complaints her work was too virile and strong for a woman artist.

Hilda took this as a complement since most critics regarded 'women's art' as vastly inferior to paintings by male artists.[41]

Using money from the sale of her paintings and from letting out the Sutton family home, she had the money to take a short lease on former stables and coachman's dwelling in the grounds of *Abbotsford* and renovate them to her own design. Her new address was No. 17 Raglan Road, Mosman, and the garden behind her studio had a view of the harbour.

Hilda had a good eye and was clever at interior decoration. She employed a builder and was able to convert the disused stables and the coachman's cottage into a comfortable studio and living quarters. Mosman was an ideal place to live for an artist. Ethel Carrick Fox, now widowed, spent part of her time in a Mosman mansion owned by the Theosophists group.

Hilda painted her garden and its harbour view, and young women posing on the beach and seated under Japanese-style umbrellas, considered the height of fashion. The art critic of the Sydney *Bulletin* echoed French art critics and described the oil paintings of Hilda Rix Nicholas as being 'as vigorous as those by any man'. Celebrated Australian photographers, Max Dupain and Harold Cazaneaux photographed the attractive Hilda Rix Nicholas in her studio.[42] Having enjoyed success in France Hilda was the subject of a great deal of media attention.

But living alone, Hilda missed Elsie and her mother. Fortunately, at this juncture in her life she met Dorothy (Dodo) Richmond, who would eventually become her confidante and best friend. Dorothy was a sweet-natured and creative. She earned a modest income from writing children's stories and was more reserved than Hilda. Dodo remained calm under stress, which Hilda, who was more volatile in temperament, found very soothing.

Dorothy's good looks, peaches-and-cream complexion and shapely figure were ideal for an artist's model. She had the ability of an actress to strike dramatic poses when required and hold the pose for a long time, something Elsie had been able to do. Hilda, missing Elsie badly, became very attached to Dorothy.

Outwardly, Hilda appeared to be recovering from her husband's death, but the hurt still ran deep. In 1922, she suffered a serious emotional setback. In memory of her late husband she entered a competition to paint a large mural designed to adorn what was in those days called the Melbourne Public Library (now the State Library of Victoria). Emotionally involved with her subject matter Hilda prepared a design showing wounded Anzacs on a battlefield (page 158). This was a theme that obsessed Hilda. She was keen to make this a tribute to Anzacs like her husband, who had lost their lives in the war.

She submitted her design to the trustees of the Melbourne Public Library. The competition was won by an artist named H. Septimus Power, who had fought at Gallipoli. His design celebrated the bravery of the Australian Light Horse. Privately, Hilda was told that many judges preferred her design but political correctness meant they selected the one by Septimus Power, preferring images of glory and victory rather than images of suffering Anzacs.

Hilda was devastated by their choice. An angry 'digger' wrote to the director of the Melbourne Public Library, claiming that Mrs Rix Nicholas's design should have won, outraged that Australians could forget how the Anzacs had suffered. His letter aroused public indignation and the rejection of Hilda's design became a *cause célèbre*. The trustees of the Australian War Memorial showed scant interest in the idea of a mural showing the sufferings of Anzacs and rejected Hilda's offer to paint an idealised Anzac in battle dress.

However fashions in art change, Many years later the Australian War Memorial *did* purchase Hilda's portrait of an Anzac in battle dress. It now hangs on the walls and is one of the War Memorial's most haunting and popular images.

Quixotically, having rejected Hilda's portrait of an Anzac, early in 1921, the trustees of the War Memorial bought an oil painting Hilda had made eight years previously before the war began, to which they gave the title *A Mother of France*. The painting shows a careworn peasant woman in a white cotton cap and blue skirt, the blue echoed by the row of *faience* plates behind the woman, who was presumed to have lost sons in the war. Having been painted before World War One started, this could be called a fanciful attribution.

Hilda insisted that the War Memorial place a notice beside her painting of the elderly French peasant indicating that it had been 'painted by the widow of Major George Nicholas, DSO, who had died fighting for freedom on the Somme'.

In 1923, after the Mosman mansion in Raglan Street was sold by the owners, Hilda lost her studio and the money she had spent on converting it into a comfortable home. Lacking a home or studio, left her free to travel around and paint. So she bought a car and paid for the boot to be fitted with racks to hold her paintings and named it 'The Paintbox'.

In an era when young women rarely ventured into the outback without a male escort, Hilda and Dorothy Richmond toured rural New South Wales and stayed with friends. They visited the Snowy River area where Hilda painted pastoral properties, boundary riders on horseback and attractive landscapes of the southern Monaro area. They stayed with Dorothy's married cousin Jocelyn, where they met two bachelors, Edgar and Ned Wright, both young graziers, tall, athletic with laconic senses of humour. Hilda and Dorothy went riding with Ned and Edgar. Hilda made an unforgettable impression on both bachelors while Dorothy preferred another Wright cousin named Walter, who eventually she would marry.

Hilda painted Ned Wright on horseback and called her portrait study *In Australia*. To paint his portrait, she nailed the canvas to a tree, leaving her hands free, but a sudden gust of wind seized the half-finished work. Hilda grasped the canvas while clinging onto her paint brushes and managed to save it.[43]

Hilda painted Dorothy's married cousin Jocelyn with her young daughter on her lap, titled *Motherhood* (see page 158). Such a tender painting is rare in Australian art which is rich in landscapes but unlike French and Italian art has few good depictions of motherhood.

Hilda and Dorothy returned to Sydney with finished canvasses in their storage racks. In August 1923, Hilda held a successful exhibition at Anthony Horden's Gallery. Reviewing Hilda's Sydney exhibition, *The Daily Telegraph*'s art critic, William Moore, praised Mrs Rix Nicholas for catching 'the Australian atmosphere so well. Her work is a genuine example of the courage of Australian women'.[44] But other critics claimed she was infringing on male territory. However, Hilda refused to change her style or her subject matter.

Since she was homeless following the sale of *Abbotsford*, Hilda was thinking about returning to France. She proposed to take Dorothy, who had never been overseas, as her companion and assistant. Her friend was thrilled by the idea.[45]

In high spirits, the two women left for France on the ss *Ormonde* with crates of Australian paintings. Hilda, about to turn 40 looked much younger. She had succeeded in leading life on her own terms but as yet had no wish to settle down or remarry.

At no 84 rue d'Assass, overlooking the Luxembourg Gardens Hilda rented a studio with two bedrooms, a large living area and a kitchenette. Dorothy was disgusted by the lavatory which consisted of a cupboard containing a bucket. Hilda explained to her friend that many Parisians lived without bathrooms or proper toilets and the concierge was paid to empty the bucket each morning.

A foreign writer, who lived close to Hilda and Dorothy under similarly primitive conditions, was Ernest Hemingway. With his first wife, Elizabeth Hadley, Ernest lived in a walk-up apartment in the rue Notre Dame des Champs, a few streets away from the rue d'Assass and Hilda's studio. Hemingway's young American wife was also horrified to find their toilet was a bucket that had to be emptied each morning.

Hilda and Dorothy as well as Hadley Hemingway and her baby took daily walks in the Luxembourg Gardens on fine days. Hemingway's reminiscences, *Paris is a Moveable Feast*, record how he had renounced journalism and was living in Montparnasse on very little money. Hemingway wrote for *The Transatlantic Review*, an influential magazine, published by Ford Maddox Ford, a British expatriate writer also residing in Montparnasse. Ford Maddox Ford lived with the South Australian artist Stella Bowen, who had borne Ford a daughter and was using her private income to help fund Ford's literary review. Stella also took long walks in the Jardins de Luxembourg. These expatriate Australian artists knew each other by sight. Hilda and Dorothy may have attended one of the many parties Stella gave for expatriate writers and artists to promote Ford's literary magazine. Hemingway's memoir, *Paris is a Memorable Feast*, describes the charm of Montparnasse at the time when Hilda and Dorothy lived there.

Hilda decorated the living area of her Montparnasse studio in the style of the period with colourful Persian rugs on the floor. On the wall behind her desk, hung a portrait of her late husband. Hilda wrote the occasional letter to the young grazier, Edgar Wright, but she had no time or inclination to pursue a deeper relationship — the loss of her husband was far too painful to contemplate remarrying.

Hilda, with Dorothy as her assistant, had to support both of them and pay the costs of transporting her paintings from Australia by sea and road to Paris and find a gallery to exhibit them.

The art galleries Hilda contacted recalled her successful exhibition of Moroccan paintings before the war but regretted they were booked out for several years with exhibitions by younger *avant-garde* artists.

Hilda left her card with the address of her studio in Montparnasse and asked to be contacted if they had a cancellation. In October 1924, the prestigious Georges Petit Galerie in the centre of Paris advised her they had received a cancellation so were able to host an exhibition of her Australian paintings in a few months' time. If Madame Nicholas would bring in her paintings they would have them framed for a solo exhibition in January 1925 at their gallery in the rue de Sèze. Georges Petit Galerie was one of the most prestigious galleries in Paris. Its domed glass ceiling was a talking point and ensured that during the day paintings were seen to good advantage by natural light.

The founder of the gallery, the great Georges Petit had died four years earlier and been famous for organising major exhibitions, including a Monet retrospective, and the first showing of Rodin's masterpiece, *The Kiss*. After Petit's death the urbane Bernheim brothers, Joseph (Josse) and Gaston ran his famous gallery in addition to their more *avant-garde* Bernheim-Jeune Gallery whose stable of artists included Bonnard, Utrillo and Matisse. The Bernheim brothers were collectors as well as dealers, publisher of art books and an art magazine. Hilda was told they would publicise her work in their magazine *Bulletin de la vie artistique*. They emphasised the lure of Hilda's paintings of a country of wide open spaces which the French regarded as a very romantic place.

In January 1925, the opening of Hilda's exhibition was attended by leading political figures and members of the *haute monde*. Guests drank Moet or chilled Sancerre wine from crystal glasses. The French had warm feelings for Australians, who had fought bravely on French soil against the hated Germans. Young Madame Rix Nicholas was an attractive war widow which also endeared her to French people. Money was flowing freely during the stock market boom of the 1920s and sales were good. Hilda's opening was a great success, helped by the fact she spoke French and her looks charmed the male guests.

Suave Frenchmen kissed Hilda's hand and told her she looked *charmante*. Dorothy Richmond recorded that Hilda looked charming in a new Parisian outfit.

Gaston Bernheim negotiated a very profitable sale to a French public collection of Hilda's portrait of Ned Wright on horseback *In Australia*. Among other paintings the Bernheim brothers sold to French collectors was *Motherhood*, the tender portrait of Dorothy's cousin Jocelyn and her little daughter, to a French collector. Decades later the painting would return to Australia.

The art critic for *Le Temps* described how the paintings of Mme Rix Nicholas revealed Australia as a romantic place with a dazzling light like the coast of southern France and her rural landscapes had 'the melancholy romance of vast spaces as yet uncultivated'.[46] In spite of so much praise, Hilda kept her head. She claimed modestly, 'It's the work that matters, not *who* does it' and added that 'the true artist was born to paint and *nothing* would stop them'.

Hilda, with her good looks and vivacious personality, was invited to several important functions on the Paris arts calendar including a formal dinner at the Luxembourg Gallery, whose director had purchased one of her Australian landscapes.

An agent for a leading London gallery saw Hilda's exhibition and loved it. He arranged for any paintings that remained unsold, plus a few others specially commissioned from her, to be exhibited in a prestitious Bond Street gallery. This led to four exhibitions in suburban galleries and an extended tour of British regional galleries, an honour never attained before by any Australian artist, male or female.

Hilda learned she had been additionally honoured by being elected an Associate of the Sociéte Nationale des Beaux-Arts. She was congratulated by fellow Australian artists Bessie Davidson and Roy de Mestre. But other foreign artists working in Paris were jealous of Hilda's success. She was urged to paint more views of Australia by the Bernheim brothers, who continued to represent her for years.

Another portrait study Bernheims sold to a French collector featured Dorothy Richmond dressed for the opera, titled *The Golden Cloak*. Hilda added greenish shadows to the cloak and to Dorothy's beautiful face, in the manner of the celebrated portrait by Matisse of his wife in this striking painting. Before leaving Paris, Hilda painted another arresting study of Dorothy posing as a socialite of the Jazz era. The painting, titled by Bernheim-Jeune, *Une Australienne*, is an important representation of that period. Dorothy is depicted in long suede coat with a collar and cuffs of black fur and a red hat and matching scarf, clearly enjoying herself. She strikes a dramatic pose, hand on hip, her long elegant fingers encased in leather gloves and the painting is a memorable one. (see page 158).[47]

Hilda and Dorothy left Paris in mid-July, the start of the holiday season, and spent the early part of the summer back in her Etaples studio visiting old friends and enjoying the atmosphere of the area of France she loved.

Two months later, they went to London, where an exhibition of Hilda's works was opened by the Australian High Commissioner, Sir Joseph Cook, at a gallery on Bond Street, London's most fashionable area for art galleries and shops.[48] Hilda's exhibition, like the one in Paris, attracted many viewers. The art critic of the *Morning Post* praised her work and published an extract from the speech of Sir Joseph Cook, who claimed Hilda Rix Nicholas had 'expressed the brilliance of Australia's sunshine, its scenic grandeur and beauty... Her work marks an advance on any Australian paintings previously shown in London'.

Hilda's Australian paintings toured English regional galleries for the next two years and many thousands of Britons saw views of the outback — boundary riders, the rolling hills of the Monaro and its homesteads. At the end of the tour, several British regional galleries bought paintings by Rix Nicholas.[49] Hilda was elated by her success and, amid good wishes for her speedy return, she and Dorothy left Paris for Australia on 14 September 1926.

Hilda aimed to paint more Australian landscapes and brought several of her French paintings back with her in order to exhibit them in Australia.

On arrival in Melbourne, their ship was met by journalists who interviewed Hilda about her successful exhibitions in France and England. Hilda and Dorothy drove to Canberra and from there to the southern Monaro where met up with Edgar Wright. But in spite of his evident affection for her, at this stage Hilda did not want to commit herself to a serious relationship. She had suffered a great deal and worked hard for her success. Her work was still on show in various regional galleries in Britain and a portrait study of a French peasant, *Le Bigouden*, had been selected to hang in London's Royal Academy Summer Exhibition. In 1928, she enjoyed a successful exhibition at the Melbourne Athenaeum.

Finally, Hilda decided that she had fulfilled her ambitions. It was high time to leave the limelight and marry Edgar Wright, the handsome quietly-spoken grazier who loved her. Up to now, she had been cautious about marrying in an era when most men of substance refused to let their wives work, believing it reflected badly on their own status. But Edgar Wright was secure enough in his own career as a successful grazier to marry a woman who was successful.

Living on a large grazing property, there would be ample space for Hilda to have her own studio. They agreed she would run the house and continue to paint, while Edgar would run his sheep property with no interference from her. Edgar insisted she could use the money from her paintings to do whatever she wanted with it.

Hilda was in her forties and did not feel the intense passion that had prompted her to marry an Anzac who she had known for less than a month. This was a different and more mature relationship in which friendship and mutual respect gradually developed into love and Hilda was convinced it would endure. She cherished the dream that she might be able to have a child, which would complete their happiness.

Dorothy was to marry Edgar's cousin Walter, so the four of them would be close, a perfect arrangement for happiness.

Hilda and Edgar Wright were married in one of the side chapels of Melbourne's St Paul's Cathedral in May 1928. Hilda would spend the rest of her life in the Monaro, one of the most beautiful parts of New South Wales but hoped they would make more visits to France together.

What no one could have foreseen was the fact that in 1929, a year after Hilda married Edgar, Wall Street crashed, followed by the crashes of the French *bourse*, the Australian stock market and countless other financial institutions. Many people in France, Britain, Australia and America were ruined. Several commercial galleries went bankrupt and art prices went into melt-down.

By 1933, Rupert Bunny, once earning a very good living in Paris, had his income so drastically reduced he was forced to leave France and return home to Melbourne almost penniless. In the outback Hilda continued painting portraits and landscapes and no longer needed to support herself by their sales. She ran her home efficiently, beautifying her garden and supervising the construction of a purpose-built studio in the French Provincial style, a project that made her happy.

Most exciting of all, two years into the marriage, she gave birth to a healthy handsome boy called Rix in memory of her father, Henry Rix. Hilda fulfilled her aim and became a mother at 43, an age when most women were deemed far too old to give birth.

Little Rix appears in some of his mother's paintings, sometimes with his father and in others with his governess. Hilda painted the life around her — the homestead, her garden and portraits of her husband and her son. Rix's governess posed in a work shirt, jodhpurs and riding boots for her striking work, *The Fair Musterer*, which, along with the preliminary sketch for this painting, is now in the Queensland Art Gallery.

During World War Two, Hilda and Edgar Wright acted as surrogate parents to a young school friend of their son Rix, attending the same boarding school. The boy's parents were living in wartime London and were very grateful to Hilda and her husband.

In 1944, a year before the war ended, Hilda painted a superb portrait of Edgar Wright titled *The Fleece*, sometimes known as *The Grazier* (page 159). In this painting, the strong image of Hilda's husband, examining a strand of wool, is framed by the vertical lines of the woolshed. The painting is now regarded as an icon of the era when Australia lived 'off the sheep's back' and depicts the importance of the Australian wool industry and the skill and knowledge of Australian graziers.

Once World War Two ended, fashions in art underwent a huge change. Revelations about the Nazi concentration camps and the Jewish Holocaust had a profound influence on artists from countries occupied by the Germans. The horrors of Word War

Two and the influence of Freudian psychology, changed ideas of art in many parts of the world, including Australia. Josl Bergner, who had migrated from war-torn Europe, demonstrated new concepts of art to young Australian painters like Arthur Boyd, Albert Tucker and Sidney Nolan.

From Vienna and Prague, Stanislaus Rapotec emerged as the leader of Sydney's new school of Abstract-Expressionism and the fine draughtsmanship and mastery of line, which Hilda represented, no longer appeared relevant. Russian-born Danila Vassilieff urged his students to paint like children.

Living on a remote sheep property, Hilda continued to paint figures in the landscape in her distinctive style but there were now fewer and fewer buyers for her work. Artists of her period who had been greatly loved, such as Augustus John and Dame Laura Knight, were no longer so popular. Like Hilda Rix Nicholas, they are now being rediscovered and praised.

In 1950 Hilda returned for a visit to war-torn France with her husband and son.

In old age, Hilda had problems walking and started to suffer from the characteristic tremors of Parkinson's disease. An operation on one of her feet proved unsuccessful, with the result that her walking problems worsened and she was no longer able to stand at her easel. She died in 1961, survived by her husband and her son and at the time of her death, her artistic triumphs and her trailblazing work were almost forgotten.

Now, half a century after her death, the wheel of fashion has turned again — the best works of Hilda Rix Nicholas are once more under the spotlight. The brilliance of Hilda's brushwork and her drama of her portrait studies received renewed appreciation from critics and public alike. Women's art of high quality and fine draughtsmanship has received the respect it merits. In April 2010, a successful retrospective of Hilda's French and Australian works was held at the Bendigo Fine Art Gallery, accompanied by an excellent catalogue.

In August 2010, *The Golden Cloak,* Hilda's dramatic portrait of Dorothy Richmond in an opera cloak, was chosen to adorn the invitation to the opening of an important Sydney exhibition titled *100 Years of Women's Art*. The exhibition was a treasure trove of paintings by Australian women and a tribute to their skill and dedication.

Designed to commemorate the life and work of gallery owner, the late Eva Breuer, it was held at Sydney's S.H. Irwin Gallery of the National Trust. Drawn from the best works by women in three private collections, was opened in the presence of more than 1,500 guests. As so many people wanted to attend the opening, an enormous marquee had to be erected in the grounds of the National Trust Headquarters to house them.

The exhibition contained major works by trailblazing women artists of the calibre of Margaret Olley, Grace Cossington Smith and Judy Cassab. Hilda's large oil, *The Golden Cloak*, occupied a prominent position, visible to all those entering the exhibition. Beside *The Golden Cloak* hung another brilliant portrait of a woman, painted by Stella Bowen, a contemporary of Hilda, also working in Montparnasse in the 1920s.

Stella Bowen, a brilliant Adelaide-born artist, was weighed down by domestic responsibilities and a demanding lover and enjoyed less success than Hilda. But times have changed and today both women are regarded as highly talented artists.

The exhibition was opened by Her Excellency Marie Bashir, Governor of New South Wales.[50] In her speech she praised the strength and courage of Australia's female artists. How Hilda Rix would have loved to see her work hanging in an exhibition which proved what she had claimed for decades — women artists could paint in oils just as well as men.

Hilda's lithographed poster for an exhibition of artists at Le Touquet Plage in 1913. Rix Wright collection.

Pencil drawing of Major George Nicholas before he returned to fight in France. Rix Wright collection.

Hilda Rix Nicholas as a war widow, 1917. Pastel drawing. Bega Valley Art Society.

Hilda Rix Nicholas. Festive costume of woman from Finistère, pastel drawing, 1925-26. Private collection.

Pastel drawing of a boy from a Moroccan souk, 1914. Rix Wright collection.

Motherhood, c 1922-23, oil, exhibited in Paris. The model was Dorothy Richmond. Private collection.

Projected mural for the Australian War Memorial, (Detail) 1922. (Original destroyed)

Une Australienne, oil. Model Dorothy Richmond. Private collection.

Right: *The Fleece*, 1944. Arguably Hilda's most important Australian painting depicts her second husband, Monaro grazier Edgar Wright, in a woolshed. Private collection.

Below: *The Fair Musterer*, painted in oils in 1935. Hilda wanted to show the important role of women on the land. Queensland Art Gallery.

ALL PAINTINGS AND DRAWINGS BY HILDA RIX NICHOLAS ON PAGES 157–159 ARE REPRODUCED COURTESY OF HILDA'S GRANDDAUGHTER, BRONWYN WRIGHT.

CHAPTER 5

Sister Anne Donnell (1875–?)

SISTERS IN WAR ON LEMNOS ISLAND

Things are just too awful for words. We are the first women to have come here and find only a bare piece of ground with wounded men still in their clothes lying on it, filthy, bloodstained and in pain. Matron Grace Wilson, head of Anne Donnell's unit on the island of Lemnos.

Anne Donnell, a senior nursing sister from Adelaide, decided to enlist in the Australian Army Nursing Service (AANS) after a group of bronzed young men in uniform waved at her from a troop train. Seeing her uniform, they called out, 'Hullo, nurse! Wish us luck. We're off to France!'

As their steam train started to move the bronzed young Australians began to sing *It's a Long Way to Tipperary*. Several blew a farewell kiss to Sister Donnell. None of them appeared to have a care in the world.

Anne Donnell waved them farewell but feared they could be embarking on a journey which would see many injured or killed. Through the train windows, Anne saw laughing young soldiers. She looked for uniformed nurses, but could not see a single one.

Anne could not sleep for thinking about that trainload of young recruits with no one to look after them if they were sick or wounded. She had no ties and was an experienced nurse. Why not enlist? A few senior nurses had been allowed to enlist in the Boer War, so surely the Army would have women nurses in this war rather than male orderlies? She wrote a letter of application to the director of the Australian Army Nursing Service, one of the first to volunteer her services.

In this war, there was considerable resistance against sending women to war. After a long delay and a medical examination, Sister Anne Donnell was finally pronounced fit and accepted by the AANS. Her age was recorded as 39 years and 7 months on her enlistment form. On 20 May 1915, she was assigned to the Third Australian General Hospital or 3 AGH.

Since the senior army doctors, most of whom had served in the Boer War, preferred to work with male orderlies, initially far too few nurses were enlisted. The AANS accepted only senior nurses and insisted they had to be single and had wide nursing experience. In addition to working as a theatre sister, Anne Donnell had done her midwifery training, a skill she did not expect to be of use as an army nurse.

On her application form, Anne gave her address as Cherry Gardens, Adelaide. She named her brother, Stewart Donnell, as her next of kin and her religion as Anglican.[1]

Among the upper echelons of the Army Medical Services, fears were expressed that unmarried women might fall pregnant. Exceptionally strict rules were laid down about the appearance and conduct of army nurses, whose uniform had to be as sexless as possible. Anne was issued with two ankle-length uniform dresses with stiff white collars and cuffs which had to be starched, two short scarlet capes, a long grey cape, white aprons to wear over her wool serge uniform, a pair of button boots and a pair of canvas ward shoes. For outdoor wear, there was an old-fashioned black bonnet with long trailing silk ribbons. Looking at herself in the mirror, Anne felt it made her look like one of Florence Nightingale's nurses off to the Crimea rather than a modern young woman braving convention to work for the army in northern France.

The price to pay for serving her country was that Sister Donnell suffered a loss of seniority and for six months would be demoted to the rank of nurse and would be paid less than an army corporal, but would be responsible for the lives of her patients. But at least she would see London, where a short stay was scheduled for induction talks and to learn some French. In 1914 only relatively affluent women could afford overseas travel and Sister Donnell, though from a family who valued education, was not wealthy.

Before leaving, Anne had arranged with a group of friends from her local church that they would send gifts for her patients such as cakes and chocolate. In return, she would write them long letters about the war which would be circulated around members of the group.

On 25 April 1915, a month before Anne was due to leave for France, the newspapers reported that an Anzac force had made a successful landing in the Dardanelles, an area of Turkey the papers called the Gallipoli Peninsula, on their way to capture the ancient city of Constantinople. To Anne, excited by the idea of seeing France, it all seemed very remote. Rigid military censorship had kept the knowledge of the full death toll from the Australian public, fearing enlistment figures would drop were the full extent of casualties and the difficulties the Anzacs faced become public knowledge. There was no hope of establishing a military hospital there. In spite of all the efforts of Major Neville Howse, who headed the Australian Army Medical Service, the War Office had not provided nearly enough hospital ships to take the wounded to Alexandria, five days away by sea, where they were being nursed.[2]

On 20 May 1915, Anne Donnell and other nurses from her unit, 3 AGH, clad in heavy winter uniforms and those antiquated bonnets, embarked from Sydney on the ss *Mooltan*. Anne and many of her colleagues had purchased French phrase books believing they would eventually be working in northern France near the battlefields on the Somme.

Anne's unit arrived in Britain in June 1915 as the War Office was making secret plans to establish two British and two Australian tented hospitals on the island of Lemnos, some 80 kilometres away from the Gallipoli Peninsula — as a staging post for assessment of wounded men, with the worst cases taken by hospital ship to Alexandria. Anne's unit was one of those selected to serve in a hospital which to date had no tents, no beds and no medical equipment. After sitting through a series of induction talks Anne and her colleagues were delighted to do a little sightseeing in London, unaware their destination was being altered.

What none of the administrators at the British War Office had foreseen was that the profusion of corpses, flies and the lack of sanitation on the Gallipoli Peninsula would cause outbreaks of dysentery and typhoid among the Anzacs. There was a lack of lavatory paper, which, in view of the fact that the new hospital in Lemnos specialised in cases of dysentery, was a real problem for the patients.

Wood was prohibitively expensive on Lemnos and in such short supply it would have to be imported to build huts for the nursing staff should the war be prolonged into the bitterly cold winters on this small island. The War Office believed they could solve the water and food shortage on Lemnos by shipping out a small desalination plant or condenser as well as crates of tinned fruit and vegetables, along with tents and medical supplies. However, just as they had done with the nurses' summer uniforms, which did not reach them in time, the British administration was so chaotic that the troopship delivering the desalination equipment and essential food and medical supplies destined for Lemnos was diverted to another port.

From England, the Australian nurses, unaware of the chaotic situation on Lemnos, were told plans had been changed. They were now to embark for the port of Alexandria before proceeding to Lemnos. In yet another War Office bungle, summer uniforms were ordered but did not reach them in time. All they had were the heavy woollen winter uniforms they had been issued in Australia. As temperatures soared, they lived in those heavy woollen serge grey dresses in which they were bathed in perspiration aboard ship long before the invention of air conditioning. Their starched collars and cuffs turned to rags in the heat. However, in Alexandria, so great was their discomfort that the starched collars were replaced with linen collars and cuffs.

This was another mistake by administration staff of the British War Office. As a result of so many bungles, Lemnos would acquire the dubious reputation of being the worst provisioned of all the army hospitals.

The male staff of 3 AGH sailed ahead of the nurses and arrived on the bleak hillside selected as the site of the new hospital on 29 July 1915. The Anzac attack on the Sari Bair ridge saw a large number of casualties arrive on Lemnos before the tented hospital had been properly established.

Anne and her fellow nurses were kept in the dark about the bungled arrangements, excited to think they would be serving in a brand new tented hospital on a Greek island. They were told they must wait in Alexandria to give time for the British supply ship *Ascot* to arrive on Lemnos with tents, medicinal equipment, tinned food and the precious desalination plant. In Alexandria, Anne saw how wounded soldiers and those suffering from dysentery had overwhelmed the military hospitals set up in converted buildings or former hotels in Alexandria and Cairo.

Nurse Donnell's unit, 3 AGH, was commanded by elderly Colonel Thomas Fiaschi, a veteran of the Boer War. Colonel Fiaschi had been born in Italy and worked as a surgeon in Sydney and was typical of the old school of army doctors. He was convinced women were not strong enough mentally or physically to work at the front line. The nurses were determined to prove him wrong. The colonel bent the rules to suit himself and made an exception for his young pregnant wife who he adored, having lost his first wife and two sons to illness. She was allowed to accompany him to Alexandria and the couple lived in luxury in one of the city's most luxurious hotels.

Making it quite clear he regarded the enlistment of female nurses as a waste of money, Colonel Fiaschi did not endear himself to Matron Grace Wilson and the nursing staff of 3 AGH. Anne was disappointed rather than flattered when told Colonel Fiaschi had selected her to deliver his young wife's first baby. This meant she had to remain behind while her unit sailed without her until the baby was several weeks old. There was no point in appealing. Anne (now given back her former title of Sister Donnell) had to obey orders or face a court martial.

So Anne waved her nursing colleagues goodbye and spent her days with young Mrs Amy Fiaschi, a former nurse. After talking to her at length, Anne saw a softer side to the elderly colonel who so desperately wanted this child and loved his wife very much. There were no problems and Sister Donnell delivered Mrs Fiaschi of a healthy girl.

Meanwhile, the nurses of 3 AGH had arrived at Mudros Harbour aboard the ss *Simla* on 7 August 1915, the day after the Anzacs attacked Sari Bair. They were shocked to find nothing had been done for their arrival and were ordered to wait on board their transport ship. Alongside them were white-painted hospital ships, with red crosses on their bows to prevent German planes bombing them, carrying hundreds of wounded men. But the tents had not arrived to accept the wounded Anzacs, although the French and Canadians had been better organised and managed to erect a tented hospital for their wounded soldiers.

Before the war, Matron Grace Wilson had been in charge of the Brisbane General Hospital (forerunner of today's Royal Brisbane) and was very popular with her nurses. She was angry and upset to learn about what was potentially a disastrous situation for the wounded and for 'her' nurses. Believing medical equipment was arriving from London, all the nurses had brought with them in their kit were a few rolls of bandage and cotton wool and bottles of aspirin. One of the nurses had a small methylated spirit stove. Colonel Fiaschi was too busy looking after his army doctors to worry about the nurses, who he had never wanted on Lemnos in the first place.

The nurses were told to stay on board for 24 hours. Finally, when Colonel Fiaschi issued orders to disembark, the nurses were met by a Scottish staff sergeant playing the bagpipes. In true military style, he marched them for miles over rough stony ground to a bleak hillside. They found hundreds of wounded Anzacs lying in rows on stretchers on the open ground and no tents to shelter them. There were very few trees and hardly any shade, so most of the patients had to be left out in the blazing sun.

Matron Grace Wilson and her nurses were horrified to think these poor men must be nursed in the open and sleep on stony ground. The few beds that had arrived were reserved for critical cases. Many of the wounded, especially the dysentery patients, were lying in their own ordure, some of the wounded stuck fast to their stretchers with dried blood, many delirious with pain and fever.

The nurses had no morphine to alleviate pain, only the few bandages and bottles of aspirin they had brought with them and the drinking water British warships in Mudros Harbour could spare them.

Food was scarce due to the non-arrival of the supply ship. Instead of bread, they were given large square army biscuits, so hard some nurses broke their teeth trying to eat them. The nurses and their patients had to sleep on the hard ground without even a mattress under them, there were no changing tents in which to dress or undress and only one latrine for nurses and patients to use.

Back in Alexandria, unaware of the chaos on Lemnos, on 23 September 1915, Anne told her friends,

> I am now ready for Lemnos and for what I came here for, to nurse the wounded from Gallipoli. As transport ships sail every day I imagine myself already there. I know you are eagerly watching for a letter telling you about our work, though, you know, as far as war news goes, one cannot write freely. [Anne was referring obliquely to the fact that military censors read

every letter and took out any remarks critical of the administration or that could betray the position of the Anzacs to the enemy.] I do not in the least mind roughing it. I am off to my final destination in a day or two. My address will be No. 3 AGH, A.I.F., Turk's Head Peninsula, West Point, Mudros, Lemnos, via Alexandria, Egypt.[3]

The fact that Anne's address *giving the exact site* of 3 AGH on at Mudros was not blacked out by the military censor indicates censorship at Alexandria was less strict than on Lemnos or at Gallipoli. Meanwhile, Anne fretted that she was not with her colleagues. A shortage of transport ships, busy ferrying the wounded from Gallipoli, delayed her departure for Lemnos.

Not until 12 October 1915 was Anne able to board a ship for Lemnos and arrived at Mudros Harbour the following day. Lemnos was not far from the Gallipoli Peninsula, so she could hear the booming of the big guns across the water.

The harbour was full of British warships and had been heavily netted to prevent attacks on them by German submarines. Anne's ship, the ss *Simla*, would be used to transport many more patients back to Alexandria, so great were the number of casualties from the Anzac attack on Sari Bair.

> We were in the harbour all night singing 'God Save the King' after Evening Service. The ss *Kanowna* was waiting alongside us. converted into a hospital ship. The staff of ten nursing sisters on board are English, with the exception of one Australian and one New Zealander… Colonel Fetherston, three officers (Australian) and myself are here as guests. Colonel Fetherston is over from Australia on a tour of inspection and making for the 3rd Australian General Hospital to inspect it. From what I could gather in conversation with the colonel last night, he is not too pleased with the accommodation and lack of comfort of our nurses. Colonel Fetherston [later General Fetherston] thinks all nursing sisters should be on an equal footing with the officers.[4]

Sister Donnell's letters revealed many of the distressing conditions she and her colleagues were facing. Their pay was relatively meagre compared to Australian soldiers and that of army nurses from Canada, who were paid almost double the Australian rate. Their low rate of pay made it hard for them to supplement their meagre diet with the figs and oranges and scarce local vegetables offered by impoverished Greek hawkers keen to make a profit.

Fortunately, Anne's seniority and professional experience was recognised and she was once again made a nursing sister. She would inspire younger nurses working under her with her professionalism in the difficult months that lay ahead. But as she arrived at Mudros Harbour on 13 October she had no idea of the harsh conditions in which she would work or that two nurses on Lemnos Island, like so many of the patients, would die of dysentery.

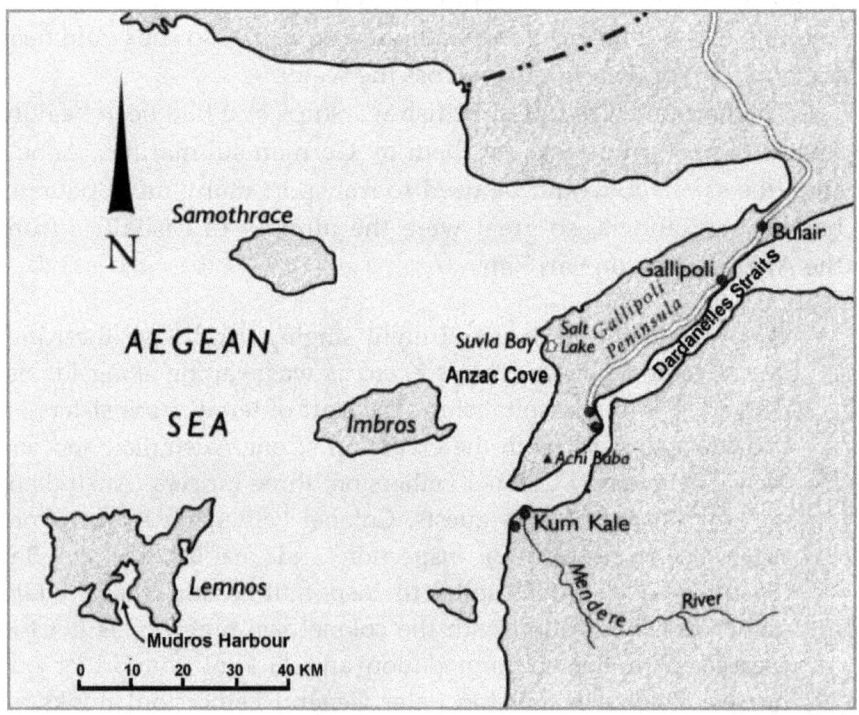

Map showing the location of Lemnos (with Mudros Harbour), Imbros, the Gallipoli Peninsula and Anzac Cove

October 13th.

Yesterday at 4 pm we anchored in the outer harbour of Mudros. Here we are still waiting calmly and patiently for orders from the ss *Aragon*. There seems no hurry where things military are concerned. The harbour is beautiful, and it's a fine sight to see all the different kinds of ships — destroyers, sub-marines, etc… Last night two crowded troopships passed us on their way out, but, instead of turning to the left (the port side), as is usual, they turned right. This makes us wonder if something fresh has arisen. If Greece has entered the war the ships are bound for Salonica [Thessaloniki]. We are anxious for news. Lemnos Island from here looks barren, not a sign of vegetation to be seen, only tents to the north-east and west, and windmills in the distance on the hills.

This was Anne's first intimation that conditions were harsh on Lemnos. It did not help the nurses that British generals, ambivalent about the status of Army nurses, had refused to grant them 'honorary' officer status like the Canadian nurses. The Australian nurses were paid as soldiers rather than officers. Amid the chaos on Lemnos they had a great deal more responsibility than nurses in civilian hospitals and worked far longer hours. Yet they never complained, keen to prove they were as good as any man there.

Such high casualty rates, far higher than expected, meant the idea of evacuating the Gallipoli Peninsula was raised on 11 October 1915. However, evacuation was opposed by the British commanding officer, Major-General Hamilton. He did not seem alarmed by the enormously high casualty rate and the difficulties of evacuating the wounded due to the shortage of hospital ships. What General Hamilton feared most was the damage to British military prestige, not the loss of his troops so nothing was done.

Anne's next letter reported her first meeting with Colonel Fiaschi, the senior medical officer whose baby she had delivered. Although very grateful that Sister Donnell had delivered his baby girl safely, in general the colonel showed scant concern for the welfare of nurses under his command and cared only about his doctors.

> October 14th.
>
> Early this morning we received our orders and immediately started for the inner harbour. Everyone brought their cameras and many snaps were taken of the ships. On anchoring Colonel Fiaschi was soon alongside in a little Red Cross hospital boat to meet Colonel Fetherston and myself. Colonel Fiaschi was pleased to hear the latest news of his wife and delighted with the photos I had taken of her and his baby girl and thanked me profusely. Now that I have actually rejoined my Unit [and seen conditions there] my regret about staying behind has vanished.

Rigid censorship meant Anne could not record her shock that most nurses still had neither beds or mattresses and had to sleep on the hard ground wearing their uniform and wrapped in their grey cloaks.

The tented hospital had originally been intended to be used for lightly wounded troops and those suffering from dysentery. After being nursed for a few weeks, dysentery patients were expected to return to duty. But as many of them were very ill indeed in an epidemic of dysentery, their recovery was often delayed. Patients needing amputations and major surgery were supposed to be shipped to Alexandria to be treated in hospitals there or sent on to Cairo, but soon these Egyptian military hospitals were overflowing. As a result, the wounded had no option but to remain in the primitive facilities available to them on Lemnos. Anne's unit, 3 AGH, was made up of 30 medical officers under Colonel Fiaschi and 96 nurses under Matron Grace Wilson, a brave and determined woman who did her best for her nursing staff in continual battles with Colonel Fiaschi and War Office officials.

Anne was told by her colleagues how appalled they had been at the sight of hundreds of wounded men lying in the open, some so ill they were delirious with pain and fever. Although finally the diverted transport ship, the ss *Ascot*, had arrived at Mudros bringing a small desalination unit, some tents and beds, due to more bungling by the British War Office in London they were still very short of sheets, bandages and toilet paper (so vital for dysentery patients) and had no mosquito nets. Anne spent her first nights on Lemnos sleeping on the hard ground at the mercy of mosquitoes and flies surrounded by wounded Anzacs, many of them suffering severe pain.

Over 50,000 wounded men or patients suffering from severe attacks of painful dysentery or weak with typhoid fever needed care and attention. Many were so weak they could not reach the latrines that had been dug for them and the stench was indescribable. Had Anne described the scene, no doubt, the censor would have removed it from her letters. Those who were wounded by grenades or shrapnel had deep wounds that needed cleaning and draining and the nurses worked around the clock trying to cope under extremely difficult conditions.

Anne was horrified to see the high rate of gangrene among wounded men who had spent days lying in the burning sun on the beach at Anzac Cove before being loaded onto polluted horse barges and sent to Lemnos. They often arrived delirious on Lemnos from lack of water. Some had tongues so badly swollen from thirst that they could not fit inside their mouths. Many were so badly infected with gangrene there was no hope they would survive. As the nurses lacked sulphonamide drugs (the forerunners of antibiotics) all they could do was drain the wounds of pus and watch helplessly as the wounds continued to fester.

'We could do little for many of our patients except help them die,' wrote Matron Grace Wilson in despair.

Anzacs arriving aboard hospital ships had usually been cleaned by the nursing staff who lived on board. Those who arrived by barge had received very little attention. The barges had not been disinfected after transporting horses so horse dung was a breeding ground for infection, the patients lay there among bits of straw amid the reek of dung. They were 'filthy, bloodstained and in pain' on arrival. Some had wounds infested by maggots, many were crawling with lice. Cleaning them up was an unpleasant job for the nurses, especially as water was rationed.

The number of dysentery cases from Gallipoli increased. In a letter written early in October Anne described her dysentery patients in guarded terms so as not to upset the censor, but wondered how

> ... human frames, so gaunt and grim, could hold on to life for so long, as their life literally drained away. Many did recover even though we had no sulphur drugs. [By this, Anne means sulphonamides, which were not nearly as effective as antibiotics but these did not come into use until World War Two].

In addition to the 3 AGH, there were the No. 2 Australian Stationary Unit, several British military hospitals and two Canadian military hospitals, a convalescent depot and the Sarpi rest camp. At the 3 AGH, one small condenser unit was struggling to provide enough drinking and washing water for so many patients and staff, so water was strictly rationed.

At first, Anne was undaunted by the conditions around her, convinced things had to improve. On 21 October 1915, she described life on Lemnos in an optimistic letter to her friends in Adelaide.

> How interested you would all be in our field hospital could you only pay us a visit. Entering it by the main thoroughfare, 'Macquarie Street,' with its marquees and tents on either side, you would see, instead of flower gardens in the spare patches in front, decorations made with white stones in the form of maps of Australia, an emu, and the kangaroo to remind us of home. We have beds for 1,040 patients, but, as we have far more patients than beds, some are still on mattresses on the ground. ...I am working with a sweet Sister and as she has no red tape about her I am very happy. We hope soon to be fully equipped, but know we must be patient. We are roughing it, but are happy to know we are doing what we came to do. As long as we can serve our boys and make them comfortable and contented we do not mind. Our chief luxury is exercise and fresh air, and as we get these in

abundance, we nurses bring a keen appetite to our tinned provisions served on enamel plates.

I warn you not to expect [us to be] dainty ladies on our return as we may well be weather-beaten hags... this expression is appropriate when we look in the glass. While we enjoy our work here and know it is vital in saving lives... we are helped by letters from you all and by parcels from the Red Cross. You and they provide a strong link between us nurses and our sunny home, for no other name sounds as sweet to us as Australia.

Their patient load per nurse was nearly double that of civilian hospitals in peacetime. In her next letter the stoic Sister Donnell made, only one mention of the poor living conditions (probably fearing the censor would delete her words if she revealed the full horror of life on Lemnos or even destroy her letter).

So, instead, Anne describes preparations for the onset of the severe wintry weather that was expected.

Huts are being prepared for us two miles away, in a more sheltered spot. We [nurses] may get there, we may not. I have an inward feeling that we will not be able to weather it here, for various reasons, one being that we are put on half rations for bread and firewood, and the latter only used for cooking purposes. Then with the gales predicted I wouldn't be surprised to hear of shipping being suspended. We think of ourselves [and our discomfort] but there are the boys just across from us in the same latitude on the [Gallipoli] Peninsula who won't even have the same shelter and comforts as we do. When the Unit first arrived on Lemnos a good deal of surgery was done, but now we have chiefly medical cases. One of our best surgeons left us today. I could tell you a lot of interesting tit-bits, but they would border on the critical, so will reserve them for the fireside next winter.

When Anne wrote that last sentence, she was aware that her letter would be censored.

The nurses still ate unappetising food from chipped enamel plates while the doctors ate far better food, served on china plates in the officers' mess which as females the nurses were not allowed to enter. Anne's colleague Sister Evelyn (Tevie) Davies described the biscuits as resembling 'plaster of Paris, you had to bang them on the table to break them, and they do not always break, so you gnaw small pieces off the corners. Our girls were breaking their teeth on them.'

Although often hungry themselves, many of the nurses unselfishly donated their one egg a week and their small pat of butter, to their critically ill patients to assist their recovery.

Unlike the doctors, the nurses had no batmen to care for them and had to wash and iron their uniforms and those wretched collars and cuffs while the officers had batmen to keep their uniforms clean, do their washing and polish their shoes. It seemed very unjust to Anne and her overworked 'sisters in war' that a corporal in the Army Medical Corps was earning double the pay of a skilled female nurse.[5] The Australian nurses were annoyed that Canadian nurses had been awarded officer rank as early as 1901 while their status was still under discussion in London.

One of the disadvantages of living on Lemnos was that all meat and vegetables had to be imported. Greek hawkers still offered fresh fruit like figs and green vegetables, but, poorly paid as they were, Australian nurses could not afford them except as a rare treat. The Australian nurses bore their hardships stoically, determined to show Colonel Fiaschi and his doctors, women could cope with hardships just as well as men. The attention to personal hygiene showed by the nurses ensured they had a lower death rate than army doctors.

Water continued to be scarce. When finally they had sheets they could often not be laundered due to lack of water. They could not use sea water as the soap would not lather and the soiled bedding of the dysentery patients sometimes had to be burnt on bonfires.

Cooking was done on open fires — hot water reserved for sterilising medical instruments used in operations had to be boiled by the nurses in coppers out in the open air. Hurricane lanterns were the main form of lighting, but a small emergency operating theatre was lit by battery lamps. Eventually, 'bell tents' arrived by another transport ship and were erected for the nursing sisters.

Meals were miserable affairs. Blowflies were so numerous the nurses had to keep plates of food and cups of tea covered as best they could. Their mess room had only a table and some planks laid across boxes to act as benches. The nurses were delighted to receive Red Cross parcels to supplement their meagre diet.

Anne Donnell's letter of 21 October 1915 mentioned how grateful she was to receive two parcels delivered through the good offices of the Red Cross. Items like chocolate and tobacco went to the patients. She was thrilled with gifts of hand-knitted sweaters and warm fleecy dressing gowns for herself and other nurses and sheets that arrived from her friends in South Australia.

> Yesterday I opened a Red Cross box from Toowoomba, Queensland. Such useful comforts of [every] kind of socks, mittens, mufflers, and the cigarettes tied up in the socks delighted the boys immensely. Then on going on duty in the Officers' ward I find a pile of soft white sheets from South Australia, each one marked with 'May health attend you.' Yes, it is through your efforts that we are able to carry on our work. and we do appreciate to the full what you are doing. Even the Sisters are not forgotten and receive presents of sweaters and dressing-gowns. They say we'll need all this warm clothing as soon as the winter sets in. It's as cold as possible now, the beginning of autumn days (It's such a change for you to hear of anything apart from the heat from me).

Complaints were made about the poor hygiene of the Army's portable kitchens. The nurses still lacked a bath tent so when their hair became dirty and they caught lice from their patients, some nurses cut their long hair close to the scalp in an effort to solve the problem.

Greek villagers at Kastro and elsewhere were pitifully poor but were friendly towards the nurses since for centuries they had hated the Turks who they regarded as enemies. Many villagers were so poor they did not even have an aspirin and only home-made remedies to cure their ailments. Most wore shoes made from untanned animal skins.

The ss *Aragon* was a former luxury passenger liner, rumoured to have been chartered by the British Admiralty at vast cost to act as a floating headquarters for the British Communication's staff. The officers and crew on board had large and delicious meals. The *Aragon* was viewed with resentment by some of the nurses and doctors struggling with the lack of food and the primitive conditions on Lemnos. The officers aboard, feeling sorry for the hungry nursing sisters, sometimes arrived at their campsite with gifts of a piece of steak, an orange or a chocolate bar which were regarded as luxuries by the hungry nurses. They worked long hours, hours that today's nursing union would never permit. They were out in weather which varied from the autumn heat to cold and wet and winter snow. The warm autumn weather ended in October, replaced by storms and rain. But at least they had tents and a few wooden huts to shelter them.

However Anne and the other nurses spent much of their spare time keeping their tents pegged down when the November winds began to blow. As the temperature dropped dramatically at night the nursing sisters were issued with gum-boots (Wellingtons), men's riding-breeches and woolly balaclavas. Those who could afford them bought rough sheepskin coats from the Greek villagers or used the Army greatcoats of dead soldiers. It was goodbye to nursing bonnets and they wrapped their heads in woolly scarves to keep warm.

The Canadian, Australian and French units occupied the western side of Mudros while the British units occupied the eastern side of the harbour. All of them were at the mercy of the elements and many tents were blown away in howling gales. Photographs show the unfortunate nurses struggling to re-erect their tents. Anne described how

The weather is terrible, bitterly cold, with a high wind and rain. We are nearly frozen, even in our balaclavas, mufflers, mittens, cardigans, raincoats and Wellingtons. It's a mercy we have ample warm clothing else we should perish. Last night *five* tents blew down, one ward tent and four Sisters' tents. I asked one of the nurses who was late coming on duty if she had overslept.

She was indignant and replied 'No. If *your* tent had blown down and half your clothes blown into the sea *you'd* be late too!'

The Canadian nurses are installed in huts with paraffin heaters and the 2nd Stationary [Unit] are very comfy. We, the poor old 3rd Battalion that set out from Australia so splendidly equipped, full of patriotism and high ideals, have had a lot of difficulties and shortages to contend with...

The hospital of 3 AGH is situated on a long elevated piece of land that projects into the harbour. On one side two rows of little bell-tents extend along the bank to the water's edge — the Sisters' Quarters. The view on either side is beautiful. There are scattered picturesque Greek villages; but the harbour is the chief attraction. Straight before me now, without looking to the left or right, I can count 100 ships of different kinds. One is reminded of Sydney, but in place of harbour ferries and picnic boats, there are warships.

Just opposite, across the bay, are the Rest Camps of Sarpi for our boys coming from the Peninsula. The sisters say they have never seen sunrises and sunsets to equal those over the harbour and the long grey granite hills in the distance.

Extending landwards from ours is the 2nd Australian Stationary Hospital then come the 1st and 3rd Canadian Hospitals, and, further on, the Convalescent Camps. There are English-run hospitals at Mudros and East Mudros.

Lemnos was so overcrowded with patients that eventually hospital ships had to bypass the island and go direct to Alexandria. As the wards overflowed at Alexandria and Cairo, it became necessary to send crowded hospital ships as far as the old and crumbling British hospital on the island of Malta.[6]

In spite of the devotion of the nursing sisters many wounded men died needlessly, having been left on the beaches of Gallipoli for days before a hospital ship arrived so that their wounds became infected. At 3 AGH most of the patients were Anzacs although some British and French troops were admitted for nursing.

Anne's South Australian friends kept their side of the bargain and continued to send out parcels containing sheets and bandages as she confided these were *still* in short supply. Anne thanked her friends in a letter asking for more bandages. She explained how she and her nursing colleagues had been forced to cut their cotton petticoats into strips as the supply of bandages had run out.

In a letter dated 31 October 1915, Anne reveals a lighter side to Army life.

> The camps across the bay often invite the nursing Sisters to their entertainments, and we, of course, just love going there…
>
> October 18 was the anniversary of the day those Australian troops left Sydney. Our boys celebrated it by giving a concert for the nurses at Sarpi Camp.

Anne described how, off duty, she and four other nursing sisters were collected by three officers who sailed them across the harbour. With much difficulty the small sailing dinghies made headway against strong winds and they arrived late.

> … the concert was half finished when we arrived. Reserved seats were held inside but we couldn't wedge our way through the crowd, so instead were taken to the O.C.'s tent and entertained there. Captain L. Lloyd was allotted to me and I enjoyed his conversation immensely. He is only twenty-four years of age and has won the Military Cross. Time passed quickly and it must have been nearing midnight when we had a delicious cup of cocoa and left. Arriving at the rocky jetty we found the pier master drunk, so a boat was pinched to take us across, but we couldn't get it to start. At last our coo-ees brought a motor boat to our rescue.

The party waded ashore by moonlight, Anne and the other nurses carried by the young officers amid stifled laughter. Great care was taken not to let the long, grey skirts of their uniforms get wet while keeping up decorum by not revealing their black-stockinged legs. After having enjoyed themselves, the nurses returned home in the early-morning hours.

The Army's strict rules as to how nurses were to behave off duty were rigidly enforced on Lemnos. Lipstick and rouge were regarded as provocative and were forbidden, as was dancing in public with an officer. Nurses could only 'walk out' with officers and were strictly forbidden to fraternise with 'other ranks' even if they were brothers or cousins. Male visitors (officers only) were restricted to the nurses' sitting room and the door had to be left open at all times.

In public, when off duty, the nurses were obliged to wear their high-necked ankle-length uniforms even when having picnics on the beach.

There were few diversions and the long hours, poor diet, poor sanitation and harsh conditions took their toll on overworked nursing sisters. Anne in despair at sickness among her nursing colleagues dared to brave the wrath of the censor and told the truth that some nurses were so ill with dysentery they had faced death.

> ... a large number of our Sisters have fallen ill with dysentery. We nearly lost one, but she has recovered now. It's terrible this amoebic dysentery and has been the death of a Canadian Matron (Margery Jaggers) and one of the Canadian nursing sisters. They were buried with full military honours about a month ago.
>
> Dear old Colonel Stawell was very ill all the time he was here and has now been sent to England. Several Sisters have gone too, but only for the change of the trip. Many of our doctors have been drafted to other spheres, and the outlook generally seems anything but bright.

Even Anne's spirits suffered after working so hard without a break. She described one happy evening when she and two others were invited to the officers' mess for a decent meal, a rare event on Lemnos.

> As we were on our way up to dinner we overheard an officer exclaim that he had orders to claim three Sisters, and we almost immediately found ourselves in the Mess Tent of the Headquarter Staff of the Brigade, where we had a very nice time with the O.C. and two Captains. The table was set for six, with bright polished cutlery (quite a luxury). The Australian flag waved over us and then came a dinner... of soup, steak and kidney pie, green peas, potatoes, marrow and onions, asparagus and butter sauce, custard and jellies, followed by grapes, apples, walnuts and chocolates. Fancy that on Lemnos!

She and the others felt so sorry for the soldiers who had to return to the carnage on Gallipoli although in the strictly censored press in Australia it was implied wounded soldiers could not wait to get back to the fighting on the peninsula. Anne told a very different story and may have written at length but this was removed by the military censors.

> October 26th, 1915.
>
> This morning we heard the band playing. It was the 1st Brigade on its way back to Anzac Cove after a rest. They came down the main street of our field hospital. We sisters gather up all the cigarettes and chocolates and all the tins of food we can and throw them to the smiling faces as they march by. They are brave and apparently cheerful, though we all know how in their inner heart they dislike going back to all they remember there. It makes us feel terribly sad.

The nursing sisters watched with heavy hearts as the young Anzacs they had nursed back to health returned to the dangers of the Gallipoli Peninsula. Anne and her colleagues, in spite of reports in the Australian and New Zealand press that victory was imminent, realised that these boasts were nothing but propaganda. Gallipoli was a military disaster. It was almost impossible for the

Anzacs to reach the Turks, safely ensconced on high ground above the narrow beaches held by the Anzacs.

October 29th.

The reinforcements for the 4th have been quarantined on account of mumps and measles. I wonder why this island is so unhealthy, yet I don't suppose it is the island so much as the flies and the want of suitable food. It is truly heart-breaking when we have serious cases to fight for.

Anne Donnell could not celebrate her birthday on 31 October as she was rushed off her feet nursing 'her boys'. But the following day she received an unexpected present.

November 1st, 1915.

Dear Friends,

Yesterday proved a very happy day. At noon the mail was sorted and I had such a number of nice letters, the very nicest birthday present I could have had. In the afternoon Sister Rush brought us some lovely cake. It is the first and only cake I have tasted here (it came from the Navy men in the Harbour; they are awfully good to us). Then I had a message from Colonel Fiaschi to say he would like to see me. He really wanted to hear all about Mrs. Fiaschi and little Elisa. The snaps I had taken have been enlarged and framed, and they look well. He looks very poorly, but will not give in... I fear a serious breakdown. I peeped into the colonel's tent to see if his bed was nice and comfortable, but found that he was roughing it like the soldiers, sleeping between sparse blankets, with no pillowslip and on a hard pillow. I tried to get him to stay in bed but...ill as he is, he still goes down the steep bank at 6.30 a.m. for his daily dip in the sea.

Anne, having delivered Colonel Fiaschi's baby, saw a softer side of the irascible old soldier than the other nurses, many of whom loathed him. She felt sorry for the elderly colonel when, finally, as she had predicted, he collapsed under the strain of running a military hospital under terrible conditions and had to be invalided back to England. However, some of her colleagues rejoiced as they saw Fiaschi as someone who had done little to help them and favoured his doctors at their expense. They preferred the colonel who would replace him.

> November 3rd.
>
> This morning on going into our mess tent for breakfast the following [announcement] meets my eye from the colonel. 'November 3rd, 1915. Compelled by sickness I reluctantly leave to-day for England. I bid you all temporary good-bye and wish to thank all of you for the noble way in which at all times you have fulfilled your duties and helped to make our Hospital the great success it is I am leaving, Lieut.-Colonel de Crespigny to take my place and feel you will extend to him the same loyal obedience as you did towards me.'
>
> I went across to bid Colonel Fiaschi farewell and found him sad and depressed. I thought what a shame, remembering the man he once was and the man he is today. Later I saw him carried away on a stretcher to the hospital ship *Mauretania* bound for England. [Fiaschi was suffering from dysentery and berri-berri.] We fear he will not return, and the general opinion is that he will not live to reach England; but perhaps he will, now that he is relieved of worry and anxiety, and the hope of being met in England by his wife and baby will help him. I hope so anyway.
>
> Our unit is breaking up fast... We sisters on the whole are standing it much better than officers. I was so pleased to be able to take a snap of Colonel Fiaschi, the day before he went away. He just managed with my help to crawl to the door of his tent.
>
> Truly the little camera you gave me is giving me more pleasure than I can say. When off duty my hobby is remembering my friends and photography [taking photos of soldiers]. There is nothing I can think of that would gladden a mother's heart more than a peep at her soldier boy so far away, and already have been able to give many of our boys a photo to send home for Christmas, and they were delighted.

Like many other nurses, Anne supplemented her own photographs by purchasing some of those taken by Private William Savage, who, in peacetime, had been a commercial photographer.

He was now taking the opportunity to sell his photos taken on Lemnos to nurses, doctors and soldiers as a way of earning extra money.

The reason most of the sisters remained reasonably healthy, unlike the medical officers, was attributed to the nurses' insistence on high standards of personal hygiene and the fact that, unlike some of the army doctors, they did not submerge their stress in drinking a great deal of alcohol.

In another letter, Anne, who was feeling ill and homesick, described how badly she missed family, friends and her dog.

November 10th, 1915.

> To-day in the lines I passed a dear little dog, stopped and played with him, then it suddenly dawned on me what a changed life we are living, and are indeed even growing accustomed to. No little children to love, no trees, no flowers, no pets, no shops, nothing dainty or nice, practically no fruit or vegetables, butter and eggs once in a month, twice at most. Please don't infer from this that I am complaining, far from it, and we have much to be thankful for, but how we wish that we could give our serious cases the very best of foods and delicacies. Of course it's only natural too that we should wish, for our own health's sake, to have some nourishing food. I see food in my dreams at night. I visit the most beautiful fruit gardens and pick the sweetest flowers. Don't smile, it's true... Just for once I wish I could be transferred home for a couple of days. For a week the prevailing sickness here has been troubling me. [Anne does not give details but it may have been a mild bout of dysentery].

Early in November, Lord Kitchener arrived to visit the soldiers on Gallipoli and the tented hospitals on Lemnos. His visit would have important consequences.

November 12th, 1915

> Yesterday morning, as things were going on in the same even tenor, one of the patients calmly called out 'Sister, come and see Lord Kitchener arriving'. Sure enough, there the general was just

landing down at the wharf about 500 yards away. There was the guard of honour and half a dozen motor cars in waiting. Presently the motors start our way and we see Lord Kitchener, General Monro and General Birdwood in the first car, the remaining cars containing other military notabilities.

Yes, up they came, slowly entering our hospital the back way, and stopping when they came to C2 Ward. Lord Kitchener entered the first marquee and spoke to each patient in bed there.

In the other two marquees Lord Kitchener spoke a few words in general, shook hands with the nursing sister, and turning to the multitude of boys in blue (the pyjamas issued to the patients) who had gathered outside said: 'Well, boys, I hope you'll soon be well.' The general saluted us, and was off. The visit took about five minutes. One had scarcely time to realise what the sudden commotion was. Indeed the Sister didn't recognise it was Lord Kitchener until he shook hands. I thought 'Oh, for a snapshot,' went to my tent for the camera, arriving back just in time to see him shaking hands, but I couldn't focus it quickly enough and was only able to get the back view of Kitchener as he sat down in the car.

When the cars halted our Colonel was busy in the Infections Ward and had his [surgical] gown on; so his batman was sent post haste for his 'Sam Browne' belt and he hastened to the scene. We learnt later that Lord K. had inspected the men in the camps across the bay. He gave us a personal message from the King, how the monarch was very proud of them. Lord K. claimed that our boys were among the bravest soldiers in the world.

After Lord Kitchener's visit the decision was made to withdraw before the onset of winter, a decision slow to be implemented. Just as the British journalist Ellis Ashmead Bartlett and other, had warned, when it finally snowed, soldiers froze to death at their posts.[7] It would take another six weeks before all troops had been evacuated from the peninsula.

Anne found that the wintry days on Lemnos had their own beauty.

November 22nd, 1915.

The gales are still here. I won't describe them for they don't improve Lemnos, or us. However, it's not all unpleasant, for when the weather is calm and fine it makes one feel good to be alive, but to-day is the most impossible day I have ever known. I am on duty as I write but all work is suspended *pro tem*, on account of wind and dust. The poor boys are buried under the dust storm. If you step outside you are blinded. We are just managing to give them nourishment but any minute we are expecting the marquees to be blown down. Surgeon General Babtie was to have inspected the Hospital to-day. I wish he would, and would realize the miserable conditions we are struggling against but expect it is too rough for him to land... I don't think Florence Nightingale at Scutari had stranger experiences than us nurses — her followers on Lemnos.

Our boys are telling me what the Turks say about Australians when shells are flying [through the air]. They say: 'The Indian, he runs behind a bush, the Englishman, he lies flat down on the ground, but the Australian stands up, looks around and says, "Where the Hell has that one gone!" ' The name they have for our boys is 'The Great White Gurkhas' [Gurkha regiments being renowned for their bravery].

We see the most gorgeous sunrises and sunsets here, in the former the colouring is of the softest pink and amber toning,... and reflects down into the harbour below. What I love most are sunsets where the intense crimson flame throws its flakes over half the sky. One feels they cannot move away until the red disc has sunk beneath the horizon. These clear Eastern nights seem to hold a world of mystery...How I wish you could see us in long Tommy greatcoats with putties wound round our legs.

The last week of November found the nurses shivering through three chilly sleepless nights and even Anne's valiant spirit began to flag.

There were high winds, rain and sleet. It all seemed so pitifully hopeless... Our thoughts are with the boys on the Peninsula. The wards are dark both day and night and we are nearly frozen in spite of balaclavas, mittens, mufflers, cardigans, greatcoats and wellingtons.

A week later winter set in with Australian nurses in their unheated tents chilled to the bone. Even Anne, once so optimistic conditions on Lemnos would improve, gave way to despair. Two of her toes were badly frostbitten and she feared they might have to be amputated, though in fact this was not necessary.

What depressed her and her nursing colleagues was the needless waste of lives of young Anzacs, some frozen stiff in their trenches on Gallipoli, others arriving with feet so frostbitten they had to be amputated.

> December 6th, 1915. On night duty.
>
> I haven't written for some days. The truth is I have felt too downhearted and miserable, the foundation of it being the weather, still the weather, and through it we are indeed experiencing the grim realities of this awful war. The 26th, 27th, 28th, and 29th of November will never be forgotten. We all suffered terribly with the cold, and with all our warm clothing we couldn't get warm day or night. Personally, I shivered for three nights without sleep. I have chilblains and my two small toes are frostbitten. In the daytime most of us just hobble about. I heard one boy say as I was trying to get my gum-boots and myself along in the sticky mud 'She won't stick the winter through'. He exactly expressed my feelings. In that terrible weather, with wind travelling a hundred miles an hour and rain and sleet, all seems so pitifully hopeless. The wards inside are dark both day and. night, the boys cold, and I would defy anyone to call the outlook bright. How I envied those sisters able to rise above their own feelings and keep bright and happy. They are dears; and one has saved me from being downright sick. I will send you a snap I took of her while cooking some soup for her boys in the dixie.
>
> During those fearful days our thoughts were constantly with the boys on the Gallipoli peninsula, wondering how they were faring; but little did we realize their sufferings until the wind abated and they began to arrive with their poor feet and hands frostbitten. Thousands have been taken to Alexandria, hundreds,

the boys say, were drowned because their feet were so paralyzed that they could not crawl away to safety in time. They endured agonies. Sentries were found dead at their posts, frozen, and still clutching their rifles. And even among those who were able to keep their blood in circulation by moving about, many could only grin at the Turks because their fingers were too frozen to pull the trigger. And some we have in Hospital are losing both feet, some both hands. It's all too sad for words, hopelessly sad.

The summer heat had been almost unbearable, but the cold winter was equally grim. Blizzards expected in mid-January arrived early accompanied by one metre of snow. By November, the huts had only been partially completed. Frostbite and cases of 'trench foot' caused by living for weeks in damp boots and socks multiplied as men in the trenches were exposed to the elements.

Trench foot, which caused foot rot, needed specialised nursing. The gangrenous toes had to be amputated by the nurses due to shortage of staff. On Gallipoli, the Anzacs and the British soldiers scrounged for firewood to boil their billies and were too preoccupied trying to keep warm to shoot at the enemy. The unfortunate stretcher bearers suffered badly. Many of them, knee-deep in mud and icy water, fell sick wearing the same wet clothes for days on end. During four days of blizzard conditions, about 16,000 cases of frostbite were received on Lemnos, mostly from Suvla Bay. Army hospitals in Egypt and Lemnos were stretched to the limits.

Three days after her previous letter, Anne described a large number of wounded men were expected any moment but sounded more optimistic as the food had improved and for the first time the army had given them oranges to eat.

December 9th, 1915.

Last night we could hear distinctly the bombardment over on the Peninsula, and on getting up today we find preparations under way to take in a thousand wounded, whom we are expecting to-morrow. I got up early to go to the village of Portiana — such dirty, primitive places these Greek villages are, but I think I have discovered someone who will do laundry which is one of our greatest difficulties here. We are allowed a gallon of water a head per day, and it doesn't go far when you do your own washing.

Huts are springing up fast and improvements going on in all directions as at present there is a tremendous Army population on this island. Perhaps I shouldn't say so [the censor again] but even railways are in course of construction.

We are faring much better now as regards food. Several more canteens have opened, oranges are procurable, fresh too, and we have butter rather than margarine and occasionally some fresh meat. There have been such drastic results from the lack of proper nourishment that we appreciate getting these things... even though they are an exorbitant price.

Rumours of the evacuation of the Gallipoli peninsula had reached Lemnos as the military authorities had finally acknowledged the extent of the disaster on Gallipoli and on Lemnos.

December 17th.

Such a spirit of unrest everywhere; the troops are arriving here as fast and as crowded as the ships can bring them from Anzac and Suvla Bay. They say the evacuation will be completed by Sunday night... The Hospital is being kept as empty as possible to be prepared for any emergency [thousands of casualties were feared but in fact none were received on Lemnos].

We night Sisters are beautifully comfortable now in tents. It is such a treat after the crowded huts where my dressing and sponging space was 36 x 18 inches. My old cabin mate of the *Mooltan* is one of those sharing our [tent]. On going to bed this a.m, I see her corner in a perfect litter. She is busy sorting, packing and repacking all her things. I exclaim 'Goodness gracious, what *are* you doing?' She replies emphatically, 'We are likely to be taken prisoners of war at any minute. I'm preparing to flit.' It's hard to take that view of things with so many soldiers and battleships around to protect you. However 'forewarned is forearmed'. To-morrow will see me sorting my treasures!

In a letter written just after Christmas, Anne described the evacuation of the Anzacs from Gallipoli and preparations made to celebrate Christmas and raise the morale of their patients.

> December 27th.
>
> Over a week and not a line to you, though the place has been full of interest. First, the safe arrival of the last retreating party from the evacuation on Monday morning, the 21st and wasn't it great? It was carried out with only three casualties. A few of us night Sisters were sitting on the bank watching them land opposite, at Sarpi Camp. One couldn't take in all that it meant. The stories that they have to tell are very interesting, how, when they were far out at sea, they could see the Turks bombarding and shelling the empty trenches. Then, in the morning, they found one trench empty, then another and another, and so on until they reached the beach. Then, for a grand finale, our battleships got to work on them.
>
> Now to prepare for Christmas and give the boys a good time while we have the opportunity. Christmas Eve came, the carol singers went around with a piano in a motor lorry. It was a calm, starry moonlight night, followed by a glorious sunrise and the most beautiful day we have had at Lemnos. Nature seemed to give us a good omen. Australia was here, the billies, the bags and tins were all waiting to be distributed, and I think every soldier on Lemnos got one. It was my joy to act as Santa Claus in F2 Ward, and to see them open their presents at 5 a.m. You couldn't possibly have made the day happier for them. I think the reflection of grateful thoughts must have been wafted down to our sunny land. Yes, for the time, war was forgotten, and we were perfectly happy. I heard one English soldier remark as he opened his parcels, 'Well, I say, God bless the people of Australia,' and the other Englishman seconded that. These two, later in the day, went away aboard the *Aquitania*, but before going one said to me, 'Sister Donnell, if I'm alive and you visit my home in twenty years' time, you'll see this tin on my mantelpiece.' [8]
>
> My table for Christmas tea was with eight privates from the camps. I don't think they will ever forget it. We Sisters

entertained everyone all, from generals to privates, under the same marquee, and opposite our party sat a party of officers. It was the real Christmas spirit, wasn't it? I know the boys enjoyed it. In the evening we went for a long walk, and how pretty the harbour looked with a few hundred ships and ten hospital ships all lit up.

With the successful evacuation of the Anzacs it was clear that the work of the nursing sisters on Lemnos was nearly over. Even though there had been no official notification everyone knew that they would soon be leaving the island.

Anne took the opportunity to explore the island that had been her home for three traumatic months. She visited Greek villages, going there by donkey as there was no other form of transport.

At times, some of the nurses' underclothes had disappeared when hung out to dry. Such things were impossible to replace on Lemnos so their loss had been an additional annoyance for the overworked and often hungry nursing staff. The thief was a wary bird and for some time evaded capture.

However, two orderlies made an excursion to one of the Greek villages and noticed a number of people paying admission to a small stone house. Being curious, they joined the queue, paid their admission fee and inside the house found a display of the missing undergarments pinned to the walls. Great interest was shown by in the trimmings of lace and fancywork on some of the undergarments. Observing the name of one nursing sister on some underclothes, the soldiers told the sisters about their discovery. The thief had done well very financially out of his exhibition, but, under Greek law, was jailed for a month. The recovered undergarments were piled outside the nursing sisters' quarters, so they could recover their own possessions.

Anne visited a Greek village and was horrified to learn of the primitive birthing techniques used by the midwives who wore baggy, bloodstained trousers which were seldom washed due to shortage of water. If the birth was delayed, the midwife tied a live octopus to the woman's stomach to bring on the birth quickly. After cutting the umbilical cord, they would place either crushed garlic or a poultice of fresh manure on the baby's navel. Anne talked to a priest who spoke a little English and suggested better ways of helping mothers give birth, as many died in childbirth.

Another aspect of island life which upset Anne was the cruelty shown to animals by the impoverished villagers, who maltreated their donkeys.

> I have a great admiration for donkeys since coming here. The poor, wee patient beasts are cruelly treated; they whip them and the poor little beasts stagger under very heavy loads.
>
> Five of us received permission and passes to go to Kastro, the capital of the island. It was a most enjoyable day. A Greek with a dilapidated carriage, the only one on the island drawn by mules, was here ready to take us at 9.30 a.m. for the fourteen miles drive to the other side of Lemnos.
>
> It was delightful to be driving again, and the scenery became more rugged, volcanic, and picturesque as we neared Kastro. We passed a few small villages, and Thermos, where the hot mineral springs are. I can imagine what a beautiful island this must be in the springtime and they say the wild flowers and poppies make it like a huge flower garden. Kastro is larger and cleaner than the other villages and nestles in a sheltered spot by the sea, with the forts on one side and the rugged mountains on the other. We had dinner at a small hotel; it consisted of a small fish, a little meat and potato, an orange, and a cup of tea, in all 3/9 each. We reached home in time for me to have an hour's sleep before going on duty. A break and change of scene refreshed one wonderfully.

Over the next few weeks the tented hospitals on the island of Lemnos were gradually closing down. Patients still very weak from dysentery were placed on hospital ships bound for the military hospitals in Alexandria and Cairo or for repatriation to Australia. The sisters' workload eased considerably — they packed up and at last had a little more free time.

> New Year's Day.
>
> We had a party last night to welcome the year in, and just on the stroke of midnight the volume of sound was immense. All the sirens, bells, and whistles from the ships in the harbour pealed. Rockets went up from the camps all around. We clasped hands and sang, 'Should Auld Acquaintance'. So was the New Year heralded in at Lemnos, and I'm sure it was the inward wish of all that the war would be over soon. Cape Helles has been evacuated but we still have 110,000 British, Canadian troops [and French troops] on the island. Our Australians have gone.

Early in the morning of 14 January 1916, 102 Australian nursing sisters assembled to board the hospital ship *Oxfordshire* bound for Alexandria. Their winter uniforms were patched and shabby. They wore cloaks, raincoats and any kind of hat available, since their orders stipulated hats must be worn. These courageous 'sisters in arms' who had endured deprivation with courage and dignity huddled together on the quay in a howling January gale so Private Savage could take photographs of them. On board the ship Anne wrote to her friends in Adelaide whose support and gifts of sheets, blankets and food parcels had been so magnificent.

> We have just seen the last of Lemnos. Of course we are glad but there are things we will miss, the unconventional freedom and the unique experiences, the glorious sunsets, the beautiful stars at night and the harbour surrounded by hills. But when we think of the cold wind and dust storms we are thankful we are not going to pass the winter there. In fact this would have been impossible. The night we left Lemnos, fortunately when we were safe aboard the ship, a hurricane arrived and by morning not one tent was left standing. It was fortunate that our patients were gone. Good bye Lemnos! I would not have liked to miss you, yet I have no desire to see you again. Over 7,400 patients were treated here in 7 months and the death rate was just over 2 percent. Not one of our Australian staff died although two Canadians did. Many of the Australian staff were seriously ill but we nursed them through and are proud of the fact none of them died.

Sister Donnell was posted back to Egypt in January 1916, where she nursed at the Deaconess Hospital, in the old Abbassia Barracks. Eventually, she was posted back to Britain and worked at the Kitchener Hospital in Brighton, living in a deserted school some way from the hospital.

In April 1917, Anne and her colleagues were posted to a military hospital at Abbeville near the killing fields on the Somme. This hospital admitted soldiers whose lungs had been affected by gas attacks. Many of the patients died a terrible death, choking for air. This army hospital had both tents and wooden huts for the staff but very little cutlery. Initially, Anne and her nursing colleagues improvised and drank their morning tea out of jam jars and ate meals with their fingers. However, war had brought the nurses more freedom. Serving in France, they were allowed to shorten their skirts, wear tin hats and gumboots rather than bonnets with long trailing ribbons and those stiffly starched collars — starching them had proved impossible.

Weather conditions in winter were so severe that the nurses unselfishly gave up their paraffin stoves to keep their patients warm. Living under damp conditions Anne suffered a severe attack of Spanish flu' during a world-wide epidemic. She was shipped out on a stretcher to a London nursing home especially for nursing staff. Although very ill, such was her devotion to her 'boys' that she felt guilty she was leaving them.

> ... In spite of my pleas to remain here Matron insists I must leave and be sent to the station in an ambulance. I am to go to a convalescent home in London's Southwell Gardens, the convalescent home for Army nurses.

After recovering from what could have been a fatal attack of Spanish flu, Anne's letters from April 1918 come from a large military hospital established in the grounds of *Harefield*, a Georgian mansion owned by an Australian family. A series of tin Nissen huts in the grounds and around an ornamental lake had been erected by the Australian Army and it was there that the patients and the nursing staff lived. Harefield Park Military Hospital specialised in patients who had lost one or more limbs.[9] Some patients were now quadriplegics in wheelchairs. Those who had lost both arms could not feed themselves and had to be assisted to eat and in other ways. Those who could not walk depended on the overworked nurses to push them around. The amputees often had psychological damage as well as physical damage and needed very careful nursing.

Finally, when the Armistice was declared, nurses and patients observed two minutes silence in memory of dead colleagues.

Anne Donnell and other nurses received an invitation from King George and Queen Mary to attend a function at Windsor Castle. As there were as yet no Australian medals Sister Donnell was awarded the British Campaign and Service Medal and the British Victory Medal.

In February 1919, Sister Anne Donnell, aged by what she had experienced during the war, arrived back in Adelaide on the ss *Marga*. She and the other nurses found the wharf crowded with friends waiting to greet them. Anne felt very emotional at the warmth of their reception and wrote,

> As I go up the gangway to them and set my foot on my own native land again, I inwardly breathe a word of thanksgiving.

The letters Sister Donnell had sent to her friends formed a valuable record of life on Lemnos. Anne was asked to publish a selection of them by Angus and Robertson of Sydney. Even though the war was over, military censorship still operated. Anne was obliged to submit her manuscript and her original letters to the Military Censor for South Australia, who insisted that any passages critical of the British War Office overlooked by the censor be deleted. In 1920, Angus and Robertson were allowed to publish *Letters of an Australian Army Sister*. Today, Anne's letters are regarded as an important eye-witness account of life in a military hospital lacking water, medical equipment or bandages and a record of the devotion of the Australian nurses who served there.

The photograph by a former professional photographer turned soldier, James Savage, shows Anne's unit arriving at Mudros Harbour on the island of Lemnos. James Savage later sold copies of his photographs to the nurses and Anne Donnell purchased many of them.

After having lived in crowded huts, the nurses were rehoused in 'bell tents' along the exposed shores of Mudros Harbour. Photographed by Private Savage.

As Lord Kitchener inspected the conditions at Anzac Cove, he realised that it was time to evacuate. Australian War Memorial, Canberra.

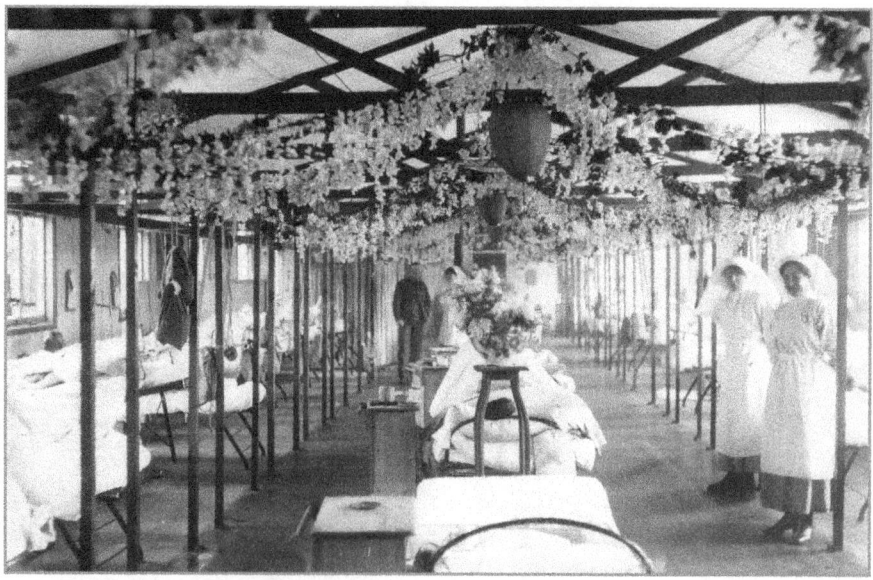

Celebrating Christmas and the imminent departure from Lemnos. Photograph by Private William Savage sold in multiple copies to the nurses.

CHAPTER 6

Lydia Ellen (Nell) Kerensky (née Tritton) (1899–1946)

THE BRISBANE WRITER WHO MARRIED A RUSSIAN LEADER IN EXILE

In February 1917, a charismatic barrister named Alexander Kerensky became Prime Minister of Russia's Provisional Socialist Government after the abdication of Tsar Nicholas II.[1] Kerensky hoped to give Russia a democratically-elected government, but was ousted by Lenin, who wanted him killed. Lenin was replaced by the even more murderous Stalin. Living in exile in Paris Kerensky ran a Russian newspaper. His supporters in France and America regarded him as Russia's rightful leader. They were convinced that Communism would eventually fail and Kerensky would return in triumph to Russia and establish a democratically elected parliament.

Thousands of kilometres away in Brisbane, Nell Tritton, in her final year of school at Somerville House, dreamed of living in Paris, working as a journalist and marrying a famous man. Her dreams would come true but the reality was not quite what she had imagined.

Frederick Tritton, Nell's father, was a successful businessman with a fascination for powerful cars. Born on the island of Jersey, Fred Tritton worked in England where he married Eliza Ellen Worrall. Fred Tritton, his wife and brother William migrated to Brisbane where Fred and Eliza bought a house in East Brisbane and had three children. Fred and his brother had little capital but plenty of drive and initiative.[2] The Tritton brothers opened a store in the Brisbane suburb of Woolloongabba and sold furniture which was designed and made in their own factory. Unfortunately, Brisbane's 1893 floods caused a great deal of damage to their store.

Six years later, on 19 September 1899, Frederick and Eliza Tritton's fourth child, Lydia Ellen (always known as Nell, a derivation of Ellen) was born. In the same year, the Tritton brothers opened a second store in the centre of Brisbane. Their George Street store, named 'Trittons', was much larger, sold furniture and furnishing accessories and had a small art gallery on the top floor. Trittons became a Brisbane landmark long before Myers and David Jones opened branches in the Queensland capital. Frederick Tritton worked hard, invested his profits in prime land and became seriously wealthy.

Nell and her siblings Charles, Lillian and Ida Jane were born in a small house in East Brisbane. Like many homes in the Federation era, the exterior and veranda rails were painted with lead-based paint, to which the children were exposed. But, at the time, doctors were ignorant of the dangers of lead poisoning.

By the time Nell was four years old, her family moved to a much larger property in exclusive Clayfield. Frederick Tritton had purchased the Federation style residence, named *Elderslie*, from Edgar Harris.[3] The property included several blocks of land at 151 Adelaide Street, Clayfield. Under the house was a latticed garden room or fernery and the extensive grounds contained a tennis court and a swimming pool. Resident staff at *Elderslie* included a chauffeur, a cook, a cook's assistant, a gardener as well as housemaids and cleaners.[4]

In addition to Nell and her three older siblings, Eliza Tritton bore more two boys, Roy and Cyril.[5]

The George Street store and the factory were so profitable that Fred Tritton was able to send all six children to Brisbane's best private schools. With domestic staff to care for her home, Mrs Tritton sat on the board of various charities and would eventually be awarded an OBE for her charity work.

By the time Nell was in her teens, the comings and goings of Mr and Mrs Frederick Tritton were reported in the social columns of the Brisbane *Courier* and *The Daily Mail* (forerunners of today's *Courier-Mail*). Family life at *Elderslie* revolved around croquet, tennis and swimming. They played bridge and had the occasional musical evening in which Eliza Tritton and her attractive dark-haired daughters participated. Eliza took the girls by a chauffeur-driven car to Sydney to buy ball gowns at the Model Dress department of David Jones.

Nell was not only attractive but very intelligent. For several years running she won the school prize for English composition and was commended by the headmistress, Miss Constance Harker, for her debating skills. She was also good at sport, winning cups for tennis and swimming.

In her final year at Somerville House (originally known as the Brisbane High School for Girls), Nell read the history of the small island of Jersey, where relatives of the Trittons were farmers and fishermen. She learned that during the French Revolution an aristocratic French girl had fled to the island and married one of her father's ancestors.[6] Nell was thrilled to think she had an aristocratic French forbear and claimed to her classmates she wanted to change her name to Nellé, believing this to be the French equivalent of Nell.

Several girls, jealous that Nell's father had made so much money, sneered at the idea of a French aristocrat marrying a fisherman. Nell was hurt by their mockery but claimed that she preferred her classmates laughed at her rather than ignoring her.

For her social debut at Brisbane's Government House, Nell Tritton wore a white ball gown and long white gloves. She waltzed and flirted with young men but did not take her admirers seriously. She had no wish to marry young and the idea of settling in Brisbane, at the time no more than a large country town, had no appeal for her. Nell craved a life of adventure and excitement.

While living at home, she enjoyed a round of dances and parties. She played tennis, went swimming and loved bushwalking. Having persuaded her father's chauffeur to teach her to drive, Nell won several car rallies, an unusual hobby for a girl of her era.

Nell, who had plenty of leisure time, wrote poems and described the beauty of flowering jacarandas in New Farm Park and the 'solemn grey Anglican cathedral of St John', where she had been confirmed. Some weekends she drove herself along the narrow winding road to the north coast and went climbing one of the Glasshouse Mountains. In her poem, *From Coochin*, Nell described reaching the summit of Coochin and the beauty of the coastline spread out below her.

In one poignant poem, written during the Great War, Nell revealed her anguish at seeing a young cousin in his khaki uniform and slouch hat marching down Queen Street, having volunteered to join the Anzacs. Her cousin fought at Gallipoli where so many of his comrades were killed and was later sent to fight in the trenches of northern France. For months his family did not know whether he was alive or dead but he returned safely when the war was over.

Mrs Tritton hoped that her three pretty daughters would find suitable husbands and settle in Brisbane. But Australian men bored Nell who was fascinated by everything French. She took French conversation lessons and subscribed to the newspaper *Le Figaro*.

A major influence for Nell's desire to live in Paris was reading the journal of Marie Bashkirtseff, a talented young Russian girl whose family came from St Petersburg. Marie had enjoyed success as a painter in Paris at the time when young women of good families did not exhibit their work. Marie Bashkirtseff died young of tuberculosis and did not have the opportunity to paint many canvases. Those she did paint were memorable and the celebrated artist Manet praised her work. Marie's beautifully written journal recorded her unrequited love for the famous French writer Guy de Maupassant and her fascinating life among artists and writers in late nineteenth century Paris.

Reading Marie's journal made Nell even more determined to go to Paris as soon as she gained access to her own money. She hoped to meet some Russian expatriates as she had become fascinated by Russian culture and literature. Nell knew that when she turned 25 she would receive an annual income from the family company, money invested in a trust fund set up in her name by her father, and would be free to live a less conventional life in Paris.[7]

In 1919, tragedy struck the Tritton family when Charles and Lillian died in a flu epidemic. Lillian died on 19 September 1919, aged 26. Charles, the eldest son, died on Christmas Eve 1919. His death certificate cited 'chronic nephritis' or liver damage as the secondary cause of death, influenza being the principal cause.[8]

As toddlers, Nell, Charles and Lillian had been exposed to lead-based paint on the woodwork of the Tritton's East Brisbane house, causing lead poisoning. Eventually, this resulted into chronic nephritis or kidney disease.[9]

Nell and the rest of her grief-stricken family had to attend two family funerals within the space of three months. To make matters worse Charles left behind a young wife in the last months of pregnancy and a toddler. From 1919 onwards, Christmas became a bleak period at *Elderslie*.

***

Late 1920, Brisbane received an official visit from HRH Prince Edward, the eldest son of King George V and Queen Mary. The bachelor prince was making an Australia-wide tour to thank Australians for their courage and sacrifice in World War One.

By now, Nell and her family were out of mourning and she was allowed to attend the fancy dress ball to welcome the Prince of Wales to Government House. Nell was dressed as Shakespeare's romantic heroine Juliet Capulet who dies for love of Romeo. She wore a long flowing gown of rose pink silk and her hairdresser had woven pearls and pink flowers into her long dark hair.

The Prince of Wales, attracted by Nell's beautiful heart-shaped face and curvaceous figure, asked her to dance. Nell was an excellent dancer and she and the prince made such a handsome couple on the dance floor that spectators applauded.

When the heir to the throne asked Nell for a second dance the gossips had a field day. However, this was an innocent flirtation. Unknown to his subjects, the handsome Prince of Wales had severe sexual difficulties after suffering a mumps orchitis. He was involved in a passionate affair with Freda, the wife of a senior British politician, the Right Hon. William Dudley Ward, Chief Whip of the Liberal Party and a Privy Councillor. The prince's clandestine love affair with a married woman with two children had to be kept secret from the public. And so the heir to the throne was packed off to New Zealand and Australia by his father in the hope he would abandon Freda and marry Princess Frederika, his German cousin.[10]

Nell, unaware of the Prince of Wales's passion for Mrs Freda Dudley Ward, enjoyed dancing with Prince Charming, the heart-throb of his era, but she never saw him again.

By now Brisbane's social round was starting to become boring and rally driving became Nell's hobby and her passion. At weekends she and other enthusiasts competed or drove to Wellington Point or stayed overnight at Redcliffe, where Nell's family had their beach house.[11]

Unlike most of her classmates Nell wanted a career. To her parents' dismay she insisted on applying for a traineeship on Brisbane's *Daily Mail,* a post usually reserved for young men. Nell's quick intelligence, her skills at dealing with people, and her warm personality meant she was awarded the coveted training post.[12]

Nell worked with a senior journalist (identified by the initials 'WFW') and he taught her interviewing techniques and how to strengthen her writing style.[13] Nell showed WFW her poems, asking if he thought they were good enough to be published. WFW, who was by now fond of his attractive young trainee, recommended to the editor of *The Daily Mail* that they publish one of the poems. He advised Nell to have the rest of them published privately and warned her that it was virtually impossible to make money from poetry. She should stick to writing articles or short stories if she wished to survive as a writer.

Eventually, a limited edition of *Poems by Nellé Tritton* bound in green leather with a photo of Nell as the frontispiece, was printed in Brisbane. It was self-published and paid for by Tritton family money.[14]

At the age of 24 Nell finally wore down her parents' opposition to the idea of her leaving home. She moved to a rented apartment in Sydney's Eastern suburbs, shared with another young woman. She did some freelance journalism for the *Sydney Guardian* and wrote for a small but prestigious arts magazine named *Triad*, which could only afford to pay its writers a pittance.[15] But Nell, who enjoyed writing about art and theatre, was happy to work for it.

She wrote articles and reviewed books at a time when women journalists earned a great deal less than their male counterparts. She defied the rigid conventions that insisted marriage was every girls ultimate aim and upper-class or middle-class girls should not leave home before they married.

In 1925, on the invested income from her trust fund, Nell booked her passage to London. Arriving there after a long voyage, she visited relatives and made contact with magazine editors, telling them she was a freelance correspondent for the *Sydney Guardian*. She asked the editors if they wanted articles about Paris, but received little interest in retaining her services, as most magazines and papers already had Paris correspondents.

Undeterred, Nell went to Paris where she, like her heroine Marie Bakshkirtseff, lived in Montparnasse, the *quartier* of artists and writers who had by now forsaken Montmartre for the Left Bank which was close to the university and the Luxembourg Gardens. Nell rented a small apartment near the rue de Vaugirard. She took a course of private lessons to perfect her command of spoken and written French. She supplemented the monthly income from her trust fund by freelancing for several American magazines, having learned that editors of these magazines paid more than their Australian or British counterparts.

Nell's articles were published under a variety of pen names, one of which was 'An American Girl in Paris', designed to please American editors. Like most foreign writers in Paris, Nell had favourite cafés. She sat for hours over a *café au lait* to read the wide selection of French newspapers provided by the *Café de Flore* and *La Rotonde*. She shopped for food in narrow cobbled streets in *charcuteries*, small grocery shops and bakeries where *baguettes* were freshly baked twice a day.

The *émigrés* who had fled from the Russian Revolution and civil war added a cosmopolitan flavour to the Left Bank. In her local *boulangerie* Nell made friends with Nina Berberova, a talented young writer from a privileged background in St Petersburgh, now living a hand-to-mouth existence in exile. Nina and her ailing, neurotic husband, the poet Vladimir Khodasevich, could only afford a sparsely furnished room near the Boulevard Raspail. Nina supplemented the money she earned from writing short stories, by stringing beads in a factory and by embroidering Russian traditional patterns on linen. She told Nell she was working on a biography of Tchaikovsky and a novel about expatriate Russians in Paris.

Nell was drawn to this talented young woman with her dark soulful eyes and long black hair. Aware that Nina was living a hand-to-mouth existence, Nell bought her meals and coffee at *La Rotonde*. Nell felt she had found a soul mate. They spoke in French, the second language of most educated Russians. They discussed writing and talked about writers from Proust to Claudel, Kafka and Virginia Woolf, which Nina had read in a French translation.

Nina's coming-of-age party in St Petersburg had coincided with the start of Alexander Kerensky's revolution. When Lenin ousted Kerensky in the October revolution, Nina and her poet escaped from the ensuing civil war to Paris where they met Kerensky.

Exiled White Russians (anti-Bolsheviks, as opposed to Red Russians as the Bolsheviks were termed) detested Kerensky as much as Lenin, because they believed Kerensky's February socialist revolution had destroyed their leisured way of life. Nina claimed Kerensky's tragedy was that he had left the law and academia to become a politician and taken control of the army with no military experience. He deserved praise for ridding Russia of the last vestiges of serfdom and halting Tsar Nicholas's persecution of Russia's Jews. He had tried to save the life of the Russian royal family by offering them a safe conduct to the border.

Nina was grateful to Kerensky, who had published her first short stories in the Russian language newspaper he ran in Paris.

Stalin hated Kerensky because his paper *Dni (Days)* disclosed that, under Stalin's regime, Russian peasants were suffering from famine due to the inept distribution of corn from Russia's collective farms.[16] Kerensky's revelations infuriated Stalin who had ordered several attempts on his life, which had all been foiled.

Nina Berberova, a novelist and biographer, told Nell that liberal-thinking Western authors were deluded in regarding Communist Russia as a paradise for writers. Stalin had no use for writers or poets, unless they were mouthpieces for Communist propaganda. Writers who refused to co-operate were jailed, murdered or declared insane and incarcerated in mental hospitals.

Nina introduced Nell to the world of exiled White Russians, living in cheap rented rooms and trying to remain dignified in spite of their poverty. She told Nell about former White Russian generals driving taxis at night and writing their memoirs by day and ex-cavalry officers waiting at restaurant tables, surviving on the leftovers from the plates of diners in the restaurants. Nell, aware that Nina was too proud to accept money from her, frequently invited the young Russian writer to lunch. In return Nina took Nell to a birthday party given by White Russian *émigrés*, who were splurging for a special occasion. Vodka, smoked herrings and cucumbers in sour cream were served.

Nell met a tall handsome former White Russian officer named Nicolai Nadejine. He told her that his grandfather had been a professor who compiled a French-Russian dictionary. His father, General Nadejine, had lost everything in the revolution and the ensuing civil war, been transported to Siberia but managed to escape.[17] Nicolai earned a pittance in Paris, singing in cafés, but dreamed of becoming an opera singer.

Intrigued, Nell went to one of the cafés where Nicolai Nadejine was singing. At the end of his performance, he announced that his final song would be *The Song of the Volga Boatmen*, which was dedicated to 'La Belle Australienne'. Amid applause he sat at Nell's table and made every effort to charm her. Unknown to Nell, Nicolai had made enquiries about her and learned that she had wealthy parents and a private income. Clearly Nell would make a very suitable wife for a penniless exile.

As Nicolai spoke very little English, they conversed in French. He invited Nell to accompany him and a group of friends to dance and drink wine in a riverside café at Bougival. Surrounded by a group of exuberant Russians, Nell enjoyed herself. Nicolai proved to be an excellent dance partner.[18]

Nicolai went out of his way to please Nell as their romance progressed. Although he rarely opened a book, they wandered along the quays in search of second-hand books for Nell to buy. They also visited Shakespeare and Company, the bookshop-cum-lending library at 12 rue de l'Odéon.

On Saturday evenings, Nicolai took Nell dancing at the Bal Bullier, near the Luxembourg Gardens. As drinks were very cheap the dance hall was a favourite place of artists and their models. The evening usually ended in a noisy party at someone's studio. Afterwards, Nell and Nicolai would walk to her apartment through empty streets where farm carts took cabbages and carrots to the early-morning market.

Warm-hearted Nell, who had never known poverty, listened to Nicolai's stories about the tragic death of his mother in Siberia and the loss of their ancestral home. Having flirted and broken hearts for many years, Nell found herself genuinely in love. She was fascinated by Nicolai's volatile Russian nature and his romantic gestures, convinced that she had found the love of her life. With her help Nicolai would become a famous opera singer and she would write his memoirs. But Nell's devotion made her blind to her lover's insecurities and his need for money.

Keen to learn Russian, Nell subscribed to Kerensky's Russian newspaper. On one occasion they saw Kerensky, Russia's Prime

Minister in exile, surrounded by supporters eating at *La Rotonde*. As Nell was accompanied by White Russian friends, who detested Kerensky and blamed him for their losses, she did not approach him, but observed him with interest.

By now Nicolai had moved into Nell's apartment and become very possessive of her. He soon complained that her living quarters were too small for his piano, which he insisted was essential for practicing if he was to become an opera singer.

In order to please her lover, Nell rented a larger and more expensive apartment in the 13th *arrondissement* at 15 rue de la Santé and paid for singing lessons for Nicolai.

Nell organised musical soirées, wearing elegant *couture* dresses (see portrait frontispiece), and invited celebrated Russians like Olga Picasso (daughter of another exiled White Russian general) to hear Nicolai sing.[19] In spite of Nell's efforts to introduce him to influential people who might advance his career, Nicolai failed to secure a contract to appear at the Paris opera house. She was determined to support Nicolai in spite of his weakness for vodka and outbursts of rage and violence. These were followed by Nicolai sobbing bitterly, kissing her hands and feet, begging her to forgive him and assuring her of his love.

Meanwhile, in her letters home Nell did not mention the fact she was living with a penniless Russian café singer, aware how upset her parents would be.

As a Queenslander, Nell hated cold winters and missed the sun, so she rented a holiday villa for her and Nicolai on the island of Capri. Like most Russian exiles, Nicolai had been a stateless person. In 1922, over a million Russians had fled from the USSR causing huge problems in France and other countries. Dr Fridtjof Nansen, as Commissioner for Refugees, persuaded the League of Nations, to provide these *émigré* Russians and Armenians with identity cards known as Nansen passports. As Nicolai had obtained a Nansen passport he was able to accompany Nell to Capri.

Installed in a villa overlooking the sea, Nell took Italian conversation lessons and enjoyed mingling with the many artists, writers and musicians who were spending the winter in this beautiful spot. Amongst them was the wealthy and famous Scottish author, Sir Compton Mackenzie and his attractive actress wife, Faith. Mrs Mackenzie flirted with Nicolai, who responded to her advances, which annoyed Nell.

Finally, when they left Capri, Nell took Nicolai to Rome. But in spite of her efforts, her lover failed to obtain a place in an Italian opera company.[20]

After their return to Paris, Nell continued doing her best to help Nicolai. She gave her impoverished lover English lessons, hoping a knowledge of English would help him obtain an audition at Covent Garden.

Nell feared that, if they moved to London, her mother's relatives would discover the nature of her relationship with Nicolai. To forestall this, she wrote to her parents, informing them she was engaged to the son of General Nadejine and planned to marry as soon as they arrived in London. She omitted to mention that General Nadejine earned his living driving a taxi and that her impecunious fiancé had no job and lived off her money.

Eliza Tritton, believing that her daughter was marrying an established opera singer, planned a big wedding so her British relatives could attend. Nell's sister Ida Jane, by this time married, was delegated to substitute for her parents and go to London with her husband and act as hostess and matron-of-honour. Nell's father paid for Nell to have an extended honeymoon in a luxury suite on a passenger liner, bringing the couple to Australia.

As staunch members of the Anglican Church, Nell's parents were unhappy that her wedding would take place in a Russian Orthodox church. Nell wanted to please her husband and found the music of the Orthodox liturgy hauntingly beautiful. However, she did not intend to upset her Anglican parents by converting to the Russian Orthodox faith.

Nell's wedding took place in London on 11 December 1928, with a ceremony in the Russian Orthodox church in Buckingham Palace Road, followed by a civil ceremony in Kensington Registry Office and a reception in a Mayfair hotel.[21] In traditional Russian fashion, at one stage during the ceremony, the bride and groom wore small crowns on their heads. A photo taken when Nell and Nicolai emerged from Kensington Registry Office (page 238) shows Nell wearing a white bridal veil. *The Brisbane Courier* ran a story headed 'London Society Wedding — Miss Nell Tritton the Bride'.

There were long delays in getting to Nell's homeland, due to Nicolai's lack of a French or Russian passport. The Australian authorities refused to accept his travel documents, but eventually matters were sorted out.

Finally, Monsieur and Madame Nadejine arrived in Australia and spent several months with Nell's parents in Clayfield. The weather was magnificent. Nell borrowed one of her father's cars and drove her husband up the coast to the small settlements of Maroochydore and Caloundra to swim in the sea.

Miss Constance Harker and Miss Marjorie Jarrett, joint principals of the former Brisbane High School for Girls (now renamed Somerville House) gave a tea party for their star pupil to meet her classmates. Guests included Orma Howard Smith, the Gargett sisters, Isobel Walker and Dora Littledike as well as Nell's English teacher. On 6 May 1930, *The Brisbane Courier* described how Mrs Nell Nadejine at Somerville House had worn 'a stylish black dress with a white collar and cuffs with a red and black embroidered skirt'. *The Brisbane Courier* implied that Nadejine was a successful opera singer, information provided by Mrs Tritton, keen to present Nicolai in as good a light as possible.

However, Frederick Tritton was worried that Nadejine relied on his daughter's money and made plans to help his son-in-law by organising a Brisbane recital. Fred Tritton paid for the hire of a hall and sold tickets to family friends. Nicolai's recital would take place in His Majesty's Theatre, but tickets for an unknown singer proved hard to sell, so most of them had to be given away to friends and employees of the Tritton family.

The performance was well attended but with so many free tickets there was no profit for anyone. Nicolai sang *The Volga Boat Song* and other well-known arias. Unfortunately, he received no further professional engagements in Queensland. Nell's parents were worried, aware Nicolai had no work, but, by draining Nell's income, enjoyed the good things in life.

While in Brisbane, Nell took Russian lessons from Captain Maximoff, another exiled White Russian. Nell enjoyed looking at the captain's photographs of St Petersburg in the days of the Tsar and Tsarina. She met Captain Maximoff's daughter Nina, who was supporting her elderly father by teaching German and Russian. Captain Maximoff greatly admired Nell, but he was wary of Nicolai Nadejine. She gave the captain a signed copy of her book of poems.[22]

They returned to London where Nell rented an apartment and set about trying to find her husband work at Covent Garden or other venues. As this proved far more difficult than she had imagined, they continued to live on Nell's money.

※

More than three years elapsed before Monsieur and Madame Nadejine made a second Australian trip in another attempt to promote Nadejine's singing career.

On 23 August 1934, soon after they arrived in Sydney, Nell arranged interviews for herself and Nicolai with *The Sydney Morning Herald* and *The Canberra Times*, in which she praised her husband's wonderful baritone voice. Nell had hired a concert hall in Sydney for Nicolai's recital, but once again, ticket sales were poor. Nicolai Nadejine's performance disappointed critics and opera lovers. As a result of his failure, Nicolai turned sullen, drowned his sorrows in drink and refused to speak to anyone.

From Sydney the couple took a train to Melbourne, where Nell had rented an apartment at the top end of Collins Street, hoping that Nadejine would be more successful in music-loving Melbourne than in Sydney. If he received offers of further performances they would consider living in Melbourne permanently. Nell was interviewed by the *Argus* and gave readers details of the forthcoming recital. But in spite of all her efforts, Nadejine's Melbourne recital was poorly attended and no further engagements resulted.

After a brief visit to Nell's parents — who were worried by Nicolai's heavy drinking — Mr and Mrs Nadejine returned to London. Nell now angled for her fellow Australian, Nellie Melba, to help her husband. Melba was very busy but she put Nell in touch with someone on the board of Covent Garden. This titled English lady claimed to have considerable influence with the board. She promised faithfully to do everything in her power to see that Nadejine was given a role in one of Covent Garden's productions. The aristocratic lady, who was considerably older than Nicolai, asked Nell's permission to take her husband to musical soirées and introduce him to fellow committee members. Hoping this would secure Nicolai a part at Covent Garden, Nell agreed.

However, after Nicolai spent several days and nights away from home, Nell heard rumours that the aristocratic lady was besotted by her husband. In response to these rumours, Nell had the couple followed by a private detective, whose report confirmed Nell's suspicion that Nicolai and the lady were lovers.

Nicolai had been spending hours in a hotel room with his aristocratic supporter. Nell, incandescent with rage, consulted lawyers and started divorce proceedings. In her divorce petition, she stated that her husband had deceived her with a 'crazy elderly English woman who was rich and idle'.[23]

Divorce was scandalous and took a long time. Although there were no children of the marriage or any property to fight over, it cost Nell a great deal of money. Finally, in 1936, Nell managed to obtain her decree absolute and was free at last. Nell's divorce was handled discreetly and kept out of the papers to spare embarrassment to her family. Feeling that work would be the best solution, she wanted to find an interesting job to take her mind off her disastrous marriage and divorce.

※

While in London, Nell had become friendly with a wealthy White Russian by the name of Flora Solomon (née Benenson). Flora's Russian-Jewish father had owned tea plantations in Ceylon and she had inherited his fortune. She had a brilliant and original mind and enjoyed spending her fortune on humanist causes. Flora's husband, a leading British Zionist, was semi paralysed and in a wheelchair.

During the depression years of the 1930s, Flora Solomon provided financial assistance to many White Russian exiles and helped Spanish refugees escape from Franco's Fascist regime. She also donated funds to help Jews who had fled from Nazi Germany and Russia. Flora told Nell she was a friend of Alexander Kerensky and saw him when he came to London. They discussed political matters and projects to aid Russian refugees.

Nell would learn much later that Flora had a sexual relationship with Kerensky. Their affair had began in 1927, after Kerensky had made an emotional speech about Russia to a large audience. Flora had been so impressed she invited him back to her hotel suite for a chat over a glass of wine. As Kerensky did not speak English they conversed in Russian. The result was that he became homesick and emotional and they ended up in bed together.

In return for payment, a member of the hotel staff tipped off the press and told them that the celebrated Alexander Kerensky had spent the night in the suite of wealthy philanthropist Mrs Flora Solomon. The next morning, journalists were waiting in the hotel lobby to interview Kerensky, so he had to be smuggled out of Flora's suite and leave the hotel by the rear entrance.

Shortly afterwards, Flora's ailing husband died, leaving her all his money in addition to the fortune left by her Russian father. Flora and Kerensky continued seeing each other when he came to London. But Kerensky, a man with a high libido, also had several other mistresses.

Kerensky told Flora Solomon he was looking for a suitable person to translate the French edition of one of his books into English. This meant the book could be published in America, where he had many supporters who hoped Communism would fail and Kerensky would return to Russia as Prime Minister.

Aware that Nell was bilingual in French and English and spoke a little Russian, Flora thought she would be perfect to translate Kerensky's books and pamphlets. As Nell had a private income, she did not need a large salary, which was an important consideration. Kerensky's first newspaper, *Dni* or *Days*, although influential, had failed financially and its replacement, *New Russia*, needed all the money his supporters could raise to keep it going.

Nell, still emerging from the stress and pain of her divorce, was thrilled by the idea of working for Kerensky. Tired of London, she longed to return to Paris and enjoyed the idea of translating books from French into English. Flora decided to arrange a meeting between Alexander Kerensky and Nell Tritton, so the terms of employment could be discussed.

The next time Kerensky visited London, Flora introduced him to Nell, having told him that she was bilingual, spoke a little Russian and was happy to work for very little money. The interview was conducted in French. Kerensky was impressed by Nell's intelligence, her command of the French language and her knowledge of the press, which could be useful to him. He offered Nell a job but regretted he could not pay her very much. Living on the income from her trust fund Nell accepted Kerensky's offer and made plans to return to Paris.

A month or so after her meeting with Kerensky, Nell started her new job in Passy, an elegant tree-lined suburb which stretched from the Right Bank of the Seine as far as the Champs Elysées. Nell found a small apartment to rent near Kerensky's combined office and apartment. Passy had the advantage for her that it was close to French fashion houses where she enjoyed buying *haute couture* clothes.

Using her journalistic skills, Nell talked to Kerensky's Russian and Armenian friends, many of whom who worked for him in an unpaid capacity, convinced that, one day, he would return to Russia in triumph. Gradually Nell built up a picture of his background.

※

Alexander Kerensky was the son of a school principal and a wealthy mother. After studying history and law at the University of St Petersburg he had gained a reputation as a brilliant barrister with liberal ideas. He often defended socialists and those persecuted by the Tsarist regime, and did not charge for his services.

In 1912, Kerensky was elected to the Fourth Duma (the Tsarist very restricted version of a parliament) leading the SPF, a moderate socialist opposition party. The SPF abhorred the Tsar's secret police as well as the Tsarist persecution of Jews and wanted an elected parliament to replace the corrupt Tsarist regime.

However, Kerensky had no intention of murdering the Tsar and his family and hoped they would seek exile in England. He was shocked that Lenin had ordered their execution.

Olga Baranovska, Kerensky's serious-minded wife, was also a committed SPF party member. The couple had two small boys, Oleg and Gleg, but Olga refused to accompany her husband when he fled from Lenin and remained in Moscow with their sons.

Kerensky inspired great loyalty from his supporters and financial backers (mainly wealthy Russian Jews with money outside Russia) who treated him with deference. His followers were convinced that Communism under Stalin was bound to fail and Kerensky would be invited back to Russia to form a democratically elected government. Some of his older and more naïve supporters claimed that Kerensky would enter St Petersburg in triumph on a white horse, hailed by cheering crowds.

The failure of Kerensky's marriage was due to his love affair with Olga's younger and more beautiful cousin, Lilya Biriukova. Lilya, trapped in an arranged marriage to an elderly White Russian general, consoled herself by having a sexual fling with Kerensky.

But Kerensky became obsessed with the beautiful Lilya and begged Olga to divorce him so he could marry her cousin. Lilya, who was expecting Kerensky's child, left her elderly husband but Olga refused to divorce. Kerensky divided his time and attention between Olga and Lilya, a state of affairs that pleased neither of them. He installed Lilya in luxurious rooms next to his presidential suite in St Petersburg's Winter Palace, and left his wife and young sons in Moscow, which alienated those supporters who had been fond of Olga.

As Prime Minister and head of the Russian Army, Kerensky was dismayed to find that the Russian Treasury lacked money to pay for food or winter uniforms. Russian soldiers turned against Kerensky, having been made to fight under appalling conditions.[24] Lenin promised Russian soldiers he would make peace with Germany and redistribute land from wealthy White Russians to the peasants, a promise that won him wide support.

When the garrison of St Petersburg mutinied, Lenin's Bolsheviks seized power in what became known as the October 1917 revolution. When Lenin issued orders to kill Kerensky, he fled from St Petersburg to Berlin in the uniform of a Russian sailor, wearing a pair of aviator's goggles to disguise his face.

In revenge Lenin ordered several of Kerensky's supporters and friends to be shot. Exiled in Paris, Kerensky was joined by Lilya and their baby daughter, while Olga and her two sons chose to remain in Moscow under the Bolsheviks.

Lilya Biriukova and Kerensky lived together briefly in Paris before their relationship broke down and she left him. The love of Kerensky's life had been Lilya who had deserted him. She was working as a nurse and refused to have any more to do with him.

※

Nell found working for Kerensky in his office-cum-apartment on the rue de Vineuse interesting and enjoyed the hint of danger. The apartment had strict security due to constant danger from Stalin's paid killers. All the windows were protected by bars. Only those who knew the secret password, which was changed daily, could enter. Kerensky's friends and supporters took turns to act as his bodyguard. Since he continued to denounce Russian Communism and Stalin, Kerensky had many enemies. But the dangers of working for Kerensky did not worry Nell. At last she was having what she had always wanted — a life filled with excitement, purpose and danger.

Kerensky, who regarding himself as Prime Minister of Russia in exile — as did many of his supporters — was a brilliant orator but not easy to work for. He was prone to bark orders at his staff and did not seem to notice that his new translator was a attractive female.

Having been chased by Stalin's gunmen, Kerensky never drove himself. He always took one or other of his supporters with him in the car, looking out for potential assassins, while Kerensky crouched low in the rear seat and made himself almost invisible from the street or from another car.

Nell had always enjoyed driving fast cars. As a former rally driver she volunteered to become one of Kerensky's team of chauffeurs, and her offer was accepted. She had to drive Kerensky around Paris, while a bodyguard with a gun sat beside her.

Although Kerensky was considerably older than her, now in his mid-fifties, Nell found him attractive with his deep blue eyes, a muscular body and hair cut *en brosse* (French for crew cut), which made him look younger than his age. Whenever they were alone in the office Nell did her best to flirt with her employer. She was disappointed that he regarded her purely as a translator and part-time chauffeuse. This piqued Nell — she was used to men admiring her and this made her all the keener to be noticed by Kerensky.

Nell was determined to forget that she had ever loved Nicolai and had no idea where he was. In fact, having failed to secure a role at Covent Garden, he had returned to the island of Capri. Hearing that Sir Compton Mackenzie and his wife were living apart, Nicolai felt he might have a chance of marrying Faith Mackenzie, who would be very wealthy if she and her husband divorced.[25]

However, his plan failed. Faith Mackenzie rejected his advances and returned to her husband. When Nicolai's funds ran out he returned to Paris to live with his father and go back to singing in cafés. Realising how much Nell had done for him and missing the pleasant life her money had provided, he gained admittance to Kerensky's office by a ruse, claiming it was vital he obtained his ex-wife's signature on a legal document.

On seeing Nell, elegantly dressed seated behind her desk, Nicolai tried to kiss and embrace her and promised to stop drinking if she would take him back. But Nell had trusted Nicolai's promises for too long and repulsed his advances. As he sobbed and ranted she ordered Kerensky's bodyguards to eject him from the office.

The drama of this scene made Kerensky more aware of Nell and for the first time he saw her as a desirable woman. It was the catalyst that started their romance. When they became lovers, Nell stayed the night and then took up permanent residence in Kerensky's apartment and never left.

On learning of the new arrangement, Flora Solomon was furiously jealous. What she had failed to recognise was the fact that Nell, with her dark hair, magnolia complexion and curvaceous figure, was exactly the same physical type as Lilya Biriukova, Kerensky's great lost love. Flora told her son, Peter Solomon how much she regretted having introduced Nell and Kerensky to each other.[26]

Years later, Flora boasted to her son that Kerensky had proposed marriage during a boating holidays at Lake Annecy, but *she* had refused *him*. This was probably a desperate attempt by Flora to salvage her pride in front of her son. Flora's jealousy was responsible for spreading the myth that Nell Tritton was Kerensky's 'secretary', hoping to denigrate her role to that of a humble typist-cum-mistress and maintaining the fiction that she, Flora Solomon, was Alexander Kerensky's real love and his intellectual equal.

When Nell found out that Flora Solomon was one of Kerensy's mistresses she was dismayed. But it seemed he admired Flora more for her generosity to refugees and her intellect than for her physical attractions. Flora was matronly, had red hair and a plump figure. Kerensky favoured petite slim, dark-haired women.

Knowing the truth, Nell was jealous when Kerensky visited London. But he assured her that these visits were made to consult with Foreign Office staff on the Russian desk. He said that his visits to the London home of Flora Solomon were purely platonic, which, by that time, was the truth.

All the love and energy Nell had poured into those unhappy years with the alcoholic Nadejine were now invested in supporting Kerensky, the famous man she had dreamed of meeting and marrying. She translated one of his books on the Russian Revolution as well as his magazine articles and speeches.[27] By now head over heels in love — Nell never did things by halves — she continued to drive him around Paris often risking her own life to do this. She was aware that one of Kerensky's kidneys had been removed, so he was on a strict diet and never drank alcohol. Nell did her best to care for her lover and make his life as easy as possible.

Nell loved theatre, ballet and opera, but Kerensky refused to accompany her, claiming he was in mourning for Russia and had no time for such frivolities. So Nell often took Nina with her to the theatre or the opera. However, she and Kerensky used to listen to Russian classical music on gramophone records. He would on special occasions take her to a restaurant in Passy where the waiters received handsome tips for calling him 'Monsieur le President'.

Although Kerensky refused to share many things Nell enjoyed, she was convinced they were compatible. She claimed they both enjoyed the same kind of books and classical music, had friends in common and complemented each other. Kerensky introduced Nell to the world of politics and Russian history. Her years of experience as a journalist and her skills as an excellent translator of French into English were valuable to him.

Kerensky became more and more reliant on Nell who wrote his press releases in French and English and sent them to newspapers. The term 'media advisor and translator' describes Nell's work more accurately than Flora Solomon's scornful term of 'typist-secretary', which was pure jealousy on Flora's part. In reality, Nell's typing skills were scarcely better than those of Kerensky, but she was a trained journalist and an excellent translator.

Nell made light of the dangers of working for Kerensky, although she was aware that Stalin had an entire department organising the assassination of his enemies.[28]

Nell adored Kerensky and, in spite of his high-handed attitude, wanted to spend the rest of her life with the man she called 'my beloved unicorn'. This was a private joke between them, which implied that Kerensky resembled a mythical animal reputed to be rampantly male, horny and unique. Nell did everything possible to please him and even learned to cook her lover's favourite Russian dishes. Aware of his kidney problems she adhered to his diet with great care and made certain he drank a great deal of water.

After spending eighteen months as Kerensky's mistress, Nell realised that her parents were bound to learn the truth and be distressed and worried. She knew her alleged love match with the money-grubbing Nicolai had been a disaster, so it pleased her that Kerensky was not interested in her money. He lived from writing books and successful speaking tours in America and did not want to touch Nell's private income.

Nell wanted to be Kerensky's wife, not his mistress. It seemed to her that he was using the difficulty of obtaining a divorce from his wife as an excuse for not marrying her. Jealousy of the women who flirted with Kerensky played a part in Nell's decision to issue Kerensky with an ultimatum. She insisted he obtain a divorce from Olga — who was now living in south-west London with their adult sons — and set a wedding date. Otherwise, she would return 'home' to Brisbane and start a new life.

Faced with this ultimatum, Kerensky at last took Nell's wishes seriously. Aware how much he relied on her to run his office efficiently and deal with the press, he engaged the law firm of Bourgeois and Bourgeois and started divorce proceedings. But divorce was a slow and complex procedure in Catholic France, especially as there were two children from Kerensky's marriage to be considered.

Olga's lawyers argued that Kerensky's heirs should benefit from any future sale of his private papers and manuscripts. Due to increasing interest in the Russian Revolution, Kerensky's notes, manuscripts and his records of events were now worth a great deal of money to an university library, especially one in America.[29]

But Kerensky's lawyers claimed that his sons did not need financial support. They were adults — qualified engineers, earning a good income. Oleg, the eldest son, was designing bridges for the British firm of Dorman Long and would soon move to Australia and work on the Harbour Bridge. Gleb, Kerensky's second son, had translated two of his books before Nell was employed to do this and Gleb was now working as an engineer. The lawyers considered that the sale of Kerensky's manuscripts and papers should not be part of the divorce settlement.

Nell grew tired of the prolonged legal wrangling. She spent ten weeks with Kerensky in New York, where they stayed with Mr Kenneth Simpson, leader of the Democratic Party and his wife. Kenneth Simpson was working on a scheme to pay Kerensky a handsome annual fee as a government consultant on Russian affairs.

In America, with its Bible belt and strong religious affiliations, Nell was in a difficult position socially. She found it embarrassing when being entertained in private houses that their hosts were not sure whether to acknowledge their relationship or treat Nell as Kerensky's employee. The Simpsons had a different attitude and treated her as Kerensky's wife. However, many Americans were narrow minded and puritanical and their wives did not bother to disguise what they felt about the fact that Nell Tritton was Kerensky's mistress.

The time had come for Nell to make a stand — she no longer wanted to be Kerensky's mistress-fiancée and have the wives of American politicians treat her with disdain. Fortified by her private income Nell could do as she pleased, so returned home to Australia.

On 9 March 1939, she arrived in Sydney on the steamship *Manunda* and was interviewed by several journalists. No doubt, they suspected she was Kerensky's mistress but addressed her as 'Madame Tritton'.

Her interviewers acknowledged her as a fellow journalist, knowledgeable about world politics, and sought her views on recent events in Europe.[30] Nell discussed the Munich pact with

Hitler and the tension this was causing in government circles in America. She voiced Kerensky's fears that Hitler in his desire for *lebensraum* might invade his neighbours and the dangers this posed to peace in Europe. Nell implied she would be returning to Australia for good, praising the beauty of the country and its safety and did not mention she had promised Kerensky to join him in America as soon as he set a firm date for their wedding.

Nell took the train to Brisbane and enjoyed the opportunity to catch up with family and friends. She was wearing a ring given her by Kerensky but played down its significance, saying she had been given it as 'a token of their friendship'.

By 1939, the situation had become even more dangerous for Kerensky, because Stalin was stepping up his efforts to silence his political enemies. Both Alexander Kerensky and Lev Davidoff Trotsky had written books and pamphlets about the situation in Russia which revealed the truth about Stalin's *gulags* and murders of his former friends. Trotsky's eldest son Sergei had been caught by Russian Communists and tortured to extract an admission of his father's guilt and shot at Vorkuta camp. Trotsky's other children had been harassed and threatened by Stalin and died prematurely.[31] Meanwhile, Trotsky and his wife had left Paris for Mexico at the invitation of the Communist painter Diego Rivera. Diego had accepted a well-paid commission in New York and left his beautiful and talented wife, the artist Frida Kahlo, to look after their distinguished guest at *Casa Azul*, their Mexico City home.

In May 1939, Diego Rivera returned from painting murals in New York and learned that Trotsky had an affair with Frida while staying at the *Casa Azul*. Diego was angry, but he could scarcely complain as he himself was a serial philanderer.

Diego Rivera, who admired Trotsky for his political stance, decided it was best if Trotsky and his wife moved away from the security of the *Casa Azul* to a rented house at Coyoacan, on the outskirts of Mexico City. The Moscow headquarters of the GPU (the secret police) soon learned of Trotsky's move and made their plans accordingly.

Assassins, employed by Stalin, entered Trotsky's rented house at Coyoacan and fired bullets into his bed. Trotsky and his wife had heard the assassin coming and managed to escape by hiding under the bed. They were shaken but unharmed. Trotsky informed the Mexican press that his home had been invaded, but Stalin's spin doctors responded by accusing Trotsky of staging the attack himself to attract publicity.

Nell read about the attempt on Trotsky's life and was worried that Kerensky, still in America to publicise his latest book, faced increased danger of being assassinated.[32]

Early in July 1939, Nell received a telegram from Kerensky begging her to join him in America. His divorce was almost through so they could marry as soon as she arrived. Relieved and delighted by the news, Nell informed her family and packed her trunk with the clothes she felt suitable for a second wedding and a honeymoon. At the first opportunity she took the boat to New York.

On arrival in America, Nell was angry to find that, although the decree nisi had been granted, Kerensky's final decree absolute had still not come through. She felt she had been tricked and lured back under false pretences and knew how upset her parents would be. She hired a car and drove to another hotel and from there wrote to her lover,

> I am deeply wounded that you made me leave my country without reason when you know I refused to return [and] continue playing *'la comedie de la fiancée'*.

Kerensky rushed to see her and did his best to assure Nell that his decree absolute from Olga would soon be through. She replied with dignity that she had heard that particular story before. She refused to continue to play the role of mistress. She would return to Australia until Kerensky was able to set a firm date for their wedding. Then she went back to her own hotel.

A few days later, Nell was mollified to learn that the divorce papers were nearly ready. Kerensky had arranged a private venue for their wedding at the home of Harry Stein, a Justice of the Peace who lived in Pennsylvania. Mr Stein could conduct the wedding ceremony without any risk of the American press being there.

Kerensky's divorce was finalised on 29 July 1939 but it took several weeks for the divorce certificate to arrive. On 20th August 1939, Nell and Kerensky were driven across the state of New Jersey, accompanied by Russian-born David Soskice, a former aide to Kerensky who acted as their bodyguard and witness. They arrived at the small town of St Martin's Creek, Pennsylvania, where Harry Stein conducted the wedding ceremony at his home.

At the ceremony, Nell gave her age as 38 while Kerensky stated he was 58, but both looked younger. Nell was elegant in a black suit by a leading Paris couturier feeling it would be hypocritical to appear in a traditional white wedding dress. She wore her long lustrous dark hair high on her head in traditional Russian style. Their wedding was followed by a celebration lunch, after which the couple returned to New York for their honeymoon. The press had been tipped off by the perfidious Harry Stein, who hoped to see his name in print.

Nell and Kerensky were interviewed by *The New York Times* who headlined their marriage, news which was repeated in other papers. At the interview Kerensky warned the world of the dangers posed by Stalin and advised that the Hitler-Stalin pact, which had just been announced, was a 'betrayal of democracy'. Kerensky feared that the pact had been arranged so that Stalin and Hitler could invade Poland and carve up the country between them and would liquidate all Poles capable of resistance and Polish Jews. Subsequent events proved him right.

Not until September 1939, did the *Australian Women's Weekly* publish an account of Nell Tritton's marriage to Kerensky, headed 'AUSTRALIAN GIRL WEDS FAMOUS RUSSIAN EXILE'. Nell's mother was interviewed and did her best to cover up the fact that Nell and Kerensky had been living together for well over a year and claimed

> ... when Nell arrived in Brisbane to visit us last February she wore two magnificent rings given her by Kerensky. She had met

him in France some years ago. Having retained her interest in international politics she enjoyed long discussions with him. She told us that she liked him because he was a highly intelligent man of the world. We suspected that their mutual interest might develop into a romance.

Clearly, Mrs Tritton had realised that Nell and Kerensky were lovers but avoided mentioning this.

Shortly after the wedding, Kerensky occupied the same platform as the Nobel Prize-winning author Thomas Mann, both pleading with the American people to enter the war. Kerensky urged the Americans 'to join the Allied cause and fight not only for freedom but for the liberty of the entire democratic world'.

But, even in America, exiled Russians were not safe from Stalin. A former White Russian General, Walter Krivitsky, allegedly a double agent working for Stalin *and* exiled White Russians, was murdered in a Washington hotel on the orders of the Kremlin.

Trotsky was the next victim of Stalin. At the second attempt on his life he was murdered in his rented house in Mexico City by one of Stalin's agents. Trotsky's killer fooled the security guards by entering Trotsky's house with an ice-axe hidden under his coat. Claiming he had written a book on Stalin and wished to show the manuscript to Trotsky, the young assassin entered Trotsky's office and buried his ice-pick deep in Trotsky's skull. The victim was rushed to hospital but died several days later. It was a grim warning to Nell and Kerensky that he was next in line to be assassinated.

**

Early in 1940, Monsieur and Madame Kerensky returned to Paris by sea. At a party given by Kerensky's supporters to celebrate his marriage, Nell met up with her old friend Nina Berberova, who was no longer starving in a garret in Montparnasse but had become an acclaimed writer. Her lover, Khodasevich, had run off with another woman, leaving her free. Nina had married a more affluent Russian who owned a country house outside Paris, called Longchêne, surrounded by a beautiful garden fringed with woods.

Nina's memoirs recall t Nell was 'beautiful, calm and intelligent with shoulders and a bosom like Anna Karenina' and she enjoyed having Nell and Alexander Kerensky to stay. Nell loved visiting Nina at Longchêne, picking mushrooms in the woods with her hostess, cooking meals together when Nell chopped tomatoes and talked about her Australian childhood. She enjoyed the nights when all four of them sat on a terrace under the stars and talked.

When she asked Nina if she believed Kerensky would one day enter Moscow on a white horse, Nina replied, 'this will never happen', but Nell chose not to believe her. Holding on to Kerensky's dream of power and glory was what mattered.[33] Nell's pleasure in returning to Paris did not last long. Kerensky's fears there would be a second world war came true.

In July 1940, Germany invaded France, Belgium and Holland. The British government sent troops to halt the advancing German troops in the north of France. But the British were outnumbered and forced to flee and regroup on the beaches of Dunkirk. German planes flew low over the beaches and bombed and strafed British soldiers. Those who survived were rescued by a fleet of British fishing boats and yachts.

As German tanks and soldiers advanced on Paris, thousands of frightened Jewish families sold off their possessions cheaply, piled portable valuables into their cars and headed for Spain or to stay with relatives in southern France.

Nell knew she must act quickly to save her husband's Jewish employees. Using her own money she paid a large bribe to an official at the Spanish Consulate to give her blank visa forms stamped with the Consulate logo. She phoned their Russian Jewish employees and told them to come to the office. She had their birth dates and parentage filled in with the aid of a Spanish friend and the requisite identity photographs added. The completed forms were given to eight past and present employees and their wives and children s so they could escape by train to Hendaye and cross the Spanish border to safety in Spain before German soldiers arrived to arrest them, as had happened to Jews in other occupied countries but deliberately made no record of who had the forged visas. .

Nell and Kerensky were invited to spend the weekend with Nina Berberova and her husband on the outskirts of Paris. On the night of 11 June 1940, they heard on the radio that German soldiers were advancing and would soon be in Paris. Kerensky, who had denounced Hitler as a 'murderer of Jews and intellectuals', knew he was on the Nazi's death list. The news made Nell, normally so calm, burst into tears. She sobbed to Nina that her husband was certain to be jailed or shot like Dolfuss, the former Chancellor of Austria, who had been gunned down by Nazis in his office.

They decided not to return to their Passy apartment and head south immediately. At dawn on 12 June, they put the few clothes they had taken with them for the weekend in their car, said a fond goodbye to Nina Berberova and her husband who gave them some food for the journey. Nina would never see Nell again.

With Nell at the wheel they became part of a mass exodus of cars, bicycles and farm carts loaded with people and livestock, all of them desperate to escape the German army.[34] Their car inched forward at a snail's pace as all roads south were gridlocked with traffic.

On the second day of their journey, German planes flew overhead and started to bomb the cars and farm carts travelling south. Amid the screams of the wounded and the dying, Nell and her husband left their car and crouched in a ditch until the German planes had departed.

As they walked back to their car, feeling shattered by the events, Nell saw two small girls dragging the corpse of their father over the grass verge to a ditch and attempting to scrape earth over it with their bare hands. Nell took pity on the girls and helped them bury their father.[35]

She climbed back into the car as the long convoy still had not moved. The food Nina had given them was finished and Nell and Kerensky were hungry and desperately thirsty. The convoy moved off again but all the inns and restaurants along the road were deserted — their owners had fled by car and taken their supplies of food and mineral water with them. Clean drinking water was a problem as that part of France had a polluted water supply. Notices in public lavatories said 'Eau non potable' and warned of the dangers of drinking water from the tap as typhoid was endemic in the area. They spent several miserable days without food or water until Nell found a bar of chocolate and two bottles of mineral water in a deserted house.

The following day, foraging in another deserted farmhouse, Nell found a loaf of stale bread but no more bottled water. German planes reappeared each morning and strafed them with bullets. All along the grass verges lay corpses riddled with bullet holes or shrapnel. Finally, they were so thirsty they were reduced to drinking water from ditches, giving them stomach cramps and diarrhoea.[36] They spent a couple of days recovering in a deserted barn before joining the long convoy of cars and farm carts on the crowded road, inching forward at a snail's pace.

Each time German planes returned and bombed more cars before flying away. Nell regarded it a miracle they were still alive.

On one occasion when it seemed as though the German Army might catch up with them, a kindly Frenchman hid them in his cellar. The Frenchman had recognised Kerensky from a photograph and, as a keen admirer, offered to help the man he hailed as the real leader of the Russian people. Nell never revealed this Frenchman's name, fearing that the Germans would retaliate as he remained in German-occupied France.

The lack of water on that nightmare fortnight journey south had unfortunate effects on Nell's kidneys, already weakened by the fact that as a toddler she had been affected by the lead in the paintwork at their East Brisbane home — the same lead-based paint that had caused the kidney disease from which her older brother and sister had died.

Nell should have taken care of her own health and shared whatever water was available with her husband. But as always her concern was for Kerensky, knowing that as young man he had had an operation to remove one of his kidneys. Unselfishly, Nell made certain that her husband received the lion's share of any food and drinking water, unaware that by depriving herself her own kidneys would be affected.

Finally, when they managed to reach the Spanish border at Irun, Franco's *guardia civil* looked at Nell's British passport and waved her through.[37] But Kerensky, who was a prominent socialist and had denounced Fascism, figured on a list of Franco's enemies and was stopped by the border guards.

Nell got out of the car and spoke to the guards with Kerensky at her side. In spite of her anguished pleading that they were only passing through Spain en route to England, Kerensky was denied entry. As a result, Mr and Mrs Kerensky were escorted back to their car by *guardia civil*, armed with pistols.

Tired and hungry, Nell turned the car round and drove back along the same route, hoping that at the fishing port of St Jean de Luz or at the larger resort of Biarritz they would find a French fishing boat prepared to take them to England. By now their money was running as low as was their fuel. But none of the petrol stations they passed had gasoline.

Fortunately, Nell had taken a roadmap with her, so they were able to follow secondary roads, where they found a petrol station that still had fuel available. At night they slept in barns or under hedges or remained in the car, doing their best to sleep. They had worn the same clothes for eighteen days and were exhausted, hot and dirty by the time they reached the fishing port of St Jean de Luz.

It was up to Nell to arrange their escape, Kerensky being too weak to help. She entered a bar to try to find a captain of a fishing boat who would be prepared to take them to England. Nell managed to find the captain of a sardine boat and begged him to take her and her husband to safety.

The captain retorted that this was impossible, because the English Channel had been mined by the German Navy. 'I have refused two fortunes already, but have a wife and children and must stay alive to protect them,' he insisted.

Recounting the story later, Nell observed with dry humour, 'Unlike some English expatriates we had no fortune to offer, so he and his family were safe from harm.'

Their spirits lifted when they learned that the British government had sent a warship to St Jean de Luz to take British subjects including the famous Mrs Alice Keppel, mistress of the late Edwad VII and her husband back to England.

As they arrived at the quayside they saw a dense mass of people, laden with piles of luggage. The crowd surged towards to a counter where Customs officials were inspecting their belongings. More well-dressed people arrived by car to join the long queue of those desperate to escape. The ones on stretchers or in wheelchairs were turned away to the distress of their relatives. Some British people offered bribes to get to the head of the queue.[38]

Nell demanded to see the captain, claiming that her husband was an important Russian politician wanted for consultation with the British government. He had made passionate speeches against Hitler who had him on a death list. He *had* to reach Britain. The captain was moved by Nell's words as well as by her looks and he allowed them to board the ship. Without doubt, Nell's quick wits and dramatic skills saved Kerensky's life.

They had to leave their car behind. Nell tossed the keys to a startled peasant in a blue beret telling him the car was his. So in addition to his donkey cart the Frenchman found himself the owner of a motor car and called down blessings on his benefactors.

It was dusk by the time Nell and Kerensky boarded the ship. They were both exhausted, starving and thirsty and looked forward to a cabin and a bunk with clean sheets. However, a steward informed them that no cabins were available, not even for a Prime Minister of Russia in exile. The only free cabin had been commandeered by Alice Keppel, former mistress of Edward VII and her husband, the Hon. George Keppel.

Nell and Kerensky spent a cold night sitting on a hard metal deck eating a few stale cheese sandwiches and drinking clean water from tin mugs. They prayed they would not be blown up by a mine or torpedoed by a German submarine.

Soon after they arrived and were put up at a hotel in London, Kerensky went to see his sons, Oleg and Gleb, who were living in Putney, but he did not take Nell with him. The Kerenskys had no plans to stay in England and wanted to reach the United States as soon as possible. But all the passenger liners bound for America were fully booked and had long waiting lists.

Fortunately, as Kerensky had supplied confidential information about Stalin to the Foreign Office and the British Secret Service, he received preferential treatment. A Foreign Office official procured the former leader of the Russian people in exile and his wife a cabin on a liner bound for New York.

On 12 July 1940, Mr and Mrs Kerensky arrived in America to a triumphal welcome organised by *The New York Times*. Crowds of exiled Russians surrounded them and showered Nell with flowers. Friends and supporters helped the couple move into a small rented apartment at 1060 Park Avenue, a fashionable part of New York. Kerensky was consulted by American officials dealing with foreign affairs who hoped that Stalin might, if properly handled, change sides and fight against Hitler, as would soon happen.

Russian-Jewish friends, Simeon and Manya Strunsky, took them to their holiday cottage in the rural area of New Canaan, about 40 miles north-east of New York.[39] Nell liked this picturesque area so much that the following year they rented a summer cottage there.

By 1942, Kerensky's books and political pamphlets, translated into English by Nell, had made sufficient money to buy a charming old country house, recently renovated, on the border between New York State and Connecticut. Nell's artistic talents were given full rein and she created a beautiful home for them. One friend remembered how idyllic the Kerenskys' married life appeared in their attractive country house filled with books, antique furniture, Persian carpets and Russian ornaments.

Nell enjoyed playing the role of political hostess and she entertained many important visitors to elegant dinner and luncheon parties. In summer, tea was served to visitors on the lawn.

Due to the war, Nell's income from her investments was greatly reduced. To make money, Kerensky had to continue his America-wide lecture tours. Communist Russia had changed sides after Hitler attacked the Soviet Union, so Americans wanted to know about Russian history, the Russian revolution and Stalin. Living in an English-speaking country and aided by lessons from Nell, Kerensky's command of spoken English improved. When he was on a speaking tour in Texas, Nell received his first letter written entirely in English, which pleased her enormously. She replied in her vivid style,

> I loved your letter, like having a new beau. Simeon [Strunsky, a Russian friend] was very impressed. He said you'd probably come back with a western accent wearing a ten-gallon cowboy hat.[40]

However, most of the time they wrote to each other in French. In one affectionate letter to her husband Nell claimed, *'Avec toi, mon amour, j'ai bu de la fontaine de la vie'* (With you my love, I have drunk from the fountain of life). She felt that her second marriage to the famous man of whom she had dreamed had brought her happiness and made her feel truly alive.[41]

Kerensky returned from one of his many lecture tours in time to celebrate Easter 1944. Nell had gone to great pains to make it a real Russian Easter. Using stencils of traditional Russian designs, she drew and painted on eggs dyed in bright colours and baked a *paska*, the traditional rich spicy Easter bread. They enjoyed a memorable feast with Russian friends.

Nell always enjoyed swimming at the Roton Point Beach Club on Long Island, but noticed that she was not as strong a swimmer as before. She started to suffer from palpitations of the heart and felt weak and nauseated. She and her doctors failed to understand that her kidneys and heart had been damaged by the lack of water during the nightmare journey from Paris. She suffered from nightmares in which she saw dead bodies lying on the grass verges of the roads and German planes strafing them with bullets as they flew low over their car.

At first, Kerensky, thought his wife was being neurotic and had little sympathy for her. Only as Nell's health problems became worse did he finally become worried. As Nell's strength declined, they moved to a smaller house at Rowanton, which was closer to New York and far easier for her to manage with only a little domestic help. As the winter of 1944–45 was exceptionally harsh, Nell became increasingly miserable. She spent weeks alone at Rowanton while Kerensky was away lecturing, his main source of income. He still hoped to obtain a professorship which would give him financial security.

Nell, who longed for a warm climate and wanted to see her parents, made plans to return to Brisbane. Kerensky reluctantly agreed to accompany her. Shortly before their departure, Nell suffered a mild heart attack which delayed their travel plans.

Finally, in October 1945, Nell and her husband sailed to Australia on the ss *City of Durham*. The following month they arrived in Melbourne and stayed in a hotel on Collins Street.

Nell was interviewed by the Melbourne *Argus* and several other papers and mentioned that, many years ago, she had visited Melbourne with her first husband who had sung at Melbourne's Town Hall, but she kept quiet about her divorce.[42] She said she was happy to be back in Australia, but disclosed nothing about her deteriorating health, as she did not want to worry her parents.

Kerensky hoped that the University of Melbourne, intending to establish a Russian Department, would appoint him as head of department. Clearly, he was a suitable candidate with degrees in history and law from the University of St Petersburg and the author of many reference books on Russian history and politics. Nell persuaded him to apply for the position.

Nell's cousin, Corbett Tritton, who had worked as Private Secretary to Prime Minister Robert Menzies and for the ABC in London, supported Kerensky's application to become the first head of the new Russian department at Melbourne University. Corbett was delighted at the prospect of Nell returning to live in Australia.[43]

Having received tuition in spoken English from Nell, Kerensky believed his interview, conducted in English and Russian, had gone well. He felt that his curriculum was impressive and was convinced he would be appointed head of the new department. While awaiting the outcome of Kerensky's interview, they visited Sydney briefly and then flew to Brisbane.[44]

But by the time they arrived at *Elderslie*, Nell was exhausted. Her damaged kidneys caused her blood pressure to rise. Her weakened heart muscles meant she felt tired all the time. It was the end of her favourite walks at the Glasshouse Mountains or trips to Surfers Paradise, which she had always loved in the past. Nell spent much of the day resting on a day-bed, but was delighted to catch up with former school friends and relatives when they arrived at *Elderslie* to visit her.

With a dash of her old fire, she managed to give an interview to *The Courier-Mail* for their article headed 'Nightmare Ordeal in France'. She talked about their time in Paris and admitted she had been 'conscious of being shadowed by agents, because of my husband's well-known anti-Fascist and anti-Communist beliefs'.[45]

Nell and her husband were very disappointed when the University of Melbourne chose Nina Christesen to head their new Russian department. Nina (now the wife of Clem Christesen, editor of the literary journal *Meanjin*) was the daughter of Nell's former Russian teacher, Captain Maximoff.

Kerensky was incensed by the fact he had been rejected. He claimed Nina Maximoff had not attended a Russian university or written authoritative books on Russian history as he had done. And eventually wrote an article for a Swiss newspaper, pointing out that European intellectuals who hoped to work in Australia were not welcome. Nell, already low in spirits, was upset by the decision, convinced that for political reasons her husband had been denied a job for which he was well qualified. She believed that pro-Communist Australian writers and others with political motives were responsible for Kerensky's rejection.

Nell was gradually becoming weaker and Brisbane's finest medical specialists could do nothing to improve her condition. She rested on a sofa and went to bed early. Each night after dinner, Kerensky paced the veranda, doing what he called 'meditating', pondering his uncertain future. He was depressed that the doctors could do little for Nell and was haunted by the news of Trotsky's assassination. He feared that, even in Australia, Stalin's gunmen were after him. Each night he slept on the veranda outside Nell's room, wanting to be near her, aware she slept so badly he could not sleep beside her. He took the precaution of sleeping with a gun under his pillow.

Nell, near death herself, still worried about her husband. She invited her former Russian teacher, Captain Maximoff (whose daughter had gained the coveted professorship of Russian) to come to her family home and meet Kerensky. She confided that her husband was miserable and isolated and would welcome the chance to talk in Russian.

What Nell had overlooked was the fact that Captain Maximoff, as a White Russian, loathed Kerensky for overthrowing the Tsarist regime and did not wish to meet him. Neither was Kerensky sympathetic to the man whose daughter had gained the job he wanted. However, Maximoff realised that Nell was very ill indeed, so went to visit her at *Elderslie*. He sat beside her bed and shook hands with Kerensky, pretending to be his friend for Nell's sake and took a sad farewell of Nell.[46]

In February 1946, Nell suffered a massive stroke. Her speech became confused and she needed professional nursing day and night. In order to be close to her Kerensky continued sleeping on the veranda outside her room.

Kerensky realised that his wife was dying and that he had failed to appreciate the full extent of her love for him and felt guilty he had not been kinder to her when she first told him of her symptoms. All too late, he realised how much he loved her but had been unable to express it, mistakenly believing the great love of his life had been Lilya.

On 11 April 1946, Nell Kerensky died in her bedroom at *Elderslie*, the house she loved.[47] As her body was placed in her coffin, Kerensky was convinced she smiled at him — 'a sign from beyond' he called it. Although he had flirted with atheism as a radical student, he had returned to the Orthodox faith of his parents and wore a miniature icon on a chain round his neck.[48]

Kerensky insisted that, according to Russian custom, Nell's coffin was left open all night before her funeral. Following the precepts of the Russian Orthodox Church, he kept an all-night vigil beside his late wife. Nell's coffin lay on a bier surrounded by hundreds of red roses, which was a final attempt by Kerensky to show her family how much he had loved her.

The room where Nell lay was lit by long wax tapers in the Russian fashion. Kerensky, the grieving husband, remained awake all night beside Nell's body in its open coffin.

In accordance with her parents' wishes Nell's funeral took place in an Anglican church rather than Brisbane's Russian Orthodox one. Kerensky made no objection as he did not like the priest in charge of the Orthodox church or the priest's political views.

Nell was cremated and her ashes placed in the Dutton Park Cemetery at Annerley Road, in the same grave where her brother Charles and her sister Lillian were buried. On the marble block over their resting place Nell's name is inscribed as 'Lydia E. Kerensky'.[49] Eventually, Nell's parents were buried in the same grave and their names and dates of death are also inscribed in the block of marble over what became the Tritton family grave.

Kerensky, aware that Stalin had paid assassins to kill Trotsky, feared they would hunt him down in Brisbane.[50] Nell's cousin, Corbett Tritton, arranged for him to join his family at his beach house at Surfers Paradise.[51] Kerensky told Corbett of his fears he might be shot or stabbed, as had happened to Trotsky. One night, he was convinced that an assassin was prowling around the beach house. After he told Corbett of his suspicions, a search party was organised. Although they were unable to find an intruder, Kerensky was so rattled he insisted on returning to the Tritton home in Clayfield.

Passenger ships were crowded in wartime, so it took some months before Kerensky, still grieving over his wife's death, returned to America. He took up a professorship at the Hoover

Institute of Stamford University, gave lectures on Russian history and wrote more books. Still attractive to women, he enjoyed brief affairs with wives of university colleagues, but never forgot Nell and never remarried. In old age he went blind and was very unhappy, feeling the promise of his early years had been unfulfilled.

Alexander Kerensky died in 1970. His memorial service was celebrated on Madison Avenue, but it was considered unwise to bury him in New York. There were fears that Stalin's supporters would damage his grave or desecrate the corpse of the man they regarded as a traitor.

Kerensky's body was flown to Britain, but London's Russian Orthodox Church also disliked the idea of having a former revolutionary leader buried in their graveyard, believing that Tsar Nicholas II was a saint and Kerensky had played a significant role in his overthrow.[52] They ignored the fact that Kerensky had done his best to save the Tsar and his family from being murdered and had urged to send them into exile.

Priests blamed Kerensky and Lenin for the Russian revolution and the persecution of the Orthodox Church by Communists, even though Kerensky had embraced the Orthodox faith again in mid-life. There were fears that KGB agents would harass or damage the two Russian Orthodox churches in central London, so the church leaders rejected having Kerensky's body there for burial.

Kerensky was buried in a non-denominational churchyard in the London suburb of Putney Vale, where his sons and his first wife lived.[53]

It might have been more appropriate to have buried Kerensky beside Nell, his devoted second wife, at Brisbane's Dutton Park Cemetery who had saved him and others by her courage, resourcefulness and determination. . .

Baby Lydia Ellen (Nell) and her three older siblings.
Courtesy Mrs Lavinia Tritton

Frontispiece of Nellé Tritton's
volume of poems.
Courtesy Mrs Lavinia Tritton

Alexander Kerensky in his mid-
thirties when he led the
1917 Russian Revolution.

In February 1939 Nell Tritton returned to *Elderslie*, her parents' home in Clayfield. Jake de Vries photographed the house in its present location at Pullenvale.

Glamorous Nell in a Parisian dress.
Courtesy Mrs Lavinia Tritton.

A wedding photograph of Nell Tritton
and Nicolai Nadejine.
Courtesy Mrs Lavinia Tritton.

Nell and Alexander Kerensky on a domestic flight in Australia.
Photo courtesy Mrs Lavinia Tritton.

In 1945, four months before her death, Nell and her husband returned to stay with her parents at their home in Clayfield. Courtesy Mrs Lavinia Tritton.

The headstone on the Tritton family grave. The inscriptions record the deaths of Lydia (Nell) and her brother Charles.
Photograph Jake de Vries.

CHAPTER 7

Marie Louise Mack
(1870–1935)

THE LIFE AND LOVES OF THE FIRST FEMALE WAR CORRESPONDENT

Possessions are not important, Life is the big adventure. Live it to the full.
Louise Mack.

Louise Mack was beautiful, talented and highly unconventional, nothing like the traditional image of a clergyman's daughter in the reign of Queen Victoria. The Reverend Hans Mack, his wife Jemima, and their 10 surviving children lived in genteel poverty in a series of rented parsonages in Hobart, Adelaide, Morpeth and Windsor. Finally, the family was moved by the Wesleyan Methodist church to a mission in inner-city Redfern, where the Reverend Hans wore himself out helping the poor and destitute.

Louise and her siblings were made to attend morning and evening service to hear their father preach on the joys of heaven, the dangers of materialism and the horrors of hellfire.

Louise's mother, Jemima Mack, taught her four daughters to read and made them learn by heart passages from the King James

Bible and the novels of Dickens and Dostoevsky. Louise resisted all attempts by her father to make her a devout Methodist but was convinced great literature had the power to redeem lives.

Overworked and underpaid, the Reverend Hans Mack died from cerebro-vascular disease when Louise was 16. Her eldest brother, named Hans after his father, won a scholarship to study medicine in London and worked there in a teaching hospital. Sid Mack, always Louise's favourite brother, studied law while Louise hoped to become a writer. Fortunately for these fatherless children, Jemima's father had left a bequest to allow them to attend private schools. But economies were vital, so Louise and her siblings wore shoes bought at jumble sales and made their own amusements.

Louise enjoyed writing little plays for her brothers and sisters, which they performed in the garden of their large shabby house in Redfern. She and her younger sisters, Alice, Florence and Amy, attended Sydney Girls High School. Louise showed talent for writing and was appointed editor of the school magazine while her equally talented classmate, Ethel Turner, edited a rival magazine.

While at school, Louise started a semi-autobiographical novel. Lacking a desk, she had to write seated at an old washstand. Louise had hoped to study literature at Sydney University, but lack of funds meant only her brothers attended university and she had to work as a governess, a job she disliked.

Determined to enter the world of publishing, Louise sent some of her poems to Alfred Stephens, the Literary Editor of *The Bulletin*, and signed the accompanying letter 'M.L. Mack'. Believing they were the work of a talented young man, Stephens asked the author to come to his office and was amazed that 'M.L. Mack' was an attractive girl. Louise created such a favourable impression she was given a job as a trainee journalist.

Louise was head over heels in love with dashing Jack Creed, who was nine years older than herself. He was tall and broad shouldered with dark curly hair and deep blue eyes and a mature-age student at the law school of Sydney University. Jack's closest friends at university were Louise's brother Sid and the shy and dutiful Herbert Curlewis. Jack was newly arrived from Ireland, so Sid invited him home and told Louise that Jack's father had owned an estate near Cork, but was such a heavy drinker the family property had to be sold. Jack Creed had visited London, France and Italy and appeared a man of the world to the unsophisticated daughters of a Methodist clergyman.

Amy, not nearly as pretty as Louise, had a crush on 'Handsome Jack', but Jack was attracted to Louise and treated Amy like a younger sister. The 20-year-old virginal Louise with her flowerlike beauty and bubbly personality fascinated Jack. She found his Irish charm and devil-may-care approach to life exciting and was convinced he was the love of her life.

Mrs Jemima Mack, a teetotaller, was worried by the fact that Jack Creed spent much of his time in pubs. She warned her romantic and impractical daughter that Jack would not make a good husband. Headstrong and impetuous, Louise refused to listen to her mother.

After graduating, Sid Mack and Herbert Curlewis found places in legal chambers as juniors, but Jack Creed had taken a part-time clerical job at the Law Institute of New South Wales, which paid a pittance. Jack claimed he would receive briefs from the solicitors with whom he drank in various pubs.

Louise assured her mother that Jack was so clever he was bound to succeed — it was only a question of time. She and Jack were soul mates, neither of them cared about money or bourgeois concepts like bank loans and home ownership. Once Jack was established as a barrister they would visit Montparnasse, Florence and Rome.

Louise was thrilled that her first novel, *The World is Round*, had been accepted by London publishers, Fisher Unwin. *The Bulletin's* Literary Editor, Alfred Stephens, had a soft spot for the gorgeous Miss Mack and promised that the publishing arm of the magazine would publish her poems in a small anthology to be titled *Dreams in Flower*. He would write an introduction to the book.[1]

Louise worked hard to learn the business of magazine publishing and was eventually given her own column for women. It was very popular and Louise expanded it to include reviews of books, plays and art exhibitions.[2]

As the only attractive young female in an office full of male journalists and illustrators, Louise was the subject of considerable speculation over her sexual availability. Alfred Stephens warned the young men on his staff that Miss Mack should be treated with the greatest respect. Louise was convinced that with the support of Alfred Stephens and *The Bulletin*'s senior editor, J.F. Archibald, once she was married to Jack and able to give up work, she could dedicate herself to writing poems and novels.

For years, the shy and unprepossessing Herbert Curlewis had pursued Ethel Turner without much encouragement. Spurred on by Louise's success when *The World is Round* was accepted by the London publisher, Ethel finished her novel about a motherless Australian family. London publishers Ward Lock were certain Ethel's book *Seven Little Australians* would sell very well. They invested a large sum in advance publicity and Ethel's first novel was to appear the following year just as she and Herbert were engaged. After a failed romance, Ethel realised how dependable Herbert was and what a good husband and father he would make. She announced she and Herbert Curlewis would marry as soon as they had enough money for a nice house.[3]

Sid was doing well at the bar and, having met his future wife, was also saving for a house. 'Handsome Jack' still had no briefs and did not save a penny. Jack's heavy drinking failed to impress Sydney solicitors and they did not send him any briefs. Loyal to the man she loved, Louise maintained that love and a stable home would cure Jack's drinking habits.

So, at 25, by which time most of her school friends were married, Louise wore down her mother's objections to Jack Creed and their engagement was announced. Jack was 34 but still had no briefs, but Louise did not care.

⁂

By that time the Mack family had moved to Neutral Bay to live in another large shabby house, but their home had a beautiful garden. In January 1896, to save money, the garden became the venue for the wedding of Jack and Louise. Herbert Curlewis was the best man and Ethel Turner was Louise's bridesmaid. All the guests said what a handsome couple Louise and Jack made.

As the newly-weds lacked money for a honeymoon, they loaded their double bed, table and four chairs onto a horse-drawn cart and set off for the primitive weatherboard cottage at Chatswood which they had rented. Louise claimed she did not mind the cottage was uncomfortable, convinced that 'love would find a way'. They would soon be off to Europe, anyhow.

In 1896, Chatswood was a remote bush area reached by the tram from the lower North Shore. Their 'cottage' or bush shack had no piped water or interior sanitation. It lacked any of the comforts Ethel and Herbert Curlewis took for granted — they had rented a comfortable house in Mosman.

Ethel's first novel, *Seven Little Australians*, became a best-seller, so she and Herbert could soon afford to buy a prestitious house and employ a well trained maid to help at their dinner parties.

Having given up work, Louise was short of money and could not think of employing a maid or a cleaner. Never domesticated when she lived at home, she found that boiling water to wash dishes, cooking meals on an iron range in a dingy kitchen and heating flat irons in the fire was boring. After a few months as a housewife, she longed to be back at work with a bunch of creative, amusing young men who teased her affectionately and invited her out to lunch.

Nevertheless, Louise was happy to stay at home and write poetry and novels. Her novel for young adults, *The World is Round*, was published and made a little money. She then wrote a sequel called *Teens*. Like *The World is Round*, it was semi-autobiographical and the heroine, Lennie Leighton, was Louise's alter ego. *Teens* was published in 1897 by the Sydney firm of Angus and Robertson, who were known as 'Anguish and Robbery' by their authors for the miserly amount of royalties they paid them.

Jack's lack of money did not prevent him from buying expensive clothes, books and fine wines on credit to keep up with his barrister friends. To pay their bills, Louise started a third teenage novel, *Girls Together,* once again featuring the adventures of Lennie and the Leighton family. It was published by Angus and Robertson in 1898, but to her chagrin did not enjoy the publicity and financial success of Ethel's book, *Seven Little Australians.*

By the end of 1898, Louise was still waiting for her royalties from Angus and Robertson, while Jack's debts were mounting and his creditors demanded payment. To make ends meet, Louise went back to work at *The Bulletin.* When she tackled Jack about his drinking, he insisted she was being ridiculous. Everyone in the legal profession drank in pubs, the best way to obtain briefs.

Louise retorted that Sid and Hubert obtained briefs without going to pubs. In response, Jack accused her of nagging, slammed the door and went to the pub. Louise realised with a sinking heart that she had been wrong — love and marriage had not changed Jack at all.

Working longer and longer hours, in an attempt to pay off their debts, Louise found commuting to the city very tiring. The more popular her column became and the more hours she worked, the more her marriage suffered.

Each evening, Louise returned home tired, after which she had to cook dinner and clean the house. Hours later Jack would arrive, reeking of alcohol, and eat the dinner Louise had left for him in the oven, drink more beer and go to bed. Their sex life, once so good, became a disaster. Jack would paw Louise ineffectually and weep that he was a failure.

By now, they argued fiercely about everything. When Louise tackled Jack over his debts, Jack would become abusive or sob on her shoulder and promise to stop drinking. He would remain sober for a few days before stealing money from her purse and going to the pub. He no longer went to work at the Law Society, sat at home drinking and tried to hide the empty bottles.

Louise's publishers, Angus and Robertson, owned several bookstores and they informed her that Jack had been caught stealing books from one of their shops. To prevent her husband from being prosecuted, Louise paid for the stolen books.

In the first years of her marriage, Louise had hoped to become a mother, but now, with Jack's soaring debts, a baby was the last thing she wanted. Only when her brother Hans, now an experienced doctor, returned from London on a visit, did Louise break down and confide her problems to him. Hans had seen many alcoholics in his time and warned Louise that unless Jack stopped drinking he would die from liver damage.

When Ethel Curlewis confided she was pregnant, Louise congratulated her, but kept quiet about her marriage problems.

To raise cash Mr and Mrs Creed pawned their furniture, left Chatswood and moved to a cheap lodging house in Redfern. Finally, Jack admitted he had lost his job at the Law Institute. When Louise insisted he had to get another job, he told her he hated her and they should never have married.

Louise sought advice from her brother Sid, who was now happily married. He warned Louise that, if Jack were declared bankrupt (as seemed inevitable), his bankruptcy notice would appear in the Sydney papers and he could be jailed.

After Jack had told Louise that he hated her, she realised that their marriage was over. A divorce seemed to be the only way out, but how much would it cost? Sid warned his sister that divorce proceedings were prohibitively expensive and only within reach of the seriously rich. Reputable barristers felt divorce was a very sordid branch of the law and many refused to take divorce cases.

Sid could not lend her money as he was paying back a high loan on his house in Wandella Avenue in the exlusive Sydney suburb of Hunter's Hill.[4] He also needed funds for extensive renovations to his house and for the expense of their mother's eye operation, which he had agreed to pay.

According to Sid, it would be best for Louise to leave Australia before Jack was declared bankrupt. Fortunately, she had no assets or children to fight over. From royalties due to her, she could buy a passage to London and claim to be a widow. As a wife who had left her husband, she would find it hard to gain employment, so she must not tell anyone the truth.

Louise took her brother's advice. As Louise said goodbye to Ethel, she broke down in sobs and at last admitted to her friend that her marriage had failed with no chance of reconciliation.

Jack blamed Louise for their marriage breakdown, ignoring the fact she had supported him for years. To anyone who would buy Jack a drink, he complained that his wife was leaving him because she was determined to go to London.

Worried about her mother's health, Louise said nothing to her about the marriage breakdown. Louise told her mother she was going to London for six months and would return to Sydney once her 'literary' novel was published. Amy, still jealous of Louise for marrying Jack, reproached her sister for leaving her husband. Keen to avoid recriminations, Louise wrote a little poem on the flyleaf of her latest novel and asked her mother to give it to Amy.

This is my last goodbye,
This side the sea,
Goodbye! Goodbye! Goodbye!
Love me. Remember me.

As Louise was a popular member of the staff, her colleagues — including *The Bulletin*'s cartoonist, Norman Lindsay — collected money for her farewell party. They were told she was going to London to write her first adult novel and they all wished her luck.

Meanwhile, Jack Creed had been declared bankrupt. He was tried for failing to pay his debts and, being found guilty and unable to settle his debts, went to jail. Louise and her estranged husband never saw each other again.

Early in 1901, Louise Creed sailed for Britain. On the long sea voyage Louise had hoped to meet cultivated people who would talk about European art and architecture and teach her a great deal.[5] Instead she travelled in steerage class with 'business people, butchers, bakers and ironmongers', who talked about nothing but making money.

Meals were tasteless, her cabin was cramped and dark and the P & O liner had no laundry facilities for steerage passengers.[6] When the ship arrived at Naples, Louise went ashore and lingered a long time in a restaurant, watching the sun set over the Bay of Naples. Because she had been so absorbed, she arrived late at the docks and found her ship and her luggage had sailed for Marseilles.[7] So she had to spend her precious money on a train ticket to Marseilles to rejoin the ship. However, Italy and the Italians fascinated Louise and she vowed to return once she had enough money to do so.

In May 1901, Louise landed at Tilbury docks. She found a cheap attic to rent in a lodging house in Bloomsbury's Keppel Street facing the British Museum, whose reading room became her research library. Louise started writing her 'serious' novel, hoping to establish a career as an adult author. Meanwhile, she existed on black tea, toast and marmalade.

The British summer came and went and, to eke out her meagre savings, Louise put a shilling in the gas meter only when her hands were too cold to continue typing her manuscript.

Fisher Unwin, the British publishers who had published *The World is Round*, gave her no advance but agreed to publish *An Australian in London*. The novel for adult readers, written in the form of letters, was well reviewed by a few London critics, including the illustrious *Review of Reviews*. Unfortunately, *An Australian in London* was poorly promoted and did not sell well.[8] *Dreams in Flower* was published by *The Bulletin* in Sydney, but, being poetry, earned only a pittance. Clearly literature did not pay as well as journalism.

Louise now had six months to wait for her royalties and was desperate for money to pay her landlady. She could not ask her brother Hans for money — as a poorly paid doctor in a free hospital he was struggling to support his wife and children.

Journalist friends advised that Lord Northcliffe's *Daily Mail* was looking for someone who could write romantic fiction to appear in serial form. The job would pay a handsome salary. In response to her letter of application, Louise was asked to come for an interview at Northcliffe House with the *Daily Mail's* Fiction Editor and to bring references from papers she had worked on.

Louise lacked the money to take an omnibus to Fleet Street. It was pouring with rain and she feared that, if she walked there, she could catch a cold and the worn soles of her shoes might drop off. So Louise decided to take a horse-drawn cab and charge the fares to the newspaper.

Having pawned most of her good clothes and jewellery, she put on her only presentable dress. Standing in front of the mirror, she fluffed up her dark blonde hair and applied a red wax crayon to her pale cheeks (at a time when only prostitutes and chorus girls wore make-up). She descended the stairs to Keppel Street and hailed a hansom cab which clip-clopped off to Fleet Street.

On reaching the steps of the Northcliffe House, Louise dazzled the doorman with her smile, asked him to pay the cab driver and charge it to the *Daily Mail*.[9]

Impressed by her looks and air of authority, the doorman did as she asked. A messenger boy showed her into the office of the Fiction Editor and she sat facing him in a low chair.[10]

The Fiction Editor looked at her with cold, fishy eyes and advised that when writing romantic serials she must never forget the most important thing was to keep 'the sympathy of the reader'. Louise nodded agreement.

The Editor outlined his requirements. Her serialised romance had to divide into five instalments, one for each day of the week. On Monday, the handsome hero and the beautiful but penniless girl — orphans were very popular with readers — must meet under romantic circumstances. After a series of misunderstandings involving a 'bad woman' who wants the hero for herself, they discover they love each other and make plans to marry.

Louise, reared on the novels of Dickens, Dostoevsky and Tolstoy, was amazed to think anyone would read such twaddle. But, as her stomach was rumbling with hunger, she kept quiet. It was vital she obtained this well-paid job or the landlady would throw her out. If she could make a success of it and last the course, she could earn enough to go to Italy. It meant *adios* to any hopes of writing anything of quality. This would upset her mother and Amy, but at least she would have enough to eat as well as buy new clothes and send her mother presents.

The Fiction Editor asked where she planned to set her romances. Louise thought of English stately homes or villas in Italy but realised she knew so little about them it would be hard to make her stories convincing. She suggested setting a story on an outback sheep station or an island in the South Seas. To her surprise, the Fiction Editor liked her suggestions. He said that his readers were tired of romances set in castles and stately homes and would like something new.

He commissioned a story set on an island in the South Pacific. If her story 'held the sympathy of the reader', the job was hers. Louise was so relieved she could have burst into tears. Instead, she smiled politely as the Fiction Editor arranged with the Pay Office to grant her a cash advance to write her first romance.

The money meant Louise could take a hansom cab to her Bloomsbury lodgings, pay her landlady and eat a decent meal for the first time in weeks. She sat at the rickety table in her bedroom or lay on the bed and worked on the first romance she had ever written. Having been a virgin when she married Jack Creed, she had a limited experience of love to draw on. But she had a vivid imagination and found it easy to write about tall, dark heroes with broad shoulders and dazzling white teeth. She shut her eyes and pictured Jack standing beside her at the little altar in their garden at Neutral Bay, before alcohol bloated his handsome features.

Raised in inner Sydney, she had never had enough money to visit a Pacific island, but she did have a vivid imagination. Louise was helped by memories of a *Bulletin* journalist who used to regale her with tales of life on a copra boat going from island to island. As a child, missionary friends of Louise's father had told her about Fiji and the New Hebrides — the cannibal feasts, native dancing and kava drinking from a ceremonial bowl, descriptions which she used in her story. She made her handsome hero the manager of a large coconut plantation Her heroine was a penniless orphan who answered an advertisement placed by the hero for a young lady to come by boat from England to act as governess to his younger sister.

Louise handed in the story, hoping the Fiction Editor would like it. After a few anxious days she received a telegram asking her to come to Northcliffe House and was told she would receive a two year contract to work for the Northcliffe Press at a salary so high it amazed her. The Northcliffe Press reserved the rights to sell her stories to book publishers who specialised in paperback romances, from which she would earn a further 10 percent in royalties on top of her salary.

When Mrs Creed was introduced to her new colleagues, she pretended to be widowed. She was given her own desk in the area called 'The Hen Coop', which was reserved for female journalists. The women who sat there were much older and were only allowed to write serialised romances and articles on fashion and cookery.

Readers loved Mrs Louise Creed's romances set on sheep stations where bronzed men rode tall in the saddle and owned properties larger than Wales. Some of the stories were re-published as books by Gerald Mills and Charlie Boone or their rivals, the New Circulating Library Press. As large royalty cheques arrived Louise took hansom cabs everywhere, bought new clothes and soon had admirers happy to dine and wine her.

Her mother, who had taught Louise to love great literature, was disappointed that her daughter earned her living writing escapist rubbish. Amy was writing short stories and children's books about bush animals and wrote Louise a letter warning her older sister she was prostituting her literary talent and that it was her fault Jack had been jailed. Louise was furious. What would Amy know? She was about to marry Launce Harrison, who had a secure university post, so *she* would never have to pawn her possessions and live on black tea and biscuits.

Mrs Creed, now a very merry widow indeed, was invited to dine at elegant restaurants like Rules in Maiden Lane and the Café Royal and to first nights at Covent Garden, where Melba and

Adelina Patti enthralled their audiences. It was an era of arranged marriages, when wealthy husbands amused themselves with beautiful mistresses. Louise was careful to say nothing about the men in her life in letters home to her mother and sisters. Instead she told them about visits to the theatre and her new friends Willy and Gemma le Queux (a Norman name pronounced as 'Lekew'). Willy was one of Britain's highest-paid and most prolific authors who had his spy stories serialised in *The Daily Mail*. Louise had been introduced to Willy when he brought in his latest story for the Fiction Editor to see. On hearing Louise was from Sydney, Willy, an enthusiastic traveller, invited her to diner to meet his young Italian wife. Louise was slightly apprehensive but found she and Gemma got on famously and they became close friends.

Willy was away a great deal, travelling to remote parts of the Balkans, the trouble spot where he found background material for mystery stories about spies and armament dealers. Gemma, who had no children to occupy her, was delighted to accompany Louise on shopping excursions.

Urged on by Gemma, who adored clothes and had excellent taste, Louise bought beautiful outfits from Paris and expensive furs for the London winter. She sent money to her mother each month, lavished presents on her nephews and nieces and enjoyed meals with Hans and his family.

As a successful romance writer, Louise moved from her chilly attic in Bloomsbury into a centrally heated Mayfair apartment and employed a lady's maid. She enjoyed wearing her new elegant clothes and the large picture hats that were so fashionable. She consoled herself that her romances brought pleasure to millions of women who led dull and boring lives.

Her only 'serious' novel, *An Australian in London*, had made very little money, but received a glowing review in *The Review of Reviews*. This had won Louise the friendship of the celebrated media tycoon W.T. Stead, who owned the magazine.[11]

She was joined in London by her younger sister Alice, who had been sent there to recover from a broken romance. At parties given by Willy Stead, Louise met leading members of the literary world, including John Galsworthy, author of the *Forsyte Saga*, George Bernard Shaw and H.G. Wells. Louise, raised on the Bible and the tenets of Methodism, was now a free thinker — one of George Bernard Shaw's 'New Women'. She embraced the fashionable concept of free love but was careful not to make any mention of this in letters to her family in Sydney.

Towards the end of 1904, encouraged by her Italian friend Gemma le Queux, Louise gave up her job and her London apartment and moved to Florence. She told her family she was going there to work on a novel titled *Children of the Sun*.

Life in Florence for those with foreign currency was cheap and pleasant. The city, surrounded by hills and olive groves, had a resident community of English and Americans, who rented or bought large villas or apartments in the city and could afford to employ village girls as servants. In addition, swarms of visitors flocked to Florence to admire the treasures of Renaissance art bequeathed to the city by Duchess Anna Ludovica, the last of the Medici. Louise loved the Uffizi Gallery, the Pitti Palace and Florence's frescoed churches. Intoxicated by the art around her, she told everyone she had found her spiritual home at last and would stay in Florence forever.

Louise and a group of art-loving friends attended literary soirees or met for coffee at Donney's in the Via Tornabuoni. Sometimes they visited Sieber's English bookshop and browsed the shelves for the latest English books.

At first, Louise stayed at a villa converted into a *pensione*, but a few months later she rented a riverside apartment at No 20 Lungarno Acciaioli with a view over the Ponte Veccio on one side and over Michelangelo's Ponte Santa Trinitá on the other. At night, Louise could lean out of her window and see the lights from the shops along the Ponte Veccio reflected in the water.

As a talented linguist, Louise soon learned to speak Italian fluently. Meanwhile, she was busy writing her novel, *Children of the Sun*, with chapters set in Sydney and others in Tuscany.

She was invited to write articles and review books for the English language publication *The Italian Gazette*. While on holiday in Britain, the English owner-editor of *The Italian Gazette* died, with the result that the English-language magazine lacked an editor.[12] Louise, with her journalistic experience, was invited to take over as editor. Aided by a committee of English expatriates who enjoyed seeing their names in print, Louise ran *The Italian Gazette* for several years, writing editorials, theatre and book reviews and stories about the doings of the expatriate British community in Tuscany. Louise had to claim she was English as the board of *The Italian Gazette* insisted they did not want a 'colonial' as editor.

Members of the English-speaking community in Florence were snobbish and cliquey. In order to be invited to their parties Louise had to hide the fact she was Australian and had left her husband. She still had no idea whether Jack Creed had drunk himself to death or had returned to Ireland.

Louise wrote to her mother and siblings in Sydney, telling them how she adored life in Florence, a city where art and literature were appreciated. From her family's letters, she learned that Amy had married Launce Harrison and was living in Mosman. Jemima was almost blind and lived with a paid companion, whose salary was paid by Sid.

As editor and arts reviewer for *The Italian Gazette*, Louise enjoyed interviewing writers like Ouida, Mrs Humphrey Ward and Marie Correlli. The name of the city's resident literary lion, Gabriele D'Annunzio, was on everyone's lips so, naturally, Louise hoped to meet him.[13] While in London, she and Gemma had seen one of the many plays by D'Annunzio, in which the leading role was played by the celebrated actress Eleanora Duse. Louise, impressed by D'Annunzio's talent, described the play in a letter to her family in Sydney. Louise's friend Gemma le Queux, who had grown up in Florence, told her that Eleanora Duse was the principal mistress of D'Annunzio, but as she was years older than the celebrated writer, Florentine gossips claimed the long affair was over, but Gabriele and Duse were still friends and business partners.[14]

In 1905, Louise's wish to meet Gabriele D'Annunzio came true, but as she did not keep a diary there is no record of how or where they met. D'Annunzio had abandoned his wife and two sons long ago, but by law had to support them, as well as an illegitimate daughter by one of his mistresses.

Gabriele enjoyed the company of beautiful, intelligent women and usually invited ladies he wished to seduce for a private poetry reading in his bachelor flat in the centre of Florence. He liked to have at least two mistresses at one time. He enjoyed observing their feelings of anger and jealousy and incorporated these in his plays and novels.

It seems likely that Louise met the playboy-poet at a poetry reading in his 'love nest'. Now in her early 30s, Louise was still beautiful with her slim figure and big blue eyes and appeared years younger than her age. Gabriele D'Annunzio had read in *The Italian Gazette* that Louise was an English widow. He wanted to learn enough English to be interviewed by the British press in London where he wished to promote his latest play. Gabriele was 40 and at the height of his fame. He had melting brown eyes and a lean, muscular physique, which he kept trim and fit by fencing with an instructor. Although going bald on top, he was still very attractive to women.

D'Annunzio owned the *Villa della Capponcina* at Settignano, a hill village near Florence. The imposing villa, built from local stone, was surrounded by vineyards and olive groves. Italy's greatest writer had spared no expense to furnish it with antiques, Persian rugs and Renaissance tapestries.

To run the olive groves and vineyards on his estate and deal with the farm workers, Gabriele employed Bernardo Palmieri to act as his estate manager and handle his business dealings. He also employed a private secretary, called Tomas (Tom) Antongini, who, after Gabriele's death, would become his biographer.

Tomas Antongini related that Gabriele D'Annunzio was always 'extravagantly generous' to his latest lady friends and gave them expensive presents as proof of his love. He lavished them with flowers delivered by a special messenger and leather-bound editions of his works, dedicated to them.

When a lady in whom Gabriele was interested made her first visit to his love nest in Florence, his valet was instructed to serve the finest wines in crystal goblets and then retire from the room.[15] Protestations of undying love from a famous writer of love poems meant many women fell in love with Gabriele and were happy to become his mistress even though they knew he could never marry them — Louise Creed was one of these women.

There are good reasons for believing that Louise may have borne D'Annunzio a child while living near her lover in Settignano.

In 1924, on a form put out by the Registrar of Births, Marriages and Deaths in Victoria, Louise claimed to have 'one child, still living', which implies that she had a child born out of wedlock.[16]

In 1906, D'Annunzio leased the neighbouring *Villa di Doccia* in Settignano and the name of the tenant on the lease was Signora Louise Creed.[17] The three-year lease was signed by D'Annunzio's estate manager, Bernardo Palmieri, on behalf of his employer. The other signatory was the Tuscan agent of Lord Westbury, the debt-ridden aristocrat who owned the *Villa di Doccia*.

Louise told her family she had given up the job she enjoyed, had moved out of her apartment in Florence and gone to live in the isolated *Villa di Doccia* at Settignano, but gave no reason for this. The villa's garden was surrounded by a high wall and from a small tower there was a superb view over olive groves and cypresses. It was an ideal spot to hide for a woman who had fallen pregnant to the man whose villa was nearby. A baby could have been born at *Villa di Doccia* without anyone knowing about it.

Antongini wrote in his biography of D'Annunzio that 'an English lady, living at Settignano, of whom the writer was fond, had no husband so D'Annunzio gave her a pedigree dog to keep her company'. Without doubt, the English lady was Louise Creed.

Decades later, Louise admitted to a journalist on *The Australian Women's Weekly* that she had known Italy's famous writer years previously, but now detested him and called him 'a cad'. Some of Gabriele's other discarded mistresses called him far worse names. Louise also revealed intimate details about D'Annunzio, such as the fact that he had over 100 hand-made suits hanging in his wardrobe at the *Villa della Capponcina*.

As a 'respectable English widow', Mrs Creed could not have admitted to her friends in Florence that she was pregnant — neither could she have told her devout Methodist mother and her church-going sisters that she was expecting a baby.

Living in seclusion at the *Villa di Doccia*, Louise was waited on by a cook whose husband, Torquato, acted as the gardener. When Louise needed something from Florence, her gardener walked to the village of Fiesole where he caught the tram to Florence and did the necessary shopping for her. Louise would jot down the amount of money she had given Torquato in a small notebook.

So what became of the child Louise claimed was still living in 1924? Louise, raised a Methodist, was unlikely to have entrusted her baby to a Catholic orphanage. Adoption was a possibility. I examined the adoption register of the Protestant orphanage, run by Isabella Gould in Florence's Via de Serragli. By law, the name of the relinquishing mother had to be entered in the register. But it contained no entry for a mother called Louise Mack or Creed between 1907 and 1910, after which time Louise had left Florence for London.

One can assume that Louise would have wanted the best for her child. Her affluent friend and fellow author Willy le Queux had married 27-year-old Gemma Cione in 1902. Willy, having made large sums from his novels, owned a Mayfair apartment, a country house in Norfolk, a house in Florence's Viale Michelangelo and a summer villa at Ardenza, a seaside village near Livorno. Louise wrote to her family about Willy and Gemma visiting her in Florence and driving with them to other parts of Tuscany in Willy's red sports car.

Willy and Gemma, who longed to have children, adopted 4-year-old Frances Chatfield in 1906. Frances' working-class father had died of tuberculosis and her poverty-stricken mother could not afford to keep the little girl. In 1907, Willy and Gemma adopted another daughter, but Willy's biographers did not give any information about this child. There is a strong possibility that the couple adopted Louise's baby and raised it as their own along with their first adopted daughter.[18]

※

In May 1910, Louise left Tuscany and returned to London. Her lease on the *Villa di Doccia* had expired and Lord Westbury wished to sell the property.

In the same year, D'Annunzio had a brief affair with Giuseppina di Mancini, the attractive but unstable wife of the Count di Mancini, owner of the *Villa di Giove*. It ended in tragedy when Giuseppina told Gabriele she was pregnant by him and demanded to move into the *Villa della Capponcina*. This idea terrified Gabriele and he ended the affair in a telephone call after his mistress threatened to kill herself. Giuseppina walked to the nearest village and had hysterics, screaming curses at D'Annunzio for making her pregnant. The local priest phoned her husband, who sent his carriage and footmen to collect his pregnant wife and had her committed to a private asylum for the rest of her life.

Later that year, *Villa della Capponcina* and its expensive furnishings were auctioned in a forced sale, because D'Annunzio was heavily in debt. There was so much antique furniture and so many books to sell it took a week to dispose of everything. From the proceeds of the sale, the poet's debtors were paid, but by then Gabriele D'Annunzio had fled to Paris to continue writing and womanising.[19]

Back in London, Louise resumed her old job, writing romances for *The Daily Mail* as well as a few feature articles. In June of that year she met her former best friend and bridesmaid, Ethel Curlewis. Ethel was on holiday in London with her husband, now created Judge Herbert Curlewis. Louise had dinner with them, but found that their former intimacy had vanished.

Ethel noted in her diary that Louise looked 'stouter than before' and spoke English with a strong Italian accent. Her husband told Louise that Jack Creed had left Australia, but he did not know if Jack was still alive.[20]

※

Early in August 1914, the Kaiser's army invaded the neutral kingdom of Belgium en route to attack Paris. Lord Northcliffe had warned the British Cabinet for years that Germany was preparing for war but they refused to believe him.

Bound by a treaty to support Belgian neutrality, Britain declared war on Germany on 4 August 1914 and sent troops to Belgium. The bulk of Britain's small peacetime army was sent to the area around Mons on the Franco-Belgian border, trying to halt the German advance on Paris.

Lord Northcliffe was determined to cover the conflict in detail and sent a group of journalists from his London papers, *The Daily Mail* and *The Evening News*. The journalists were to take the ferry to Ostend with instructions to proceed to Antwerp where the Belgian Army was holding out against a large detachment of German troops who had taken possession of the Belgian capital of Brussels.

Somehow, Louise — or Willy le Queux, a close friend of Lord Northcliffe — managed to persuade the media magnate to let Louise join his group of journalists heading for France. Arguably, Louise became the first fully accredited female war reporter.

Dutch journalists claimed that unarmed Belgian civilians in the towns of Aerschot and Louvain had their houses torched by drunken German soldiers. Several families, who took refuge in their cellars, had been burned to death. Louise was instructed to interview war victims and to leave the accounts of battles and armaments to the male journalists.

When Louise and the other war correspondents arrived at the port of Ostend on 16 August, the station master warned them the Germans were only an hour's march away. Kaiser Wilhelm, incensed by reports of German atrocities in the Dutch press, issued orders that all captured foreign journalists would be shot by a firing squad as enemy spies. When the leader of Northcliffe's group of journalists heard about the Kaiser's proclamation, he immediately ordered them to return to London. Louise did not want to leave but had to comply.

On 17 August 1914, she and the rest of the group took the ferry back to Folkestone. Louise returned to her London apartment, packed her belongings and gave up the lease.

Ten days later, Louise once more boarded the Ostend ferry, determined to return to Belgium for the duration of the war. With her she took two trunks filled with summer and winter clothes, her favourite books and the latest novel on which she was working. She also took that precious letter, signed by Lord Northcliffe, appointing her as an official war correspondent for *The Daily Mail*.

From Ostend, she went by train to the port of Antwerp, where the Belgian Army had retreated and were facing an attack by German forces and their aeroplanes. King Albert of the Belgians had asked Britain to send more troops to help him, but was told that British soldiers were fighting German soldiers on the French border so only a handful could be spared.

From Antwerp's railway station, Louise took a hansom cab to the Hotel Terminus, where she knew she would find other war correspondents. In the lobby, while waiting for a room to be prepared for her, she met Major Livingstone Seaman and his wife, who were heading the war relief activities of the Red Cross in Belgium. They asked Louise to tell her readers of their crying need for funds to provide aid to victims of German atrocities.

She also met Frank Fox, an Australian who had worked with her in Sydney and was now working for a British newspaper. He was astounded to find a woman reporting on war. Frank Fox warned she must escape before German soldiers arrived or she was in danger of being raped. Frank Fox was amazed to find that Louise intended to remain in Antwerp even if the Germans did arrive.

As a war correspondent, Louise was given the use of an army staff car with a driver so she could visit towns torched by the Germans as a warning to other towns and cities to co-operate with them. A photograph shows Louise seated in the open staff car, wearing an elegant Paris-inspired outfit. A group of young officers crowded around the car to talk to Louise, amazed to find such an attractive woman working as a war correspondent.

Louise asked the chauffeur to drive close to the front line, find a place without sentries and cross into German-occupied Belgium. At first, the chauffeur refused, saying it was too dangerous. As Louise retorted 'one could only die once', he reluctantly agreed to take her into the danger area.

Driving past a railway station, Louise saw a passenger train labelled 'Aerschot' from which the passengers were descending. Impulsive as always, she told her driver to stop. She jumped out of the car, crossed the track before the driver could stop her and boarded the train. She took her handbag containing her precious notebook, but left behind both trunks containing all her winter clothes and her unfinished novel and never saw them again.

As the train rumbled on to Aerschot, those passengers who spoke English confirmed that Belgian homes had been torched by drunken German soldiers. The Germans, incensed that Belgian patriots had blown up a couple of bridges to impede their progress towards France, took their revenge after a drinking spree. They had torched houses in the centre of the ancient walled towns of Aerschot and Louvain and watched with glee as the houses and the ancient library of the University of Louvain burned to the ground.[21]

Arriving at Aerschot, Louise thought the centre of this historic city looked 'as though an earthquake had hit it'. The beautiful gabled houses, for which the town was famous, were charred ruins. The streets were littered with empty wine bottles, evidence that German soldiers had been drinking.

The Germans had left sentries behind and Louise feared that, with her British passport, she could be arrested as a spy. She found a discarded German greatcoat and draped it round her shoulders.

She interviewed a sobbing woman whose husband had been taken away by the Germans and feared she would never see him again. Apparently the church had been the scene of a drunken orgy. Once inside it, Louise saw where German soldiers had stabled their horses and how the marble floors were covered with straw and excrement.

More empty bottles bore witness to the fact that Germans must have raided someone's cellar. The sacristan who showed her around was clearly in shock. When Louise told him she was a journalist, he showed her a 14th century Madonna with the head chopped off. Some soldiers had set fire to a superb carved figure of Christ which was badly charred down one side. Oil paintings of the Nativity and the Crucifixion had been used for target practice.

Pinned to the door of a small votive chapel was a notice in German saying 'Private, Keep Out'. The sacristan grimaced as he opened the door. Inside were women's undergarments, tossed on the floor, doubtless torn from their wearers. What Louise had seen confirmed the rumours of the atrocities the German had inflicted. She had to take the train back to Antwerp and wire a report of her findings to *The Daily Mail*.

Back in Antwerp, Louise tried to wire a story of the German atrocities to *The Daily Mail*'s News Editor. To her dismay she found the German Army had not only disabled the city's water supply but had cut the telegraph wires as well.

Louise was determined to get her front page story to London. Homeless refugees were paying fishing boats to take them to Dover so, if necessary, she could pay the captain of one of these boats to take her report with him or hope a Dutch foreign correspondent might take it with him and send it on to London.

By now, most foreign correspondents, fearing the Germans would shoot them as spies, had left. However, Louise was utterly determined to stay and observe how the Germans behaved. Would they act as they had done at Aerschot and Louvain and torch the historic centre of Antwerp with its gabled houses, libraries and art museums containing masterworks by Rubens and other Flemish painters?[22] Unable to wire her office, Louise kept a journal, an abridged edition of which is reproduced here.

Sunday, 4 October 1914

Crowds of frightened peasants are pouring into the city with their cows, their valuables piled on farm carts. All day long the cannons boom. Sometimes they sound so near that one imagines a shell must have burst in Antwerp itself; and sometimes they grow fainter.

Eventually we lose interest in the booming cannons, and go about our business. Our small group of war correspondents dine together at the Terminus Hotel.

A notice pasted up everywhere reads *Pas d'eau!* [No water.] Apparently German cannon balls and shells have smashed the Municipal Waterworks at the village of Wavre Sainte Catherine. As a result our bathrooms and toilets reek and are flooded with carbolic disinfectant. We drink and clean our teeth in mineral water.

The nights are stiflingly hot and mosquitoes are so bad that I put eucalyptus oil on my pillow to keep them away. How strange that this terrific canon fire has not frightened them off! I reach the conclusion that mosquitoes are deaf.

The curious thing is, no one can tell, from looking at Antwerp, that the city is being bombarded by German guns. The shops are still open. People sit in crowded cafés sipping coffee or beer. Calm prevails. A curfew ensures lights go out at seven and by ten o'clock the city is asleep, save for the coming and going of clattering troops and horses along paved streets. Yesterday a rumour reached us foreign correspondents that Antwerp is on the verge of surrender rather than run the risk of being destroyed, just as the historic cities of Louvain and Aerschot were destroyed. [At Louvain the ancient university library and all the books in it were torched by German soldiers].

The British Legation has received notice the Belgian Government is about to relocate to Ostend. Crowds of people hurry out of Antwerp in motor cars. On Sunday the news spreads like wild-fire that English troops are coming!

Monday, 5 October 1914

The historic towns of Liége, Louvain, Brussels, Aerschot, Namur, Malines, and Termonde have fallen, one by one. The small

Belgian Army is still indomitable but very tired. Haggard, hollow-eyed, exhausted, the weary soldiers revive as if by magic under the knowledge that British troops are coming to help them in the struggle for Antwerp.

At the Belgian War Office, Count Chabeau has given me a special permit to go to the ruined village of Lierre. As we drive past the village of Mortselle, I notice a Belgian lady in black among a crowd of soldiers. Her dress is elegant yet simple. I admire her furs, and I wonder what on earth she is doing here in the battle zone where ladies are rare. She comes towards me, drawn by the fact that we are both caught amid the turmoil of war, leans across the open window of my car and tells me her story.

Just down the road, a little further on, in the area we may not enter is her villa, which has been requisitioned by the British. In a hurry yesterday, Madame packed up, and hurried away to Antwerp to arrange accommodation there. This morning she has returned to fetch her dogs. But *voilà*! She reaches this checkpoint and is stopped. The way is blocked. No one can pass without a special *laisser-passer* which she does not have.

So here, hour after hour, since six o'clock in the morning, Madame stands there waiting pitifully for a chance to get back to her villa and her dogs, who she fears may be starving.

'*Mes pauvre chiens!*' she keeps exclaiming.

And now a motor car approaches from the direction of Lierre, with an English officer sitting beside the chauffeur. I tell him the story of the dogs and ask what can be done.

The officer does not reply. He merely turns his car round and flashes away along the white tree-shadowed and cannon-lined road that he has just traversed. Ten minutes go by, then another ten.

Then back along the road flashes the grey car with Colonel Farquharson, cool, calm and unperturbed. And behind him, in the car, barking joyfully at the sight of their mistress, are three big dogs.

Out of the burning village of Lierre a canary and a grey Congolese parrot are handed over to my care by a couple of English soldiers who found them in a burning house.[23]

'The poor parrot is starving!' says a Tommy compassionately. 'It'll be better with you, ma'am.'

I bring the birds back in the car to Antwerp.

As I write this, the parrot and canary sit here on my table, the parrot perching on the canary's cage.

Tuesday, 6 October

From a terrace on top of the hotel I look across the city towards the points where the Germans are attacking us. Through the clouds four aeroplanes can be seen, black as birds, moving hither and thither. Far below lies the beautiful old town, with its medieval towers and Gothic buildings, art galleries full of masterworks by Rubens, and the river running to meet the sea.

I go down to the Belgian War Office to see Commandant Chabeau. He looks pale and haggard. His grey eyes are full of infinite sadness.

'To-day it would be wise, *chere madame*, you do not go out of the city,' he says gently. '*C'est trop dangereux!*'

One o'clock strikes. We learn that the fighting outside is increasing.

Two o'clock. Cars come flying into the city and the drivers tell us that shells are falling about five miles out, on the village of Vieux Dieux.

Three o'clock. A man rushes in and says that all is over; the last train leaves Antwerp to-night; the Belgian Government is moving to Ostend. It is our last chance to escape.

'How far *is* Holland?' asks a voice.

'About half an hour away,' another answers.

Holland sounds very near. Am I going to stay in Antwerp and see the Germans enter? It seems *impossible* that such an ancient walled city as Antwerp can fall to enemy hands.

'The Germans will be burning Antwerp in twenty-four hours,' says one young man, as he calls for another drink.

'The Germans will *never* dare,' says a choleric Englishman. Outside, the sun is waning and the cannon fire has ceased. One hears only the loud shrill cries of the newsboys and women selling Antwerp papers. [Foreign newspapers could not enter as

Germans held the surrounding roads and were trying to jam English radio broadcasts].

A strange silence hangs over the besieged city. I go outside to see what is happening. Antwerp has filled up with terrified refugees. Everywhere, bareheaded women, hollow-cheeked men, little girls and boys with bundles, some pathetically small, in white or blue checked cloths under which they stagger through the streets. Overhead a magnificent sunset is spreading over the deserted city. Shop-windows glow like rubies, the gilding on the Gothic buildings burns like crimson fire. Then night falls; the red fades from the sky and Antwerp turns grey and sombre.

Wednesday, 8 October
Last night the moon was so bright that my pet birds, rescued from the ruins, woke up and began to talk. Or was it the big guns that woke the canary, and the grey Congo parrot?

Sometimes the whole city seemed to shake. As I lay in bed I wondered who were firing — Germans, Belgians or English troops?

At four in the morning, unable to sleep, I rose, dressed and went downstairs. In the dim, unswept palm court I saw a bearded man walking feverishly up and down, while the sleepy night porter leaned against a pillar yawning, watching for the cab. It came at last, and the bearded gentleman, with a sigh, stepped in, and drove away into the dusky dawn, a look of unutterable sadness on his face.

'Il est triste, ce monsieur la,' commented our voluble Flemish porter. 'He is a Minister of the Government, and must leave Antwerp for Ostend. His boat leaves at five o'clock this morning.'

'So the Belgian government really *is* moving out,' I think.

A little boy runs in from the chill dawn-lit streets.

It is only half-past four, but he throws the Flemish paper *Het Laatste Nieuws* on the table where I sit writing. I struggle to find out what message lies behind those Flemish headlines.

De Toestand Te Antwerpen Is Zeer Ernstig.

Is it good? Is it bad? I don't know the meaning of the word 'ernstig'.

The night porter translates. 'The situation facing Antwerp is very serious,' he says. 'The bombardment of Antwerp is imminent. But our resistance will continue to the end!'

So now we know. Antwerp will *not* surrender but fight to the death.

And now the hotel wakes up, and dozens of sleepy, worn, hollow-cheeked officers and soldiers in dirty boots come down the red-carpeted stairs clamouring for their *café-au-lait*.

The morning is cold, and they shiver but feel better after drinking coffee and smoking cigarettes before hurrying away.

The sun is up and floods of golden light stream over the city, where crowds are moving backwards and forwards. Cabs drive up continually to the great railway station opposite my room with piles of luggage. People are going away in hundreds, in thousands, quietly, calmly. Processions of black-robed nuns file along the avenues under the trees whose leaves are fading and turning yellow. Long lines of Belgian cyclists flash by in an opposite direction in their gay yellow and green uniforms. The blue and red of the French and English banners never looked brighter as the sunlight sparkles on them, while the great black and red and gold Belgian flags lend a note of sombre dignity to the crowded streets.

My God, what these people are going through! What suffering! How can they bear it? Where do they get such heroism?

Antwerp Shelled

That morning seated in wicker chairs in the palm court, all [of us] war correspondents who are left held a counsel of war. The question is whether the Hotel Terminus is too dangerous for us to remain here. Its proximity to the main railway station made its shelling almost inevitable when the bombardment of the city began in earnest. We argued. One suggested one hotel, one another. We know the shells will come from the south.

British journalists, Mr. Cherry Kearton, Mr. Cleary, and Mr. Marshall, decided to move to Queen's Hotel, near the quay thinking it would be easier to escape from there. Mr. Robinson and Mr. Phillips refused to move from the Hotel Terminus. The

Australian Frank Fox, Arthur Jones [a handsome fellow Northcliffe Press journalist], myself and Monsieur Lucien from a Belgian paper chose the Wagner Hotel, as being the nearest to the Breda Gate, which leads to Holland.

In the moonlight, after dinner, taking my canary and parrot with me, I moved to my new quarters in the Wagner Hotel. Precisely at eleven the first shell fell somewhere near the spire of Antwerp Cathedral.

It scarcely seemed possible to endure that noise and come out alive. Other shells followed in quick succession. Sleep was impossible. I crept down into the vestibule. It was dark, save for one little light at the porter's door. I got a chair, drew it close to the light and sat down. I had a note-book and pencil, and to calm myself made notes of what people said and sat there all night long.

Every now and then doors would burst open and men and women would rush in. Once it was two slim, elegant ladies in black, with white fox stoles who ran from their home because a shell had set fire to the house next door. They came into the pitch-black vestibule, moving about by the little point of light made by their tiny electric torch and asked for a room. There was none. So they asked to sit in the empty restaurant. I saw them disappear into that darkened room where many refugees were already sleeping on chairs and floors and tables. Next a man passes through the swing door who asks the porter,

'Is Monsieur L. here?'

'*Oui, Monsieur*,' replies the porter.

'Where is he?'

'In bed.'

'Go and tell him that a shell has just fallen on the Banque d'Anvers (Bank of Antwerp). Tell him come at once. He must come and save papers before the bank burns down! Tell him Monsieur M., the Manager, came for him.'

With this the Bank Manager disappears through the swing door and into the night with its burst of cannon fire. An English war correspondent comes down the stairs behind me, his long overcoat flapping.

'What an evil smell!' he says to the porter. 'Is gas escaping?'

'No, sir,' says the porter.

'It *is* gas!' persists the war correspondent. 'I *know* that smell. There must be a leak somewhere.' He opens the door and a horrible whiff of burning petroleum and smoke comes inside and a Belgian soldier enters.

'What's the smell?' repeats the war correspondent

'The Germans are dropping explosives on the city, trying to set fire to it,' answers the soldier.

'Good Lord, must have a look!' says the war-correspondent and goes out.

Two wounded officers come down the stairs behind me.

'Bill, please, porter. How much? We're off to inspect the forts!'

'I can't make up your account,' says the porter. 'I'm new, the other man ran away, afraid of the shelling. *Pas de probleme*, pay me later, Messieurs!'

'*Bien!*' say the officers. They swing their cloaks across their shoulders and go out, most probably never to return.

An elderly man limps in on the arm of a young Sister of Mercy.

'He's deaf and dumb,' she says, 'I found him wandering and brought him here. He will be killed if he stays on the streets.'

The nun's sweet smile is unforgettable. She leads the old man into the darkened restaurant and sits with him through the night.

Once again the door swings open. 'The petrol tanks have been set on fire by the Belgians!' says a man with a big moustache who is the hotel proprietor. 'This is the end.'

From the stairs behind us that lead down into the cellars, comes his elegantly dressed wife, wrapped in furs.

'I am going. I cannot stand it. I shall drive little Marie to Holland. I fear for our child!'

A quick kiss, and she and little Marie flee away through the night towards the Breda Gate and the safety of a village across the Dutch border.

I open the swing-doors and run to the corner of the Avenue de Commerce. Casting a swift glance right and left, I see a panorama of scarlet flames leaping from the Marché aux Souliers (the mediaeval Cobblers' Market) close to the main street. I hear the shrieking rush of one shell after another, any one of which might have fallen where I stood. But I felt as safe and secure as if I had been at home in faraway Australia.

Thursday, 9 October
Refugees leave for Holland and England.

A strange day accompanied by the shriek and whine of shells and shrapnel. The shells sound like millions of mosquitoes on the attack as they whine overhead. High-explosive shells pour down upon the city, deafening, stupefying, until at last, by the very immensity of their noise, they lose their power to affect one.

I listen with annoyance to the creaking of our lift, which makes noises exactly like those of the shrapnel outside. In fact, when I am in my bedroom, and the lift is going up and down, I don't know which noise comes from the ancient lift and which noise comes from shrapnel.

I breakfast in the café, and forget the bombardment.

A waiter brings coffee and I stand at the bar to drink it and look about me. The café has big glass doors onto the street and through these doors I see thousands and thousands of people hurrying past. As time goes on their numbers increase, until they are flowing by in a ceaseless black stream, most of them moving towards Holland and escape.

Men, women, children, nuns, priests, motor cars, carriages, cabs, carts, drays with creaking wheels, trolleys, perambulators. Every species of human being and vehicle goes hurrying past these windows, vehicles laden with terrified human beings and the poor scared animals who do not understand what is happening. A mighty city in flames is being evacuated by a million inhabitants and the hotel cook is calmly making soup in his kitchen.

Thousands of people, a ceaseless black stream, move towards Holland. Among them I see some poor pathetic animals, moving along in bewilderment — a sheep, a dog, a donkey, a cow, a horse. Cows trudge along behind desolate little groups of peasants with their belongings tied up in a big blue-and-white checked tablecloth. Over their heads go the shells and with each fresh shock the vast concourse of fleeing people hurries forward.

It seems to me as though the end of the world must resemble today's events. A huge gun-carriage, crowded with people passes me, twenty feet long, drawn by two great Flemish carthorses. Sitting in the cart with great wood stakes fixed along the edges to keep them from falling out, are several families escaping to Holland. Fathers, mothers, children. Dozens of beautiful dogs, bereft in this final parting with their masters, run wildly back and forth along the road. Belgian Boy Scouts in khaki, with yellow handkerchiefs round their necks, flash past on bicycles. A man pushes a dog-cart with his three children in it, while a dog trots along underneath, his tongue lolling out. A black-robed priest rides by, mounted on a chestnut mare, with a scarlet saddle cloth.

It is a procession of broken hearts, of desolate lives, of blighted hopes, and grim, grey despair. A pall of black smoke hangs from the leaden sky.

Sometimes I find tears streaming down my cheeks, and as they splash on my hands I look at them stupidly. I see a young nun guiding a tottering, white-bearded man who is dumb as well as deaf who can only walk with short, little, halting steps. Is the nun really going to try and get that old man to Holland?

The clock strikes ten. We know the worst. Antwerp is doomed. Nothing can save her, poor, beautiful, historic city that seemed so impregnable. The evacuation goes on but the crowds fleeing northwards are diminishing because some five hundred thousand souls have already departed. The great avenues, with their autumn-yellow trees and white, tall, splendid houses, grow bare and deserted. Over the city creeps an aspect so poignant, so pathetic, that it reminds me of a dying soldier.

All the bright, gay, cheerful, optimistic life of this city that I have grown to love during the weeks that I have spent within her fortifications is dark with despair.

Of the arrival of the Germans there is no longer any doubt, but the question is whether they will set fire to the houses.

I put on my hat and gloves, and go out into the streets.

For the moment the bombardment has ceased entirely. I rush along the Avenue de Commerce, trying to get back to the

Terminus Hotel where my belongings are. I run into three war correspondents with their arms full of bags, overcoats, and umbrellas, and for a moment or two we stand there opposite the Gare Central talking.

It was only last night at seven o'clock that we all dined together at the Terminus Hotel. We all have amazing tales and fling out disjointed remarks.

'How are you going to get away?'

'And you, how will *you* get away?'

A tall, slight young man with a moustache, Mr. Jeffries, also on the staff of *The Daily Mail* has been staying at the Hotel de l'Europe. With him is Mr. Perry Robinson of *The Times* and Mr. P. Phillips of *The Daily News*.

Mr. Jeffries tells me. 'There is not a ghost of a hope. We must get away at once.'

'I'm not going,' I say. In vain they argue and tell me I am mad to stay. I give Jeffries of *The Daily Mail* the story I have written to take back to London. Then they say goodbye.

Louise's report about the torching of Aerschot and the siege of Antwerp appeared on the front page of *The Daily Mail* on 3 September and the editor of the paper claimed that it as 'one of the finest pieces of war journalism ever written'.[24] Readers were told that Mrs Creed had chosen to remain in Antwerp, now in German hands. Fears were voiced she might be shot by the Germans as a British spy. Louise was unaware that all over Britain people were discussing her courage in remaining in Belgium to obtain information for her newspaper.

Friday, 10 October 1914

All hope of defending the city is over. Antwerp has surrendered and the Germans are coming.

'Well,' says Monsieur Lucien to Arthur Jones, in a discussion between him, Frank Fox and myself, 'As you have decided to stay, I'll give you this key. It belongs to the house of some wealthy Belgians who have fled to England. There is plenty of food and you might take shelter there.'

He gave me the key and the address and tells me to remember it.

With a lump in my throat, I stand on the hotel door-step, watching the English journalists on their bicycles whirl away down the Avenue de Commerce. They were swallowed up in the black pall of cloud and smoke that hung above the city.

I am alone in the ill-fated city.

I realised that I could go ahead with my plans without causing anyone distress.

Turning back into the big, dimly lit deserted restaurant, I went to look for the *patronne*, the sister of the owner. Her eyes widened in surprise at me, a war correspondent in a dark blue suit with a white veil floating from my little black hat.

'*Eh bien, Madame*! They told me *les deux Anglais* have departed. Why are you not with them?'

'Madame! I need help. I have stayed on to write about the war. Seeing the Germans arrive in Antwerp is a sight I must not miss. I must stay!'

'*Mais, c'est tres dangereux, Madame! Vous êtes Anglaise!*'

'Well, right now I'm *Belgian*. I need to pretend I'm a servant in your hotel. I'll put on a cap and apron, do anything you like; and I'll be able to see for myself. It'll only be for a few hours. I'll get away this afternoon by motor car but I must see the arrival of the Germans before I go!'

The old woman seemed too bewildered to protest.

Just at that moment Henri, my loyal Belgian friend and chauffeur, drove up and stopped the car in front of the Hotel Wagner, looking more dead than alive. His face was hollow, his lips were dry, his eyes staring and he was so exhausted he could scarcely step out of the car.

'Sorry I'm late,' he groaned, '*C'etait impossible, vraiment impossible.*'

'You needn't worry about me, Henri,' I whispered to him reassuringly. 'I'm not going to try to get out of Antwerp for several hours. I'm staying to see the Germans enter!'

Henri showed no surprise.

'*Bon!*' he said. 'To tell you the truth, Madame, I couldn't go out of the city again. Reaching Holland,' he went on, between gasps as he drank one cup of coffee after another, 'is like trying to get through Hell. I've been seven hours driving four miles. All the roads are blocked. A million people out there, struggling, fighting, and trying to get to Holland,…some dying on the road.'

And with that Henri sat down, put his head on the table and fell fast asleep.

The sharp crack of rifle fire woke him. We rushed to the door to see what was happening.

A nerve-racking sight! Across the square, through the grey of early morning, dogs were rushing, their tongues hanging out with thirst. The gendarmes pursuing them were shooting them down to save them from starvation that would overtake them if they were left alive in the deserted city at the mercy of the Germans.

Madame Lenore, a sad, distinguished-looking woman, a homeless refugee from the bombardment of Liege, whose house had been shelled and left roofless implored Henri to take her old mother in his car to the nearest hospital. [Louise is careful not to cite the full names of her Belgian friends in case the Germans identify and shoot them for collaborating with a British journalist.]

Madame Lenore says 'My mother is eighty-four and ill. We tried to take her to Holland, but it was impossible. Now the bombardment has ceased it seems wiser to remain. In the hospital my mother will surely be safe! As for my husband and I, having lost everything, there is nothing left to fear!'

I offer to take Madame Leonore's mother to the hospital. We climb into the car, Henri and I, and the elderly Flemish woman and the family servant, young Jeanette.

In the Marché aux Souliers — putting out the fires

We drove along the Avenue de Commerce, down the Avenue de Kaiser, towards the hospital. Not a soul to be seen. The Marché aux Souliers was still burning and the magnificent Taverne Royale only a pile of rubble on the ground. Next to it was the Hotel de l'Europe, bomb-shattered and imposing even in its ruined state. I thought of Mr. Jeffries of the *Daily Mail* and shivered; he had been staying in this shattered building. The air reeked of petrol and acrid smoke.

At last we got to the hospital. The door-step is covered with blood. As I went in, an unforgettable sight met my eyes. In the great, dim ward, with the beds full of wounded and dying soldiers; as I enter, a white-robed Sister of Mercy was bending over a bed, giving the last rites to a dying man. All the civilian nurses had fled. Only the Sisters of Mercy remained.

Death held no terrors for these women in their white robes. Trained nurses, devoted as they undoubtedly were, had left the city, either accompanying patients or in fear of the Huns' brutality to unprotected females.

The Sisters of Mercy showed no fear. The Cross stood between them and anything that might happen to them. Madame Lenore's mother is given a bed in a ward full of children.

'*Les pauvres petites!*' said one of the sisters, 'They've been left behind; there's no one to claim them, so we brought them here to look after them.' [Louise was shown about 40 children, varying from six months to five years.]

Out of the hospital again, over the blood-stained door-step, and back into the car with Henri. There were a few devoted doctors and priests standing about in silence outside the entrance to the hospital, waiting for the Germans to arrive, standing there in their white coats and long black cassocks, staring down the passage. A great hush hung over everything, and through the hush we slid into the ruined streets with the rubble of beautiful houses around us on the ground and the shriek of shells.

Before we had gone far, we heard shouts, and turning my head I discovered wounded soldiers, limping along begging us to give them a lift towards the boat. We filled the car with wounded soldiers. Bandaged heads and faces were all around me, more bandaged soldiers rode on the foot-board, clinging to the door handles as we moved towards the quay. It was heartbreaking to have to deny room to scores of limping, broken men who shouted to us to stop. As soon as we had deposited one load we went back and picked up others and ran them back to the quay. We did this time after time. A few of the men were our British Tommies, but most were Belgian.

Backwards and forwards we rushed. Henri's eyes were shining, his sallow face lit up, he no longer looked tired but afire with excitement. And still the car raced like mad backwards and forwards, backwards and forwards, venturing right to the forts and back again to the quay. But eventually tiredness overtook him and Henri was obliged to drive the car back to the hotel, where he fell asleep, his head resting on a table in the restaurant.

As we came in *la patronne* (the owner's elderly sister) handed me a note.

'While you were out,' she said, looking at me sorrowfully, 'M. Fox and M. Jones returned on bicycles to look for you.'

I read Frank Fox's kind message.

'We have managed to secure passages on a special military boat for Flushing and London that leaves at half-past eleven — we have a place for you. We have come back for you, but you are not here. I hope you will be all right. You have seen the bombardment through. Bravo!'

I was glad they had got away. But an irresistible force held me to Antwerp. I slipped quietly out of the hotel and made a solitary walk.

The last steamer had departed from the port. The last of the fleeing inhabitants had departed by the Breda Gate. All that was left was the empty city, waiting for the German army to arrive. Hundreds of deserted motor cars were heaped at the water's edge, useless as perambulators, because there was no petrol to move them. When the dogs ceased howling, there was only silence.

I seemed to be only living being left. I passed hundreds of stately homes, all shattered and locked, silent and deserted. I looked up and down the paralysed quays, through the yellow avenues of trees. For weeks, for months, I had seen thousands of people laughing and talking in these streets. And yesterday, and the day before, I had seen them fleeing for their lives — out of reach of the shells and the Germans.

And I wondered where they were now, those five hundred thousand ghosts. Were they still tramping the long road to Holland? Why had I not gone with the rest of them?

I had loved other European cities — Florence, Ravenna, Verona, Venice, Rome, London — and my home town of Sydney. But Antwerp I loved most because she let me share her sufferings.

Suddenly, through the lull, I heard heavy, dragging steps. Looking up a side-street opposite the burning ruins of the Chaussée de Souliers, I saw two Belgian soldiers, limping along, making for the Breda Gate. Both were wounded, and the one who was the least wounded was helping the other. They were hollow-cheeked, hollow-eyed, half-starved, and the ravages of smoke and gun powder all over their faded blue uniforms. They were dazed, worn-out, famished, nearly fainting.

But as they hurried past me the younger one asked, 'Is the city captured?'

It sounded like a line from the pages of Homer, so epic, so immensely tragic.

I ran forward and walked beside the men. I offered my arm to the younger soldier, who took it mechanically, without thanking me. We hastened through the greyness along the Avenue de Commerce, towards the Breda Gate and neither of my companions said a word. Sometimes, without speaking, one of them would turn his head and look backwards at the red flames reflected in the black sky to northward.

Suddenly, to our amazement, we saw a cart coming down a side-street, containing a man and a little girl. I ran towards it, terrified lest it should pass, but the man in the cart had halted for the wounded soldiers and offered to take me too.

'*Quick, quick, mes amis!*' he said. 'The Germans are coming in at the other end of the city! The *petite* here was lost, and thanks to *le Bon Dieu* I have just found her. This is why I'm so late.'

10 October — German troops enter Antwerp

I am back at the Hotel Wagner. My watch says it is half-past one. But all the clocks on public buildings in Antwerp have stopped due to the shelling and their hands point to a dozen different times.

The owner's sister gave Louise a maid's uniform and employed her because they were shorthanded as many staff had fled. What Louise did not know is that the owner feared the Germans would shoot him as a traitor if they found a foreigner disguised as a maid in his hotel. She started serving the remaining guests — Henri, Monsieur and Madame Lenore, the unnamed refugees from Lierre and their maidservant, Jeanette, plus the proprietor and his sister, his two little grandchildren, their father, the porter, and a couple of elderly Belgians who seemed to belong to nobody in particular.

> What seems extraordinary is that there is any food left in the beleaguered city! Suddenly the waiter cries out from the far side of the restaurant: *'Les Boches!'*
>
> We all spring to our feet, petrified. Through the uncurtained windows of the hotel we see one grey figure, and then another, walking along the side-path up the Avenue de Commerce. After a moment's hesitation M. Claude, the proprietor, and his elderly sister move out into the street. We follow as if afraid to be left alone.

'My Son the Soldier'
And now through the livid sunless silences of the deserted city, still reeking of gunpowder, shrapnel and burning petrol, the Germans are coming down the Avenue de Commerce — a long line of foot-soldiers and men on horses with pink roses or carnations in their grey tunics.

> Suddenly, a baker's cart dashes across the road wheeled by a poor old Belgian woman, whose face is contorted by grief. I whisper as she passes close to me:
>
> 'Is somebody ill in your cart?'
>
> Without stopping, her eyes full of despair, she mutters: 'Dead! My son! He was a soldier' and points at the shattered corpse. Then she hurries on to find a spot where she can bury her beloved son before the Germans take possession of the city.
>
> All along the Avenue de Commerce, on the grey pavements, are little groups of Belgians from Antwerp.
>
> Am I dreaming? Or are those people *smiling* at the Germans?

To my horror, I see two old men waving gaily to that long grey line of soldiers and horses. A young woman flings a posy of flowers to an officer, who catches them.

Along the Avenue the grey uniforms slowly march past, headed by fair, blue-eyed, arrogant officers on splendid roan horses, and the clang and clatter of hooves breaks the silence. The Germans wear pink roses, or carnations or have pink flowers wreathed about their horses' harness or round their gun-carriages and the lorries carrying provisions. It is obvious that the enormous buildings of Antwerp, and its wealth take away their breath. They cannot quite understand how they come to be in possession of this rich and beautiful city.

They look left and right, their blue eyes full of curiosity. I think of Bismarck's remark about London: 'What a city to loot!' the same remark Napoleon made as he advanced on Moscow. The same thought [strikes] these thousands of Germans as they take possession of Antwerp. Suddenly without warning they burst into song.

To see this beautiful city possessed by Germans is terrible. Standing there in the beautiful Avenue de Commerce, I weep. I have lived for weeks among the Belgians and respect their courage.

I stand in the Avenue du Commerce with tears rolling down my cheeks, watching the passage of the grey uniforms. Looking up, I see a young Prussian officer laugh as he rides by. He laughs again and looks away, looks back and rides on, still laughing at the Belgians, weeping over the destruction of the city.

Germans on parade in the Grand Place and Belgian Traitors
I see people gathering round the Germans as they halt at the end of the Avenue, Belgians stroke horses' heads, and old men and young men smile and bow.

A group of grey-clad officers hurry towards the Hotel Wagner and begin parleying with Monsieur Claude, the proprietor. I expected to see him turn icy and refuse to receive them. But to my surprise *le patron* seems affable. He smiles, is eager, deferential and friendly even to the point of fawning over them. Turning, he flings open the doors with a bow, and in a few minutes German soldiers are crowding into his restaurant.

Cries of '*Bier, bitte*' resounded on all sides.

A few minutes later, inside the restaurant I witness extraordinary encounters between German officers and Belgian spies. I hear the clink of gold, and see the handing over of German bank notes, and watch the flushed faces of Antwerp men who are offering note-books to the German officers, drinking beer with them, to the accompaniment of raucous laughter.

Outside, on the walls of the Theatre Flamand, the Huns are posting notices in Flemish and French, warning the inhabitants their city will be destroyed if any resistance is shown. The notices tell the inhabitants of Antwerp that 'The German Army is in your town as a conqueror. None of your citizens will be disturbed and proprieties respected on condition you abstain from hostile acts. Any resistance will be punished according to the laws of war and can lead to the destruction of your beautiful town'.

Disguised as a Belgian peasant in a large blue-and-red check apron with a black shawl over my shoulders, my hair twisted into a little knot on the back of my head and a checked handkerchief under my chin [I am working] in the restaurant. I busy myself washing and drying glasses behind the counter.

The restaurant is a splendid observation point. But sometimes the soapy beer glasses nearly fell from my fingers, so agonising were the sights on the afternoon of Friday, October 9th. Old men and young men crowd round the Germans, sit at tables with them drinking, laughing, and showing them information in their note-books, which the Germans examine. These were Belgians who had been spying for the Germans and were now seeking financial reward.

Louise saw three men, who seemed familiar, sitting at a table with three German officers. With a shock, she realised these were the three alleged British Marines who had called at the hotel the previous day. Thinking they were English she had asked them to restrain their dog, who was trying to attack the cockatoo she had rescued. They told her in perfect English they were serving with the English Flying Corps and never for a minute had she suspected they were German spies. Now she saw them (still wearing their British uniforms) laughing and drinking and talking faultless German. Obviously, they had stolen English uniforms and were trying to obtain British secrets. Antwerp had become a nest of German spies.

> Two priests have been brought in as prisoners (the Germans are convinced that Belgian priests allowed snipers to climb their church towers to shoot at them, as happened in the Franco-Prussian war). None of the prisoners are handcuffed. They look as if they are free. It is difficult to realise the truth—one move towards the door and they will be shot down like dogs!
>
> The invading Germans make themselves as charming as possible. Obviously these are their orders and Germans *always* obey orders. Extraordinary indeed is the discipline that can turn the former brutes of Louvain and Aerschot into the lamb-like beings that took possession of Antwerp.
>
> Almost the first thing some Germans did was to find the piano. Strains of German music are heard and the Germans burst into song to the music of 'The Blue Danube' and the German song 'Wacht am Rhein'.
>
> About four o'clock, Jeanette, Madame Lenore's maid, whispers that Henri wants to speak to me in the kitchen.
>
> 'A great misfortune, Madame!' said Henri, agitatedly. 'The Germans have seized my car. I shall not be able to take you away from Antwerp this afternoon. *Courage!* To-morrow I will find a cart or a *fiacre*. To-day it is impossible to do anything, there is not a vehicle of any kind to be had. But to-morrow, Madame, trust me to get you away, never fear!'
>
> Half an hour after he reappears looking miserable.
>
> 'The Germans have shut the gates all round the city. No one is allowed to go in and out without a German passport!' he said.
>
> This was serious. As dusk fell and the lights were lit, I retired into the kitchen and busied myself cutting bread and butter, and continuing my observations. On the table lay piles of sausage, and presently in came two German officers, an old grey-bearded General, and a dashing young Uhlan (cavalry) lieutenant.

'We want three eggs each,' said the Uhlan officer roughly, addressing himself to me. 'Three eggs, soft boiled, and bread with butter, *und viel* (much) butter!'

I nodded but dared not answer.

The red-faced young Lieutenant, thinking I did not understand him, ground his heel angrily, and muttered *'Liebe Gott! Eine Dumkopf!'*

But when he saw the sausages on his plate his expression changed.

'Wurst?' he exclaimed. *'Wunderbar!'*

The soldiers bent over that German sausage, their eyes bulging with greed and delight.

Saturday, 10 October 1914 (evening)
The saddest thing in Antwerp is the howling of the dogs. Thousands have been left shut in the houses when their owners fled, and all day and night these poor creatures utter desolate cries that grow louder and more piercing as time goes on.

Strange things have happened. When I went to my door just now, I found it locked from the outside. I tried the other door. That is locked, too. What does it mean?

Here I am in a little room about twelve feet by six, with a window looking on to the back wall of one of the Antwerp theatres. I hear the sounds of cannonading going on in the distance, but the noise within the hotel is so loud as to deaden the sounds of battle. Germans are running up and down the corridors, shouting, singing, stamping, and the pianos are going, too.

Nobody comes near me. I knock at both the doors gently, for I am afraid to draw attention to myself. Nobody answers. The old woman and the two little children have left the room on my right, the old man has left the room on my left. I am all alone in this little den. I dress as well as I can, but the room is tiny, there are no facilities for making one's *toilette*. I have to do without washing my face.

I lie down on my mattress and wonder what is going to happen. Hour after hour goes by. In a corner of the room I discover an outdated English newspaper with an account of the fighting. Lying there, I read strange stories. German soldiers claim to the Belgians they never wanted war. It was the English who wanted war not them, the wicked English who had made the first attack. How twisted truth becomes in wartime.

Voices outside my room reach me from the corridor.

Two elderly Belgians are talking.

'*Ce sont les Anglais qui ne veulent fas rendre les forts!*' says one implying the fault lies with the English who do not want to surrender the forts but fight to the bitter end. Fighting continues as the Tommies have refused to give up.

My head aches! I am hungry; and the booming of those big guns and the whining of so many shells make my head ache even more. I am weary of fighting. Anything for peace, for an end to terror and that soul-racking thunderous noise.

I am so tired. I have not slept for five nights, and feel as if I shall never sleep again.

It's five o'clock and darkness has set in.

Nobody has been near me, I'm still here, locked up in this little room.

I roam about like a caged animal and look out of the tiny window. The blank back wall of the Antwerp Theatre meets my eye. I see three tiers of windows facing me and hastily move away. All those rooms house Germans. What if they glance down here and discover me? I pull the curtains over my window, and move back into the room.

It is Saturday afternoon, October 10, 1914, and all of a sudden I realise that it is my birthday. Lying there on the bare mattress, on this dreary October day when the Germans have conquered this magnificent city, I realise I am in danger. If the Germans capture me I will be shot.

I lie there in the darkness, forgetful of time and hunger, until I hear voices in the next room. The old woman opens my door, and two golden-haired children stare at me curiously. The old woman gives me some grapes out of a basket and a glass of water.

'*Ma pauvre enfant!*' she says. 'I am sorry I can bring no food, but the Germans are up and down the stairs all day long, and I dare not risk them asking me, "Who is that food for?"

'What has happened? Please, tell me the truth.'

'*Alors, Madame.* You recollect that German officer who leaned over the counter for a long time when you were washing glasses?'

'Yes'.

'He said to me "That young woman never speaks!" '

'Who did he mean?'

'*Madame,* he meant you!'

My lips turn dry because a German soldier has noticed me. It is absurd.

I force a smile.

'Perhaps you imagined it,' I said.

'No, today he asked me "*Where* is that girl who never speaks?"

'What did you tell him?'

'She is deaf. She does not hear what is said when *anyone* speaks to her!'

'So *that's* why you locked me up.'

'*C'est ca,* Madame. My brother, *le patron,* ordered it. He is afraid. And now, Madame, good-night. I must put the little girls to bed.'

'How long am I to stay here?'

She pushed the girl out of my room with the intention of locking me in again. But just then someone knocked at the outer door.

It was Madame Lenore the refugee from Liege, who came in, drawing the bolt behind her. I looked in her weary face, with its white hair, and beautiful eyes and saw sympathy and sincerity.

She said, 'My husband has been talking in the restaurant with a friend of his, a Danish doctor, a Red Cross doctor, he is sorry for you, Madame, and he thinks he can help you to escape! He wants to come to see you for a moment.'

'Will you bring him up,' I said.

There was a gentle tap at the door. Madame Lenore and the Danish doctor entered. The doctor was a young fair-haired man with blue eyes, he seemed kind and sincere [and was] wearing the Red Cross badge on his arm. I told myself he was to be trusted.

In perfect English he said, 'I heard there was an English lady here who wants to get away from Antwerp?'

I interrupted 'Please don't speak English! The Germans are up and down the corridor. They may hear!'

He smiled at my fears, but switched to French to reassure me.

'No, no, Madame! You mustn't be alarmed. The Germans are too busy to think of anything else. I want to help you. Your Queen Alexandra is Danish and has kept the bonds close between Denmark and England. If you will agree to pass as my sister I can get a pass for you from the Danish Consul which will enable you to leave Antwerp in safety.'

'May I see your papers?' I asked. 'I am sure you are sincere. But I would like to see your papers.'

'Certainly!' He brought out his papers and I saw that he was Danish, working under the Red Cross for the Belgians.

Having examined his papers I let him examine mine.

'And now I must ask you one thing,' he said. 'Your passport. I want to show it to my Consul, in order to convince him that you are of British nationality. I am afraid that without the passport my Consul may object.'

I had been told a hundred times by a hundred different people that the one thing one should never do, under *any* circumstances, was to part with one's passport. And here was this Dane pleading for mine, promising me escape if I would give it. I looked up at him as he stood there, tall and grave. I was not quite sure of him because he had spoken English and I still thought that handing over my passport was a dangerous thing to do. I stood there breathless, stupefied, trying to think. Madame Lenore watched me in silence.

'Well, I shall trust you,' I said slowly, and put my passport into his hands.

His face lit up and in that agony of doubt, I told myself that he was genuine.

'*Madame*, thank you for trusting me!'

He bent and kissed my hand and put the passport in his pocket. 'To-morrow at three o'clock I will come here for you. Trust me. I will arrange a peasant's cart or a *fiacre*, and will myself accompany you to the Dutch borders. *Courage*—you will soon be in safety!'

Ten minutes after he had gone Monsieur Claude, the proprietor burst into the room.

His face was working with rage.

'What is this you have done?' he cried in a hoarse voice. *'Le Danois parle avec les Allemands dans le restaurant!'*

'It's not true,' I cried. 'It can't be true.'

'The Dane is talking to the Germans in the restaurant,' he repeated. Clearly I was endangering his business. He flung on the table some English papers I had entrusted to him to hide for me. 'Take these! I have nothing more to do with you. You are my sister's concern.'

I seized him by the arm. But he flung me off and left the room. It was clear now. That Danish doctor had gone down to the restaurant to betray me with the evidence of my passport. What a fool I had been! My folly had led me into this trap. At any moment now the Germans would come for me. With my passport in their possession. I could deny nothing.

I barricaded the door with a chair and looking in the glass saw a white face gazing at me in the mirror. 'Prepare yourself! You cannot hope to escape, it's imprisonment or death!'

I lay down on the mattress and was so tired I knew no more, till a knocking at my door awoke me, and I saw it was morning. A light was filtering through the window blind.

I jumped up, fully dressed, having fallen asleep in my clothes.

'Madame!' whispered a voice. *'Ouvrez la porte, toute suite.'* It was the sister of the *patron*.

I pulled away the barricading chair, and let her in.

Over her shoulder I saw a man. It was not a German but dear Henri, my friendly Belgian chauffeur, in a grey suit with a white-and-black handkerchief round his neck.

Behind him were the two little girls.

'Quick, quick!' breathed the old woman, 'you must go, Madame, at once! My brother is frightened; he refuses to have you here any longer. He is terrified lest the Germans should discover that he has been allowing an Englishwoman to hide here!'

She threw the apron on me, and hurriedly tied it behind me, then brought out the black shawl and flung it round my shoulders. Then she picked up the blue-and-white check scarf lying on the table, and nodded to me to tie it over my head.

'You must go at once, leave everything behind you. We will see about your things afterwards. You must pass as Henri's wife. There! Take his arm! And you, Henri, take one of the little girls by the hand! And you, madame, you take the other. There! *Courage, madame*. Oh, my poor child, I am sorry for you!'

She kissed me, and pushed me out of the room.

Next moment, hanging on to Henri's arm, I found myself in the corridor walking towards the staircase.

'*Courage!*' whispered Henri in my ear.

Suddenly I ceased to be myself; I became Henri's wife. These little girls were mine. I leaned on Henri, and clutched the little girl's fingers. I felt utterly unafraid. I became the woman I was supposed to be. And in that new personality I walked down the wide staircase with my husband and my children, passing dozens of German officers who were running up and down the stairs. They moved aside to let us pass, the poor peasant, his anxious wife, the two children with flowing golden hair.

The hall below was crowded with Germans. I saw their florid faces and grey uniforms. But I was a peasant, a little Belgian peasant. Fear had fled and the sight of the sunlight as we reached the street was reassuring.

'*Courage, madame,*' whispered Henri.

'Call me Louise!' I whispered. 'Where are we going?'

'To the house of a friend.'

We turned the corner and crossed the street. Everywhere there were Germans, seated in the cafés, in motor cars, looking as if the Germans had lived there forever.

We entered a café. I clutched Henri's arm. The place was full of German soldiers, seated at little tables and drinking beer and coffee.

'Take no notice of them,' whispered Henri. 'Trust me.'

We walked through the restaurant arm in arm, with the little girls clinging to our hands.

'My wife has arrived from Brussels,' announced Henri in a loud voice to the proprietor.

'How are things in Brussels, *madame?*' enquired an elderly Belgian. [Louise spoke French, but feared that her Australian accent would betray her to the Germans.]

I pretended not to hear him and followed Henri through the little hall at the far end of the café. I found myself in a big kitchen, introduced to a tall dark haired woman called Ada. Her eyes were swimming with tears, she came towards me, her arms open.

'Oh, poor *madame,*' she said. 'I told Henri to bring you here. You are safe with me. We are from Luxembourg. We *hate* the Germans. I have sent my two little ones away to England for safety.'

In the big featherbed in the spare bedroom of Ada's house I did my best to sleep. My windows looked out on a long narrow street of empty houses and from those houses came louder and louder the sounds of imprisoned dogs howling. Their cries were terrible, they were starving and perishing of thirst and through all that noise the Germans slept. They made no attempt to give them food and water. They were to be left there to die. Hour after hour, I buried my head in the pillow but I could not shut out those awful sounds, they penetrated everything. The dogs were giving up, they could suffer no longer. They understood at last that mankind, the friend who had received all their faith and love, was deserting them. They howled and cried. They shivered, shrieked and wailed but all in vain. It was the most awful night of my life.[25]

Thanks to the bravery of Henri and Ada, the sister of the hotel owner and Monsieur and Madame Lenore, Louise was not arrested by the Gerns and shot as a spy.[26]

Louise and Madame Lenore and her husband spent five days hiding in the deserted Belgian home whose key she had been given by the Belgian journalist Monsieur Lucien.

Then she was smuggled over the Belgian-Dutch border in Henri's car. Louise wore dark glasses and a headscarf and did her best to resemble Madame Lenore, whose passport she had been loaned so she could cross the Belgian-Dutch border.

Louise and Henri crossed the border without any difficulty, driving through neutral Holland, where she saw over a thousand Belgian refugees whose homes had been torched camping in the forests in tents supplied by the Dutch authorities. These refugees had lost everything they owned when the Germans burned down their houses. The mayors of Dutch towns near the Belgian border established soup kitchens to feed the penniless refugees and supply them with second-hand clothes.

The terrible sights she had witnessed in Belgium made Louise determined to repay the courage of the Belgians and to give the Belgian Red Cross any money earned from her account of the invasion of Belgium by the Germans and their atrocities.

The Danish doctor Louise feared had betrayed her to the Germans still had her British passport. In fact he had *not* betrayed her and was merely chatting to the Germans to allay their suspicions. On learning Louise had left Antwerp, he sent her passport to London through the Red Cross and eventually the British Foreign Office returned it to Louise who, by that time, had become famous after her newspaper article was published.

From Holland, Louise was driven by friends of Henri, the chauffeur, to the French port of Dunkirk. There she watched with fascination as German and British planes attacked each other before catching a ferry to Dover.

It was the end of October 1914, when worn out from lack of sleep and stress, Louise arrived in London. She was welcomed by the editors and staff of *The Daily Mail*, who had feared she was dead. Louise was thrilled to find that her despatch from Antwerp had made her an overnight celebrity.[27]

Fisher Unwin, the publishers of two of Louise's earlier novels, *The World is Round* and *An Australian Girl in London*, realised that her war story would be very popular. She had no money and no clothes and no home to return to so Fisher Unwin provided a generous advance so she could live in a hotel and write a book to be titled *A Woman's Adventures in the Great War*.

But Louise was exhausted and writing was not easy. She was haunted by nightmares of burning towns, sobbing people and the howls of deserted dogs. She shut herself away in a hotel bedroom, wrote day and night and told Amy (who had arrived in London with her husband) that she needed to take a holiday.

Louise left her manuscript with Amy — who had been editor of the Children's Section of the *Sydney Morning Herald* — to give it a final check. Amy complained that Louise's manuscript was full of grammatical errors and spelling mistakes and was filled with hatred of the Germans.

A Woman's Adventures in the Great War was published in 1915 and became a runaway best seller. Amy insisted that some of the success of Louise's book was due to the fact she (Amy) had edited it. Ever since Jack Creed had preferred Louise to her, she had been jealous of her elder sister. Both of them were writers, but Amy's bush tales, though popular with children, were never going to obtain the kind of success Louise's war memoir received.

Louise's account of German atrocities was vindicated in recent years by historians detailing the atrocities inflicted on Belgian civilians by the Germans. Her war memoir has been republished in several American anthologies of war literature and it was used as support material by the Boyce Commission into German Atrocities in World War One, convened by the British Prime Minister.

Backed by the support of the Northcliffe press, Louise gave fund-raising talks to raise money for the Red Cross as they, as well as the Quakers, were the only organisations providing aid relief to war victims. Her interest in the work of the Red Cross dated from the time of that initial meeting with Major Livingstone Seaman, head of the American Aid Services, at the Hotel Terminus in Antwerp.

Louise, always warm-hearted, was suffering from what we now call 'survivor guilt', haunted by her memories of Belgian suffering. From Major Livingstone Seaman and other friends in the Red Cross she learned that Belgian families under the German occupation were starving. their harvests, their farm equipment and their cars confiscated and sent to Germany.

This information made Louise donate the major share of her royalties from *A Woman's Experiences in the Great War* to the Red Cross fund for Belgian war relief and to Belgian refugees in England. Amy regarded her sister, who now had no home, husband or savings, as sentimental and impractical in giving away the greater part of her royalties.

Late in 1915, Louise returned to Sydney on the troopship *Malawa* and received a warm welcome, mainly due to the success of her war memoir. The family home in Neutral Bay had been sold and her mother, now totally blind, lived with a companion (paid for by Sid Mack) in a small unit in which there was no room for Louise.

Alice, Florence and Amy, all married and affluent, also thought Louise mad to have donated her royalties to the Belgians. Amy claimed if her sister had any sense she would have bought a house in London or Sydney. Louise infuriated Amy by claiming money was unimportant. She insisted her time in London and Tuscany had given her experiences money could not buy. Louise claimed life was what mattered rather than owning an expensive home in the suburbs, another dig at Amy.

To raise more funds for Belgian refugees and those suffering under the German occupation, and to sell more copies of *A Woman's Experiences in the Great War*, Louise travelled to Melbourne and other Australian cities and gave talks about her war experiences. Next she visited remote parts of the Australian outback talking about her book and raising more funds.

Then she travelled to New Zealand to tour the country and raise funds for the Red Cross. In the city of Wellington Louise was aided by Captain Allen Leyland, a well-educated young Anzac veteran whose lungs had been damaged by a German gas attack in northern France. Captain Leyland, having been invalided out of the Army, was now a volunteer helper with the Red Cross. Louise discovered that Allen Leyland, the son of an Auckland lawyer, had similar tastes for books, music and art to her own. Although there was a large age difference, they soon fell in love with each other.

As far as Louise was aware, she was still legally married to Jack Creed, so marrying Allen was out of the question. After touring together for some years, during which Allen acted as Louise's manager, they set up house together in Melbourne. Meanwhile Louise kept quiet about their relationship to her family.

In 1924, Louise received the death certificate of Jack Creed and learned that her husband had been dead for 10 years. The confirmation of Jack's death made it possible for Louise to marry Captain Allen Leyland. The wedding took place in September 1924, but it took Louise more than four years before she introduced her second husband to her family, which was typical of Louise's secretive nature.

Louise's conventional sisters expected to be introduced to an elderly husband. They were amazed to find that Louise, in her late 40s, with her good looks gone, but still vivacious and amusing, had married a very handsome man 21 years younger than herself.

In spite of their initial disapproval of such a disparate union, Louise's sisters soon found they liked Allen very much. In spite of the difference in their ages, Louise and Allen lived together — hard up but happy — in a series of inexpensive rented homes in Chatswood and Mosman. Allen did all the housework and Louise wrote and lectured for a living. Most Australians deeply distrusted foreign foods, but Louise cooked Italian food from recipes the cook at Settignano had taught her. Her siblings wondered how she could bear to settle in shabby accommodation in Chatswood (and later in Mosman) having lived somewhere as beautiful as the *Villa di Doccia*. When Louise came to live in Mosman, snobbish Amy was horrified that her Mosman friends might meet the bohemian Louise.

At Christmas 1931, Allen's damaged lungs filled with fluid and he was fighting for his life. Although Louise nursed him devotedly, Allen died in July 1932, leaving his wife broken hearted. It turned out that Allen Leyland had been the Great Love Louise had dreamed of and she would never love another man.

In 1934, Louise, in an attempt to earn money, wrote a novel for girls, called *Teens Triumphant*. Unfortunately, the book's publisher,

'Inky Stephenson', went broke, so Louise made nothing from it. The following year, in another attempt to make money, she dashed off a sentimental romance called *A Maiden's Prayer*, which was published, but Amy mocked unmercifully.

Louise's other sisters, Alice and Florence, had successful husbands and expensive homes. Alice lived in Clifton Gardens and Florence in Mosman near Amy's home. Sid Mack, now a well-known criminal barrister, adored Louise and, unlike Amy, was always happy to see her. Amy, by now a widow, complained that Louise was eccentric, wore bohemian clothes, had 'modern' ideas on love and marriage and larded her conversation with Italian phrases. To annoy Amy, Louise would arrive unasked at her sister's elegant bridge evenings, dressed in flowing skirts and hoop earrings, looking like a gypsy.

In her 60s and still short of money, Louise was on occasions asked to write articles for *The Bulletin* and *The Australian Women's Weekly*. Louise confided to a journalist on *The Women's Weekly*, who asked about her time in Florence, that D'Annunzio was 'a vile seducer'. She related intimate details about him, including how many hand-made suits and pairs of shoes the famous writer had in his bedroom at *Villa della Capponcina*. By the time she made this statement D'Annunzio had been discredited for his support of Mussolini and his reputation as a writer and poet had diminished.

At the age of only 65, Louise died from cerebro-vascular disease, the same disease that had killed her father and her brother Sid. Louise's sisters discovered that, at the time of her death, she was virtually penniless and they had to pay for her funeral and cremation. When disposing of her few possessions they found Louise's declaration to the Registrar of Births, Marriages and Deaths, which disclosed that she had 'one child still living', which shocked her sister.

In her final years Louise had mentioned to her niece, Nancy Creaghe (later Mrs Phelan), that her life had been a success and thanks to Allen Leyland she had experienced the great love affair she had dreamed about as a girl. This was more important to her than any amount of possessions or money in the bank.

⁂

POST SCRIPTUM.

In the summer of 1996, while in Florence on a Churchill Fellowship, I and my husband met the English author and lecturer Rupert Hodson, who lived at Bellosguardo on the other side of Florence from Settignano. Rupert's neighbour, Joan Haslip, the biographer of Empress Josephine, Marie Antoinette and Emperor Maximilian of Austria, had died at Bellosguardo two years previously, appointing Rupert as her literary executor. He told us how he had found Louise's notebook among her papers and a copy of the lease on *Villa di Doccia*, signed by D'Annunzio's agent Bernardo Palmiere, citing Louise Creed as the designated tenant of the villa, proof of a connection between them.

Rupert told us that Joan Haslip had leased the *Villa de Doccia* in the 1970s.[28] Haslip had kept the copy of the lease and Louise's notebook as they could be useful were she to write a biography of D'Annunzio. After Haslip's death, her papers were sorted and catalogued by Rupert and passed to his wife, Lorna Sage, who, as Professor of English Literature at the University of East Anglia, was compiling a reference book on female writers for Cambridge University Press.

Left and above: Louise Mack as a trainee journalist working in Sydney in the 1890s. Courtesy the Manuscript Dept. National Library, Canberra, and a private collection.

Below: In Florence, Louise rented an apartment overlooking the Arno and the Ponte Veccio.
Private collection.

Gabriele D'Annunzio at the
Villa della Capponcina.

Villa di Doccia, Settignano, rented
by Louisa Mack.
Photo Laura Maggini of Florence

When German soldiers entered Antwerp after bombing the city, Louise recorded most Belgians looked angry while a few of them who had been collaborators actually welcomed the German soldiers. Photo private collection.

Enid Burnell (Lyons)

CHAPTER 8

Trailblazing Women in Politics

Margaret Ogg (1863–1953)
Emma Miller (1879–1913)
Vida Goldstein (1869–1949)
Edith Cowan (1861–1932)
Irene Longman (1877–1964)
Dame Enid Burnell Lyons (1897–1981)
The Right Hon. Julia Gillard (born 1961)

Women will never give up the struggle for the right to vote and sit in Parliament. Margaret Ogg.

Julia Gillard is tough, she's smart, she's funny and she works bloody hard.' Nicola Roxon, Minister for Health, *The Age,* 21 June, 2003.

In 1902, Australia became the first country in the world to grant women the right to vote in national elections. It would take a further seven years for Australia's state parliaments to grant women the vote, Queensland being the last state to do so.

In 1920, after Western Australia removed legislation which banned women from actually sitting in Parliament, Edith Cowan won the seat of West Perth and became the first woman to sit in a state Parliament. In 1943, Enid Lyons made history as Australia's first female Cabinet Minister and over half a century would elapse before Julia Gillard would oust Prime Minister Kevin Rudd and become Australia's first female Prime Minister.[1]

In the nineteenth century the idea that a woman could become a Member of Parliament provoked male ridicule and derision. Few men imagined there could ever be a female Prime Minister. This was a century when women were denied access to higher education as it was believed that, women's bodies being smaller than those of men, their brains must also be smaller and incapable of reasoned thought.

Male politicians claimed women could not be trusted to use the vote wisely, let alone head the nation. They found the mere idea ludicrous and insisted that women should never be given the vote. One woman who dared to speak out against these sexist ideas was Margaret Ogg, who grew up in Brisbane's Ann Street Presbytery. As a clergyman's daughter, Margaret saw many sad cases of worn-out, poverty-stricken women struggling to raise more than a dozen children. Her father was often called to the bed of women dying in childbirth at a time when the sale of contraceptives to married women was illegal.

After leaving school, Margaret Ogg worked as a journalist on a rural Queensland newspaper. The recession of the 1890s resulted in bank failures, breadwinners losing their jobs and their families being evicted for non-payment of rent. Margaret helped her father give out food parcels and second-hand clothes to homeless families for whom there was little or no government assistance. A compassionate young woman, she became convinced if only women had the vote and could sit in Parliament they would demand measures be implemented to help working families who were in desperate circumstances.

Margaret Ogg had been influenced by Mary Woolstonecraft's *The Vindication of the Rights of Women,* published centuries earlier. In her landmark book, Mary Woolstonecraft insisted that women were as intelligent as men but must have wider educational opportunities and equal rights before the law.[2]

In the 1890s, Margaret Ogg held public meetings demanding women be given the vote and wider opportunities. At that time, many parents had over a dozen children to support, often with the breadwinner out of work. Miss Ogg castigated Catholic priests who urged women to have even more children and dared to suggest that wives should receive free contraceptive advice.

Margaret's claim that Australian women would use the vote wisely and even sit in Parliament was met with jeers and laughter by men who retorted that woman's place was in the home — cooking and caring for children — and only male householders should vote. Miss Ogg was threatened with violence if she continued urging women to demand equal rights. Some of the men in her audience hurled rotten fruit at her. She described being unmercifully heckled at one public meeting after another and claimed this was done 'by gangs of paid hecklers seeking to nullify any progress towards the emancipation of women'.[3]

Miss Ogg's opponents soon devised a way of preventing her from holding public meetings. When she attempted to hire a hall, the male owner would inform her the venue was booked for months and months. Margaret refused to admit defeat, purchased a horse and buggy, advertised the date and time of her meeting and tethered the horse to the railings of the chosen hall. Using the leather seat of the buggy as a platform, she spoke to her audience by the light of kerosene lamps.

Male hecklers made lewd gestures and abused Miss Ogg but her quick wit made the hecklers look foolish as she told them sweetly, 'As you hate women so much you perhaps should refrain from wedlock, as your father did with your mother!'[4]

As roads in central and north Queensland were bad, Margaret visited ports like Rockhampton and Townsville by ship and then returned to Brisbane. Driving her buggy over bumpy roads, Margaret journeyed inland to Toowoomba and Warwick and held meetings there.

With financial help from her father and her salary as a journalist, Margaret Ogg was eventually able to buy a house at 27 Bridge Street, in the Brisbane suburb of Albion and held meetings with women who sought changes in society. Together with Christina Buisson Corrie, Margaret Ogg established the Queensland Women's Electoral League (WEL) which aimed 'to advance political knowledge among women' and demanded the right to vote for women. Miss Ogg served as Hon. Secretary of the Queensland branch of WEL for over 30 years. She also founded the Brisbane Women's Club as a forum to discuss political issues affecting women. She was elected President of the Brisbane branch of the Lyceum Club and served as State Secretary of the National Council for Women.[5]

Retiring as a journalist in 1930, silver-haired, petite Miss Ogg was given an illuminated address praising her 'sense of justice, courage and endurance in leading women along hitherto untravelled paths of public life'.[6]

She deserves to be remembered for the bequest she made in her will. A fund established in her name helped Irene Longman enter the Queensland Parliament and Annabel Rankin the federal Parliament. This fund was increased by money provided by the Queensland branch of the WEL, the organisation which, decades earlier, she had founded.[7]

Campaigning for the female vote among working-class women was widowed Emma Miller (1839–1917), who was employed in a Brisbane sweatshop making shirts. Emma had emigrated to Brisbane from Britain and campaigned for equal pay and better conditions for working women. Feisty Emma became president of the Women's Equal Franchise Association and a keen member of the Worker's Political Association.

Emma Miller became famous when participating in a march on Parliament House to demonstrate in favour of the women's vote. She halted a charge of mounted police attempting to mow down the demonstrators. Emma bravely stepped forward and stuck her hatpin into the flank of the leading horse, which fell over and the police officer fell on the ground. The result was that the line of charging men and horses came to a halt.

Emma Miller's statue stands in Brisbane's Trades Hall today.

※

The talented and outspoken Vida Goldstein was younger than Ogg and Miller. She led a campaign to obtain the female vote in her home state of Victoria and did her best against strong male opposition to enter Parliament. Vida was a cosmopolitan Australian. Her father had Jewish, Polish and Irish roots, while her mother, Isabella (née Hawkins) was the eldest daughter of a Scottish-born squatter. Vida's mother was a suffragist who firmly believed her clever daughters were entitled to a good education, at a time when women were excluded from Melbourne University due to their gender. Vida's father did not believe women deserved the vote, so her parents' marriage was far from happy.

As a star pupil at Melbourne's Presbyterian Ladies' College, Vida matriculated in 1886. After her father lost money in the bank crashes of the 1890s, Vida and her sisters supported themselves by establishing a primary school in which they taught their pupils.

Vida believed that women could hold ministerial office or become Prime Minister. She demanded a change to unfair divorce laws which favoured husbands and resulted in a divorced wife losing all rights over her children. In the 1890s and for several more decades, legally children remained under the control of their fathers after a divorce. In some cases a male judge banned mothers from seeing their children again.

Vida Goldstein's election campaign provoked male jeers and catcalls. Vida was told she needed a husband to bed her and was searching for one in Parliament. Tall, slim and attractive, Miss Goldstein had already turned down several offers of marriage. Her parents' matrimony was very turbulent and they remained together only because divorce was scandalous and extremely expensive, which may have been the reason why Vida was weary of marriage.

The dauntless Miss Goldstein stood for election five times between 1903 and 1917. However, men sabotaged her campaign, insisting women lacked the intelligence and the stamina to cope with the stresses of political life. In 1911, Vida was invited to tour England by British suffragettes and her brilliant speeches in favour of the vote drew large crowds. She remains an important figure in women's struggles to secure the vote in both countries.

In 1921, Edith Cowan, a hard-working volunteer social worker married to a lawyer, became the first woman elected to the West Australian Parliament. Edith had been opposed by the West Australian Attorney-General, Mr T.P. Draper, who claimed that electing a woman was absurd. Ignoring his rude comment, Edith Cowan campaigned for reforms to improve the lives of women and children, including the establishment of free infant welfare clinics for deprived families.

Edith Cowan had been a founding member of Perth's Karakatta Debating Club and Education Section and lent her support to the establishment of the District Nursing Society to provide home nursing for women who could not afford this luxury. Her voluntary social work took her into Perth, and Fremantle's worst slums, where sanitation was rudimentary. One of her reasons for wanting a seat in the West Australian Parliament was to provide better living conditions for the poor, who received no government assistance. Later, she became a hospital almoner (now known as a social worker).

In 1921, a year after the ban on women sitting in the West Australian Parliament was finally lifted, women voters elected Edith to that parliament convinced she would improve the situation for women. Although Edith Cowan's children were by now grown up, obtuse male MPs argued that she should be at home supervising them. They deliberately humiliated silver-haired Mrs Cowan by discussing in her presence what a waste of public money it would be to install a female toilet for her use. She retaliated by insisting (at a time when few women worked outside the home) wives should be legally entitled to a share of their husband's income and financially recompensed in any divorce. Mrs Cowan achieved success with other bills that benefited women and children, but, after concerted male opposition, she lost her seat in the 1924 election. When she died, crowds of women attended her funeral and today her portrait appears on Australian banknotes.[8]

⁂

Mrs Irene Longman, a former teacher in north Queensland, was in 1929 nominated by the Queensland Country Party for the seat of Bulimba. She promised to improve schools and give them libraries and more books.

Her opponent, Mr A.W. Wright, sneered at Mrs Longman's chances of getting into Parliament, claiming, 'I've only got a *woman* standing against me, she'll *never* get in.' However, this boastful man lost his seat and Irene Longman became the first woman to gain a seat in Queensland's State Parliament.[9] But even then Irene Longman was banned from eating in the Parliamentary dining room and was told it was reserved for men, as were the toilets. She had to walk across the road to use the ladies' toilet in the nearby Bellevue Hotel.

As promised, Irene Longman MLA did improve schools and ensured that women were allowed to enter the Queensland police force, but lost her seat during the depression years of the 1930s. She is commemorated by an electorate named 'Longman' after her.

⁂

Australia's first female federal Cabinet Minister was Enid Lyons. She had married Joe Lyons, who became Prime Minister, but when she became a cabinet minister she was widowed with several dependent children. Her life as a Catholic mother of 12 children is in striking contrast to the unmarried and childless Julia Gillard, who would become Australia's first female Prime Minister. One thing these clever hard-working women share is the fact that both came from working-class backgrounds. Both received a good start in life, mainly because their mothers taught them to read before they attended school.

When Enid managed to enter Parliament she did her best to improve the plight of working-class women. Memories of her parents' financial struggles also moulded the character and political beliefs of the equally determined Julia Gillard.

Enid Lyons was born into a religious household and raised as a Methodist by her mother, Eliza Birnell (née Taggart). Enid was taught to venerate the Holy Bible and distrust Catholics in an era of religious sectarianism and intolerance. Understandably, Mrs Eliza Birnell was very upset when her 15-year-old daughter announced she wanted to marry Joe Lyons, a Catholic politician almost old enough to be her father.

At the age of 18, Eliza had made a turbulent marriage to handsome William Burnell, an uneducated sawyer and woodchopper. William did not share Eliza's Methodist zeal for self-improvement. In the early years of the marriage, Eliza's husband worked in remote timber mills in Tasmania. Eliza was left alone in the town of Burnie with Nellie, her first baby, Enid's elder sister.

With her husband frequently absent, the penniless Eliza became a supporter of Tasmania's fledgling Labor Party and received a loan from an unknown source.[10] This money may have enabled Eliza to buy a block of cheap land at Co-ee beach and build a shack, which she ran as a tea room to support her daughters. Enid watched her mother working hard, but during a financial recession in Tasmania Eliza's tea rooms at isolated Co-ee beach ran at a loss.

The only way Enid could continue her education after she turned 14 was to become a pupil teacher, a post reserved for the brightest and most dedicated students. As a badly paid pupil teacher, Enid had to keep order in the school playground and help younger children with reading problems. By working long hours in return for additional coaching, Enid managed to win a scholarship to a teachers' training college in Hobart.

In 1923, Enid attended a Labor Party rally in Hobart where she was thrilled to hear the Minister for Education, the Hon. Joe Lyons, announce his plans for building more secondary schools and abolishing school fees. Joe Lyons was the eldest son in a large Tasmanian family of devout Irish Catholics and had started his career as a schoolteacher.

Enid, an attractive 15-year-old, was mature for her age and looked at least three years older. She was so excited by the minister's ideas on educational reform that she waited in a queue to talk to him. When it was her turn, Enid asked the minister several searching questions. Despite the queue of people waiting for their chance to speak to the Minister for Education, he spent considerable time talking to Enid.

At that time, Joe Lyons was 34 years old and a bachelor. Supporting his ailing mother and his siblings, he had been far too preoccupied with work to devote his time to girls. But the attractive Miss Burnell, who seemed to share his aims to improve the teaching profession, took Joe's fancy. He was so fascinated by this confident young woman that he suggested they continue their discussion the following day. He wanted to hear more about Enid's ideas to improve conditions for pupil teachers.

At their second meeting, Joe Lyons dismissed his aides. He and Enid spoke in private for a long time before an aide tactfully reminded him that he was due to attend another meeting. Joe said goodbye reluctantly and promised to write, unaware Enid was under age. This was a critical time for Joe Lyons. His mother had recently died, leaving him lonely and wanting a home and a family. He was convinced that in the extroverted attractive Miss Burnell he had found a soul mate. With her charm, good looks and an extroverted personality she would make an ideal wife for an ambitious Labor politician.

Enid knew that her mother, a staunch Methodist, would not see a Catholic politician as a suitable husband, even though she was a keen Labor supporter. So Enid hid the letters from the Minister for Education, which arrived at her home almost daily, claiming that he loved her and wanted to marry her.

***

Joe's father, Michael Lyons, had lost all his money by betting on a horse he dreamed would win the Melbourne Cup. After drinking a great deal, Michael went to Flemington racecourse and put his life savings (plus a sum of money borrowed against the surety of his house) on the horse he had seen in his dream, convinced it would win.[11] Joe's father, claiming inner voices told him what to do, was probably suffering from schizophrenia and the 'inner voices' were symptomatic of his psychiatric illness.

When the horse lost, the bank repossessed the family home. Michael Lyons suffered a nervous collapse and spent the rest of his life in mental hospitals. With no welfare measures to help his family, Joe, the eldest boy, had to leave school to support his mother and seven younger siblings by doing farm work and later worked as an errand boy in Ulverstone.

Two unmarried aunts intervened to help the family so that young Joe could return to school. Like Enid, he was offered the post of pupil teacher and, in 1907, won a scholarship to attend Tasmania's first teacher training college and then taught in Launceston before moving to Hobart. Elected Labor Member for Wilmot in 1914, the hard-working popular Joe Lyons was appointed State Treasurer as well as Minister for Education.

Eventually, Enid plucked up the courage to tell her suitor she was only 15 and a Methodist, rather than Catholic. Considering that his supporters were mainly Irish Catholics, Joe realised that his relationship with a Methodist girl, 17 years younger than himself, would cause a scandal. In a letter to Enid, he pleaded with her to add a couple of years to her age or people would think he was mad even to think of marrying her. After such an unhappy childhood, he could not bear to renounce his chance of happiness with the only girl he had ever loved.

Enid loved Joe too, but she had strong principles. She refused to lie about her age and protested that what mattered was the fact they loved each other — she did not care about their age difference, so why would anyone else? But, being a minor, Enid needed her parents' written permission to marry. Enid's mother, a staunch Methodist and Labor supporter, was appalled by the prospect of her young daughter marrying a Catholic, even though he was a

Labor Cabinet Minister. Enid's parents opposed the marriage and forbade her to continue her correspondence with Joe Lyons.

But it was too late. Several days previously, on Co-ee beach, Joe and Enid had kissed for the first time. We 'plighted our troth and swore to be true to each other', Enid would recount in her memoirs. Joe was her first and only love.

The Lyons family were no keener on Joe marrying a Methodist than the Burnells were on having a Catholic son-in-law. However, as soon as she turned 16, Enid became unofficially engaged to Joe Lyons with the promise she would not marry until she was 17.

Eliza Burnell relented, realising that opposition would achieve nothing and risk losing her daughter. She understood that Joe Lyons needed to marry in a Catholic church or lose many of his Catholic supporters. Clearly, Joe adored Enid and would make a very good husband, but Eliza realised that her daughter had to have the same religious beliefs as Joe Lyons.

Eventually, Eliza agreed that her underage daughter could take instruction from a Catholic priest. Overjoyed, Enid wrote to Joe telling him of her mother's change of heart.

In February 1915, Enid Burnell and Joe Lyons became formally engaged. Joe visited Devonport to buy land and engaged a builder to drew up plans for a house. Enid took instruction from a priest and converted to Catholicism. On 28 April 1915, they married at St Brigid's Church, Wynyard.

Enid accompanied her husband when he attended a Premier's conference in Sydney. The couple had a short break in Melbourne before returning to their weatherboard house at Devonport. That first Premiers' Conference was Enid Lyons' introduction to the Byzantine complexities, feuds and shifting alliances of the Labor Party. (Julia Gillard would find this out for herself when involved in overthrowing the Labor Prime Minister, Kevin Rudd.)

In spite of misgivings from Joe's supporters over their age difference, he and Enid confounded their critics by having a happy marriage. They lived at *Home Hill*, the house Joe had built for them at Devonport. Initially they did not have a telephone, so Enid wrote her husband long letters whenever they were apart. Joe wrote back every day with equally long and passionate letters.

In 1916, when Enid was pregnant with their first child, she joined her husband on the campaign trail in Tasmania.

In 1920, when Enid was 23, she made her first public speech. Joe realised that his young wife's good looks, warm personality and quick wit made her a political asset and encouraged her to speak at Labor rallies.

Eventually, their small weatherboard house had to be enlarged, because their family grew and grew. Enid, being petite, suffered difficult pregnancies, possibly due to a childhood case of rickets from a diet deficient in essential vitamins.

Joe was a loving husband and father, but, with so many children to feed, clothe and educate, they were often short of money. The births of Gerald in 1916, Sheila in 1918, Enid Veronica in 1919, Kathleen in 1920 and Moira in 1922 gave Enid a huge amount of work, as they still could not afford live-in servants. Joe was unusual for his era as he did not mind helping Enid with housework. On Sundays, he would cook the family dinner and read to Enid while she did the ironing.

The births of her children were so difficult that Enid was left with a slight crack in her pelvis, which caused her a great deal of pain as she grew older. As a devout Catholic who refused to use contraceptives, Enid bore Joe Lyons 12 children in an era when politicians were poorly paid and their wives did not work outside the home. Enid, who could not afford a maid, had to cope with mountains of laundry, housework and child minding. In addition to her domestic chores, she still managed to find time to write brilliant speeches for her husband.

Enid was a trailblazer, standing as a Labor candidate in 1925. But the cliché that women had no place in politics, meant she failed to win a seat in the Tasmanian Parliament, losing by 60 votes. From 1923–25, during Joe Lyons' second term as Premier of Tasmania, she bore four more children, Kevin, Garnet Phillip (who died very young), Brendan and Barry. Kept from the public was the fact that after giving birth Enid often suffered episodes of postnatal depression due to an undiagnosed crack in her pelvis.

After the turmoil caused by the stock market crash of 1929, the political beliefs of Joe and Enid underwent a change. The Australian economy, based on wool, wheat and dairy products, seemed to be heading for financial disaster while Labor seemed unable to deal with the crisis effectively. Joe Lyons was Acting Treasurer of the Labor Party when many thousands of Australians lost jobs and homes in the Great Depression. Joe switched from Tasmanian to federal politics and joined the Scullin Labor government as Postmaster-General and Minister for Works.

With so many men out of work, Enid and Joe ceased subscribing to the union journal *The Australian Worker*, finding it 'too bitter in its denunciations, too intolerant and too biased'. By now the federal Labor government was desperately short of funds. Joe and Enid believed that the crisis caused by the Wall Street crash of 1929 could have been overcome by financial economies and a general tightening of belts.

In the 1930s, there was no mining boom to help Australia weather that particular financial crisis. The Lyons government reduced government expenditure, although many of Joe's Labor colleagues wanted to spend massive sums they did not possess and run Australia even deeper into debt. Joe, supported by Enid, refused to go with Labor policy. As an austerity measure, Joe demanded a reduction in the salaries of leading public servants, which caused a furore among his Cabinet colleagues.

In the election campaign of December 1931, as recession started to hit public confidence in Labor's ability to handle the crisis, Joe Lyons and Enid changed their views. In spite of anguished requests for Joe to remain as Labor leader, after much soul-searching he resigned from the party and became the leader of the newly formed United Australia Party (UAP) believing they represented the only hope of solving the financial crisis. Joe Lyons was seen as betraying the Labor Party and, forever after, was vilified for it.

In January 1932, Joe Lyons was sworn in as UAP Prime Minister. Enid did not attend the ceremony, because one of her children was very sick. Remembering how little Garnet Philip had died, she wanted to nurse the sick child herself.[12] The night after the swearing-in ceremony, Joe found time to write to Enid telling her how much he missed her and emphasised that 'whatever honours or distinctions accrue, they are ours not mine'.

Once her sick child was better, Enid and their younger children moved into The Lodge in Canberra but the hatred and verbal abuse of the couple continued. Senior members of the Labor Party cut Joe dead and labelled him a 'traitor' and the Lyons received sacks of hate mail. Few people expected Joe Lyons to last more than one term as Prime Minister. But by using the relatively new medium of radio, Joe surprised everyone by winning three successive elections.

Enid disliked having to divide her time between Canberra and Tasmania, where several of the older children were still at school. She longed for her extended family to be together.

During the Great Depression of the 1930s, Joe consolidated an alliance with the Country Party which enraged his former Labor colleagues even more. Encouraged by Enid, Joe Lyons was tough on Communism, aware some former Labor colleagues supported Stalin. Joe had always distrusted Joseph Stalin, convinced that he was a brutal dictator. Some Labor members believed that Stalin was a benevolent leader rather than a monster responsible for the death of millions of men, women and children in *gulags* in Siberia.

Enid travelled around Australia speaking to women's groups in spite of the assertions of Robert Menzies that she should remain at home in the kitchen. Like Julia Gillard, Enid had a remarkable talent for public speaking and related well to her audience. If asked a difficult question, Enid was unfazed. She just smiled and ignored the question and continued speaking about the topic in hand, a technique Gillard employs successfully on television.

From 1934–1935, Enid accompanied her husband to England for the Golden Jubilee of King George V. She dreaded the formality of the grand state and social functions, but managed them very successfully.

Joe and Enid Lyons sailed to the United States to stay at the White House with President Roosevelt and his wife. Enid also dreaded meeting the formidable Eleanor Roosevelt, but discovered that they had much in common. Both were determined to improve conditions for working-class wives with husbands out of work, struggling to feed their families during the Great Depression.

On their return to Australia, Enid gave a series of popular radio talks, describing their overseas tour. She was an excellent performer on the radio and her talks were very popular.

In 1937, after the abdication of the uncrowned Edward VIII (created Duke of Windsor), Joe and Enid Lyons made a second trip to Britain to attend the coronation of George VI and took the opportunity to visit Anzac cemeteries in France. The rows of graves they saw on the Somme confirmed their opposition to conscription in the second world war that would soon envelop Australia. In London, Enid was created a Dame Grand Cross of the British Empire in her own right in a private investiture at Buckingham Palace.

Back in Australia, she was henceforth known as Dame Enid Lyons and became even more popular. But her gynaecological problems became so severe she had to be admitted to hospital for a hysterectomy, then a dangerous operation. Enid recovered but her husband's health was causing concern. Joe had stubbornly refused to see a doctor, despite heart palpitations. Aged 59, he worked very long hours as Prime Minister, greatly worried by domestic political problems and the deteriorating international situation, which he feared would lead to a second world war — as it did.

Enid insisted Joe visit a doctor, who diagnosed high blood pressure. Prime Minister Lyons was advised to reduce his working hours or resign if he wanted to reach old age. In 1939, there were no drugs to lower blood pressure. Each time Joe Lyons attempted to resign, another foreign or domestic crisis occurred — as a result his colleagues pressured him to stay in office. Joe had no clear successor and feared a leadership struggle would destabilise the party. To reassure his anxious wife, Joe promised that, once the crisis ended, he would resign.

In April 1939, as the tensions between Poland and Nazi Germany increased, Joe Lyons suffered a fatal heart attack. His death proved a nightmare for 42-year-old Enid. As a widow, she found herself with no savings or superannuation to support her large number of children, ranging in age from 23 to 6 years, with the youngest still to attend school.[13]

Enid had to deal with feelings of grief and guilt that she had not insisted Joe resign from office earlier, convinced that, had he done so, he would still be alive. Out of gratitude and respect for Edith Lyons, the United Australia Party tabled a motion to give the Prime Minister's widow an annuity to educate her children. Even this relatively modest provision provoked rage among Labor stalwarts unable to forgive Joe Lyons for deserting the Labor Party.

At the time of Joe's death, Enid was still in great pain from the crack in her pelvis and suffered from sleeping problems. The loss of her husband brought on an attack of clinical depression, which was made worse by death threats and hate mail from malicious Labor supporters. She received packages containing dead rats or cockroaches and feared for the safety of her children. Eventually, Enid had a nervous breakdown and was admitted to St Vincent's Hospital for a complete rest.[14]

Once she had recovered, convinced that Joe would have wanted her to continue in politics, Enid stood for election to the federal Parliament as a United Australia Party candidate. Although Labor won the election, Enid's popularity, mainly due to her radio talks, was so great that she managed to defeat her male rival. She entered federal Parliament in August 1943 as member for Braddon, which gave her a much-needed income and reassured her she was continuing the work of her beloved husband.

In the 1940s, social benefits were minimal, so Enid aimed to obtain a pension for widows as well as government housing for families in need. In a Parliament famous for male histrionics and searing insults, Enid Lyons remained calm and polite, no matter how much she was provoked, another trait shared with Julia Gillard.

Enid Lyons trebled her majority in the 1946 election and quadrupled it in 1949. She was proud of her role in securing government endowment for all Australian children. Having no secretarial assistance, she had to write her campaign speeches by hand. Her workload was heavy and she wrote how 'I look at the men around me and envy them for having wives. [Do] any of those politicians wash their own socks?'

For Enid Lyons, interstate travel was slow and uncomfortable. During World War Two it was dangerous to go by boat between Tasmania and the mainland, because the waters of Bass Strait were mined. But Enid ignored the danger and travelled tirelessly, addressing scores of rallies and meetings and attending political functions all over Australia.[15]

Suffering severe exhaustion after the 1946 election campaign, Enid's health deteriorated. With two goitres in her throat she needed a life-threatening operation. Although the operation was successful, her neck was wrapped in bandages, so doctors ordered her to limit her speaking engagements. But so great was Dame Enid Lyons' political expertise and popularity that she was appointed Vice President of the Executive Council. Due to her declining health, she did not accept a portfolio and retired from federal Parliament in 1951.

After taking a long period of rest, she agreed to become an ABC commissioner. In 1973, her memoir was published under the title *Among the Carrion Crows* (a code name for political journalists). She made plans to leave *Home Hill* and some of its contents to the National Trust on condition the Trust would maintain the house and open it to the public. The Lyons' family home at 66 Middle Road, Devonport, was surrounded by extensive gardens on which Enid, who loved gardening, had worked extensively as a hobby.

On 2 September 1981, Enid Lyons died in a hospice at Ulverstone, the town where her husband had once worked as an errand boy. At her request she was buried beside him.

⁂

With her working-class background, political views and a pleasant way with people Julia Gillard has much in common with Enid Burnell Lyons. Like Enid, Julia is the second daughter in a family without sons, so parental ambitions were directed to both clever girls to achieve something in life. At school, both of them were studious, motivated and ambitious and developed a talent for public speaking, using everyday language that wins the hearts and minds of ordinary people. Initially, like Enid Lyons, Julia Gillard hoped to become a teacher before deciding on a career in law. Both women were drawn into Labor politics by their commitment to social justice.

However, in other respects, the differences between these two remarkable women could not be greater. While Enid was a devoted Catholic with a very large family, Julia has never pretended to be religious or want to marry and have children.

Her late father, John Gillard, grew up in the town of Barry in the Vale of Glamorgan in South Wales. Lack of family money meant that John, who had gained a scholarship to a grammar school, could not take it up and had to work in coal mines to help his family. Her father's deprived circumstances would motivate Julia Gillard to study. Once she had become a politician, she wanted all Australian children to have good schooling and the possibility of access to higher education.

In 1965, the Gillard family migrated to Australia from Wales on medical advice, because 4-year-old Julia was suffering from chest infections and bouts of bronchial pneumonia. As assisted migrants, the family arrived in Adelaide, hoping its milder climate would improve Julia's health.

The Gillard family obtained subsidised accommodation in a bleak migrant hostel on the outskirts of Adelaide. Eventually, Julia's father was able to take out a mortgage and buy a house.[16] John Gillard retrained as a psychiatric nurse, but often had to work double shifts to pay off the mortgage. His wife, Moira, found cleaning work in an aged care facility and at times looked after neighbours' children to earn extra money. John and Moira hoped their daughters, Alison and Julia, would do well academically and sent them to Mitcham Demonstration School. Later, Julia attended high school in the Adelaide suburb of Unley, where she worked hard, hoping to become a teacher.

Anthropologist and mother of four Mrs Marlene Pilowsky, wife of the celebrated Jewish psychiatrist Issie (Isaac) Pilowsky, became an important influence on Julia. Marlene encouraged young Julia to aim high and become a lawyer rather than a teacher, insisting 'You're good at debating, good at ideas, logical thinking and argument. Law is the career for you'.[17]

In 1979, with government assistance for her tuition fees, Julia enrolled in a course in Arts-Law at the University of Adelaide. As a student, she joined the Labor Club within the Australian Union of Students and was eventually elected as president. Moving to the University of Melbourne to finish her law degree, she worked as secretary of the left-wing Socialist Forum.[18] At the time, she was known as 'Red Julia' for her political opinions and her wild mop of hair.[19]

As Julia matured and obtained her law degree, she moderated her extreme views to those espoused by the central faction of the Labor Party. She was popular with her own group, but some party members claimed she was a pragmatist, keen to be on the winning side and could not be trusted. Paul Henderson, also employed by Melbourne law firm Slater and Gordon and a colleague of Gillard, recalls that Julia did not secure the right to do 'articles' (the term for an apprenticeship in a law firm) and had enrolled in an expensive postgraduate course at Melbourne's Leo Cussen Institute, which provided practical tuition in the workings of the law and whose graduates did very well. It has never been revealed who helped to pay the hefty fees. As part of the course, Julia spent a few weeks working for Slater and Gordon, who were so impressed they offered her a job in their industrial law department, which had trade unions as clients.

Ar 29, Gillard's intelligence, her capacity for hard work and the high standards she set herself, were responsible for her being created a salaried partner in Slater and Gordon. Acting for the unions, she secured better wages and conditions for underpaid workers in the clothing trade, many of whom were migrants, being exploited as 'sweated' labour by their employers.

When questioned about her feelings on marriage, on radio she replied, 'It's not that I have anything against the institution of marriage, it's just that the accumulation of a set of life choices has led me to this point.'[20]

Gillard's final years at Slater and Gordon were marred by the fact her boyfriend, union official Bruce Wilson was investigated by the Victorian police for misappropriating union funds. Gillard admitted she had worked with her boyfriend setting up a special 'slush fund' for this purpose but neglected to tell Slater and Gordon what she was doing. She severed her relationship with Bruce Wilson and departed from Slater and Gordon. Faced with investigation by a royal commission, Bruce Wilson and his friend Ralph Blewitt seemed likely to face criminal charges for conspiracy. Julia repeatedly denied she had received money from the Union 'slush fund' to pay for her home renovations. At a Royal Commission into Union Corruption in 2014 others swore on oath that cash *was* paid to builders who were renovating Gillard's Altona home. Her conduct as a lawyer was questioned by the legal counsel who was assisting the .Royal Commission.

From 1996 to 1998, Julia worked as chief of staff to John Brumby, Victoria's opposition leader. Brumby praised Gillard as a person of great ability, with a lovely way with people and a good sense of humour. She helped establish 'Emily's List', a network committed to place Labor women in politics and donated money to this cause. She made three attempts to enter federal Parliament,succeeded on the third attempt and became the member for the working-class electorate of Lalor in 1998, at the age of 37. Once again, her intelligence and her capacity for hard work were recognised and she was promoted to Shadow Minister for Population and Immigration in 2001. Two years later, she became Shadow Minister for Health, Reconciliation and Aboriginal Affairs. [21]

Early in 2005, Senator Bill Heffernan, known as a political dinosaur rudely labelled Julia Gillard 'deliberately barren' after she was photographed sitting beside an empty fruit bowl in her Altona kitchen (fruit being a symbol of fertility in Renaissance art). Julia was defended by female colleagues, friends and professional women without children.

On 3 December 2007, the Labor Party under Kevin Rudd won the federal election with a sweeping majority, ending the long Prime Ministership of John Howard. Ms Julia Gillard was sworn in as the first female Deputy Prime Minister by Governor-General Ms Quentin Bryce. She took on a large portfolio, being responsible for the 'super ministry' of the Department of Employment, Workplace Relations and Social Inclusion.

On 11 December 2007, Gillard became the first woman to assume the role of acting Prime Minister, standing in for Prime Minister Kevin Rudd when he was in Bali attending a United Nations Climate Change Conference. She was determined to abolish Howard's 'Work Choices' and replace it with her own 'Fair Work Bill', which passed the Senate in March 2009. In the same year, , Gillard oversaw the grandiosely named *Building the Education Revolution.* The Labour government allocated $16 billion for the construction of new classrooms, libraries and assembly halls. Unfortunately, the program failed to provide additional teachers and funded some schools about to close.

Confidence in Kevin Rudd's leadership plummeted in the first half of 2010. Criticism of the Prime Minister's performance intensified in debates over his projected 40% mining tax and its effect on the Australian economy. Questioned by TV interviewers about her future, Gillard smiled at the camera, insisting glibly she was *not* interested in becoming Prime Minister.

On 23 June 2010, Rudd was asked to resign or to hold a leadership ballot in the 115-member Caucus to be held the next day. Meanwhile, former Trades Unionist Bill Shorten and two senior Labor politicians y assured Julia Gillard that, as a result of phone calls, she had the requisite numbers to become Prime Minister and Gillard agreed to replace Rudd whose mental stability shes subsequently queried. Rudd resigned after learning he faced a humiliating defeat if he insisted on remaining in office .Gillard, created history by becoming Australia's first female Prime Minister although not elected as such. Her overthrow of a sitting Prime Minister aroused a political furore comparable to the one caused by Joe and Enid Lyons in 1931, when they abandoned the Labor Party to join the United Australia Party.

She faced probing questions as to whether her partner would live with her at the Prime Minister's official residence in Canberra.. When Enid Lyons stood for Parliament in the 1940s, such admissions would have been political suicide. But, in 2010, few voters seemed to care about the Prime Minister's marital status, Gillard's attitude to religion, her keen sense of ambition and her views on marriage were a complete contrast to the selfless, deeply religious character of Enid Lyons. Gillard admitted she had been raised in the Baptist tradition, but when questioned as to whether she believed in God answered candidly, 'No, I don't. I'm a great respecter of religious beliefs, but they're not *my* beliefs.'[22] Gillard revealed that she had enjoyed a two-year relationship with Craig Emerson, a Labor Minister who had left his wife and children. Gillard, asked if their liaison took place *before* or *after* Emerson broke up with his wife, replied evasively 'That's a set of issues between Craig and his wife that I wouldn't want to canvas'.[23]

In August 2010, shortly after being chosen as Prime Minister by a small majority, Julia Gillard and Tim Mathieson, a divorced former hairdresser moved from Altona to The Lodge in Canberra. When Enid and Joe Lyons occupied The Lodge, a Prime Minister 'living in sin' with a divorced partner and a daughter born out of wedlock would have caused so much a scandal the Prime Minister would have had to resign but it was clear attitudes had changed.

It was hard for Gillard'a spin doctors to gloss over the fact that she had shown disloyalty to Kevin Rudd, the man who had made her Deputy Prime Minister. Asked why she had given Rudd little warning before replacing him Julia Gillard adroitly side-stepped this embarrassing question by claiming she had taken over the reins of government because 'I came to the view that a good government was losing its way'. On her visit to Western Australia, the new Prime Minister received a warning of Labor's decline in popularity when an egg was thrown at her.

ABC interviewer Kerry O'Brien asked Gillard why, having worked with Kevin Rudd for so many years, she had not sent him a get-well card when her colleagues was hospitalised for a serious operation. When Gillard pleaded lack of time, Kerry O'Brien asked sardonically if she could not have spared two minutes to phone the hospital to enquire after the man who had appointed her as Deputy Prime Minister. Gillard, usually brilliant at evading awkward questions, was unable to wriggle away from O'Brien's question,. In office Gillard became a controversial figure, admired by some and loathed by others but had to put up with insults about her appearance and dress sense no one in politics should have to face. As a polished performer in Parliament, she managed to keep calm, often under difficult circumstances. She put through a great deal of legislation in her time in office in what was later seen as a triumph of quantity over quality.

Gillard's concern for the most vulnerable members of society was seen as one of her strengths. But this was under question when it was alleged Kevin Rudd proposed to raise the age-pension by $30 a week and Gillard opposed the raise because 'elderly voters did not support Labor'.[24] Such a revelation, even if invented by Rudd and relayed to the publio by Laurie Oakes, did not go down well with voters and probably cost Gillard votes in the 2010 election.

Accusations of inadequate supervision of Gillard's $16 billion school building programme continued to be raised. The federal election of August 2010 saw an 11-seat swing against Labor, resulting in a hung Parliament but Gillard's negotiating skills saved the day for her and she managed to convince three independent MPs and one Green MP to support Labor, thus giving her a slim majority.[25]

On 14 September 2010, Prime Minister Gillard was once again sworn in by the Governor-General.

Julia Gillard's negotiating skills managed to oversee the passing of controversial legislation for the National Broadband Network. But grave problems establishing the NBN, which had never been properly costed by the Rudd Government would lead to serious problems and the whole project fell behind schedule and ran over budget. There was delay in implementing the 'My Schools' website, due to the number of errors the website contained. Tbis in turn led to accusations that the Gillard government was more about spin than substance.

Gillard's nasal voice was not an asset her when speaking on television. Asian Australians claimed they had difficulty understanding her as did some of those she met overseas. She was also criticised for her dress sense, criticisms which would not have been applied to a male prime minister. On 30 June, 2010 she revealed she did not support of gay marriage. She usually performed well in Parliament with her ready wit and wry sense of humour and demonstrated a capacity for hard sustained work and rarely took a holiday.

In January 2011, widespread floods devastated parts of the eastern states of Australia. Julia Gillard showed great empathy with the flood victims and was quick to offer financial support to the affected areas.

In November 2011 the Gillard government's Clean Energy bills were passed by the Senate, under which polluting industries were made to pay $23 per tonne of carbon emissions from 1 July 2012, (legislation which was repealed by the next government). In the same month plain packing laws for cigarettes were passed under which cigarettes would be sold in dark green packets with a health warning, and Australia was the first country to implement this. Gillard gained popularity in November when she instituted the National Disability Insurance Scheme (NDIS) but the costing of this scheme was poor, having no provision for disabled housing which presented a problem for those who had to implement the scheme. By now the Chinese mining boom was starting to decline and Australia's debts and the interest payments were soaring but Gillard appeared to ignore both these important factors and history will be her judge.

In February 2012 Kevin Rudd resigned as Foreign Minister to challenge Gillard for the leadership of the Labour Party.. Gillard called a party meeting on 27 February, 2012 and asked for and won a leadership vote, receiving 71 votes to a mere 31 for Rudd. Several ministers resigned including Treasurer Wayne Swan and Peter Garrett, trying to distance himself from several deaths of young men in the 'pink batts' scandal. Other resignations were received from Greg Combet, Joe Ludwig, Craig Emerson and Stephen Conroy so Prime Minister Gillard appeared to be leading a government desperate to find new policies to implement in order to try to win votes.

The Gillard government celebrated the passing of a controversial mining tax which came into effect in July 2012 which failed to raise as much money as expected and was later repealed by Tony Abbot's government when they replaced the outgoing Labor government..

On 26 June, 2013, amid Labour party tensions, Gillard announced a second leadership ballot and undertook to stand down if she was unsuccessful. Rudd defeated Gillard in the ballot so she resigned as Australia's first female Prime Minister and gave a very dignified withdrawal speech. Kevin Rudd was sworn in as Prime Minister for the second time on 27 June, 2013 which destabilised the Labour Party before losing the next election to his political rivals.

Above left:
Margaret Ogg in old age.

Above right:
The young Vida Goldstein. Detail of a portrait painted from a photograph. National Library of Australia.

Right:
The Goldstein sisters and their younger brother. Private collection.

Enid Burnell Lyons.

Julia Gillard.

CHAPTER 9

The Honourable Dame Quentin Bryce, AD CVO (born 1942)

AUSTRALIA'S FIRST FEMALE GOVERNOR GENERAL

A lot of the things I do best, I do quietly. Quentin Bryce.

Her Excellency Ms Quentin Alice Louise Bryce made history as the first woman to be appointed Governor-General of Australia, a post intended to 'encourage, articulate and represent those things that unite Australians as a nation'.[1] The position of Governor-General was inaugurated by Queen Victoria, who planned to fill it with minor members of the Royal family or retired British generals or former British diplomats. No Australian was appointed until 1965.

As the Queen's representative, a Governor-General can appoint or dismiss a Prime Minister. Should an election result in a hung Parliament, it falls to the Governor-General to decide which party should govern. The position was created to ensure the continuance of stable government so it is vital that the Governor-

General is above politics and seen as having no political affiliations.

When Her Excellency Quentin Bryce, Governor of Queensland, was chosen to be the next Governor-General by Prime Minister Rudd, she was well known in Queensland but people in other states knew little about her. She set up a website to inform the public of the scope of her duties and engagements. So good was the delivery of her speeches and so polished and elegant her public appearances, that Queenslanders felt very proud of their Queensland-born Governor-General. In 2010, an internet poll was conducted by News Limited to choose Queensland's most glamorous female celebrity and Her Excellency Ms Quentin Bryce was the winner.[2]

***

In 1975, soon after arriving from London I started work at the University of Queensland library. The fact that civil liberties under the Bjelke-Petersen government were abused shocked me. Dr Janet Irwin, trailblazing Head of the University's Student Health Centre, told me that street marches were forbidden and those who sought social change, as she did, were blacklisted and had their telephones tapped by the police.[3]

Dr Janet Irwin, a friend of Quentin Bryce, introduced me to her. When I first met the glamorous Ms Bryce she lectured at the T.C. Beirne Law School, was in her thirties and had five school-age children. She stood out from other feminists on campus. Most of them were wearing t-shirts printed with feminist slogans, long cotton skirts or blue jeans and rarely wore make-up. In contrast, Ms Bryce wore tailored suits in brilliant colours, high heels and bright red lipstick. Her elegant suits were made by a male tailor in Brisbane out of exquisite materials. To enliven her wardrobe, Quentin enjoyed visiting op-shops where she used her keen eye for fashion to find fascinating 'pre-loved' items like hand-embroidered waistcoats.

Dr Irwin told me that 'Quentin Bryce is an excellent speaker, a very private person and a perfectionist. She adores her children and is good at networking with other women, which is vital if we are to change things in this backward state.'

Even as early as the 1970s, the achievements of Ms Bryce were impressive. With an arts degree as well as a degree in law, she was one of the first women to be admitted to the Queensland bar. Instead of practising as a barrister, she became the first female lecturer at the Faculty of Law.

Years later, attending a conference on mental health, the high achieving Ms Quentin Bryce admitted to having had 'dark nights of the soul'. Unable to sleep, she lay in bed 'shrouded in fear' and worrying she might have a nervous breakdown. She was thinking of tasks still to be done, wondering how she could cope with family commitments as well as holding down a demanding job. At times she had a hacking cough, which she feared might turn into pneumonia. Had her mother and her husband not been so supportive, she could have had a breakdown.

This frank admission from a woman who was widely admired made other women feel better about their own weak moments. Quentin Bryce had been forced 'to rid herself of the Superwoman concept' of doing everything perfectly — being the perfect hostess, the perfect wife and mother and the perfect community worker'.[4]

'You *can* have it all,' Quentin Bryce told younger women she mentored. 'But *not* all at the same time.' She advised working mothers to give priority to their own health in order to safeguard their families.

Often a particular item will trigger memories of the past. To Marcel Proust, author of *Remembrance of Things Past*, a small cake known as a *madeleine* aroused memories of his childhood. The triggers for Quentin Bryce to remember her happy childhood are the sweetly scented flowering stocks that her mother raised and tended in their garden at isolated Ilfracombe. This was a remote settlement in the Queensland outback where her father managed the Ilfracombe wool scour.

Like most outback people, Quentin's parents experienced good and bad times. At the Ilfracombe wool scour, whose owner was the town's largest employer, men scoured or cleansed the wool sent there by local graziers.

By today's standards, Quentin's father had a tough childhood. Norman Strachan came from a family of six children and money was often short. Quentin's paternal grandfather, Cornelius (Neil) Strachan, was a master carpenter who had migrated from the small town of Strachan, near Aberdeen, which was named after his family. Neil Strachan had settled at Austinmer, near Wollongong.

Norman Strachan was clever and under normal circumstances would have done well at Wollongong High School, which he attended for only one year. Lack of money meant he was about to be withdrawn from school and, to support his siblings, would have to work in the local coal mines. A stroke of luck saved Quentin's father from this fate.

As a strong swimmer and a keen surfer, Norman Strachan became captain of the Austinmer surf club and in this capacity risked his life to save a child from drowning. This was his lucky break as the child's wealthy parents were so grateful they offered Norman Strachan a job at their Botany Woollen Mills, where he learned about wool processing. Norman Strachan worked hard and was eventually appointed manager of the Ilfracombe wool scour, near Longreach, owned by the wealthy Whiddon family.

In 1936, on a visit to Winton, Norman Strachan met attractive Naida Wetzel from Brisbane. Naida had attended All Hallows School and Brisbane's Teacher Training College and worked in the small school in Winton. Naida's father, Edward Wetzel, had migrated to Queensland from Germany and was in charge of Brisbane's Spring Hill swimming baths. After Norman Strachan married Naida Wetzel, they went to live in the manager's house in Ilfracombe.

Quentin's mother had a natural elegance that she passed on to her daughters. Her slim figure and excellent fashion sense made her stand out in a crowd. Naida taught her daughters to read and write and impressed on them the importance of appearing elegant.

Sending away by post to buy fine cottons and delicate lawns, Naida made her pretty little girls exquisite dresses, fit for princesses, some with rows of delicate hand smocking on the bodice.

In 1940, Norman Strachan managed the Carrar wool scour before returning to Ilfracombe, resuming his post as scour manager. The production of wool was regarded as a strategic war activity, so Quentin's father and his employees were exempt from war service.

Naida Strachan's first daughter, Diane, was borne in 1937, two years before the outbreak of World War Two. On 23 December 1942, the Strachans' second daughter was born in Brisbane.[5] They named her Quentin, a name people would not easily forget. In 1944, Naida's third daughter, Revelyn, was borne and three years later she had another girl who was named Helene.

For almost 10 years, the Strachan family lived in the manager's house on the outskirts of Ilfracombe. In spite of the harsh conditions of outback Queensland, Naida Strachan managed to create a beautiful garden with herbaceous borders and a lily pond. During the blistering heat of summer the children paddled in the lily pond. There was also a tennis court on which family and friends enjoyed playing.

Older residents of Ilfracombe remember the generous bush hospitality provided by Mr and Mrs Strachan. Families from surrounding areas gathered at their home, bringing food and drink with them.[6]

In the 1940s, Ilfracombe had little in the way of amenities. Quentin's father, as a councillor of the Ilfracombe Shire, did his best to secure reticulated water and electricity for the area. Local mothers taught their children with the aid of correspondence courses and, as an experienced teacher, Mrs Strachan was often consulted by mothers who had problems teaching their children.

To give her own daughters the best possible start in life, Mrs Strachan schooled her four daughters at home. Her dedication to education benefited her children's future. Naida Strachan played the piano well and her husband played the violin and they hoped to impart a love of music in their daughters.

Norman Strachan told his daughters, 'You can be whatever you want — just work hard when you are at school and never waste your time.'

Like many children of that era Quentin may have suffered from a condition known as rickets. But, whatever the reason, she had to wear cumbersome callipers or leg braces as a child, which made her sympathetic to the plight of the disabled.

Quentin's elder sister Diane (Craddock) recalls,

> Quentin had a knee problem as a child so had to wear heavy leg braces but the braces seem to have solved the problem because there is no trace of it now. I think that the experience left Quentin with a particular sympathy for people who have disabilities.

By 1949, prices for raw wool were declining, which had its effect on the income from the Ilfracombe scour. Determined their daughters would have the benefits of secondary — and if possible tertiary — education, the Strachans left Ilfracombe. In the Brisbane suburb of Belmont, Norman became manager of another scour for Morris Woollen Mills.

Subsequently, the Strachan family moved to Launceston, but later returned to Belmont. Quentin, who was 9-years-old by that time, attended Camp Hill School. There she met Michael Bryce, the elder brother of one of her school friends, who was in the school's top class.

In 1956, Quentin's parents stretched themselves financially to pay the fees for her to become a boarder at Brisbane's Moreton Bay College. Quentin was very happy there, made good friends and enjoyed acting in plays. She did extremely well scholastically and matriculated with flying colours.

She described her headmistress as an excellent role model.

> ...a well educated, professional woman, highly regarded. Widowed with two children, she ran a home and a school. She got on with whatever needed to be done, assiduously and without fuss. Her forthright example assured us of our capacity

> to do anything we chose while teaching [us] to share its rewards well and beyond our fortunate selves.
>
> My education was the greatest advantage of my life. I know how hard my parents worked to give it to me. My chance discovery that Dad had continued to pay off my school fees long after I had left Moreton Bay College profoundly affected me. It disclosed my parents' quiet resolve, their commitment to my lifelong advancement and well-being and their tacit anticipation that I would make something decent of their investment. I had a clear sense it was my duty to do what I could to secure the same for those who were less advantaged, particularly women... Feminism was for me a natural and necessary consequence of those days.[7]

While young Quentin was at Moreton Bay College, the Strachans moved to Tenterfield, where Norman Strachan attempted to become a grazier. But in spite of working extremely hard, Norman's rural property suffered from a series of droughts and floods, so he lost a great deal of money. As a result, he took other employment out in the bush.

So that her daughters could continue their education, Naida Strachan and the girls moved to a small house in St Lucia, where Mrs Strachan worked as a remedial teacher at the Brisbane Spastic Centre. Quentin frequently accompanied her mother when she took disabled people on outings, which increased her understanding and sympathy for the problems disabled people face.

At the University of Queensland, far smaller than it is today, Quentin enrolled in the Bachelor of Arts course. As a university student, she took several part-time jobs, such as baby sitting, and earned some extra pocket money.

In 1962, Quentin completed her Bachelor of Arts. She stayed on to study law and became involved in student politics.

Quentin, by now a tall, slim young woman, started to date Michael Bryce. Ten years previously, she had met Michael when they both attended Camp Hill School. When they met again, Michael Bryce was studying architecture and also active in student affairs. The couple had several rendezvous in romantic surroundings at the Gold Coast. Quentin was sun-tanned and her blonde hair was bleached almost white by the sun. After some time, Michael Bryce realised he wanted to spend the rest of his life with this remarkable young woman. His feeling were reciprocated.

They did some of their courting at dances and parties at Government House in Brisbane. Michael, who had joined the University Air Squadron, was *aide de camp* to the Governor, Sir Henry Abel Smith. Sir Henry and his wife approved of Quentin and told Michael he had made an excellent choice of fiancée.

On 12 December 1964, Michael Bryce and Quentin Strachan had a traditional white wedding at St John's Anglican Cathedral in Brisbane. They set up house in Swan Road in the university suburb of St Lucia, where Quentin had lived as a student.

After Quentin had her first baby in 1966, Michael had a chance to go to London to work for a leading firm of architects. So the couple and young Michael, (always known as 'Jack') moved to London. In the 1960s. a period known as the 'Swinging Sixties' the role of women changed substantially. In London Quentin saw enterprising young women establishing flourishing businesses and found it an exciting place. Australians Germaine Greer and Carmen Callil were working there. Callil established the Virago Press to publish books by women and broke the male stranglehold on publishing. In the front of each book by this important small publishing house was the feminist manifesto: 'It is only when women start to organise in large numbers that we become a political force and can move towards the possibility of a truly democratic society'.[8]

Quentin, always a voracious reader, read all the latest feminist books while baby Jack slept. She contemplated what she would do once she and her husband returned to Australia.

In her second year in London, Quentin fell pregnant. In 1967, she had a little girl, who was named Revelyn (Revvy) after Quentin's younger sister.

With her keen eye for fashion, Quentin Bryce saw the work of young designers like Mary Quant — who had a shop in King's Road, Chelsea — and Barbara Hulanicki, founder of the Biba store in Kensington. Quentin enjoyed wearing mini-skirts long before they reached the Antipodes. In 1965, Australia's ultra-conservative society was shocked when the English model Jean Shrimpton attended the Melbourne Cup without a hat, stockings or gloves, wearing a mini-skirt.

Returning to Brisbane in 1968 with two young children, Quentin found many Brisbane ladies still wearing elaborate hats and white gloves to shop in Queen Street. Married women, especially those with children, rarely had paid jobs. Mayor Rex Pilbeam of Rockhampton sacked a young female library assistant once he learned she was married.

Many people were amazed when Quentin Bryce, mother of two children, took a tutoring job in the Faculty of Law. Quentin proved so popular with her students she was appointed the first female lecturer at the T. Beirne School of Law, which was a male dominated establishment.

Many of Quentin's former students still speak with fondness of her. Ruth Nicholls, a law student working part time to fund her studies, arrived for a tutorial, looking tired and flustered, having not had time for breakfast. It became clear to Quentin that her student had trouble concentrating. On learning that Ruth had not eaten for some considerable time, Quentin went outside, made Ruth a cup of coffee in the staff kitchenette and brought it back for her with a plate of biscuits.

'None of the male lecturers would have done that,' said Ruth. 'They would not have dreamed of going to that much trouble. Quentin Bryce *really* cared about her students.'

✳✳✳

By 1973, Quentin and her husband had five children. In addition to Jack and Revelyn, came Rupert, born in Brisbane in 1969, Clothilde (Chloe), born in 1971, and Tom, born in 1973. During those busy years, Quentin's mother was a tower of strength and helped her daughter whenever she was needed.

Around that time, I met Quentin Bryce in the university staff club, where she was chatting with several young male lecturers from the law school. Some elderly male academics were outraged by Quentin's presence there and expressed their opinion that with a husband and five children she should be at home cooking dinner.

Dr Janet Irwin defended her friend and said that Quentin and her husband were caring parents. They employed a reliable housekeeper who fetched their children from school and cooked evening meals for the family. Besides, Michael Bryce was a supportive husband who helped his wife in her career.

In the 1970s, law was regarded as a male career — there were few female law students and major law firms rarely employed women. But Quentin and a few other women like her, dedicated to change, eventually triumphed. In 2010, almost three decades later, female students in the University's Faculty of Law outnumber male students.

My granddaughter graduated from the law school at Queensland University and has now an impressive career. Had it not been for women like Quentin Bryce, stellar careers for female lawyers would have been harder to achieve.

Eventually, Quentin Bryce and her feisty female friends like Dale Spender and Janet Irwin, did win many of their battles. In the early 1970s, Ms Bryce began agitating for a *troika* of things she wished to see instituted — affordable childcare for working mothers, paid maternity leave and social justice and fairness in the workplace. When Quentin and her friends started talking about putting such things in place, it seemed like a pipe dream. But today women like her have succeeded in many of their aims.

The period of change for women continued throughout the 1970s and in the early 1980s. Dr Janet Irwin was made to suffer for her stance on Queensland's outdated abortion laws, but received a great deal of support from her feminist friends, including Quentin Bryce. Quentin's friend, Dale Spender, author of *Women of Ideas and what men have done to them* and other significant books, shared similar aims and goals for women.[9]

In 1978, Quentin Bryce was appointed to the National Women's Advisory Council under the Fraser government and left the University of Queensland for her new role.

⁂

Eventually, Norman and Naida Strachan moved to a farm at Cooroy before settling at Mount Tamborine. In 1985, Quentin's father died and her mother moved back to Brisbane.

In 1984, Quentin Bryce was appointed Inaugural Director of the Women's Information Service, then under the umbrella of Queensland's Office of the Status of Women. Three years later, she became the Director of the Human Rights and Equal Opportunities Commission of Queensland. In 1988, she became federal Sex Discrimination Commissioner within the Human Rights and Equal Opportunity Commission under the Hawke government.

Each year more than 2000 complaints were handled by the commission and Quentin had to deal with some difficult cases. One man sued Quentin for sexual discrimination after she wrote 'Another example of a male wasting our time!' at the bottom of one of his letters. After the man was informed about this he filed a law suit against Ms Bryce, but it was dismissed by the judge.

Quentin Bryce achieved a great deal, mainly because she was able to win the confidence of many different groups. Since she was always well groomed and wearing lipstick, women with traditional views on life could not accuse Ms Bryce of being a bra-burning radical. Her commitment to equal rights for women reassured her female colleagues she was not just masquerading as a reformer, but was true to feminist ideals.

Research at London's Tavistock Clinic had proved that psychological damage could be the consequence of separating young children from their mothers when hospitalised. In Queensland parents were allowed to visit sick children only at selected hours. Juvenile patients often cry when their parents leave them, so it was considered better if they visited them as rarely as possible.

Ms Bryce's concern about the welfare of sick and disabled children has always been close to her heart. The Association for the Welfare of Children in Hospital, of which Quentin Bryce was a member, lobbied for mothers to have the right to stay overnight with their hospitalised children.

When she feared her young son might be suffering from leukaemia, Quentin took a mattress and pillow with her to the hospital and refused to leave her son's room. She stuck to her guns and won the right for mothers to spend the night in hospital with their young children in the case of serous illness.

Ms Bryce was made an Officer of the Order of Australia (OA) in 1988. Later, she was awarded an Honorary Doctorate of Laws by Macquarie University and other Australian universities followed suit.[10]

In 1992, Dr Janet Irwin brought Quentin Bryce to the launch of my book *The Impressionists Revealed, Masterpieces and Collectors*. After the speeches were over, I had a long talk with Janet Irwin and Quentin Bryce.[11] It was evident that Quentin had a keen interest in art, having studied the subject before taking a law degree.

Quentin Bryce was appointed founding Chair and CEO of the National Childcare Accreditation Council and her committee skills saw her chairing the National Breast Cancer Council. She was also a member of the Australian Children's Television Foundation, which had been set up with the aim of improving television programs for children.

Towards the end of 1997, Quentin Bryce accepted the appointment as Principal and Chief Executive Officer of the Women's College of Sydney University. By now, her children were adult and her husband's architectural and design business was thriving. Michael Bryce had to travel interstate and overseas and was working on design projects for the Sydney Olympic Games.

In Sydney, Quentin enjoyed mentoring female students who came to her for guidance. She was regarded as having run Women's College extremely well. The student residents approved of the changes she had made, including the dismissal of the cook who had served stodgy food to the resident students of Women's College. The students either ate what they were offered and gained weight or starved themselves, which in both cases was bad for their health. Quentin Bryce was appalled by the unhealthy food on offer, so she hired a new chef and instituted a salad bar from which the students could serve themselves.[12]

⁂

In 1992, Canadian-born Leneen Forde was appointed as Queensland's first female governor. She made an effort to remove some of the stuffy formalities from Government House and provided a warm and friendly style of hospitality.[13] Leneen Forde instituted a warmer and less formal approach to ceremonies. Eventually, she was replaced by Major-General Peter Arnison, whose term of office ended in 2003. So who would be the next Governor?

On Quentin Bryce's 60th birthday, she received a phone call from Premier Peter Beattie, who had been one of her law students. After wishing her a happy birthday Peter Beattie asked, 'How would you like to be Queensland's new governor?' As there was no immediate reply, Beattie asked, 'Do you need time to think it over?'

Ms Bryce has never been one to dither over decisions. She told the Premier she would be happy to accept the appointment.

On 29 July 2003, Her Excellency Ms Quentin Bryce (the title by which she wished to be called in her new office) was sworn in as Queensland's 24th governor. She was thrilled that her beloved mother was able to be present to see her sworn in. In her acceptance speech, the new governor stated that she regarded her governorship as

> ... a unique opportunity to serve the community in which I was nurtured, educated, my values and principles shaped and where I was encouraged to participate in our democracy

Governor Bryce received a wide range of guests at Government House and invited many country people who had extended warm bush hospitality to her and her husband. Many of her guests were enduring tough times during a long drought and a visit to Government House was a great boost to their morale.

Like all good hostesses, the new governor thought about the comfort of her guests. She placed people around the table where there were opportunities for them to make useful connections, networking being one of Ms Bryce's strengths. She aimed to make

Government House accessible to people who had never been there before and honour those who did valuable work in the community. It was a demanding job and Governor Bryce described how

> A big box of papers would be delivered to me on Tuesdays, for Executive Council meetings on Thursdays... I wasn't going to sign anything unless I knew what it was about, so I made a point of reading all the papers in order to be well prepared for the meeting and well informed about everything that was going on but... sometimes I had to stay up all night to do it.
>
> I also thought a lot about the governor's ceremonial role... I have a strong feeling about the importance of ritual and ceremony in reinforcing democratic traditions and processes... I wanted to carry out these duties impeccably, but with friendliness. I was always grateful for my legal background, a big advantage when I was doing that sort of thing.
>
> I gained great respect for people who contribute to democracy by taking on public office. Once politicians were lofty and inaccessible. Now, they are expected to be available and responsive to every representation, every demand.
>
> Queensland is a big and far flung place and it takes all a governor's time to get around it. You have really got to take your hat off to those early governors who did so much travelling despite the difficulties of their times. Wherever we went we found people were pleased to see us and we were enriched by the people we met. Every day, everywhere, we found examples of courage, inspiration and support in the generous contributions made to our cultural, economic, political and intellectual life by remarkable people.

In her role as Governor of Queensland, Ms Bryce provided a great deal of encouragement to the disabled. Jane Steinberg, the daughter of one of Quentin's university friends, was born with a disability. Ms Bryce used to invite Jane and her mother to tea at Government House on Jane's birthday.[14] This is only one instance of Quentin Bryce's many acts of kindness, which are often overlooked. Ms Bryce claims, 'A lot of the things I do best, I do quietly.'

Jane Steinberg said, 'You realise when you are talking to Governor Bryce that she understands the special problems and difficulties of disabled people.'[15]

The governor made friends with Aboriginal women after spending time with them at Groote Eylandt and met women from the Lockhart River Aboriginal community during a conference. Later, she visited the Lockhart River region and stayed for two days in the Women's Centre there to help her understand their problems. She invited Aboriginal women from Lockhart River to stay at Government House.

Her mother's death, which occurred in the early years of her term as Queensland governor, was a sad time for Quentin Bryce. She was deeply attached to her mother, a woman greatly admired.

Ms Bryce's schedule was daunting and demanded she was in good health. As well as attending a large number of official functions, Governor Bryce kept up with some of the young women she had mentored at the Women's College of Sydney University and with representatives of various charitable organisations.

Queensland is a very large state and visits from the governor were important for bolstering morale in outback towns, especially in times of severe drought. Her Excellency Governor Bryce took a special pleasure meeting country people and this brought back happy memories of her outback childhood.

As state governor, she held breakfast meetings, received callers in the morning, ate a sparse luncheon with other visitors — hence her razor-slim figure, the envy of many women of her age. At times, she acted as hostess at dinners and receptions for as many as 200 people.

What surprised many of Quentin's friends were complaints in the press that she had held the wedding of one of her children at Government House, while paying the costs of food and drink herself. Government House was the home of Michael and Quentin Bryce — surely, they were allowed to host a wedding there.

As Governor of Queensland, Ms Bryce visited Britain to meet Queen Elizabeth II and found Her Majesty extraordinarily well informed about Australia and was surprised by her interest in everything that happens 'down under.'

Ms Bryce worked extremely hard, sometimes attending as many as six or seven events in a single day. Her day often began with a breakfast meeting, followed by organisational work during the morning. Then she would host an official lunch. After several hours of work in the afternoon she had to attend an official dinner. Amid this hectic life, Ms Bryce still found time to host functions for those who train guide dogs and a display of wheelchair dancing for the disabled. Meanwhile, she did not forget her friends or responsibilities to her children, who were now adults, some already married.

∗∗∗

Quentin Bryce, who is a great reader, is supportive of books and writers. In 2004, she was kind enough to launch my book *Heroic Australian Women in War*. In spite of her busy schedule she had found time to read my book from cover to cover, so she was able to give an inspiring and well informed speech. She mentioned Brisbane-born Sister Joyce Twedell, who weighed only four stone when rescued from a Japanese death camp along with other 'Paradise Road' nurses. After the war Joyce Twedell retrained and became a senior radiographer and radiation expert at the Royal Brisbane Hospital. The governor's brilliant speech about these brave Army nursing sisters brought tears to the eyes of many in the audience.[16]

In 2006, Quentin Bryce was awarded an Honorary Doctorate of Laws by the University of Queensland. In her acceptance speech, she said that being honoured by her own university was dear to her heart.

Several years later, Governor Bryce and I were on the same platform as speakers at a fund-raising event at Brisbane's Greek Club, organised by the Greek Consul for Queensland, Alex Freeleagus. As a lawyer in private practice, Alex had known Quentin for years and greatly admired her. The intention was to raise money for Austcare, an Australian charity with programs to help refugees in camps all over the world.

Governor Bryce looked elegant as ever and made an inspiring speech about the plight of refugees in camps and quoted passages out of my book, *Blue Ribbons, Bitter Bread*, which describes the aid work carried out by Joice Loch in the 1920s and after World War Two. This remarkable woman had worked for refugees from Poland and helped people who had escaped to Greece from ethnic cleansing in Turkey. Our joint efforts raised thousands of dollars for the valuable relief work in refugee camps, carried out by Austcare.[17]

Quentin Bryce's five-year term as governor of Queensland resulted in praise for the excellence of her speeches, the long hours she worked and her elegance, wearing clothes designed by leading Australian designers.

In 2008, Labor Premier Anna Bligh announced that Governor Bryce had been an inspiring leader and hoped that she would stay on as governor. Ms Bryce replied by saying she looked forward to an extended term, because it would take her through Queensland's important sesquicentenary celebrations.

However, circumstances prevented Ms Bryce from staying on as Governor of Queensland. In 2008 it was announced that, on the recommendation of Prime Minister Kevin Rudd, Her Majesty the Queen had approved the appointment of Ms Quentin Bryce as Governor-General of Australia.

Stating that this was 'an opportunity I could not refuse', on 5 September Ms Quentin Bryce was sworn in as Australia's twenty-fifth Governor-General. Her duties included opening new sessions of the Commonwealth Parliament, welcoming and entertaining visiting heads of state; receiving the credentials of foreign ambassadors and ministers of the Crown, entertaining representatives of community organisations and conducting investitures. In addition, Governor Bryce has to assent to every piece of legislation that goes through federal Parliament and must act as nominal head of the Armed Forces.[18]

As a former academic, when first invited by the military top brass to make inspections of the armed forces, Her Excellency was honest enough to admit that 'I was a bit nervous about uniforms at first. But they welcomed me and I gained a lot of respect for the military and made many friends among the armed services community'.

As Australia's commander in chief, the Governor-General attended several military ceremonies, visited Australian troops serving in Afghanistan and sat with pilots of Hercules transport planes. She talked with those in dangerous jobs such as detecting bombs planted by terrorists. Ms Bryce praised Australian soldiers and officers she met on her trips overseas for their courage, sense of humour under difficult conditions and their professional skills.

As Governor-General from 2008 until 2014 Quentin Bryce had even greater distances to travel by air and land. Instead of dealing with Queensland politicians and residents, she entertained ambassadors and visiting foreign dignitaries. As Governor-General she had a large staff with a high staff turnover and was given a generous dress allowance which ensured she always looked extremely elegant.

As Governor General Quentin Bryce received a great many invitations to launch projects and make speeches. An excellent and inspiring speaker, she acted as patron to several hundred voluntary organisations and charities and took an active interest in all of them.[19] She was specially concerned about the disabled people and was and is a member of several prestigious clubs for women.

She made many journeys overseas including one to the Gallipoli Peninsula for the 2010 Anzac celebrations. It was delayed after an Icelandic volcano produced so much volcanic dust airlines found it too dangerous to fly. Eventually, after long delays, the Governor-General arrived at Gallipoli, where she gave one of her most emotive speeches. In July 2010, she made an official visit to the battlefields and the Fromelles (Pheasant Wood) Military Cemetery, where in company with Prince Charles she attended a service for Anzacs who had died on French soil.

As Governor-General she made several vice-regal visits to Her Majesty Queen Elizabeth II at Buckingham Palace and at Balmoral

Castle in the Scottish Highlands. On one occasion, a scheduled 20-minute meeting between Ms Bryce and the Queen continued for nearly an hour as they found so many topics to discuss.

⁂

On 13 November 2009, the Bryce's daughter Chloe Bryce-Parkin and Bill Shorten, having divorced their respective partners, had a quiet wedding in Melbourne. A month later, the new Mrs Shorten gave birth to a little girl called Clementine, another grandchild for Quentin and Michael Bryce.

In October 2009, there was a sense of outrage in some sections of the press, as Parliament had been told that the Governor-General's African trip had cost taxpayers $700,000 to plan and implement at a time when the Australian public were being urged to tighten their belts.[20] In an article titled *The High Price of Quentin Bryce*, it was claimed that the Governor-General requested not one but *two* private jets for her entourage, but later it appeared that one was enough. The article estimated the Governor-General and her entourage cost the taxpayer $64,000 for meals and gifts and the hire of the Presidential Suite in a luxury hotel in Mauritius.

The late Susan Stratigos Wilson, another mutual friend, who moved in political and diplomatic circles in Canberra, defended Quentin Bryce and said these criticisms of her African visit unjustified. It was almost impossible for a Governor-General to refuse a request by a serving Prime Minister to make an official visit overseas. Whatever Quentin Bryce's opinions in the matter, she was obliged to go to Africa. While in Africa , she used her time wisely and demonstrated her sympathy for the underprivileged by her talks with African children in primary schools to whom she gave small gifts. She also talked at length with groups of African women and enjoyed a lengthy meeting with Nelson Mandela. On record is the fact the Ms Bryce worked hard and did not have a single free day.

Controversy over the Governor-General's role filled the papers during the August 2010 election when it seemed there could be a hung Parliament. Had this occurred, she would have been called to act as umpire and decide whether Labor under Julia Gillard or the Coalition under Tony Abbott should form government.

Concern was felt by right-wing voters over possible bias in view of Ms Bryce's close family ties to Labor. Melbourne barrister Peter Faris QC called on the Governor-General to stand aside in favour of the Chief Justice if called on to make such a major decision. In interviews with the Sydney and Melbourne press, Faris added that Bryce's son-in-law (Bill Shorten, the architect of the conspiracy for Gillard to supplant Rudd and now Shadow Labour Prime Minister was certain to gain a place in a cabinet formed by Julia Gillard (a prophecy which proved correct). Peter Faris QC ended his opinion by quoting from an essay on the role of the Governor-General: that 'Australia is entitled to a governor who is independent and above politics.'[21]

Labor voters felt that Farris had gone too far but clearly her daughter [now married to Bill Shorten would have benefitted hbad the Governor General n Bryce chosen Labor to govern'.[22]

A spokeswoman for Chief Justice Robert French added that neither he (Robert French) nor other High Court judges would advise the Governor-General, just in case the matter ended up before them in court. When Governor Quentin Bryce asked the Commonwealth Solicitor-General, Stephen Gageler, for his opinion, Gageler claimed it was totally unnecessary for the Governor-General to stand aside as there was *no* conflict of interest. The impasse resolved itself when three Independent MPs and one Green MP joined forces with Labor, ensuring Julia Gillard was able to hold on to the reins of government.

There was more public discussion of the work of the Governor-General when Senator Michael Ronaldson queried the size of the vice-regal entourage on the Governor's visits to Sydney. During the year, Ms Bryce had hosted 38 official events at Admiralty House, which is the Governor-General's second official residence at Kirribili. Parliament was assured the reason for transporting the entourage to Sydney was to *save* money, as it was cheaper than employing resident chefs or household managers at Admiralty House on a permanent basis.

In November 2010, the Governor-General received the good wishes of Australian football lovers when, as the patron of Australian women's football, she and her husband flew to Zurich as part of the Australian delegation, hoping Australia would be chosen to host the 2022 FIFA World Cup. Before leaving, Quentin Bryce announced, 'We will be presenting a very strong case to FIFA on how Australia could host a fantastic 2022 World Cup in our beautiful and friendly country'.

The Australian government had spent forty-six-million dollars of taxpayers' money in their bid to obtain the cup and believed America to be their main rival. However, FIFA officials were swayed by Qatar's suggestion of demountable sport arenas to be re-erected in Africa as well as other considerations. Australia received no more than *one* vote from the FIFA Executive. Hearing the news that Qatar would host the 2022 World Cup, the shock and distress on the Governor-General's face spoke volumes.

Quentin's husband, Michael Bryce AM, AE, who retired from his architectural practice with a string of awards and served in a voluntary capacity as adjunct professor of Architecture and Design at Canberra's National University.[23]

On 22 Novermber Quentin Bryce delivered the annual ABC Boyer Lecture, arousing controversy by appearing to support gay marriage by her statement that she would like to see an Australia where 'people are free to love and marry whom they chose'. However Prime Minister Tony Abbott support Bryce's right to comment on the topic saying she was expressing a personal view .

Quentin Bryce had been created a Companion of the Order of Austraia AC on 30 April 2003, a Commander of the Roayl Victorian Order CVO, a personal award given by H.M. Queen Elizabeth II during her royal visit and a Dame of the Order of Australia on 25 March 2014 by Liberal Leader Tony Abbott, before she retired as Governor-General the following month.

At the end of her term of office having been appointed a Dame by the government of Tony Abbott, Quentin and Michael Bryce returned to live in Brisbane and purchased a house in Indooroopilly.

Determined she would continue to make a difference to the lives of others, Dame Quentin Bryce was appointed chair of a new Queensland Government task force on domestic violence and given an office at the Queensland Institute of Technology to carry out this important task. This job is now her prime focus. Her devotion to the task in hand and her enthusiasm for her new job will hopefully make a make a substantial difference to the unacceptably high rate of domestic violence in her home state.

Above: Quentin Strachan as a schoolgirl. Courtesy H.E. The Governor General

Right: Dr Janet Irwin, AM, friend of Quentin Bryce and Susanna de Vries.

Below: Government House, Bardon, Queensland. Photo Jake de Vries.

H.E. Quentin Bryce launching *Heroic Australian Women in War* for Susanna de Vries with the late Alex Freeleagus, Greek Consul of Queensland, on her right. Photos by Jake de Vries.

H.E. Quentin Bryce receiving an honorary doctorate from the Chancellor of the University of Queensland. Photo © University of Queensland.

Acknowledgements

Thanks to Dame Quentin Bryce for allowing me to reproduce her photographs and to photographer Marcus Bell of Studio Impressions, Brisbane. Thanks to Lavinia Tritton for the use of photographs and material on Nell Tritton and to Douglas Tritton for information and to fellow art historian Bronwyn Wright for information she provided on her grandmother, Hilda Rix Nicholas, and for permission to reproduce of Hilda's paintings and drawings. . Thanks also to the staff at the Fryer Library of the University of Queensland. the John Oxley Library, Brisbane, Sydney's Mitchell Library and the New York Public Library for help with research.And special thanks to my husband. Jake de Vries fora preliminary edit of the text and for designing the cover and the interior of the book.

Endnotes

CHAPTER 1

1. Caldwell, J. C. *Australians Historical Statistics*, p. 23. Fairfax, Syme, Weldon Associates, Sydney, 1987. Gives a rate of 80 per cent of male population in rural areas.

2. Pool, Dennis. *What Jane Austen Ate and Charles Dickens Knew, the Facts of Life in Nineteenth Century England.* Simon and Schuster, London and New York, 1994.

3. Hellier Donna. *Families in Colonial Australia,* edited by Patricia Grimshaw. Allen and Unwin, Sydney, 1985.

4. See also the article on Caroline Chisholm's marriage by Patricia Grimshaw in *For Richer, For Poorer, Early Colonial Marriages,* ed. Penny Russell, Melbourne University Press, Melbourne, 1994 and biographies of Caroline Chisholm by Margaret Kiddie, *Caroline Chisholm,* Melbourne University Press, Melbourne, 1950; Mary Hoban. *Fifty-One Pieces of Wedding Cake,* Lodden Press, Kilmore, Victoria, 1976; Bogley, Joanna, *The Immigrant's Friend,* Moorhouse Publishing, 1994. The latest work on Chisholm by Carole Walker, *The Savior of Living Cargoes, the Life and Work of Caroline Chisholm,* Australian Scholarly Publishing, Melbourne, 2009 is a very detailed biography which contains Caroline's family tree, a chronology of the lectures and meetings she held in England and interesting theories about Caroline's childhood. It postulates she may have been born out of wedlock.

5. *Sydney Emigrants Journal,* 1850, cited in Kiddle, *Caroline Chisholm, Op. cit.* p.14.

6. Thierry, Judge Roger. *Reminiscences of Thirty Years Residence in New South Wales,* London, 1833. Provides a description of the Immigration Barracks.

7. Chisholm, C. *Female Immigration Considered in a Brief Account of the Sydney Immigrants' Home.* James Tegg, London, 1842 cited in Kiddle, Margaret, *Op. cit.*

8. *Ibid.*

9. *Ibid.*

10. *Ibid.*

11. *Ibid.*

12. Gandivia, E. *Tears Often Shed. Child Health and Welfare in Australia from 1788.* Charter Books, Sydney, 1977.

13. Madgewick, K. B. *Immigration into Eastern Australia. 1937.*

14 Cited by Margaret Kiddle, p. 63.

15 Lord Shaftesbury, philanthropist and reformer, succeeded in banning children under nine from working in mills, women and children from working underground in mines and the use of small boys as chimney sweeps. Shaftesbury was active in other good causes including the 'Ragged Schools' movement, legislation to provide lodgings for the poor and in supporting the work of Florence Nightingale.

16 In London, Caroline Chisholm published *Emigration and Transportation Considered,* published John Oliver, London, 1847, and *Comfort for the Poor! Meat Three times a Day!* a pamphlet urging the poor to emigrate to NSW. In 1849, she published *Family Colonization Loan Society by the Grant of Loans for Two Years or More Without Interest... to the Colonies of New South Wales, Port Phillip and South Australia by Mrs Chisholm: The ABC of Colonization having appended... the rules of the Family Colonization Society,* 1850. In 1853, her articles were reprinted under the title *Mrs Chisholm's Advice* to *Immigrants.*

17 *Household Words.* Charles Dickens vol. 1, (1850), p. 43. Cited in Kiddie.

19 Chisholm, C. *The ABC of Colonization. A series of letters addressed to the Gentlemen forming the Committee of the Family Colonization Society formed by Lord Ashley, MP, the Rt. Hon. Sydney Herbert, MP, the Hon. Vernon Smith, MP etc.* published by John Olivier, London, 1850.

20 *Argus,* 2 September 1855. Cited in Kiddle.

21 *Australian.* 19 May 1842. Cited in Kiddle.

22 For a detailed account of a group of Irish orphans with a matron in charge provided with assisted passages on a migrant ship bound for Australia in the 1880s see the first chapter of Susanna de Vries, *Desert Queen, The Life and Loves of Daisy Bates,* HarperCollins, Sydney 2008.

23 Dark, Eleanor *Caroline Chisholm and her Times,* in Flora Eldershaw's *The Peaceful Army.* WEC Publishing, Sydney, 1938.

24 M. Hoban, *Fifty-One Pieces of Wedding Cake,* p.317 and Carole Walker, *A Saviour of Living Cargoes, The Life and Work of Caroline Chisholm,* Australian Scholarly Publishing, 2009, page 110.

25 From a report in *The Times,* London, dated 8 August 1854.

26 *Illustrated London News,* 7 October 1854.

27 Letter from Governor Charles La Trobe, Trobe Papers, La Trobe Collection, State Library of Victoria.

28 *Argus,* Melbourne, 11 November 1854.

29 This part of Caroline Chisholm's work is commemorated by a park bench in Kyneton and a plaque on the Essendon Nurses Home showing the various

locations of Caroline Chisholm Shelter Sheds.

30 Pool, Dennis. *What Charles Dickens Ate and Jane Austen Knew.* Simon and Schuster, 1994 quoted this figure. The figure for Paris was even higher per head of population according to the report of Dr Parent-Duchâtelet on prostitution in the 1880s and Dr Hollis Clayson, *Painted Love, Prostitution in French Art.* Yale University Press, Boston, 1992.

31 *Argus,* Melbourne, 13 June 1857.

32 Kiddle and Walter both mention Chisholm's kidney disease but Hoban suggests Caroline Chisholm returned to London to 'finish off' the education of her daughters, which was incorrect.

33 Jules Michelet praised Mrs Chisholm's work in a chapter headed 'Femme Protectrice des Femmes' (The Woman who Protected Women) in his book, *La Femme,* Paris, 1862, p. 468.

CHAPTER 2

1 Information for this story has been obtained from a letter Elizabeth Hawkins wrote during the journey and sent to her sister Ann (Mrs Bowling) in Britain, on 7 May 1822. As it was believed that the second part of the letter had been lost, Elizabeth re-wrote that part from memory when she was 88 years old. Although she had forgotten many details of the journey, she added some particulars about her later life and her family. The letter with the second part re-written was published in 1904 in *Proceedings of the Royal Society of Queensland,* vol. XVIII, pp. 95–107. However, in 1877 the original complete letter was found. That letter was published in 1950 in *Fourteen Journeys Over The Blue Mountains of New South Wales,* Part II, collected and edited by George Mackaness.

2 Elizabeth Hawkins was born 15 July 1783 in Kent (Britain). *Fourteen Journeys Over The Blue Mountains of New South Wales,* collected and edited by George Mackaness, published 1950, Part II, p. 17

3 No date is provided for the sailing of the *Minstral* which came to Sydney via Hobart, but Elizabeth mentioned in later years that the voyage had taken six months. *Proceedings of the Royal Society of Queensland,* vol. XVIII, p. 105

4 Donkin, Nance. *Always a Lady: Courageous Women of Colonial Australia,* Collins Dove, Melbourne, 1990.

5 Pursers in the British Navy were responsible for paying the crew and checking stores, which was why Thomas Hawkins had been appointed Government Storekeeper at Bathurst.

6 A tilt is the Australian term for a large canvas canopy.

7. It is assumed that all nine men who accompanied the Hawkins were convicts. It is possible that one or two may have been soldiers acting as guards, but Elizabeth made no reference to that being the case.

8. Elizabeth does not mention her servant by name in her letter to her sister.

9. It is unlikely that they would have been staying with Sir John Jamison at *Regentville;* without doubt, Elizabeth would have written about that in the letter to her sister. They did *not* pitch their tent for the four nights stay at Emu Plains, so it is assumed that they stayed in the government's hostel.

10. The indented sections of text are extracts from the letters of Eliza Hawkins to her sister in England.

11. In her letter Elizabeth writes as the departure date Friday the 12th of April, which cannot be correct—it is either Friday the 11th of April or Saturday the 12th of April.

12. Today Springwood is a thriving town of the same name, site of the former home of artist Norman Lindsay.

13. Those must have been the hills leading up to Mount Blaxland. The sequence of events, as described by Elizabeth Hawkins, does not seem to agree with the topography of the area; accordingly, certain changes have been made to reflect the more likely sequence.

14. The total distance from Sydney Town to Bathurst, as quoted by Elizabeth in her letter, is virtually the same as that along the present-day Western Highway. However, some changes have been made to the distances they travelled on particular days, as those quoted by Elizabeth differ from the actual distances.

15. Mackaness, George, *Op. Cit.*

16. Whether any of Thomas Hawkins' cattle or sheep were killed by the Wiaradhuri Aborigines is not known.

17. There is no reference as to the type of farm the Hawkinses were running, but considering the sort of farming that took place in the area it probably would have been a mixed farm with dairy and beef cattle, but predominantly with sheep.

18. In 1851 gold was discovered at Summer Hill Creek, some 50 kilometres from Bathurst. Diggers flocked to the area and prices for mutton and beef rose sharply. The general prosperity of Bathurst (gazetted as a Town in 1833) increased dramatically. Unfortunately by that time Thomas was dead and it seems that Elizabeth had moved away from the area.

19. Information provided by the Bathurst Historical Society Inc.

20. Information provided by the Bathurst Historical Society Inc.

21 *Proceedings of the Royal Society of Queensland*, vol. XVIII, p. 107
22 Information provided by the Bathurst Historical Society Inc.

CHAPTER 3

1. Lady Katherine Swyford's descendents were denied the right to bear the name Gaunt for fear one of her three sons by Prince John of Gaunt, Duke of Lancaster, would claim the throne of England on the death of Gaunt's legitimate son, Henry IV. John, Henry and Thomas (illegitimate sons of Katherine and John of Gaunt) were given the name Beaufort after lands John of Gaunt owned in France. William Gaunt's ancestors had defied the Parliamentary edict of Henry IV and reverted to styling themselves by the name of Gaunt. William Gaunt never gave Mary precise details of his family tree. Mary started a novel about Katharine Swynford and John of Gaunt but found so many illegitimate connections that she bowed to family pressure and did not continue. Alison Weir's biography, *Katharine Swynford,* Jonathan Cape, 2007, pp 267 refers to Cardinal Henry Beaufort, the bachelor son of Katharine and John of Gaunt. Henry had an illegitimate daughter named Joan and one of her children may have been Mary's ancestor.

2. Mrs Eliza Gaunt bore William Gaunt 10 children in an era when childbirth was hazardous. After two boys and a girl died in infancy the couple had seven surviving children, Mary being the eldest daughter.

3. 'Henry' Handel Richardson's real name was Ethel Richardson. Stella Miles Franklin substituted her second name, Miles, for her first name. 'George' Elliot was born Mary Ann Evans. The Bronte sisters used the male pen names of Currer, Ellis and Acton Bell.

4. Henry Handel Richardson, in *The Fortunes of Richard Mahoney*, describes the sufferings of her father, Dr Walter Richardson, who a few years earlier had to be admitted as a public patient at the Kew Lunatic Asylum which had taken in patients from surrounding asylums and he was fed disgusting food in a tin bowl and housed under vile conditions. Even through it cost her almost all the money she had, Mary was determined that her husband would have a private room and be treated with dignity in the Kew Lunatic Asylum and she rented a house in Kew to be near him.

5. Mary Gaunt, *Alone in West Africa,* page 72

6. Mary Gaunt *Alone in West Africa,* London and New York, 1912

7. Mary Gaunt, *Reflection in Jamaica,* Ernest Benn, London, 1932, pages 94–96 incorporate some of the observations of Dr Duff on the slave trade between West Africa and the West Indies.

8. Mary Gaunt, A*lone in West Africa,* page 205

9   Mary Gaunt, A*lone in West Africa*, page 205

10   Mary Gaunt, *Alone in West Africa*, page 214. Since Mary Gaunt visited the area the Volta Dam was built, creating the vast Lake Volta and changing the geography considerably.

11   Mary Gaunt, *Alone in Africa*, page 234

12   Mary Gaunt, *Alone in West Africa*, page 243

13   Mary Gaunt, *Alone in West Africa*, page 276

14   Kumasi, in southern central Ghana, is 300 miles north of the equator and 100 miles north of the Gulf of Guinea. Today it is the second largest city in Ghana and the largest ethnic group there are Ashanti. Part of Kumasi was destroyed by British troops in the fourth Anglo-Ashanti war of 1874.

15   Mary Gaunt, *Alone in West Africa*, pages 324–5

16   Years later, Mary read in *The Times* that Matron Oram had distinguished herself nursing in France during World War One.

17   Decades later, it would be revealed the corpse of Emperor Zaitan contained abnormally high levels of arsenic. It is believed he was poisoned by persons unknown on the orders of the dying Empress Cixi so that Zaitan's proposed reforms would not be implemented.

18   Mary Gaunt's description of the Legation Compound in 1913 and its American guards are from pages 58 to 61 of *A Woman in China*.

19   Extracts from Mary Gaunt, *A Woman in China*, pages 80 and 81

20   From *A Woman in China*. Page 85.

21   Extracts from Mary Gaunt, *A Woman in China*, pages 92 to 96.

22   Born Prince Di-Zu, after taking the title of Emperor Yong Lo (Yongle), he murdered all those who threatened his succession.

23   From Mary Gaunt, *A Woman in China*, page 128.

24   In 1979, when Jake de Vries visited the Ming Tombs, he observed that in separate pavilions to the tombs magnificent golden artifacts like golden crowns, golden bowls and vases from various tombs were on view to the public. This contradicts the myth told to Mary that all these prescious objects had been stolen by Chinese soldiers.

25   Extract from Mary Gaunt, *A Woman in China*, pages 188 and 189

26   Extract from Mary Gaunt, *A Woman in China*, page 231

27   Mary referred to the Imperial Park as 'Jehol', now known as Chengde or Chengdu.

ENDNOTES

28   Extract from Mary Gaunt, *A Woman in China,* pages 288 and 289

29   Extract from Mary Gaunt, *A Woman in China,* page 306

30   The Italian diplomat and author Daniel Vare rented the Temple of the Three Mountains or San Shan Yur the summer after Mary Gaunt had departed. He arrived in Peking in 1908 and saw the overthrow of the Manchu dynasty, China swept by civil war and the effects of the Russian Revolution on China. Daneil Vare describes the temple in *The Gate of Happy Sparrows,* Methuen, London, 1937, pages 210 to 222

31   Extract from Mary Gaunt, *A Woman in China,* page 375

32   Extract from Mary Gaunt, *A Woman in China,* page 379

33   Mary Gaunt, *A Woman in China,* pages 167 to 174 deal extensively with foot binding as do parts of the sequel, *A Broken Journey.*

34   Study into foot binding by Dr Xu Ling, MD, MPH, Peking Union Medical College, Beijing, Dr Steven Cummings, MD, UCSF Professor of Medicine and Katie Stone, Department of Epidemiology of University College, San Francisco at www.sfmuseum.org

35   Extract from Mary Gaunt, *A Broken Journey,* page 81

36   Extract from Mary Gaunt, *A Broken Journey,* page 24.

37   Extract from Mary Gaunt, *A Broken Journey,* page 26

38   Extract from Mary Gaunt, *A Broken Journey,* page 31

39   Extract from Mary Gaunt, *A Broken Journey,* pages 95 and 96

40   Extract from Mary Gaunt, *A Broken Journey,* pages 120 to 123

41   Extract from Mary Gaunt, *A Broken Journey,* page 142

42   Extract from Mary Gaunt, *A Broken Journey,* pages 159 and 160

43   Extract from Mary Gaunt, *A Broken Journey,* pages 227 and 228

44   Australian troops thought they were bound for England and were surprised to find they were off to Egypt for training and then sent to Gallipoli.

45   Extract from Mary Gaunt, *A Broken Journey,* pages 234 to 238

46   Extract from Mary Gaunt, *A Broken Journey,* page 270

47   Mary would adapt the incident with the German torpedo boat as a dramatic ending to her novel *The Wind from the Wilderness.*

48   In 1925, *The Mummy Moves* was reissued in hardback by Edward Clode of New York and once again received enthusiastic reviews in *The New York Tribune,* 8 Feb. 1925, and the *Saturday Review of Literature* in the same year.

49   *The Times* (London), 'Obituary for Admiral Sir Guy Gaunt, 20 May 1953.

50   Varian Fry was an American journalist who arrived in Marseilles with a list of 200 celebrated Jewish artists and enough funds to organise false papers and their escape to New York by sea via various French colonies. The Russian Jewish artist Chagall was one of the artists Varian Fry helped to escape. Mary may have acted as a safe house at Vence for other escapees using Fry's escape route, but as her papers were destroyed in the war this has not been documented.

CHAPTER 4

1   Information on the three most popular paintings in the Queensland Art Gallery provided by Raoul Mellish, just before he retired as gallery director. Vida Lahey, born in Brisbane, studied art with Godfrey Rivers and for a brief period with Ethel Carrick Fox. Unmarried, Vida supported herself by giving art lessons, but, only relatively recently has the high quality and full range of her art been recognised. For an article of the life and work of Vida Lahey, see Susanna de Vries, *Strength of Spirit, Australian Women of Achievement*, HarperCollins, Sydney, 1998.

2   *The Fair Musterer* by Rix Nicholas was purchased by the Queensland Art Gallery in 1971. Dr John Pigot described this important painting in *Heritage*, [ed. Joan Kerr], Craftsman's House, Sydney, 1995. In April 2010, *The Fair Musterer* was illustrated in the catalogue of the Rix Nicholas retrospective exhibition at the Bendigo Fine Art Gallery.

3   Dr John Pigot, *Hilda Rix Nicholas, Her Life and Art,* Miegunyah Press at Melbourne University Press, Carlton, 2000 has excellent colour reproductions of most of Rix Nicholas' best paintings.

4   Dr John Pigot, *Hilda Rix Nicholas*, page 7.

5   Hilda Rix, London journal, entry for 13 September, 1907. Rix Nicholas Archive, National Library of Australia, Canberra.

6   Rix Nicholas Archive, National Library of Australia. *In Search of Beauty,* page 14, cited by John Pigot, page 10.

7   In 1907 Rupert Bunny's Paris studio was situated at 67 rue du Montparnasse but he later moved to other locations. .

8   Renoir's *Moulin de la Galette,* and several major Renoirs were on view in the Palais de Luxembourg as part of the Caillebotte Bequest. After World War 2 they were moved to the Jeu de Paume and are now considered among the greatest treasures of the Musée d'Orsay. The former Luxembourg Museum is now the home of the French Senate and closed to the public.

9   Susanna de Vries, *The Impressionists Revealed, Masterpieces and Collectors,*

Random House, London and New York 1998, reprinted by Time Warner, 1992.)

[10] See Susanna de Vries, *Ethel Carrick Fox, Travels and Triumphs of a Post Impressionist,* Pandanus Press, 2001, page 41. The description of Phillips Fox's studio made by Hilda Rix on 11 November 1907 is held in the Rix Nicholas Archive, National Library of Australia, Canberra.

[11] For an account of the life and work of Carrick Fox see Susanna de Vries, *Ethel Carrick Fox,* Pandanus Press, and Scribo Group, Sydney.

[12] Susanna de Vries, see endnote 9.

[13] The art school La Grande Chaumière was renamed Académie Charpentier in 1957. Its most famous pupils were the Russian painter, Tamara de Lempicka, the Italian sculptor Albert Giacometti and the Italian artist Modigliani.

[14] The Paris Salon rejected *louche* but brilliant paintings by Manet and Degas. Like Richard Miller these artists sought to highlight the prevalence of prostitution in French society and used street walkers and courtesans as models. *Café de Nuit* by Richard Miller is illustrated in colour in Susanna de Vries, *Impressionists Revealed, Masterpieces and Collectors,* Time Warner, London, 2002.

[15] Hilda's canvas *Sleepy* hangs in the McClelland Gallery, Langwarrin.

[16] Unlike the flower market sketches (*esquisses*) by Carrick Fox, the French flower market sketches by Rix Nicholas have not been exhibited.

[17] Elsie Rix. Italian journal. Rix Nicholas archive, National Library, Canberra.

[18] This unpublished essay by Hilda Rix forms part of the Rix Nicholas Archive, National Library of Australia in Canberra, donated to the library by the late Rix Wright, Hilda's son.

[19] See *Encyclopaedia of Australian Art* by Alan McCulloch, Hutchinson 1984 cites Major George Nicholas finding paintings by Hilda Rix Nicholas at Etaples..

[20] *Retour de la Chasse* [*Return from the Hunt*] hangs in Victoria's Mornington Peninsula Regional Gallery.

[21] *Work,* a large oil by Rix Nicholas, was sold to a private collection in France and from there was bought by Australia's Orica Collection, current wherabouts unknown. In the 1980s the painting was exhibited at the Queensland Art Gallery as part of a loan exhibition of French work by Australian artists.

[22] In the 1970s the painting was briefly exhibited at the Queensland Art Gallery on loan from a private collection and hung near Vida Lahey's masterwork *Monday Morning.*

[23] The Australian artist Marie Tuck was part of the Etaples group. Information provided by Bronwyn Wright from documentation in Hilda's studio.

[24] *Triad* magazine, (for which Nell Tritton also wrote articles) failed financially, so Nell Tritton did not write for its in Paris. The article by Elsie Rix, accompanied by Hilda's drawings of French peasants and market women remained unpublished and was only published in 1922 in the Australian magazine *Home*, (Volume 3, No 1, March 1922 pages 88-93).

[25] For details of Carrick and Emanuel Phillips Fox in Morocco see Susanna de Vries. *Ethel Carrick Fox, Travels and Triumphs of an Impressionist.* Pages 147-8. . A joint exhibition of the Moroccan paintings of Carrick Fox and Rix Nicholas was curated by John Pigot.

[26] In 2010 the attempt to re-open a new Luxembourg Gallery in the Luxembourg Gardens failed due to a prolonged dispute among those selected to head the new gallery..

[27] See John Pigot, *Hilda Rix Nicholas,* page 73.

[28] See John Pigot, *Hilda Rix Nicholas*, for the full story of her second visit to Morocco and Hilda's letters describing it are held in the Rix Nicholas archive.

[29] Hilda Rix Nicholas, Correspondence, Rix Nicholas Archive, National Library of Australia, Canberra.

[30] This work hangs in the Australian National Gallery in Canberra and was loaned to the 2010 Rix Nicholas retrospective at the Bendigo Fine Art Gallery. It accompanied an article titled *Rix Nicholas, The Brilliant Early Years* by Associate Professor Catherine Spark of the Art History Department, University of Adelaide.

[31] This portrait of Elsie Rix wearing a Chinese robe of the ill-fated Manchu or Qing dynasty, (deposed in 1911) hangs in the Art Gallery of Western Australia. The robe aroused admiration when worn by Hilda's granddaughter Bronwyn Wright at the opening of the exhibition of artists of the Edwardian period at the National Gallery in Canberra, later shown at the Art Gallery of South Australia.

[32] During the Franco-Prussian war, paintings by Camille Pissarro, left in his Louveciennes studio, were placed face down on muddy paths and used as stepping stones or duckboards by German soldiers billeted there.

[33] Hilda Rix Nicholas Archive, Canberra.

[34] According to Alan McCulloch's *Encyclopaedia of Australian Art* Hilda's paintings had been admired at Etaples by Major George Matson Nicholson.

[35] Three weeks was the life span of most officers in the front line, according to the poet Lieutenant Siegfried Sassoon in a letter to the Editor of *The Times*.. Military censors did their best to hide these grim realities. See *To Hell and Back, the Banned Story of Gallipoli* by Susanna and Jake de Vries, HarperCollins, Sydney, 2008.

36   Hilda Rix Nicholas to Major George Matson Nicholas, 15 November, 1915. Rix Nicholas Archive, National Library, Canberra.
37   Dr John Pigot, *Hilda Rix Nicholas,* page 30.
38   Bronwyn Wright to Susanna de Vries.
39   Dr John Pigot. *Hilda Rix Nicholas,* page 80.
40   John Pigot, *Hilda Rix Nicholas,* page 75.
41   For a fuller discussion of the way the art of Rix Nicholas was regarded in Australia over the years see John Pigot, *Hilda Rix Nicholas,* pages 35-38.
42   Photos held in the Hilda Rix Archive, National Library, Canberra.
43   Information provided by Bronwyn Wright.
44   Cited in an article by Tracey Cooper-Lavery, *The Man for the Job,* Bendigo Art Gallery, Bendigo, 2010, page 10.
45   Information from Hilda's granddaughter Bronwyn Wright..
46   Ditto.
47   In the 1990s this portrait of Dorothy Richmond in a red outfit was offered for sale by J.B. Hawkins Antiques.
48   Confusingly, the London gallery was called the Beaux Arts Gallery but had no connection with the Beaux Arts Salon of Paris of which Hilda would be made an honorary member, a rare honour for a woman and a foreigner.
49   In 1928-1929 (Hilda's 'brilliant years'), her Australian paintings were exhibited in prestigious British galleries like the Walker Gallery in Liverpool, London's Royal Institute of Oil Painters, the Whitechapel Gallery, London's Royal Institute of Arts and the Royal Society of British Painters and other regional galleries. See John Pigot, *Hilda Rix Nicholas,* page 76, for full listing.
50   *Sydney Morning Herald,* Diary 6 August 2010. In her speech Dr Marie Bashir praised the work of the recently deceased Sydney gallery director Eva Breuer, whose eponymous gallery had persuaded important clients to buy art by women at a time when paintings by women were greatly undervalued.

CHAPTER 5

1   Anne Donnell's brother, Stewart Donnell, lived in Torrens Road in the Adelaide suburb of Croydon.
2   See 'Truth is the first casualty of war — a theme that runs through *To Hell and Back, the Banned Story of Gallipoli* by Susanna and Jake de Vries, HarperCollins, 2002 and 2010.
3   Unless stated otherwise, the quotations in this chapter are extracts from

letters Anne Donnell wrote to her friend in South Australia. These letters and her diary were purchased by the State Library of New South Wales in 1919, as part of the European War Collecting Project established by the Trustees of the Mitchell Library.

4   Anne Donnell, *Letters of an Australian Army Sister,* Angus and Robertson, Sydney, 1920.

5   Richard Reid, in *Just Wanted to be There,* concerns Army nurses in World Wars One and Two and was published by the Department of Veterans Affairs, Canberra, 1999.

6   See Susanna de Vries, *The Book of Heroic Australian Women,* HarperCollins, Sydney, 2010, for the diary of Sister Alice Kitchen, who served on a hospital ship, which, following the attack on Lone Pine, had to take wounded soldiers as far as the British hospital on Malta.

7   Ellis Ashmead Bartlett was a British journalist at Gallipoli. He defied military censorship, made a cinefilm and gave lectures in Australia about his time there.

8   Nothing is known about Sister Donnell after the war ended. The archives of her publishers Angus and Robertson do not record what happened to her. Information about the rest of her life would be appreciated and can be emailed to the author. See www.susannadevries.com

9   Sister Alice Kitchen worked at Harefield Hospital. Her diary claims the mansion was owned by wealthy Western Australian graziers, the Billyaard-Leake family who had loaned the property to the Australian government for the duration of the war. For the story of Sister Alice Kitchen, see Susanna de Vries, *The Book of Heroic Australian Women,* published by HarperCollins, Sydney, 2010 and on CDs from Bolinda Audio.

CHAPTER 6

1   Using the Julian calendar the first Russian Revolution took place in February 1917 but when using the Gregorian calendar was March 1917.

2   Information on the Tritton family in Brisbane's John Oxley Library states that Frederick Tritton escaped the bank crashes of 1893 by taking his money out of his South Brisbane bank *before* it failed. The Tritton brothers retained an interest in their South Brisbane company (later known as the Coupon Furniture Store) but their George Street store was more prestigious. .

3   Notes in the John Oxley Library, State Library of Queensland state that *Elderslie* was originally built for Edgar Harris.

4   Information from email communications and phone calls between Doug Tritton and the author in September and October 2010. Doug Tritton is the grandson of Nell's brother (Frederick) Charles Tritton, who died in 1919 and

the son of Norman Tritton.

5   Information from Doug Tritton and from Mrs Lavinia Tritton.

6   Nell attended what was known as the Brisbane High School for Girls which later changed its name to Somerville House.

7   Trittons was a private company and was never listed on the stock exchange. The family's financial affairs were complex. Little is known about Nell's trust fund other than the fact it paid her an annual income on monies invested once she turned twenty-five.

8   Death Certificate No 31069 gives Charles' date of death as 24 December, the inscription on the headstone of his grave cites date of death as 23 December 1919.

9   (Frederick) Charles Tritton's death certificate cites causes of death as (1) Lead poisoning; (2) Chronic nephritis; (3) Uraemia of 3 days onset. Nell's older sister Lillian also died from the long-term effects of serious lead poisoning but Ida Jane did not seem to have been affected. Several doctors believe that Nell's kidneys were mildly affected by exposure to lead paint in early childhood before moving to *Elderslie*. This and her terrible journey through France escaping from the Nazis contributed to the fact she died in her mid forties. Adverse reactions in the kidneys and liver are often very slow according to Reith, D.M., O'Regan, P., Bailey, C., Acworth, J. Serious lead poisoning in childhood — still a problem after a century.' *Journal of Paediatrics and Child Health*, 2003, 39, 623-6.

10 In letters from New Zealand and Australia HRH Prince Edward wrote imploring his married mistress, Freda Dudley Ward to divorce her elderly husband and marry him. The Prince of Wales told Freda he planned to abdicate as he *hated* the idea of being king. These letters were edited by Rupert Godfrey, and published as *Letters from a Prince*, Time Warner, New York 1999.

11 Photographs of Nell, her friends and their cars at Wellington Point are held in the Fryer Library of Australian Literature, University of Queensland, ref UQFL F2703.

12 In the 1920s Brisbane readers had a choice of *The Daily Mail* and *The Brisbane Courier* and not until 1933 would they amalgamate under the joint name of *The Courier-Mail*.

13 Many years later, WFW (by then on the staff of the *Sydney Morning Herald*) read about Nell Tritton's marriage to Alexander Kerensky. He then wrote an article about the new Madame Kerensky, describing her as 'dazzlingly attractive and a talented writer'.

14 *Poems*, by Nellé Tritton, printed in Brisbane bore no date. Some sources give the date as 1920. A copy in Fryer Library, University of Queensland is filed with the correspondence between Joan Priest and Clem Christesen, a former

editor of *Meanjin*, gave the name of the printers as R.G. Gillies.

15 Ross Fitzgerald, Comrade in Arms, *The Weekend Australian Magazine,* 15 March 2003, cites Nell as writing for *Triad*. A short time after Nell Tritton wrote for *Triad,* the magazine went out of business.

16 Kerensky offered the Russian royal family a safe conduct to the frontier so they could gain asylum in Britain. The Tsar's cousin, King George V denied them asylum, fearing the British trade unions would organise a general strike if asylum were granted to the Tsar.

17 Translated into English, Nicolai's family name can be written as three ways. Nina Berberova refers to him as Nadezehin in *The Italics are Mine*, (*Kursiv Moi* being the Russian title). Nina's memoir taken from entries in her journal in the 1920s and 1930s remained unpublished until 1969 in America and was published in French in Paris in 1989; *The Italics are Mine* was republished in London in 1991 and 1994 as Berberova's reputation as a very important Russian writer increased after her death. The memoir was published again by Alfred Knopf of New York in 1992. Berberova stated Nicolai's Nadezehin or Nadejine was born in 1888 and died in 1958. Nina took Nell's side in the divorce and said that Nicolai was a workshy 'womaniser'. In her memoir Nina said she admired Kerensky who had recognized her talent and was the first to publish her short stories in his Russian newspaper. However, Nina claimed that Kerensky was stubborn and did not treat Nell well.

18 Entry on Lydia Ellen Tritton, *Australian Dictionary of Biography,* Volume 16, Melbourne University Press, 2002, pp. 409–410 has many glaring omissions in its account of the life of Nell Tritton. This is the first full account of her life to be published.

19 Address cited on a letter from Nell to Gladys Edds (nee Tritton) held by Mrs Lavinia Tritton, the letter refers to a very expensive European holiday with Nell's parents and Nadejine.

20 Mention of Nell's summer with Nadejine on Capri and the rented apartment on Collins Street is at http:/trove.nla.gov.au/search/kerensky/nell triton. See also the article 'Memories of Madame Kerensky' in Paris' from the *Melbourne Argus* of 24 August 1939.

21 In an article in *The Weekend Australian* Ross Fitzgerald cites the date of the Tritton-Nadejine wedding as February 1926. Other sources give the later date perhaps for reasons of respectability Nell claimed to the Australian press she married earlier.

22 The copy of Nell's poems in Fryer Library, University of Queensland, accompanies correspondence between Captain Maximoff's future son-in-law Clem Christesen and Brisbane biographer Joan Priest.

23 These were the words of Nina Berberova in *The Italics are Mine.* page 303. Other comments on Nadjeine are among Nell's letters archived in the

Kerensky papers in the University of Texas, Austin, Texas and in letters to her family.

[24] For a detailed account of Kerensky's career, see Richard Abraham's *Alexander Kerensky, The First Love of the Revolution*.

[25] Sir Compton Mackenzie's novel *Sinister Street (1913)* became a best seller in Britain and America. His novel *Whisky Galore* was filmed and made large sums as did the equally popular *Monarch of the Glen*, which would, decades later, became a popular television series. He had three wives.

[26] Peter Benenson took his mother's maiden name after his Jewish father died and founded Amnesty International. Flora Solomon's biography, *Baku to Baker Street*, Collins, London 1983, contains Flora's lie she was the only woman in Kerensky's life from 1927 to the early 1930s.

[27] Books by Alexander Kerensky translated into English include, *Prelude to Bolshevism by* A Kerensky; *The Kerensky Memoirs* (updated and republished as *History's Turning Point* by Alexander Kerensky); *The Murder of the Romanovs* by Alexander Kerensky (2nd edition appeared as *The Road to Tragedy*). *The Russian Revolution and its Aftermath* by Paul Browder and Alexander Kerensky was republished after Nell's death as was *The Russian Provisional Government 1917*. His youngest son, Gleb was paid by his father to translate two of his father's books from Russian into English while Nell translated others from French into English.

[28] *Alexander Kerensky, The First Love of the Revolution* by Richard Abraham, Columbia University Press, New York, 1987, details attempts to have Kerensky killed. Kerensky alleged that gunman Hans Bruersel was paid by the Kremlin to silence enemies of the regime like himself and Trotsky and Bruersel caused the death of the *émigré* Russian leader General Walter Krivitsky in his Washington hotel. Kerensky's major Russian supporter was the wealthy Anglo-Russian businessman David Soskice, who in 1917 was a member of Kerensky's staff. Like Kerensky himself, Soskice believed that one day the Russians would overthrow Stalin and ask Kerensky to form a democratic government. David's sons Frank Soskice (Baron Stow Hill) and Victor Soskice (later an American citizen) would also provide financial and emotional support to Kerensky.

[29] Kerensky's private papers and manuscripts were bought by the University of Austin, Texas. They reveal that from America Kerensky demanded Stalin abolish political commissars, liberate political prisoners arrested by the OGPU and end 'the reign of terror'.

[30] Nell Tritton. Interview with *The Courier-Mail*, 10 March 1939.

[31] After Lenin's death in 1924, Leon Trotsky, Chairman of the Petrograd Soviet with Josef Stalin as General Secretary of the Soviet, replaced Lenin. Stalin accused Trotsky of being a traitor to the ideals of the revolution. On 31 January 1928, Trotsky was banished by Stalin to Kazakhstan. Trotsky, his

[32] wife and son Lev were expelled from the Soviet Union in February, 1929 and spent four years on an island near Istanbul.

[32] Richard Abraham. *Alexander Kerensky*. Columbia University Press, New York, 1987. Page 367 contains references to Nell Kerensky.

[33] Nina Berberova. *The Italics are Mine*. pages 303-305.

[34] Date of 11 July 1940, cited in the entry under Lydia Ellen Tritton in *The Australian Dictionary of Biography*.

[35] From *Privations in France,* interview with Nell Kerensky, London, 17 July 1945. See http.trove.nla.gov.au. article 17674229 kerensky and nell tritton.

[36] In press interviews, the first in London, 1940 and the other in Brisbane to the ne *Courier-Mail* on 18 November, 1945 both headed 'Nightmare Ordeal in France' Nell gave some idea of the privations of the journey.

[37] Like all Australians of that era Nell travelled on a British passport.

[38] English expatriates behaved in a similar fashion trying to board a naval vessel at Cannes; Somerset Maugham recorded that 3,000 British passport holders laden with luggage fought to get on board a ship designed to take 500 passengers.

[39] Richard Abraham, *Alexander Kerensky*, page 372.

[40] Kerensky Papers, folio 191, University of Austin, Texas. Cited in Abrahams, Richard, page 372.

[41] Some of Nell's letters to her husband, catalogued under the initials LK, (Lydia Kerensky to AK, Alexander Kerensky are held in the library of the University of Texas at Austin.

[42] *The Hobart Mercury* on 6 August announced the impending visit of Mr and Mrs Kerensky. The Melbourne *Argus* interviewed them on 9 November 1945.

[43] The fact that Corbett Tritton once worked for the ABC in London appears in a history of ABC broadcasting by Kenneth S. Inglis. Corbett was the son of J.W. Tritton and is mentioned in the correspondence of Clem Christesen in the Fryer Library of Australian Literature, University of Queensland.

[44] Interviews with several Sydney papers and the Sydney representative of the Hobart *Mercury*. See newspapers.nla.gov. Alexander Kerensky.

[45] *Courier-Mail*, Brisbane, 'Nightmare Ordeal in France', 18 November 1945.

[46] Letter from Clem Christesen to Joan Priest dated 25.1.80. Fryer Library of Australian Literature, University of Queensland.

[47] Nell's birth certificate states that she was born on 19 September 1899. She died on 11 April 1946 and the inscription on the stone under which her ashes rest mistakenly indicates she was 45 at the time of her death.

48 Richard Abraham, *Alexander Kerensky*, page 375.

49 Nell's gravestone is in Section A3 of the South Brisbane Cemetery, the former Dutton Park Cemetery.

50 Richard Abraham, *Alexander Kerensky*.

51 Nell's parents owned a beach house at Redcliffe, named *Pevensey*, which, before World War Two, was seen by Brisbane people as 'the in place' to have a holiday home. Information provided by Mrs Lavinia Tritton and Mr Doug Tritton.

52 For Kerensky' life see Richard Abraham's *Alexander Kerensky*.

53 From the Wikipedia entry on Alexander Kerensky.

CHAPTER 7

1 Louise's anthology of poems *Dreams in Flower* was published by *The Bulletin* in 1901, the year she left for London. It sold very few copies, but received excellent reviews.

2 Louise Mack's column in *The Bulletin* was written under the pseudonym 'Gouli Gouli'.

3 Ethel Turner had huge financial success in Australia and overseas with *Seven Little Australians*.

4 The Georgian house Sid Mack purchased was *The Firs*, Wandella Avenue, Hunters Hill. Now demolished, only vestiges of its garden remain.

5 Louise Mack. *An Australian Girl in London*, T. Fisher Unwin, London, 1902.

6 From correspondence from Louise to her family cited in Phelan, Nancy, *The Romantic Lives of Louise Mack*, University of Queensland Press, Brisbane.

7 Louise incorporated this incident into the novel she was planning, *An Australian in London*.

8 Out of Louise's 10% royalties as a 'colonial author' the publishers made her pay the shipping costs of sending her novel to Australia which lowered the amount she received.

9 Phelan, Nancy. *The Romantic Lives of Louise* Mack, pp 119–121.

10 On her visit to Tuscany in the late 1980s, Nancy Phelan decided to concentrate on trying to find the grave of a dead child rather than looking for a couple who might have adopted Louise's 'one surviving child'. I combed the records of an orphanage in the Oltarno established by the American Protestant Isabella Gould (now the Istituto Gould in Via degli Serragli) thinking this would have been the most acceptable orphanage to Louise rather than a Catholic one. I found no entry in the registry of adopted

children to link any child with Louise or D'Annunzio.

[11] See Susanna de Vries, *Desert Queen, the Many Lives and Loves of Daisy Bates*, HarperCollins, Sydney, 2008.

[12] Phelan, Nancy. *Op. cit.* p. 145.

[13] Gabriele D'Annunzio, born in 1863, was at the peak of his fame when Louise arrived in Florence in 1904. As a writer, he was influenced by Flaubert and de Maupassant and his novels shocked some readers with plots loaded with sexuality and *fin de siècle* decadence.

[14] Lord Westbury sold *Villa I Tatti* to the art historian Bernard Berenson in December 1907 as the English aristocrat needed to pay off gambling debts. Mary Berenson, *Letters and Diary*, Victor Gollancz, London 1983, records the sale in a letter while another letter dated 22 March 1903 to Senda Berenson records a dinner party at *Villa I Tatti* attended by D'Annunzio and Duse. The famous writer flirted with the young Countess Serristori in front of Duse who was described by Berenson as 'sad and old, getting fat' and D'Annunzio 'treated her with contempt'.

[15] Tomas Antongini. *Con D'Annunzio a Settignano* refers to the Englishwoman with the dog at Settignano. This small volume was never translated into English, unlike Antongini's well-known biography *D'Annunzio*, published in New York in 1938, which contains no reference to Louise.

[16] It is most unlikely that Louise was pregnant while living in London, as her brother would have noticed and her family would have become aware of it.

[17] Louise kept a copy of this lease for reference. The lease expired in 1910 and she left Tuscany when D'Annunzio left Settignano. In her notebook, she noted down details of monies paid to Torquato, her gardener, to shop for her in Florence. Joan Haslip died two years before I spent a summer in Florence on a Churchill Fellowship and met the authors Rupert Hodson and his wife Professor Lorna Sage who helped research the Settignano side of Louise's story. The obituary of Professor Lorna Sage, from *The Guardian* newspaper of 3 Jan 2001, is on the internet and calls Lorna 'a brilliant teacher and writer.

[18] See *William le Queux, Master of Mistery* by Chris Patrick and Stephen Bouster, self-published, Putney, England, pp. 199–205, for accounts of the adopted daughters of William le Queux.

[19] In Paris, D'Annunzio had many affairs with younger women including the American artist Romaine Brooks and the bisexual Russian artist Tamara de Lempicka. He returned to Italy in 1915. In 1919, Gabriele with a group of legionnaires, occupied Austrian-owned Trieste to ensue its union with Italy. Out of gratitude, Mussolini's government gave D'Annunzio a handsome villa on the Lago di Garda. However, D'Annunzio's close connections with Fascism meant his reputation in the literary world declined.

20 Jack Creed died in 1914 but Louise would not have a death certificate for another ten years. When applying to remarry, she gave details of her 'one child, still living'.

21 The German version of events has inhabitants of Aerschot firing on German troops. The story was published in the Boyce Report into War Atrocities, which was published at the request of the British Government following an investigation led by Viscount Boyce. This report confirmed Louise's story sent back to *The Daily Mail* on German atrocities at Aerschot. Accounts of German atrocities in Belgium and deportations of young men to work in German factories in World War One are detailed by Larry Zuckerman in *The Rape of Belgium*. New York Press, New York, 2009.

22 This is an abbreviated version of Louise's journal, printed in full in *A Woman's Experiences in the Great War,* London, 1915.

23 Nancy Phelan's biography of Louise Mack abbreviated Louise's important account of the bombing and invasion of Antwerp. Nancy and I talked on the phone a year before her death when Nancy acknowledged that she had missed the significance of Louise writing about an Italian lover in a grey stone villa on the hills. *Villa della Capponcina* was as yet unpainted when Louise was in Settignano. Nancy kindly gave me written permission to use Louise's writings.

24 Louise Mack's story, taken to England by Frank Fox, appeared as 'An Englishwoman in Antwerp' in *The Daily Mail* on 3 September 1914. As there were no Australian passports Louise travelled on a British passport. Promoting Louise's story, the Northcliffe press claimed her to be English, ignoring the fact she was born in Hobart and raised in Sydney.

25 Dutch war correspondent L. Mokveld, who worked for the Dutch newspaper *De Tijd* first revealed details of German atrocities in Belgium and Northcliffe told his journalists to confirm them.

26 Brisbane-born Sister Edith Cavell had been shot in Belgium — the Germans claimed she was a British spy rather than a nursing sister.

27 Decades after Louise allegedly became the world's first female war correspondent, Martha Gelhorn, daughter of a Jewish-American doctor filed war stories during the Spanish Civil War and had an affair with Ernest Hemingway, who eventually married her as wife No 3. Martha Gelhorn was still at school while Louise made history as a women war correspondent.

28 Joan Haslip wrote award-winning biographies of Marie Antoinette, Catherine the Great and Lucrezia Borgia. In the summer of 1996, two years after Haslip's death, my husband, Rupert Hodson and I drove out to Settignano to see the *Villa di Doccia*.

CHAPTER 8

1. For a detailed chronology of women in Parliament see Senate Brief No 3, 2010, *Women in the Senate,* Kirsten Lees; *Votes for Women, the Australian Story,* Allen and Unwin, St Leonards, NSW, 1995, and Marilyn Lake, *Getting Equal, the History of Australian Feminism,* Allen and Unwin, St Leonards, NSW 1999.

2. Mary Wollstonecraft, *A Vindication of the Rights of Women,* London 1792, is still in print with Penguin Books.

3. Margaret Ogg's words cited in the transcript of the ABC TV program, *Lateline.*

4. A few years later, British suffragette Christabel Pankhurst adopted Margaret's idea but used a horse-drawn caravan as the platform for her 'Votes for Women' campaign.

5. Betty Crouchley, Ogg, Margaret Ann, *Australian Dictionary of Biography,* Volume 11, Melbourne University Press, Melbourne, 1988. Miss Ogg wrote her articles under the pen name 'Anne Dante' — a wordplay on the Italian musical term Andante as she played the viola in an amateur orchestra.

6. Text comes from the illuminated address to Margaret Ogg, held in the Fryer Library of Australian Literature, University of Queensland.

7. Dame Annabel Rankin became Liberal Government Whip and federal Minister for Housing.

8. For the full story of Edith Cowan's life and work see Susanna de Vries, *Great Australian Women,* HarperCollins, Sydney, 2000.

9. P.T. Fallon, *So hard the conquering, A Life of Irene Longman,* 2002.

10. Anne Henderson in *Enid Lyons, Leading Lady to a Nation,* postulates that Aloysius Joice, a keen Labour supporter, may have been Enid's father and the 'mysterious loan' a form of compensation for Enid's birth. However, Enid's birth certificate cited William Burnell as her father.

11. Hart, P.R. & Lloyd C.J., entry on Joseph Lyons *Australian Dictionary of Biography,* vol. 10, Melbourne University Press, Melbourne, 1986.

12. 'My heart never ceased to cry for little [Garnet Phillip]', claimed Enid Lyons in her memoirs.

13. The school-age children were Brendan, Barry, Rosemary, Peter and Janice Lyons.

14. This episode of nervous exhaustion and depression, covered up for political reasons, is cited in Anne Henderson in *Enid Lyons, Leading Lady to a Nation,* pages 252–254.

15 In a recorded interview, a copy of which is in the National Library of Australia, Enid Lyons claimed, 'It was nothing for me to go home from Parliament, have a meal and drive miles into the country. [The] workload took a tremendous toll.'

16 Interview with Julia Gillard by Julie McCrossin in 2007.

17 Issie Pilowsky, Professor of Psychiatry in Adelaide, worked on a research project with my late husband, Larry Evans, also a Professor of Psychiatry. The Pilowskys influenced many lives for the better, including that of Julia Gillard.

18 Jacqueline Kent, *The Making of Julia Gillard,* Viking, Melbourne, 2009, page 64 followed by a subsequent edition.

19 Lincoln Wright, 'Will Julia Gillard's past cause red faces?' *Herald Sun.* 7 August 2007.

20 Julia Gillard to Bryce Corbett, *The Australian Women's Weekly*, August, 2010.

21 Julia Gillard, biographical outline on Wikipedia.

22 Wright, Tony. 'PM tells it as she sees it on the God issue'. *The Sydney Morning Herald,* 30 June, 2010.

23 Julia Gillard to Bryce Corbett in *The Australian Women's Weekly*, August, 2010, page 54.

24 Laurie Oakes, *The Australian,* 28 July, 2010.

25 'Australia heads for hung Parliament' *BBC TV News,* 21 August 2010, and 'Independent MPs with seven key demands', *ABC News*, 26 August 2010.

CHAPTER 9

1 Definition by the Hon. Sir Asher Joel and Helen Pringle, *Manual of Australian Procedures and Protocol*, 3rd edition, 2008, first published by Angus and Roberson in 1982.

2 The poll was sponsored by News Ltd with the result published in *The Courier-Mail* on Saturday, 27 November 2010, together with a photograph of HE Governor Bryce.

3 Dr Janet Irwin, MB, BSc. speaking with Susanna de Vries in 1976. Dr Irwin, a graduate of the University of Otago, worked in child psychiatry in London and Edinburgh before heading the Student Medical Service of the University of Queensland. She was a member of the University Senate. She was awarded an Order of Australia for services 'to women and the community'. Dr Irwin was co-author with Susanna de Vries, Susan Stratigos Wilson and Dr Jean Sparling of *Parenting Girls.* Dr Janet Irwin died in 2009 in New

Zealand after a long illness.

[4] H.E. Quentin Bryce to Kerry O'Brien, *The 7.30 Report*, ABC TV, broadcast 23 September 2008.

[5] Some sources cite Quentin Bryce's birthplace as Longreach. However, as her mother had already lost one child, Mrs Strachan travelled from Ilfracombe to Brisbane for Quentin's birth.

[6] Cited in the chapter on Quentin Bryce, in Peter and Sheila Forrest, *All for Queensland, The Governors and their People,* Shady Press, Darwin, 2010.

[7] Quentin Bryce, interviewed for an article titled 'Reflections on a Life in Progress', *Vogue Australia*, September, 2009, was also interviewed by Peter and Sheila Forrest, authors of *All for Queensland, The Governors and their People*, Shady Press, Darwin, 2009, pp 263–264.

[8] A quote from a Virago publication, *Women, Resistance and Revolution*, by Sheila Rowbotham.

[9] Dale Spender, *Women of Ideas and what men have done to them.* Pandora Press, London, three editions.

[10] In 2002, Quentin Bryce received an Honorary D. Litt. from Macquarie University. In 2003, she became a Companion of the Order of Australia (AC) and was made an Honorary Doctor of Griffith University in the same year, followed by an honorary doctorate from the Queensland University of Technology.

[11] *The Impressionists Revealed – Masterpieces and Collectors*, by Susanna de Vries, was published in Australia and America *by* Random House and in Britain by Time Warner (Little Brown).

[12] Peter Hartscher of the *Sydney Morning Herald* lunched with Ms Bryce at Government House in July 2010 and described her nibbling her way through a chicken salad and toying with a glass of white wine.

[13] In 1995, Leneen Ford awarded Susanna de Vries a Churchill Fellowship and in 1996, an Order of Australia at Brisbane Government House.

[14] Jane Steinberg JP is the daughter of Professor Margaret Steinberg AM, who has done a great deal of work on behalf of the disabled.

[15] Jane Steinberg in conversation with author Susanna de Vries, August 2010.

[16] *Heroic Australian Women in War*, launched by Quentin Bryce, is still in print but has been retitled *The Complete Book of Australian Heroic Women*.

[17] The theme of this fundraising evening was the work among Greek and Polish refugees done by Queensland-born Joice Loch, the subject of Susanna de Vries' book, *Blue Ribbons, Bitter Bread*.

18   The Hon. Sir Asher Joel and Helen Pringle, *Australian Protocol and Procedures*. Revised third edition published in 2008.
19   The list of charities of which the Governor-General and her husband act as patrons appears on her website.
20   See Steve Lewis, *Herald Sun* and *The Courier-Mail,* October 28, 2009, *Governor-General Quentin Bryce's Africa trip cost $700,000.*
21   Quotation from Sir Asher Joel writing on the role of the governor-general.
22   Leslie Cannold's opinion appeared in an article by Nick Tabakoff in *The Daily Telegraph* of 23 August 2010 and in *The Australian*, article by Samantha Miaden and Nicola Berkovic, 23 August. Peter Faris QC was quoted in *The Sydney Morning Herald* in an article dated, 24 August 2010, repeated in *The Melbourne Age.* te.
23   Michael Bryce to Michael Sheather, *Australian Women's Weekly,* July 2010.

AUTHOR DETAILS

Susanna de Vries is an international author with 16 biographies of significant women and several art books to her credit. Born in London with Irish roots, she arrived in Australia in 1975 with her late husband, as he had been appointed professor at the Medical School of Queensland University. She attended a university course on Australian literature and worked in Queensland University Library where she met first met Quentin Bryce who at that time was a university lecturer. Research into Australian women in various libraries in Australia and overseas aroused her interest in the fascinating stories of   Nell Tritton. Mary Gaunt, Louise Mack and Anne Donnell and she was able to talk to members of their families. Susanna was made a Member of the Order of Australia (AM) in 1996 for *'services to Australian literature and art.'* By this time she was married to Dutch architect and book designer Jake de Vries, In 2001 Susanna was awarded a joint Fellowship by the Australian Literature Board and the Irish Government to write *Desert Queen*, the award winning biography of Irish-born anthropologist Daisy Bates. *Blue Ribbons, Bitter Bread, the Life of the Much Decorated Joice Loch*, set in Australia, Poland and Greece became a bookseller's choice and won Susanna a non-fiction award at the prestigious Sligo Writer's Festival and has never been out or print since it was published in 2002. For Susanna's other books see www.susanna de vries.com or full details on amazon and amazon kindle.

www.ingramcontent.com/pod-product-compliance
Lightning Source LLC
Chambersburg PA
CBHW050850160426
43194CB00011B/2098